Blackstone's Guide to the

CRIMINAL JUSTICE & PUBLIC ORDER ACT 1994

Blackstone's Guide to the

CRIMINAL JUSTICE & PUBLIC ORDER ACT 1994

Martin Wasik, LLB, MA, Barrister

Professor of Law, Manchester University

and

Richard D. Taylor, MA, LLM, Barrister

Forbes Professor of English Law and Head of Department
of Legal Studies, University of Central Lancashire

BLACKSTONE
PRESS LIMITED

First published in Great Britain 1995 by Blackstone Press Limited,
9–15 Aldine Street, London W12 8AW. Telephone 0181-740 1173

ISBN: 1 85431 401 7

British Library Cataloguing in Publication Data
A CIP catalogue record for this book is available from the British Library.

Typeset by Style Photosetting Ltd, Mayfield, East Sussex and
Montage Studios Limited, Tonbridge, Kent
Printed by Livesey Ltd, Shrewsbury, Shropshire

Contents

Young offenders
1.1 Secure training orders: outline of sentencing powers   1.2   Secure training orders: the custodial element   1.3   Secure training orders: the supervision element 1.4   Long-term detention of juveniles   1.5   Detention in young offender institution: maximum sentence   1.6   Accommodation of young offenders sentenced to custody for life   1.7   Provision, management and cost of secure accommodation for young persons   1.8   Detention of young persons after charge and remands to secure accommodation   1.9   Media restrictions in cases involving juveniles

Sentencing
1.10 Taking account of guilty pleas   1.11   Pre-sentence reports   1.12   Probation orders: provision for treatment by psychologist 1.13   Probation orders: rehabilitation period   1.14   Previous probation orders and discharges 1.15   Curfew   orders   1.16   Fines   and   financial   circumstances   orders 1.17   Confiscation   orders: variation   of   sentence   1.18   Committal   for sentence   1.19   Definition of sexual offence   1.20   Reviews of lenient sentences 1.21   Binding over of parent or guardian   1.22   Changes to maximum penalties

Bail
2.1 Bail in cases involving murder, manslaughter and rape   2.2   Alleged offence committed on bail: removal of presumption of bail   2.3   Conditional bail by the police   2.4   Bail following charge   2.5   Breach of police bail: power of arrest 2.6   Reconsideration of decision to grant bail

Juries
2.7 Person on bail: disqualification from jury service   2.8   Jury service: disabled persons   2.9   Jury service: excusal on religious grounds   2.10   Separation of jury during consideration of verdict

List of Abbreviations

BBFC	British Board of Film Classification
CJA	Criminal Justice Act
CJPOA	Criminal Justice and Public Order Act
CLRC	Criminal Law Revision Committee
CYPA	Children and Young Persons Act
DCMF	design, construct, manage and finance
PACE	Police and Criminal Evidence Act 1984
POA	Prison Officers Association

Preface

Criminal justice continues to be one of the most volatile areas of public policy. The Criminal Justice and Public Order Act 1994 is a large and wide-ranging statute, which makes changes to many different aspects of substantive criminal law, evidence and sentencing.

In the discussion of the Act which follows, we have tried both to describe the meaning of the various provisions and to access their likely impact in the courts. We have sought to identify the problems which the Act sets out to resolve and the further difficulties which it may create.

We are grateful to several friends and colleagues with whom we have discussed the changes brought about by the Act. We would also like to thank Greg Pope MP for his invaluable help with Parliamentary materials.

The speed with which this Guide has been produced is, once again, a tribute to the efficiency of all at Blackstone Press. Thanks are due to Heather, Alistair and Nigel for their help and encouragement. Thanks also to our wives, Pat and Karen, who have had to spend a further summer making allowances for writing deadlines and the unpredictable nature of the law-making process.

Martin Wasik
Richard Taylor
December 1994

Introduction

BACKGROUND TO THE ACT

The provisions of the Criminal Justice and Public Order Act (CJPOA) 1994 can be traced to a number of different sources. Much attention has been given to the Home Secretary's so-called '27-point plan to crack down on crime', which was announced in his speech to the annual Conservative Party conference in October 1993. When the CJPOA 1994 received its Royal Assent Mr Howard was able to claim that he had achieved the implementation of 19 of the 27 promised reforms, and that these were 'an important weapon in the fight against crime'. During the period up to and after the party conference the Home Secretary had been one of the members of the government most prominent in arguing for the 'back to basics' approach. Applying this philosophy to the introduction of new legislation on criminal justice, in a speech in Basingstoke in November 1993 Mr Howard called for the abandonment of '... trendy theories that try to explain away crime by blaming socio-economic factors. Criminals should be held to account for their actions and punished accordingly. Trying to pass the buck is wrong, counter-productive and dangerous'. The provisions in the Bill which were designed to increase the powers of the courts to impose custodial sentences on young offenders should also be seen in the context of the time at which they were brought forward. A *Times* leader for 18 December 1993 talks of '... a wave of disquiet about crime, borne upon a tide of government unpopularity. The litany of horrific cases – from the death of James Bulger to the sickening torture of Suzanne Capper – has helped to keep the fear of crime consistently high in the list of public concerns.'

While the political context in which the Bill was enacted is important, it should be remembered that a Criminal Justice Bill for the session had been planned for some considerable time, mainly for the purpose of implementing recommendations of the *Royal Commission on Criminal Justice*. The Royal Commission (Chairman, Lord Runciman of Doxford) had been set up in March 1991 at a time of great public concern over the appearance of an apparently endless series of miscarriages of justice, and in fact coincided with the quashing of the convictions of the Birmingham Six (who had been convicted for murder following the bomb explosions in public houses in Birmingham in November 1974). The Commission provided the impetus for much valuable research and generated a good deal of discussion, although the final Report (Cm 2263, July 1993) was regarded by many commentators as disappointing (see, for example, the essays in M. McConville et al. *Criminal Justice in Crisis*, 1994).

Many of the recommendations in the Report were accepted by the government and are now implemented by the CJPOA 1994. Examples are the replacement of committal proceedings, reform of the law relating to juries and the significance of a guilty plea to sentencing, the abrogation of requirements for corroboration warnings and the broadening of police powers to take intimate and non-intimate samples with a view to establishing DNA databases.

In making comparisons between the Royal Commission's Report and the 1994 Act, however, two matters stand out. The first is the absence from the Act of what many regard as the central proposal of the Commission, the setting up of a *Criminal Cases Review Authority*. In March 1994 the government, in a consultation paper, announced that it had accepted many of the Royal Commission's recommendations in this area, and that a new Criminal Cases Review Authority would be established by law. It was anticipated that it would be modelled on the Police Complaints Authority, with lay and legal members, and that it would use police teams to carry out investigations into alleged miscarriages of justice. The results of such investigations in individual cases would then be made available to the Court of Appeal. When the consultation paper was issued the Home Secretary had promised a speedy implementation, but there was no mention of the matter in the Queen's Speech in November 1994. More recently still the government has declared its continuing commitment to set up a review body, but no details of what is proposed have yet emerged.

The second striking difference between the Royal Commission and the Act is the treatment of the so-called 'right to silence'. The majority of the Commission, backed by the Bar, the Law Society and the Criminal Bar Association believed that (Cm 2263, ch. 4, paras 22–3):

> ... the possibility of an increase in the convictions of the guilty is outweighed by the risk that the extra pressure on suspects to talk in the police station and the adverse inferences invited if they do not may result in more convictions of the innocent.... In taking this view the majority acknowledge the frustration which many police officers feel when confronted with suspects who refuse to offer any explanation whatever of strong *prima facie* evidence that they have committed an offence. But they doubt whether the possibility of adverse comment at trial would make the difference that the police suppose. The experienced professional criminals who wish to remain silent are likely to continue to do so.... It is the less experienced and more vulnerable suspects against whom the threat of adverse comment would be likely to be more damaging.

The government, however, preferred the view of the minority of the Commission (two out of 11 members) who accepted the arguments of the police, the Crown Prosecution Service and a majority of judges that it should be possible for the prosecution or judge to invite a jury to draw adverse inferences from an accused's silence under police questioning. The controversy to which this aspect of the Act gave rise is further discussed in chapter 3 where it will be seen that some important concessions were gained by those opposed to the modifications to the right to silence, such as the limitation of s. 34(1)(a) to questioning under caution. Nevertheless, the government secured in general terms its preferred proposals which many fear will increase the complexity and costs of legal advice to suspects questioned by the police and yet at the same time increase the risk of convicting the innocent.

The introduction by the CJPOA 1994 of *secure training orders* has also proved very controversial. This new custodial sentence for 12–14-year-olds is seen by the government as being a central part of its strategy against persistent serious juvenile crime. It has been claimed that the courts are 'powerless' to deal with 'an epidemic' of serious offending by juveniles. No juvenile under the age of 15 can be given a sentence of detention in a young offender institution and, in cases where a sentence of long-term detention (under s. 53(2) of the Children and Young Persons Act 1933) is not available the secure training order offers a means of giving custody for persistent offenders under that age. Everyone seems to agree that the number of such offenders is very small, and this whole problem must be seen against the general background of a drop by one third since 1980 in the number of offenders aged between 10 and 16 known to have been committing offences, a fall more sharp than the decline in the juvenile population over that period. The creation of a new custodial sentence has been heavily criticised. One complaint has been that existing facilities have been consistently underfunded and that, in particular, secure accommodation is frequently not available to courts in their local area. A second concern is that custody for juveniles has in the past shown itself to be counter-productive in terms of reconviction rates. Home Office studies on young offenders who were dealt with in the old approved schools (later to become community homes with education or CHEs) and borstals showed failure rates in later years of between 70 and 80 per cent (see further NACRO, *Seriously Persistent Young Offenders*, 1993, and the Penal Affairs Consortium, *A Step in the Wrong Direction: The Right and the Wrong Way of Tackling Juvenile Crime*, 1993).

Central to the CJPOA 1994 is a range of provisions in part V related to *public order*, in which the government has significantly increased police powers in respect of the control and dispersal of various forms of 'collective trespass or nuisance on land'. The Act gives greater powers to evict and to remove trespassers (such as 'squatters', 'new age travellers' and 'unauthorised campers') from land, to remove from the land persons who are organising or attending 'raves', and to remove 'disruptive trespassers' (which would include 'hunt saboteurs' and other protesters) who obstruct, disrupt or intimidate those who are taking part in lawful activities. The Act also empowers the police to stop, and to turn away, pedestrians and vehicles which are heading for the site of a rave or a trespassory assembly. In an article in *The Times*, 8 March 1994, Peter Thornton, the chairman of the Civil Liberties Trust, argued that these provisions of the Act extend the law 'to a point not far short of a straight law of criminal trespass'. Some are in favour of such an approach. In the debate on the second reading of the Bill, Mr Butler MP (*Hansard*, Commons, 11 January 1994, col. 87) welcomed the changes, and expressed the hope that it would turn out to be the first step to a full law of criminal trespass. On the other hand Mr Gunnell MP (*Hansard*, Commons, 11 January 1994, col. 131) was sure that '... the clauses on trespass will create a new class of law breakers. The time and resources that the police will devote to dealing with them will therefore detract from the current use of police resources'. Perhaps the most contentious matter in this area, however, is the repeal by s. 80 of the Act of provisions in the Caravan Sites Act 1968, which had imposed a duty on local authorities to provide sites for gipsy encampments. The duty is replaced by a power, but there is widespread concern that this change will result in the police being employed simply to confront and to 'move on' gipsies who have no designated site available to which they can go.

Another controversial area of the Act, discussed in chapter 6, is the extension of the privatisation or 'contracting out' of the prison service and of prisoner escorting, a process first started with the CJA 1991. Opponents were particularly critical of the inclusion in the contracting-out programme of the new secure training units for persistent young offenders. The opposition have stated that they would halt the privatisation process if they were returned to power although existing contracts would normally be allowed to run their course.

MPs were given a free vote on an amendment to bring the *age of consent for homosexuals* into line with that of heterosexuals (i.e., to reduce it from 21 to 16), and also on an amendment to have the effect of lowering the age from 21 to 18. The legal age of consent for heterosexuals is 16, but when male homosexuality was legalised by the Sexual Offences Act 1967 the lower age limit was set at 21, which was then the age of majority. It was pointed out in the course of the debates in Parliament on the Bill that most countries have equal ages of consent, often lower than ours. In Holland, Greece, France, Poland and Sweden the relevant age is 15. In Norway, Belgium, Portugal and Switzerland it is 16. The argument for a compromise reduction in the age of consent to 18 was given by the Right Reverend James Thompson, Bishop of Bath and Wells, amongst others, who argued that many people experienced an ambivalence about their sexuality in their teenage years, and that a reduction of the age to 18 would allow time for this to be resolved while still protecting the vulnerable during the period of transition. Conflicting evidence was advanced by each side in the debate as to when young people typically become settled in their sexual orientation. The vote in the House of Commons resulted in the reduction of the age of consent for homosexuals from 21 to 18, by 427 votes to 162. The option of reduction to 16 was defeated by 307 votes to 280.

PROGRESS OF THE BILL

The passage of the Bill through Parliament provoked strong opposition to several of its provisions in the House of Lords. When the Bill completed its passage through the Lords on 19 July 1994, the upper House had effectively delayed the implementation of the Bill for several months by passing a series of fundamental amendments. The government had to recall the Bill to the Commons in the autumn to reverse their effect. This repair work was carried out in the Commons on 19 and 20 October 1994. The House of Commons eventually voted by a majority of 27 to reinstate the Home Secretary's controversial new criminal injuries compensation 'tariff' scheme, which had been voted down by the Lords before the summer (and which is still the subject of a challenge in the courts (see *Home Secretary, ex parte Fire Brigades Union* (1994) *The Times*, 30 May 1994) in which an appeal to the House of Lords is pending). MPs also reversed changes which had been made in the Lords relating to secure training units for persistent young offenders (by which their lordships would have permitted the new sentences to be served in local authority secure accommodation as well as in the proposed new units), to the preservation of the local authority duty to provide sites for gipsies, and to the introduction of a new offence of obtaining financial information by deception.

As first introduced into Parliament in December 1993, the Bill was 117 sections and 112 pages long. By the time it received the Royal Assent it had grown to 172 sections and 214 pages.

When the Bill was eventually passed there were a number of demonstrations against its provisions. On 19 October 1994 riot police confronted protestors outside the House of Commons. According to press reports, a full-scale assault on Parliament was prevented by the presence of some 2,000 police officers on duty. Parliament Square was closed, and a rally organised by the 'Coalition against the Criminal Justice Bill' was re-routed. Twelve people were arrested. The Bill completed its Parliamentary passage on 25 October, when the Lords eventually approved the Bill with the reversals made by the Commons to the Lords amendments. The Criminal Justice and Public Order Act 1994 received Royal Assent on 3 November 1994. The date was marked by a large demonstration on the site of the proposed M11 link road in east London, the purpose being to defy the creation of the new offence of aggravated trespass. No arrests were made. During the weekend of 19–20 November, about 300 demonstrators invaded the garden of the Home Secretary's own home in Kent. Several people climbed on to the roof. About 100 police officers were present on the occasion, but the demonstration was dispersed with no arrests.

IMPLEMENTATION OF THE ACT

The Criminal Justice and Public Order Act 1994 received Royal Assent on 3 November 1994.

On Royal Assent, by virtue of s. 172(4), the following provisions (together with their related amendments, repeals and revocations) came into force immediately: ss. 5–15 and schs 1 and 2 (provision, management and contracting out of secure training orders), s. 61 (removal of trespassers from land), s. 63 (removal of persons attending a rave), s. 65 (power to stop persons proceeding to a rave), ss. 68–71 (disruptive trespassers and trespassory assemblies), ss. 77–80 (removal of unauthorised campers), s. 81 (terrorism: stop and search), s. 83 (terrorism: financial resources), s. 90 (video recordings), chapters I and IV of part VIII (prison service, prisoner escorts and contracting out of prisons), ss. 142–8 (sexual offences), s. 150 (parole: recall of prisoners), s. 158(1), (3) and (4) (extradition), s. 166 (ticket touts), s. 167 (taxi touts), s. 171 (expenses under the Act), para. 46 of sch. 9 (discretionary life prisoners) and s. 172 (short title, commencement and extent).

Section 159(1), (2) and (4) (backing of warrants) came into force on 19 December 1994 (SI 2935 of 1994).

Section 82 (offences relating to terrorism) will come into force on 3 January 1995 (s. 82(3)).

All remaining sections will come into force on such date as the Home Secretary (or, in the case of ss. 52 and 53 (criminal appeals), the Lord Chancellor) may appoint by order made by statutory instrument. Different days may be appointed for different provisions, but the bulk of the remainder of the Act is expected to be brought into force in the early part of 1995.

Chapter One
Young Offenders and Sentencing

Sections 1 to 4 of the CJPOA 1994 make available to the courts a new custodial sentence for young offenders: the 'secure training order'. This chapter deals with all aspects of the new sentence, with the exception of details relating to the provision, management and contracting out of secure training centres, which are considered in chapter 6. Section 16 of the Act makes important changes to the arrangements for long-term detention of young offenders, under the CYPA 1933, s. 53(2). Section 17 of the 1994 Act increases the maximum term of detention in a young offender institution which may be imposed upon a 15, 16 or 17-year-old offender from 12 months to two years. Sections 19 to 24 make further changes to the law relating to the remand, detention after charge and secure accommodation of suspects and offenders under the age of 18. Section 49 amends the earlier law on the restriction of publicity at the trial of young offenders. Also considered in this chapter is the introduction, by s. 48, of a statutory duty for sentencing courts to take account of an offender's guilty plea, and the circumstances in which that plea was tendered, when selecting sentence. So too is the relaxation of the requirement for courts to obtain pre-sentence reports. Finally, reference is made to a range of penalty increases prescribed in the Act (most notably for firearms offences and drug offences), which are brought about by s. 157 and sch. 8.

YOUNG OFFENDERS

1.1 Secure Training Orders: Outline of Sentencing Powers

Sections 1 to 4 of the 1994 Act are concerned with the creation of a new custodial sentence for young offenders: the 'secure training order'. This has proved to be controversial: for discussion of the background to this change, and for an outline of the debate in Parliament, see the introduction to this book. Secure training orders may be made in respect of male or female offenders aged 12, 13 or 14 who are convicted of any imprisonable offence (except where the sentence for the offence is fixed by law, i.e., murder). The rather obscurely worded s. 1(10) seems to allow for the bringing into force of these new powers in stages, initially applying only to offenders aged 14, but with the extension of the powers thereafter to offenders aged 13, and then to those aged 12. For the purposes of s. 1, the age of a person shall be deemed to be that which it appears to the court to be after considering any available evidence

(s. 1(9)). For a similarly worded provision see the CJA 1982, s. 1(6). If there is a dispute about the offender's age, and hence their eligibility for the sentence, the best course is to adjourn until the matter can be properly resolved (*Steed* (1990) 12 Cr App R (S) 230).

Section 1 of the 1994 Act further requires that before a secure training order can be passed the court must be satisfied:

(a)   that the offender was aged not less than 12 (or 13, or 14, if the provision is implemented in stages) when the offence was committed (s. 1(5)(a)).

(b)   that the offender has been convicted of three or more imprisonable offences (s. 1(5)(b)), and

(c)   that the offender, either on the present occasion or on an earlier occasion, has been found to be in breach of a supervision order or has been convicted of an imprisonable offence whilst subject to such an order (s. 1(5)(c)).

When the court makes a secure training order it must state in open court that conditions (a) to (c) are satisfied. Condition (a) is unusual and offers a potential trap. Sentencers are used to considering an offender's age at the date of the conviction (see *Danga* [1992] QB 476) rather than his age at the date of the offence. Condition (b) is somewhat unclear. Must the three or more imprisonable offences all be *previous* convictions, or may they include convictions received on the present occasion? In the course of debate on this provision, government spokesman Earl Ferrers stated that 'the offences could all have been committed on one occasion, or they could have been done on two or three separate occasions ... I do not believe that it is right to tie the hands of the courts too closely' (*Hansard*, Lords, 5 July 1994, col. 1187). Can it be assumed that 'has been convicted' will be construed by the courts to include offences which have been taken into consideration? In the CJA 1991, special provision was made (in s. 31(2)(b)) to allow sentencing courts to have regard to offences taken into consideration but there is no equivalent provision in the 1994 Act. It is, of course, clear that previous formal cautions could never count as convictions, even though the sentencing court will have knowledge of them and is permitted to take account of them when sentencing. A further potential problem is that youth courts technically return 'findings of guilt', rather than 'convictions'. If s. 1(5)(b) of the 1994 Act is construed so as not to extend to findings of guilt, then the whole provision would appear to be redundant.

The secure training order is a 'custodial sentence' for the purposes of ss. 1 to 4 of the CJA 1991 (s. 1(6) of the 1994 Act), so that the criteria in the 1991 Act justifying custody and determining the length of custody will apply. It is clear, then, that satisfaction of criteria (a) to (c) listed above will render the offender eligible for a secure training order, but that such a sentence may only lawfully be imposed where the criteria in the 1991 Act are *additionally* made out. Section 1(2) of the 1991 Act (as amended by the CJA 1993) provides that a custodial sentence should not be passed unless (a) the offence, or the combination of the offence and one or more offences associated with it, was so serious that only such a sentence can be justified for the offence, or (b) where the offence is a violent or sexual offence, that only such a sentence would be adequate to protect the public from serious harm from the offender. It must be remembered that offences which have been dealt with on different sentencing occasions are not 'associated offences' (s. 31(2) of the 1991 Act). Section

1(4) of the 1991 Act will require a court which is imposing a secure training order to state in open court (and to explain to the offender in ordinary language) that either (a) or (b) in s. 1(2) applies to the case. Furthermore, s. 3 of the 1991 Act also applies to secure training orders, so that such an order cannot be imposed by a court without the court first obtaining a pre-sentence report. The relevant general law on the requirement to obtain a pre-sentence report before passing sentence is itself affected by other changes made in the CJPOA 1994; these changes are considered at 1.11 below. Suffice it to say here that, so far as secure training orders are concerned, s. 3 of the 1991 Act (as amended) will have the effect that no custodial sentence can be imposed on a person aged under 18 (unless the offence is triable only on indictment) without the court first obtaining and considering a pre-sentence report. Section 4 of the 1991 Act (additional requirements in the case of offenders who are, or appear to be, mentally disordered) also applies to secure training orders.

It may be noted that the minimum age at which a juvenile may be given a sentence of detention in a young offender institution is now 15 (raised from 14, in respect of young males, who were eligible previously, by the CJA 1991, s. 63(1)). So the secure training order can be seen as a custodial sentence targeted at persistent offenders who are too young to be given a sentence of detention in a young offender institution, but whose latest offence is not of sufficient gravity to merit their being dealt with by the Crown Court under the CYPA 1933, s. 53(2). According to Mr Maclean (*Hansard*, Commons, 11 January 1994):

> The secure training centres will not be for youngsters who have scrumped farmers' apples or stolen a few sweets from the local shop. Nor will they be for first-time offenders. They will be for offenders with at least three convictions who have breached a supervision order or offended during the period of a supervision order. We need to put in place a steady hierarchy of punishment, from a caution at the bottom to custody at the top.

A secure training order may be imposed by the Crown Court or by a youth court, but where the order is imposed by a youth court the normal restrictions upon the imposition of custodial sentences by magistrates' courts will apply. Since the minimum length of a secure training order is six months (see below) it seems that a youth court would only have power to impose an order of the minimum duration, unless the offender has been convicted of two indictable offences, in which case it would be open to the youth court to impose up to six months for each offence, consecutively.

1.2   Secure Training Orders: the Custodial Element

The new order will comprise a period of detention, followed by a period of supervision (s. 1(2)). The total length of the order is to be specified by the court, but the minimum term is six months and the maximum term is two years (s. 1(3)). The duration of the first (custodial) part of the sentence will be the same as the duration of the second (supervision) part of the sentence (s. 1(4)).

It is envisaged that the young offender will serve out the detention part of his sentence at a secure training centre. Secure training centres are defined as 'places in which offenders not less than 12 but under 17 years of age in respect of whom secure training orders have been made ... may be detained and given training and education and prepared for their release' (Prison Act 1952, s. 43(1), as amended by s. 5(2) of the 1994 Act). During the passage of the Bill through Parliament, the Home Secretary said (*Hansard* Commons, 11 January 1994, col. 24) that:

> ... the secure training centres should not be mere detention centres [but] will provide high-quality education and training designed to encourage those who benefit to lead law-abiding lives.

John Greenaway (*Hansard*, Commons, 11 January 1994, col. 65) said that when the Select Committee on Home Affairs were preparing their report in 1993, they visited Lisnevin in Northern Ireland which has provision for 40 youngsters, and is the kind of institution which is in mind. He said it provides:

> ... security, not just for the public against whom the youngsters might offend, but gives those youngsters the security of a stable environment that many of them have lacked. ... There is a clear place for challenging activity for youngsters, but it must be set in the right context. Equally there is a need to avoid turning the secure training units into oppressive Borstals or approved schools.

There is a definite air of unreality about all this discussion since, at the time of writing, no secure training centres have been built, and it seems unlikely that any will be completed within the next 12 to 18 months. Five centres are planned, each with 40 places. The centres will be built on Prison Service land but managed by the private sector subject to statutory rules to be made by the Home Secretary under the Prison Act 1952. It is not envisaged that the powers of the courts to pass secure training orders will be brought into force until the first batch of secure training centres is fully operational.

When secure training centres are built and made available to the courts, s. 2(2) of the 1994 Act will offer some alternative arrangements. If a secure training order has been imposed by the court but a place is 'not immediately available' at such a centre, the court can commit the offender to such place and on such conditions as the Secretary of State may direct. Such places are expressly stated to include accommodation made available by local authorities, voluntary organisations and registered children's homes (s. 2(5)) but might well also include young offender institutions. Committal can be for up to 28 days in the first instance (s. 2(2)(a)), but may be extended by the court on application. It is not entirely clear whether any further period of committal is also restricted to 28 days, or whether a further committal will be effective until the end of the detention period of the secure training order if no place in a secure training centre becomes available (s. 2(2)(b)). It seems from the wording that a fresh committal will be required every 28 days if no place has been found in a secure training centre.

1.3 Secure Training Orders: the Supervision Element

The latter half of the sentence will take the form of a period under the supervision of a probation officer or a local authority social worker (s. 3(2)). The category of person who is responsible for the supervision and any requirements of the offender relevant to the supervision must be written down and given to the offender before the supervision starts (s. 3(7) and (8)).

If it appears on information to a justice of the peace acting for a relevant petty sessions area (defined in s. 4(2)) that an offender subject to a secure training order has failed to comply with, or has contravened, any requirement specified in the supervision part of the order the justice may issue a summons requiring the offender to appear or, if the information is in writing and on oath, issue a warrant for the offender's arrest (s. 4(1)). If it is proved to the satisfaction of the youth court before which the offender appears that he or she has failed to comply with, or has contravened, a requirement of the supervision part of the order, the court may (a) order the offender to be detained in a secure training centre for the remainder of the order, or for three months, whichever is the shorter or (b) impose a fine on the offender not exceeding level 3 on the standard scale (s. 4(3)). The scale for fining juveniles is different from the scale for fining adults (Magistrates' Courts Act 1980, s. 36), and there are powers to require a parent or guardian to pay the fines imposed upon a juvenile (CYPA 1993, s. 55). It is not clear from the wording, but perhaps may be assumed, that if a fine is chosen as the breach penalty the supervision part of the order continues in place.

1.4   Long-term Detention of Juveniles

Long-term detention of offenders aged from 14 to 17 inclusive has in the past been ordered by the Crown Court in appropriate cases under s. 53(2) of the CYPA 1933. Section 53(2) has been subject to amendment recently by the CJA 1991 and the CJA 1993. The 1994 Act, by s. 16, makes significant further changes.

The qualifying conditions for a sentence of detention under s. 53(2) may now, once s. 16 is brought into force, be summarised as follows. The sentence is available where a person aged between 10 and 17 inclusive:

(a)   is convicted on indictment of an offence punishable in the case of an adult with imprisonment for 14 years or more, or

(b)   is convicted on indictment of the offence of indecent assault on a woman (under the Sexual Offences Act 1956, s. 14), or

(c)   (where the person convicted on indictment is aged from 14 to 17 inclusive) is convicted of causing death by dangerous driving (under the Road Traffic Act 1988, s. 1) or causing death by careless driving while under the influence of drink or drugs (under the Road Traffic Act 1988, s. 3A).

The sentence is available only where the Crown Court has dealt with the matter on indictment. In no circumstances can detention under s. 53(2) be imposed by a youth court, even where the Crown Court has remitted the juvenile to the youth court for sentence. Nor is it available where the youth court has committed an offender whom it has dealt with to Crown Court for sentence.

Prior to the 1994 Act changes the youth court had exclusive jurisdiction (homicide cases apart) over 10–13-year-olds. For offenders from 14 to 17 inclusive it had the main jurisdiction, but could commit the offender to Crown Court where the offender, if convicted on indictment, would be likely to attract a sentence under s. 53(2). The new Act extends that possibility to *all* juveniles, so that the youth court must now bear in mind the possibility of committing to Crown Court in all cases where a juvenile (of any age) has been charged with an offence punishable in the case of an adult with a maximum sentence of imprisonment for 14 years or more. Magistrates in the youth court will still retain the discretion to deal with the matter themselves. In the ordinary case, for example, of a house burglary committed by a 12-year-old the youth court will choose to exercise its own powers. Only in an exceptional case will the circumstances surrounding the burglary make committal for trial to the Crown Court appropriate.

In more detail, then, when s. 16 of the CJPOA 1994 is brought into force, s. 53(2) of the Children and Young Persons Act 1933 will be amended, with the following effect. The scope of the old s. 53(2)(a) will be expanded, so as to bring within its ambit any offender *who has attained at least the age of 10 years*, but who is not more than 17 years of age, and who has been convicted of an offence punishable in the case of an adult with imprisonment for 14 years or more, or has been convicted of the offence of indecent assault on a woman. This change should be understood in the context of the very important amendment, by para. 40 of sch. 10 of the 1994 Act, of s. 24(1) of the Magistrates' Courts Act 1980. That section formerly restricted the availability of trial on indictment for children (i.e., juveniles aged from 10 to 13 inclusive) to cases involving homicide. The 1994 Act amendment (by the removal of the words 'he has attained the age of 14' from s. 24(1)(a) of the 1980 Act), will place 10–13-year-olds charged with offences punishable with imprisonment for 14 years or more, or charged with indecent assault on a woman, at risk of being tried on indictment and receiving sentences of detention under s. 53(2). It will remain the case, however, that the offences of causing death by dangerous driving or causing death by careless driving while under the influence of drink or drugs will be capable of attracting a s. 53(2) sentence only where the defendant is aged at least 14. The old s. 53(2)(aa) will be unchanged by the 1994 Act, save that it will be renumbered as s. 53(2)(b). The old s. 53(2)(b) (child convicted of manslaughter) is redundant, given the expansion of s. 53(2)(a), and is repealed by the 1994 Act. The remaining text in the old s. 53(2) will be retained, but will be numbered as s. 53(3).

1.5 Detention in Young Offender Institution: Maximum Sentence

Section 1B(2) of the CJA 1982 prescribed that the maximum sentence of detention in a young offender institution which could be imposed upon offenders aged 15 or 16 was 12 months (unless the maximum penalty for the offence with which the offender had been convicted was less than 12 months in which case, of course, the lesser period applied). Section 1B was amended by the CJA 1991, s. 63(3)(b), so as to bring 17-year-olds within this same restriction. The effect of s. 17 of the 1994 Act is to change this maximum from 12 months to 24 months.

This increase provides much greater flexibility to the courts in prescribing custodial sentences for young offenders. The Home Secretary said (*Hansard*, Commons, 11 January, col. 24) that this change will 'give the courts the flexibility they need to deal with serious offending by that age group'. A longer custodial sentence may be available in some such cases under s. 53(2) of the CYPA 1933, but only where the offender has been convicted on indictment with an offence punishable by imprisonment for 14 years or more in the case of an adult (see further 1.4). In an ordinary case of a theft, or burglary of a shop, s. 53(2) is not available to the Crown

Court judge because these offences carry maximum penalties lower than 14 years. The maximum available custodial sentence of 12 months' detention in such cases was seen by many practitioners as unrealistic, particularly in relation to 17-year-olds.

Section 17 makes two further changes to s. 1B of the CJA 1982. Section 1B(4) prohibits the passing of a sentence of detention in a young offender institution where its effect would be that the offender would be sentenced to a total term of more than 12 months. This is clearly designed to deal with the case where the court imposes two sentences of detention of, say, nine months each on the offender, whether on the same occasion or on different occasions, but requires that the sentences should run consecutively. Section 17 again has the effect of changing the total permitted duration of sentence from 12 months to 24 months. The final change is in relation to s. 1B(5) of the 1982 Act. This currently states that where a court (in error) does impose a sentence of detention in a young offender institution in excess of 12 months upon a 15, 16 or 17-year-old, then 'so much of the term as exceeds 12 months shall be treated as remitted'. The sentence takes effect automatically as if it had been one for 12 months. Again, s. 17(4) amends the period of '12 months' to read '24 months'.

In making this last change Parliament has missed an opportunity to remedy what the Court of Appeal in *Smithyman* (1993) 14 Cr App R (S) 263 regarded as a defect in the law. In that case the Crown Court sentencer had purported to pass a sentence of three and a half years' detention in a young offender institution on a 16-year-old offender who had been convicted of false imprisonment and a very serious offence of indecent assault on a woman. Of course this was an unlawful sentence, since the maximum permissible term was 12 months. Section 1B(5) came into effect automatically, converting the sentence to one of 12 months. On appeal to the Court of Appeal there was nothing that the court could do to rescue the original sentence, even though on the facts the judge would have been entitled to pass a sentence under s. 53(2) of the Children and Young Persons Act 1933 for the longer period. Ian Kennedy J, in the Court of Appeal, suggested that the Home Office should give 'urgent attention' to the matter. If the circumstances of *Smithyman* were to recur after the 1994 Act, the original sentence would still be unlawful, but it would be replaced automatically by s. 1B(5) by a term of detention for two years.

1.6   Accommodation of Young Offenders Sentenced to Custody for Life

The sentence of custody for life is the mandatory sentence for an offender under the age of 21 who is convicted of murder (CJA 1982, s. 8(1)), unless he or she was under the age of 18 at the time of the offence, in which case the mandatory sentence is detention during Her Majesty's pleasure, under the CYPA 1933, s. 53(1). Additionally, the sentence of custody for life may be imposed on an offender aged 18, 19 or 20 who has been convicted of an offence which carries life imprisonment as the maximum penalty for an adult (CJA 1982, s. 8(2)).

Subsections (6) and (7) of s. 12 of the CJA 1982 currently state that where an offender is sentenced to custody for life, that sentence should normally be served in a prison, unless the Secretary of State otherwise directs. Section 18 of the CJPOA 1994 changes this presumption, and the relevant subsections are repealed. The presumption henceforth is that an offender serving a sentence of custody of life shall be accommodated in a young offender institution, but the Secretary of State retains a discretion to direct otherwise.

1.7 Provision, Management and Cost of Secure Accommodation for Young Persons

The Children Act 1989, s. 53(1), requires that local authorities must provide community homes for the care and accommodation of children who are being looked after by them, and for purposes connected with the welfare of children. Section 61 of the CJA 1991 further requires that local authorities must be able to provide *secure* accommodation, for the purposes of remand or committal (under s. 23(4) of the CYPA 1969) or committal to Crown Court for sentence (under s. 37(3) of the Magistrates' Courts Act 1980). Secure accommodation is defined as 'accommodation which is provided in a *community home* for the purpose of restricting liberty, and is approved for that purpose by the Secretary of State' (CYPA 1969, s. 23(12), emphasis added). The CJA 1991, s. 61(2), allows each local authority to discharge their statutory duty either by providing the secure accommodation themselves or, if this is not possible, by making an arrangement with another local authority for them to provide it. In fact, however, apparently because of problems of funding, a number of local authorities are currently unable to provide secure accommodation, either themselves or by convenient agreement. The purpose of s. 19 of the CJPOA 1994 is to ease this problem somewhat, by extending the statutory definition of 'secure accommodation' to include *voluntary homes* and *registered community homes* as well as community homes. Schedules 5 and 6 of the Children Act 1989 provide for the regulation of voluntary homes and registered children's homes. Section 19 of the 1994 Act amends these schedules, and also amends s. 61 of the 1991 Act in such a way as to permit accommodation in these homes (with the approval of the Secretary of State) to be designated as secure accommodation.

Section 53 of the Children Act 1989 is itself amended by s. 22 of the 1994 Act so as to reduce somewhat the heavy burden imposed on local authorities by the requirement to provide and to *manage* secure accommodation. Local authorities are, by the 1994 Act, now permitted to make arrangements for some agency other than themselves to take over the management of a community home. It seems, however, that whether the secure accommodation has been provided by the local authority itself, or by a voluntary association in agreement with the local authority, that authority cannot divest itself of its basic statutory obligation, under s. 53, to equip and maintain that accommodation.

Section 21 of the 1994 Act is headed: 'Cost of secure accommodation'. Section 21 inserts a new s. 61A into the CJA 1991, stating that the Home Secretary may defray the whole or any part of 'any costs incurred by a local authority in discharging their duty' in the provision of secure accommodation. On the face of it, this might be taken to cover capital costs (the building of a new secure accommodation provision, or the refurbishment of an existing building) but the note on the financial effects of the Bill, annexed to the Bill itself, indicates that this clause will allow the Home Secretary to:

> defray the costs of court-ordered secure remands ... as he may determine on a fee-paying basis. Costs are expected to be in the order of £16 million a full year for revenue payments.

This indicates revenue, rather than capital, costs. The note on the financial effects of the Bill, annexed to the Bill itself, indicates that capital grants from central government will support local authorities who design and build the secure accommodation required, although there may also be provision by the voluntary and private sectors.

1.8 Detention of Young Persons after Charge and Remands to Secure Accommodation

Section 24 of the 1994 Act amends the rules governing the detention of arrested juveniles after charge.

Section 59 of the CJA 1991 made changes to s. 38(6) of PACE 1984 dealing with the duties of a custody officer after an *arrested juvenile* has been charged with an offence, and where the custody officer is of the view that the juvenile should be detained after arrest rather than being released with or without bail. New subsections (6) and (6A) of s. 38 were substituted by the CJA 1991. The effect of this was that the custody officer must ensure (with two exceptions) that a juvenile detained after arrest is transferred to local authority accommodation rather than to a penal institution. The two exceptional situations are:

(a)   where this is impracticable (the officer must give reasons why this is so) and,

(b)   where the juvenile has reached the age of 15 and it appears that local authority accommodation would not be adequate to protect the public from serious harm from that juvenile, and no secure accommodation provision is available.

The change to these arrangements brought about by s. 24 of the 1994 Act is to *extend their application to juveniles aged from 12 to 14 inclusive.*

Sections 20 and 21 of the 1994 Act amended the rules on secure remands for juveniles. Section 23 of the CYPA 1969 (as amended by s. 60 of the CJA 1991 and as modified by s. 62 of the same Act) provides that if a court remands a juvenile who is *charged with, or convicted of, one or more offences,* and commits that juvenile for trial or sentence, and bail has been refused, then the remand or committal must be to local authority accommodation, rather than to a penal institution. Additionally and exceptionally, a court which remands or commits such a child or young person may, after consultation with the relevant local authority, require that authority to place and keep the child or young person in 'secure accommodation' (CYPA 1969, s. 23(4) and (5)). The CJA 1991 put in place arrangements for the remand and committal of young offenders to secure accommodation. By s. 23(5) of the CYPA 1969 (as substituted by s. 60 of the 1991 Act), the power to remand or commit to secure accommodation is available where the child or young person:

(a)   is charged with or has been convicted of a 'violent offence' or a 'sexual offence' (for definitions of these terms see s. 31(1) of the 1991 Act, and for an amendment of the latter see sch. 9, para. 45 of the 1994 Act and 1.19 below) or an offence punishable in the case of an adult with a term of imprisonment of 14 years or more, or

(b)   has a recent history of absconding while remanded to local authority accommodation, and is charged with or has been convicted of an imprisonable offence alleged or found to have been committed while he was so remanded.

The court must also be of the opinion that only a requirement to keep the person in secure accommodation would be 'adequate to protect the public from serious harm from him'. At present the courts are empowered to impose a 'security requirement' only when remanding 15 and 16-year-olds, though in fact the 1991 Act powers have *not* been brought into force. The further change to these arrangements, brought about by s. 20 of the 1994 Act, is to *extend their application to persons aged from 12 to 14 inclusive*. The change may be brought into effect in stages (i.e., first for 14-year-olds, then for 13-year-olds, and then finally for 12-year-olds). Section 21 provides for the costs involved in local authorities complying with court-ordered remands to be reimbursed by the government.

One further adjustment is made to s. 23 of the CYPA 1969 by the 1994 Act. This change is made (coincidentally and rather confusingly) by s. 23 of the 1994 Act, which inserts a new s. 23A into the 1969 Act. If a juvenile is remanded or committed to local authority accommodation under s. 23 of the 1969 Act then conditions may be attached to the remand or committal under s. 23(7) or (10) requiring the juvenile to comply with any conditions which could be imposed under s. 3(6) of the Bail Act 1976 if the juvenile were being granted bail. The new s. 23A(1) of the 1969 Act gives a power of arrest in a case where a police officer has reasonable grounds for suspecting that the person remanded or committed has broken any of those conditions. The new s. 23A(2) and (3) provide further details relating to this power of arrest.

1.9 Media Restrictions in Cases Involving Juveniles

By a general rule to be found in s. 49 of the CYPA 1933, the media *may not* report the name, or give any other identifying details (such as the address or school), of a juvenile charged, or any other juvenile involved (such as a witness), in criminal proceedings in a youth court. No picture of the child may be published. Contravention of this rule is an offence punishable on summary conviction by a fine not exceeding level 5. Such prohibition may, exceptionally, be lifted if the court thinks that to do so is appropriate to avoid injustice to the juvenile. The position which exists in the youth court may be contrasted with that which obtains in the adult magistrates' court, and in the Crown Court, where the juvenile's name and other details *may* be publicised unless the court makes an order to the contrary.

The CJPOA 1994 makes a relatively small change to these arrangements, as they apply to youth courts. At present the restrictions in s. 49 have the effect that the media cannot identify, or publish photographs of, juveniles who are alleged to have committed or have been convicted of offences, but who are now 'unlawfully at large', having absconded. In that particular context, the government has made clear its view that the media restrictions make the task of the police in recapturing those young people much harder. A new s. 49 of the CYPA 1933 is substituted by (coincidentally and rather confusingly) s. 49 of the 1994 Act. The changes made to the law by the 1994 Act permit juveniles 'unlawfully at large' to be named, and their photographs to be published. Before a court can make an order dispensing with the normal media restrictions in such cases, however, it must be satisfied that the relevant juvenile has been charged with, or convicted of (a) a violent offence, or (b) a sexual offence, or (c) an offence punishable in the case of adult with imprisonment for 14 years or more (new s. 49(6)). Application by or on behalf of the Director of Public Prosecutions is required, and notice of that application must be given to the legal representative of the juvenile (new s. 49(7)). 'Sexual offence' and 'violent offence' have the same meanings as they do in the CJA 1991, s. 31 (but it should be noted that an amendment has been made to the definition of the former term by para. 45 of sch. 9 of the 1994 Act; see 1.19 below).

SENTENCING

1.10   Taking Account of Guilty Pleas

Section 48(1) of the CJPOA 1994 provides that when determining what sentence to pass on an offender who has pleaded guilty, the court shall take into account:

    (a)   the stage in the proceedings for the offence at which the offender indicated his intention to plead guilty, and
    (b)   the circumstances in which this indication was given.

Section 48(2) states that whenever the sentencing court, in consequence of taking into account the matters referred to in subsection (1), 'imposes a punishment on the offender which is less severe than the punishment it would otherwise have imposed, it shall state in open court that it has done so'.

    This provision may be traced to recommendation 156 in the *Report of the Royal Commission on Criminal Justice* (Cm 2263, 1993) that: 'The present system of sentence discounts should be more clearly articulated, with earlier pleas attracting higher discounts'. The Commission, in taking up ideas that had earlier been floated in a Bar Council Working Party report (*The Efficient Disposal of Business in the Crown Court* (Chairman Robert Seabrook QC)), in fact made much more far-reaching proposals to the effect that there should be adopted in England and Wales more formalised a regime of 'plea bargaining', akin to the American system. This suggestion was made by the Commission in response to the problem of 'cracked trials', where defendants change their pleas to guilty at a very late stage because, the Commission suggested, of 'a reluctance to face the facts until they are at the door of the court' (p. 112). The Commission envisaged hearings at which the defendant could ask the judge for an indication of the highest sentence which would be imposed if the defendant pleaded guilty, and the judge could, if it was thought appropriate, provide such indication (on the facts of the case as known to the judge at that time). This exercise would be known as a 'sentence canvass'. There was much criticism of this suggestion (which would have effectively reversed the current leading decision in *Turner* [1972] WLR 1093) following publication of the Royal Commission's Report. The Lord Chief Justice, Lord Taylor of Gosforth, for one, expressed his opposition to such a development in English law, and the government abandoned plans to legislate to this effect at a fairly early stage. Retained within s. 48, however, are the vestiges of a legislative attempt to impose greater order on the existing system of discounting sentence in response to the defendant's guilty plea.

    It is a very well established principle of sentencing that a defendant who pleads guilty attracts a lower sentence than would be imposed on conviction of the identical offence after a trial. Sometimes a guilty plea may provide evidence of remorse, itself a mitigating factor. More frequently, however, the sentence discount is a recognition that the defendant has by his guilty plea avoided the need for a full trial of the issue, and thereby saved a great deal of time, public expense, inconvenience (and perhaps distress) for witnesses. The Royal Commission (at p. 112) suggested a three-point system of graduated sentence discount:

(a) The most generous discount should be available to the defendant who indicates a guilty plea in response to the service of the case disclosed by the prosecution.

(b) The next most generous discount should be available to the defendant who indicates a guilty plea in sufficient time to avoid full preparation for trial. The discount might be less if the plea were entered only after a preparatory hearing.

(c) At the bottom of the scale should come the discount for a guilty plea entered on the day of the trial itself. Since resources would be saved by avoiding a contested trial even at this late stage, the Commission thought that some discount should continue to be available. But it should be appreciably smaller than for a guilty plea offered at one of the earlier stages.

The Commission was probably only proposing a clarification of the existing principles. Many decisions of the Court of Appeal on appeal against sentence make reference to the operation of the discount in particular cases. A leading authority in the area is *Hollington* (1985) 7 Cr App R (S) 364, which covers broadly the same ground as the Commission and also recognises that variable discounts are appropriate to reflect the different stages at which the plea may be tendered. According to Lawton LJ (at p. 367):

This court has long said that discounts on sentences are appropriate but everything depends upon the circumstances of each case. If a man is arrested and at once tells the police that he is guilty and cooperates with them in the recovery of property and the identification of others concerned in the offence, he can expect to get a substantial discount. But if a man is arrested in circumstances in which he cannot hope to put forward a defence of not guilty, he cannot expect much by way of discount. In between comes this kind of case, where the court has been put to considerable trouble as a result of a tactical plea. The sooner it is appreciated that defendants are not going to get full discount for pleas of guilty in these sorts of circumstances, the better it will be for the administration of justice.

Other decisions of the Court of Appeal make it clear that there is a range of circumstances in which the normal discount may be reduced or lost (see *Costen* (1989) 11 Cr App R (S) 182), such as where the defendant has been caught red-handed (*Morris* (1988) 10 Cr App R (S) 216) or where, although pleading guilty, the defendant disputes an important element of the prosecution case so that a *Newton* hearing (see (1982) 4 Cr App R (S) 388) must be held to resolve the matter. Although nearly all discussion of the guilty plea discount relates to the sentencing of cases on indictment, it is clear that the same principles apply to magistrates' courts. The Magistrates' Association's *Sentencing Guidelines* (1993), for example, state that the sentence starting-points indicated therein should be reduced by approximately one third where there has been a 'timely guilty plea'.

In the light of the foregoing discussion, it may be thought that s. 48(1) of the 1994 Act does no more than confirm the effect of the existing case law, which already addresses the 'stage of the proceedings' at which the plea was tendered and the 'circumstances' surrounding the plea. If this is correct, s. 48(1) achieves nothing. Dr David Thomas has described the section as a 'clumsy and partial attempt to turn [the case-law principles] into statute' (*Sentencing News*, 26 April 1994). It may, however, take us somewhat further than the case law. The Court of Appeal authorities are almost all concerned with the appropriate discount from a custodial sentence, and there is very little discussion of the effect of plea on other forms of sentence, such as fines or community sentences. There is also no clear view in the cases on whether a timely guilty plea can properly save an offender from a custodial sentence, such that a community sentence can be given instead. Nothing in s. 48(1) would prevent the 'discount' operating in these ways: it speaks merely of a punishment 'less severe' than it otherwise would have been. One matter is, however, clear. Suspension of a sentence of imprisonment on the basis of a guilty plea is never permissible, since the Court of Appeal has said that even an early plea cannot constitute the 'exceptional circumstances' which must be shown to exist before a suspended sentence can be passed (Powers of Criminal Courts Act 1973, s. 22(2)(b), as interpreted and applied in *Okinikan* [1993] 1 WLR 173).

Section 48(2) imposes a new duty upon all sentencers, whether in the Crown Court or the magistrates' court. An explanatory statement must be made in open court in every case where the court has, in the light of the defendant's guilty plea, imposed a sentence less severe than it otherwise would have imposed. This obligation on the court seems a little unrealistic in the context of magistrates' courts, where the great majority of cases proceed by way of guilty plea. The requirement is yet one more matter that the sentencing court must remember to comply with when passing sentence. In a case where custody is imposed, the sentencer must now state the criterion for custody relied upon (CJA 1991, s. 1(2)(a) or (b)), the reason why that criterion is satisfied in the instant case, an explanation of this in ordinary language (CJA 1991, s. 1(4)), the reason why a compensation order has not been passed (Powers of Criminal Courts Act 1973, s. 35(1)), and now the guilty plea discount. So s. 48(2) may be regarded as a potential pitfall for sentencers but, since the section fails to specify what the consequences of a failure to comply with this requirement would be, it may perhaps be assumed that such failure would not have the effect of invalidating the sentence imposed.

1.11   Pre-sentence Reports

The CJA 1991 made the obtaining of a pre-sentence report mandatory in most cases before the passing of a custodial sentence or before the passing of certain kinds of community sentence. There has been concern amongst practitioners, since those provisions came into force in October 1992, that they were causing an unacceptably high rate of court adjournments to obtain reports in cases where the sentencing outcome was clear and the report could in practice make no difference to the disposal. Paragraph 40 of sch. 9 to the CJPOA 1994 makes important changes. These are, essentially, to water down the requirement to obtain pre-sentence reports on offenders aged 18 or over, and to permit courts to dispense with the obtaining of a report in such cases if the court is of the view that to obtain one is 'unnecessary'.

Paragraph 40 amends various subsections of s. 3 of the 1991 Act, and inserts new subsections (2A) and (4A). For convenience, s. 3 is here set out, as it will be after amendment by the 1994 Act:

(1) Subject to subsection (2) below, a court shall obtain and consider a pre-sentence report before forming any such opinion as is mentioned in subsection (2) of section 1 or 2 above.

(2) Subsection (1) above does not apply if, in the circumstances of the case, the court is of the opinion that it is unnecessary to obtain a pre-sentence report.

(2A) In the case of an offender under the age of 18 years, save where the offence or any other offence associated with it is triable only on indictment, the court shall not form such an opinion as is mentioned in subsection (2) above or subsection (4A) below unless there exists a previous pre-sentence report obtained in respect of the offender and the court has had regard to the information contained in that report, or, if there is more than one such report, the most recent report.

(3) In forming any such opinion as is mentioned in subsection (2) of section 1 or 2 above a court—

(a) shall take into account all such information about the circumstances of the offence (including any aggravating or mitigating factors) as is available to it; and

(b) in the case of any such opinion as is mentioned in paragraph (b) of that subsection, may take into account any information about the offender which is before it.

(4) No custodial sentence shall be invalidated by the failure of a court to obtain and consider a pre-sentence report before forming an opinion referred to in subsection (1) above but any court on an appeal against such a sentence—

(a) shall, subject to subsection (4A) below, obtain a pre-sentence report if none was obtained by the court below; and

(b) shall consider any such report obtained by it or that court.

(4A) Subsection (4)(a) above does not apply if the court is of the opinion—

(a) that the court below was justified in forming an opinion that it was unnecessary to obtain a pre-sentence report, or

(b) that, although the court below was not justified in forming that opinion, in the circumstances of the case at the time it is before the court, it is unnecessary to obtain a pre-sentence report.

(5) [Definitions.]

The upshot of these changes is to relax considerably the requirement on a sentencing court to obtain a pre-sentence report prior to passing sentence on an *offender aged 18 or over*. Under the former law a limited discretion was given to the court not to obtain or consider a pre-sentence report where, in respect of any offender, the offence was triable only on indictment and the court felt that to obtain one would be 'unnecessary'. This was a way of saying that custody was inevitable, and to require the production of a report would be a waste of time. The revised s. 3 broadens the court's discretion not to obtain a report, to *any* case involving an offender aged 18 or over. For offenders aged under 18, the position remains much the same as before, with the court almost always required to have sight of a pre-sentence report, unless the offence is triable only on indictment and the court thinks a report would be unnecessary. If the court fails to obtain a report and imposes a custodial sentence, it would normally be appropriate for the appellate court to receive a report but, again, the law is extended by subsection (4A) so that even where the sentencing court should have obtained one, the appellate court can waive this requirement. Suppose that the sentencing court failed to obtain a report (and there was no earlier one, or the court did not have sight of it) before imposing a custodial sentence on an offender under 18 for an offence of burglary. The sentence is certainly not invalidated by this failure (s. 3(4)), and it is open to the Court of Appeal to overlook it, by concluding that (as the circumstances stand at the time of the appeal) there is no need to obtain one (s. 3(4A)(b)).

Paragraph 40 of sch. 9 to the 1994 Act makes parallel changes to s. 7 of the 1991 Act (requirement to obtain pre-sentence report before passing certain community sentences). Formerly, the obtaining of a pre-sentence report was mandatory before the court passed a sentence of (a) probation (where the order included additional requirements authorised by sch. 1A to the 1991 Act), (b) community service, (c) a combination order or (d) a supervision order (where the order included requirements imposed under s. 12, s. 12A, s. 12AA, s. 12B or s. 12C of the CYPA 1969). Following the 1994 Act amendments, the sentencing court may dispense with a pre-sentence report in the case of an adult if it regards such a report as 'unnecessary'. Again, for offenders aged under 18, the position remains much the same as before, with the court almost always required to have sight of a pre-sentence report, unless the offence is triable only on indictment and the court thinks that a report would be 'unnecessary'.

1.12 Probation Orders: Provision for Treatment by Psychologist

Schedule 1A of Powers of Criminal Courts Act 1973 allows for the insertion into a probation order of a condition that the offender, during the whole or part of the order, shall receive treatment (either as a resident or non-resident patient) for a mental condition. For recent information on the operation of this type of probation order see the report by the Inspectorate of Probation, *Probation Orders with Requirements for Psychiatric Treatment* (London: Home Office, 1993). By para. 10 of sch. 9 to the 1994 Act, where a court inserts such a requirement into a probation order, provision is now made for that treatment to be carried out by or under the direction of a chartered psychologist, as an alternative to its being provided by a doctor. For these purposes a 'chartered psychologist' means a person for the time being listed in the British Psychological Society's Register of Chartered Psychologists.

Paragraph 10 achieves this effect by amending para. 5 of sch. 1A to the Powers of Criminal Courts Act 1973. It seems clear from the changes that have been made that while a psychologist may now carry out the relevant treatment, it will remain essential to receive the evidence of a 'duly qualified medical practitioner', approved for the purposes of s. 12 of the Mental Health Act 1983, before a probation order with a condition of psychiatric treatment can be made by the court. The evidence of a chartered psychologist would not fulfil this requirement.

Parallel arrangements for the insertion of a requirement of mental treatment also exist in relation to supervision orders for young offenders (CYPA 1969, s. 12B). The 1994 Act makes no change there, so that treatment requirements in that context can still only be carried out by a doctor, rather than by a chartered psychologist.

1.13 Probation Orders: Rehabilitation Period

By para. 11 of sch. 9 to the 1994 Act, the rehabilitation period for offenders aged 18 or over at the date of conviction who are sentenced to probation becomes five years. For offenders under the age of 18 at the date of conviction, the rehabilitation period becomes two and a half years, or the duration of the order, whichever is the longer. This change, made by amendment to Table A in s. 5 of the Rehabilitation of Offenders Act 1974, applies only to persons placed on probation after the date on which para. 11 is brought into force.

Formerly the rehabilitation period after a probation order was one year, or the duration of the order, whichever was the longer. The change to the law no doubt belatedly recognises the fact that the CJA 1991 altered the status of probation orders, so that they became punishments and sentences in their own right. The new rehabilitation period for probation brings it into line with community service orders and combination orders, which seems appropriate. In doing so, however, it certainly creates an anomaly with respect to supervision orders, made under the CYPA 1969, where the relevant period remains at one year, or the duration of the order, whichever is the longer. Offenders aged 16 or 17 are eligible to receive both supervision orders and probation orders, and there are a number of similarities between these two sentences, such that the existence of different rehabilitation periods looks rather odd.

1.14 Previous Probation Orders and Discharges

Paragraph 44 of sch. 9 to the 1994 Act makes further amendment to the much-discussed s. 29 of the CJA 1991, which deals with the relevance to sentence of the offender's previous convictions and his response to previous sentences.

The 1994 Act amendment is a minor, and absurdly technical one. It relates to previous convictions of the offender which have been dealt with by way of a probation order, or by conditional or absolute discharge. The problem here is that in the past these sentences (by virtue of s. 13 of the Powers of Criminal Courts Act 1973) were not to be regarded as amounting to 'convictions' for a range of purposes and (by virtue of s. 2 and s. 7 of the 1973 Act) were in the past not to be regarded as 'sentences' either. Section 13 was repealed by the CJA 1991 (with effect from 1 October 1992) and replaced by s. 1C of the Powers of Criminal Courts Act 1973. Section 1C has broadly the same effect as s. 13, but applied only to discharges and not to probation orders (the latter having been elevated by the 1991 Act to the status of punishments and sentences in their own right). Subsections (3) and (4) of s. 29 of the CJA 1991 were inserted by the CJA 1993, s. 66(6). Section 29(3) states that conditional discharges and probation orders imposed before the 1991 Act came into force *are* to be regarded as *sentences* for the purposes of s. 29. Section 29(3) is unaffected by the 1994 Act changes. Section 29(4) states that conditional discharges and probation orders imposed before the 1991 Act came into force *are* to be regarded as *convictions* for the purposes of s. 29. But s. 29, presumably because of legislative oversight, made no reference to *absolute* discharges (a defect noted by Ashworth and Gibson in their article 'CJA 1993: altering the sentencing framework' [1994] Crim LR 101 at p. 105). That omission is now remedied by para. 44 of sch. 9 to the 1994 Act, and so previous convictions which were followed by absolute discharges now count as convictions for the purposes of s. 29 as well.

New subsections (5) and (6) are added to s. 29 by para. 44, and all the amendments in para. 44 are made retrospective. The effect of the new s. 29(5) is that conditional discharges imposed after the 1991 Act came into force count as *sentences* (they probably did anyway, and the change is for the avoidance of doubt), and the effect of s. 29(6) is that conditional and absolute discharges imposed after the 1991 Act came into force count as *convictions*.

These amendments were described above as 'absurdly technical'. The original purpose of ss. 2, 7 and 13 of the Powers of Criminal Courts Act 1973 was to limit the impact of 'conviction' and 'sentence' upon the lives of individuals upon whom the courts had imposed lenient sentences, presumably for relatively minor matters. These provisions predated the Rehabilitation of Offenders Act 1974, but were motivated by a similar laudable aim of reducing stigma. In the event, however, it seems that they, and their statutory descendants, have achieved little of practical value. Their main effect has been to add unmeritorious complications to successive statutory changes in the sentencing sphere.

As a footnote to all this, it may be noted that the repeal of s. 13 of the Powers of Criminal Courts Act 1973 by the 1991 Act (and its replacement by insertion of s. 1C into the 1973 Act) failed to take account of the Magistrates' Courts Act 1980, s. 108(1A) (right of appeal against discharge), and this omission has now required remedy by para. 16 of sch. 9 to the 1994 Act.

1.15 Curfew Orders

Paragraph 41 of sch. 9 makes a minor amendment to the arrangements set out in s. 12 of the CJA 1991 for the use by the courts of curfew orders. Neither s. 12, nor the closely associated provision in s. 13, which permits electronic monitoring of offenders under curfew, has yet been brought into force, so this is an example of the law being changed prior to its implementation! Paragraph 41 adds a new subsection (4A) to s. 12, stating that the sentencing court shall not make a curfew order without first being satisfied that 'arrangements for monitoring the offender's whereabouts are available in the area'.

This change seems to be designed to allow an area-by-area introduction of curfew orders with electronic monitoring, if and when these provisions are actually brought into force. According to the financial memorandum which was attached to the Criminal Justice and Public Order Bill, the government is planning to conduct pilot trials of curfew orders with electronic monitoring, from January 1995, at a total cost of £1.4 million. For the rather discouraging results of an earlier experiment see Home Office Research Study No 120, *Electronic Monitoring: the Trials and their Results*, 1990.

1.16 Fines and Financial Circumstances Orders

Paragraph 42 of sch 9 to the 1994 Act makes a number of minor adjustments to ss. 18 and 20 of the CJA 1991 (as substituted by the CJA 1993). These sections contain general principles applicable to the imposition of fines by criminal courts, and they are relevant both to the Crown Court and to magistrates' courts.

The objective of the amendments seems to be to exclude non-individuals (i.e., corporations) from the normal requirement that the court must, before fixing the amount of any fine, inquire into the defendant's financial circumstances (normally by making a financial circumstances order, under s. 20). As far as corporations are concerned, however, s. 18(3) continues to apply. This imposes a somewhat less stringent requirement, that the court when fixing the amount of the fine 'shall take into account the circumstances of the case including, among other things, the financial circumstances of the offender so far as they are known, or appear, to the court'.

Paragraph 42 also amends s. 57(4) of the 1991 Act. This section deals with the circumstances in which a parent or guardian will be required in law to pay the fine of a juvenile. Such an order may be made against a local authority which has responsibility for offenders under the age of 18 who are in the authority's care. The purpose of the amendment to s. 57(4) is to exempt the court, in such a case, from being required to conduct a rather artificial inquiry into the 'means' of the local authority. This objective seems proper, but the method of achieving it is rather clumsy, and not clearly effective. Paragraph 42(4) leaves para. (a) of s. 57(4) in place, but that paragraph is not applicable to a local authority, since a local authority is not an 'individual'. Paragraph (b) of s. 57(4) is, on the other hand, to be 'omitted' and is repealed by sch. 11. This appears to leave the whole of s. 57(4) redundant where a local authority is to pay the fine. It is submitted that it is paragraph (a), and not (b), which should have been omitted.

Paragraph 43 inserts a new s. 20A into the CJA 1991, dealing with false statements as to financial circumstances. This provision is closely analogous to CJA 1991, s. 20(3), but that subsection deals with false statements made by persons *convicted*, while the new subsection deals with such statements made by those *charged*.

1.17 Confiscation Orders: Variation of Sentence

Paragraphs 28, 36 and 51 of sch. 9 to the 1994 Act make identical amendments to the confiscation order powers under the Drug Trafficking Offences Act 1986, the CJA 1988 and the Northern Ireland (Emergency Provisions) Act 1991. The sections amended are s. 1A of the 1986 Act, s. 72A of the 1988 Act and s. 48(3B) of the 1991 Act, all of which were inserted by the CJA 1993. The amended sections relate to the various powers of the courts to postpone determination required before a confiscation order can be made. The amendment to the 1986 Act has subsequently been consolidated in the Drug Trafficking Act 1994, s. 3(10) and accordingly the CJPOA 1994, sch. 9, para. 28 is repealed with effect from 3 February 1995.

The new changes state that where the court has sentenced the defendant during the specified period it may, after the expiry of that period, vary the sentence by imposing a fine (or such other penalty as is permitted by the relevant Act) so long as this is done within a period corresponding to that allowed under s. 47(2) or (3) of the Supreme Court Act 1981 (variation of sentence), or the equivalent s. 49(2) or (3) of the Judicature (Northern Ireland) Act 1978.

1.18 Committal for Sentence

By para. 15 of sch. 9 further amendment is made to s. 38 of the Magistrates' Courts Act 1980 (power of magistrates' court to commit offender aged not less than 18 who is convicted of an offence triable either way to Crown Court for sentence). This section was reshaped by the CJA 1991, and further amended by the CJA 1993. Prior to amendment by the 1994 Act a magistrates' court could commit for sentence under s. 38(2) if it was of the opinion:

(a) that the offence or the combination of the offence and one or more offences associated with it was so serious that greater punishment should be inflicted than the court has power to impose; or

(b) in the case of a violent or sexual offence *committed by a person who is not less than 21 years old*, that a *sentence of imprisonment* for a term longer than the court has power to impose is necessary to protect the public from serious harm from him. (emphasis added)

The amendments made by the 1994 Act are to remove the first italicised phrase in the text above, and to change the second italicised phrase so as to read 'custodial sentence'. It was never clear why in the 1991 Act reform s. 38(2)(b) was confined to cases of imprisonment, rather than also extending to sentences of detention in a young offender institution, particularly when s. 38(2)(a) did extend to offenders aged 18 or over. Now both limbs of s. 38(2) are applicable in respect of offenders aged 18 and over.

1.19   Definition of Sexual Offence

Paragraph 45 of sch. 9 provides a new definition of 'sexual offence' to replace the original definition set out in s. 31(1) of the CJA 1991. This definition is relevant for a number of legal purposes, but most importantly where the sentencing court is considering whether a custodial sentence can be justified on an offender on the ground (under s. 1(2)(b) of the CJA 1991) that the 'offence is a violent or sexual offence [and] that only such a sentence would be adequate to protect the public from serious harm from' the offender or is considering the appropriate duration of a longer-than-normal custodial sentence on the offender on the ground (under s. 2(2)(b) of the 1991 Act) that the offence is a violent or sexual offence and such sentence 'in the opinion of the court is necessary to protect the public from serious harm from the offender'.

Paragraph 45 amends the definition of 'sexual offence' in four respects:

(a) The first is to include the offence of burglary with intent to rape (Theft Act 1968, s. 9). The exclusion of this offence from the original definition was confirmed by the Court of Appeal in *Joszko* (1994) *The Times*, 11 August 1994 (although on the particular facts of that case the court held that the burglary constituted a 'violent offence', thereby justifying a longer-than-normal sentence in any event).

(b) The second is to include the offence of commission by a person in authority of unlawful sexual intercourse with a mental patient (Mental Health Act 1959, s. 128), an offence which also extends to the commission by a person in authority of an act of buggery or gross indecency with a mental patient (Sexual Offences Act 1967, s. 1).

(c) The third is to extend the definition to include, as well as all the substantive offences listed in s. 31(1), conspiracies, attempts and incitements to commit any of those offences. It was noted by commentators on the 1991 Act that the original provision was defective in failing to provide for this (see, for example, Wasik and

Taylor, *Blackstone's Guide to the Criminal Justice Act 1991*, 1.10). In *Robinson* [1993] 1 WLR 168 the Court of Appeal had to decide whether the offence of attempted rape fell within the terms of the original s. 31(1), and managed to find that it did. The reasoning was that although attempted rape was an offence indicted under s. 1 of the Criminal Attempts Act 1981, the maximum penalty for it was set out in the Sexual Offences Act 1956. Thus it could be said that attempted rape was a 'sexual offence' for the purposes of the CJA 1991. This perhaps rather strained interpretation can now be avoided.

(d)   It should be noted that while previously some offences contained in the Sexual Offences Act 1967 were within the definition, no offence contained in that Act is within the scope of the new definition.

The new definition of 'sexual offence' will apply to offenders convicted (but not sentenced) before that date when itis brought into force as it applies in relation to offenders convicted after that date.

1.20   Reviews of Lenient Sentences

Paragraph 34 of sch. 9 relates to the power of the Court of Appeal to review sentencing decisions of the Crown Court which are referred to it by the Attorney-General on the ground that the sentence imposed may have been unduly lenient (see CJA 1988, ss. 35 and 36). Currently the Court of Appeal may only consider such a reference where the offence for which the sentence was passed was either:

(a)   an offence triable only on indictment (see, on this, *Attorney-General's Reference (No. 3) of 1993* (1994) 98 Cr App R 275, which held that an offence which was triable only on indictment in respect of an adult, such as rape, was 'triable only on indictment' for the purposes of s. 35, notwithstanding that a person aged under 18 might be tried summarily for that offence), or

(b)   an offence triable either way and specified in an order made by the Home Secretary by statutory instrument under power conferred on him by s. 35(4). To date there has been only one such statutory instrument, the Criminal Justice Act 1988 (Reviews of Sentencing) Order (SI 1994/119), which extends the power to review lenient sentences to the offences of indecent assault on a woman or on a man (Sexual Offences Act 1956, ss. 14 and 15), threats to kill (Offences against the Person Act 1861, s. 16), cruelty to persons under 16 (CYPA 1933, s. 1), and attempting to commit or inciting the commission of any of these offences.

Paragraph 34 makes a minor (and somewhat obscure) addition to the wording of s. 35 of the CJA 1988. It extends the power of the Home Secretary to specify not only specific offences (as in the order referred to above) but also to 'cases of a description specified in an order under this section'.

1.21   Binding over of Parent or Guardian

Section 58(1) of the CJA 1991 places an obligation upon sentencers to bind over the parent or guardian of an offender who is under the age of 16, whenever the court is satisfied that to do so would be desirable in the interests of preventing the commission by the young offender of further offences. If the court is not satisfied of that on the particular facts of the case then it is required to state in open court that it is not and give reasons for that view. The court may order the parent or guardian to enter into a recognisance, in a sum not exceeding £1,000, or take proper care of the young offender and to exercise proper control over him or her (s. 58(2)). The maximum duration of the recognisance is three years, or until the young offender reaches the age of 18 years, whichever is the shorter period. The consent of the parent or guardian is required for this, but an unreasonable refusal to consent can be punished by a fine not exceeding £1,000.

Paragraph 50 of sch. 9 to the 1994 Act inserts a further power into s. 58(2) of the CJA 1991, whereby the court which has passed on a young offender a community order (as defined in s. 6 of the CJA 1991 to include probation orders, community service orders, supervision orders, combination orders and attendance centre orders) may include within the recognisance a provision that the parent or guardian shall ensure that the minor complies with the requirements of that community sentence. It is clear that a failure by the parent or guardian to comply would result in a forfeiture of the whole or part of the recognisance.

1.22   Changes to Maximum Penalties

Section 157 of the 1994 Act increases the maximum penalties available for particular offences. Subsections (1) and (2) give effect to the increases in fines set out in column 2 of parts I and II of sch. 8 to the Act. None of these increases apply to offences committed before s. 157 comes into force (s. 157(9)). The changes are as follows:

(1)   Offences under the Sea Fisheries (Shellfish) Act 1967   Fine levels are increased for offences involving fishing or dredging for shellfish in contravention of restrictions, the landing, taking or selling of certain types of shellfish, and the obstruction of officials.

(2)   Offences under the Misuse of Drugs Act 1971   The increases in drug offence penalties relate (with one exception) to Class C drugs. Class C drugs are mainly amphetamines and related substances. The maximum fine for producing, supplying, possessing with intent to supply these drugs increases from £500 to £2,500, and the maximum fine for simple possession of a class C drug is increased from £200 to £1,000. The one exceptional case is the possession of cannabis (which is a Class B, rather than a Class C, drug), where the maximum fine is increased from £500 to £2,500.

At the time when these increases were announced, concerns were expressed that they would result in a backlog of unpaid fines leading to more people going to jail. In a leader in *The Justice of Peace* for 12 March 1994 the editor of that journal commented on the views of some that:

> ... there has not been a rise in the level of fines for this type of offence for 20 years or more and the current tariff or starting-point for offences of this nature has become derisory.

The editor goes on to stress, however, that fines imposed for these offences must be kept in proportion to offence seriousness, take account of mitigation and, most importantly, the means of the offender. The Magistrates' Association's *Sentencing Guidelines*, issued in 1993, indicate that for an offence of simple possession of cannabis, the level of fine would be determined by the amount held, but that the guideline fine is £180.

The Home Secretary was quoted (in *The Times*, 15 February 1994) as saying that possession of cannabis was 'a minor offence' and could often be dealt with by way of caution on a first offence. He went on to say that the circumstances in which the maximum fine for possession of cannabis might be used would be where it was difficult to prove that persons who had been found in possession of a large amount of cannabis were in fact supplying it to others. This would be a dangerous line for the courts to take, however. If a defendant is convicted of, or pleads guilty to, possession of cannabis, it is contrary to sentencing principle to pitch the level of the fine on the basis that he was supplying the drug, but that this cannot be proved (see *Johnson* (1984) 6 Cr App R (S) 227, applying *Ayensu* (1982) 4 Cr App R (S) 248).

In future, it will be possible under s. 157(6) of the 1994 Act for the Secretary of State to make changes to these particular drug offence penalties by using the procedure under s. 143 of the Magistrates' Courts Act 1980 (power to alter sums specified in certain provisions). This will also be possible for equivalent provisions in Scotland and Northern Ireland (s. 156(7) and (8) respectively).

(3) Offences under the Firearms Act 1968 Section 157(3) of the 1994 Act specifies various increases in the maximum custodial sentences available for a range of offences involving firearms, under the Firearms Act 1968. The maximum penalty for possessing or distributing prohibited weapons or ammunition increases from five years' to 10 years' imprisonment on indictment. The maximum penalty for possessing or distributing other prohibited weapons increases from two years to 10 years on indictment, and from three months to six months summarily. The maximum penalty for possession of a sawn-off shotgun, carrying a firearm in a public place and shortening the barrel of a shotgun all increase from five years to seven years. The sentence for possessing a firearm or ammunition without a certificate or buying and selling firearms when not a registered dealer rises from three years to five years. The offence of falsifying a firearms certificate increases from three years to five years. For full details of the changes, reference should be made to sch. 8, part III.

According to *The Times* of 29 June 1994, the increases in maximum prison terms for these offences were in response to 'a series of incidents involving guns in London and Manchester which detectives suspect are related to drug dealing'.

(4) Offences involving poaching By para. 1 of sch. 9 to the 1994 Act, there are increases in maximum fines for two offences under the Game Act 1831. The first is trespassing in search or pursuit of game (s. 30), where the maximum fine is increased from level 1 to level 3. If five or more people are involved in this activity the offence becomes one of 'gang poaching' (CJA 1982, ss. 38, 46). In those circumstances the maximum fine is increased from level 3 to level 4. The second offence is that of searching for or pursuing game with a gun and using violence etc. (s. 32). In his book *Property Offences* (1994), Dr A. T. H. Smith comments that the fine for this offence was increased from level 1 to level 4 by virtue of the CJA 1988 but 'still looks surprisingly lenient' when compared to a maximum penalty of five years' imprisonment for the offence of trespass with a firearm under the Firearms Act 1968,

s. 20 (para. 13.03). The 1994 Act increases the maximum fine for pursuing game from level 4 to level 5, but the offence remains non-imprisonable. Equivalent changes are made to the Game (Scotland) Act 1832. Amendments made by para. 1 shall not apply to offences committed before that paragraph comes into force.

By para. 4 of sch. 9 to the 1994 Act, a new power is created to confiscate the vehicle of a person convicted as one of five or more convicted of 'gang poaching' under s. 30 of the Game Act 1831 (above). This new power becomes s. 4A of the Game Laws (Amendment) Act 1960. The power may be compared with the general powers of the courts to confiscate property used by the offender in connection with an offence (including the offender's vehicle) under Powers of Criminal Courts Act 1973, s. 43. The new power created in the 1960 Act is elaborately phrased (its provisions run to 12 subparagraphs) but would appear to achieve nothing which could not be done under the general 1973 Act powers. See, for example, *Buddo* (1982) 4 Cr App R (S) 268 (deprivation of offender's rights in a motor caravan in which he had driven to commit a burglary). A decision which might be of interest in the context of the new power is *Ottey* (1984) 6 Cr App R (S) 163, where the Court of Appeal held that where several offenders are implicated in an offence, and receive roughly comparable punishments, it is inequitable to punish one of the offenders further by depriving him of his rights to the car which was used in the criminal enterprise.

Additionally, the CJPOA 1994 increases the maximum penalties available for the offences of possession of indecent photographs of children (see 5.9), offences under the Video Recordings Act 1984 (see 5.13), and the offence of making obscene, offensive or annoying telephone calls (see 5.16).

Chapter Two
Procedural Changes

The bulk of this chapter is concerned with a range of further changes to the law of bail, introduced by ss. 25 to 30 of, and sch. 3 to, the 1994 Act. The new Act makes further restrictions upon the circumstances in which bail may be granted by the courts to certain defendants charged with very serious offences, and removes the normal presumption of bail in cases where the alleged offence has been committed while the defendant was already on bail. There are significant changes to the granting of bail by the police, including a new power on the part of the custody officer to insert various conditions into the grant of bail. The other substantial topic covered in this chapter is the abolition, by s. 44 of the Act, of committal proceedings, and their replacement by notice of transfer proceedings. This change is of great practical importance and necessitates a whole host of consequential amendments to the law, which are brought about by sch. 4 to the Act. Also covered in this chapter are a number of amendments to the Juries Act 1974, relating to the non-eligibility for jury service of those currently on bail, the presumption of eligibility of people with a physical disability, and the possibility of excusal from service on religious grounds. Section 44 of the Act increases from £2,000 to £5,000 the limit under which charges of criminal damage must be tried summarily. There are other changes relating to cross-border enforcement of the criminal law.

BAIL

Sections 25 to 30 of and sch. 3 to the CJPOA 1994 make further changes to the law relating to bail, an area which has already undergone a number of recent changes. All these changes have been fuelled by a fierce public debate about the level of offending committed by people who have been granted bail. This debate has led to the government's asserted determination to 'clamp down' on the so-called 'bail bandits'. The first of these changes to be implemented was s. 29(2) of the CJA 1991 (as substituted by the CJA 1993, s. 66), which imposed a requirement upon a sentencing court to regard the fact that an offence was committed on bail as being an aggravating factor of that offence. This provision came into effect on 16 August 1993. The second change, in the Bail (Amendment) Act 1993 (which came into force on 27 June 1994), gave the prosecution a right of appeal to a Crown Court judge against a decision by magistrates to grant bail in respect of a defendant charged with or convicted of an offence punishable by five years' imprisonment or more, or an offence under s. 12 or

s. 12A of the Theft Act 1968 (respectively, taking a conveyance without authority and aggravated vehicle-taking). Such an appeal can be made only where the prosecution have argued before the magistrates that bail should not be granted.

Further changes to the bail laws contained in the CJPOA 1994 were introduced by the Home Secretary (*Hansard*, Commons, 11 January 1994, col. 25) in the following manner:

> It is estimated that 50,000 offences are committed every year by people on bail. Part II [of the Bill] sets out five new measures which will restrict the grant of bail and help to ensure that it is only given when that will not put the public at risk

These five changes are now considered in turn.

2.1 Bail in Cases Involving Murder, Manslaughter and Rape

Subsections (1) and (2) of s. 25 of the CJPOA 1994 provide that if a person is awaiting trial or sentence on a charge of murder, attempted murder, manslaughter, rape or attempted rape, and he or she already has a conviction for one of those offences, or for the offence of culpable homicide, *then that person shall not be granted bail*. This is subject to s. 25(3), which requires that the relevant previous conviction must have been by or before a court in the United Kingdom and, in the case of a previous conviction for manslaughter or culpable homicide, the offender must have received a sentence of imprisonment or (if then a juvenile) long-term detention (under CYPA 1933, s. 53(2), or their Scottish or Northern Irish equivalents). It is also made subject to s. 25(5), which states that for these purposes the previous 'conviction' includes cases where (a) it was found that the person was not guilty by reason of insanity or was found to be unfit to plead or (b) the sentence for the earlier offence was a discharge or a probation order. The legislative purpose here is clearly to make relevant any previous conviction for these offences, whatever the sentence received. The exception is manslaughter, a previous conviction for which is relevant only where the offender received a prison sentence or a sentence of long-term detention under s. 53(2) of the CYPA 1933. The drafting seems to overlook the possibility of an offender having received a sentence of youth custody, or detention in a young offender institution, or custody for life, for manslaughter. Such sentences are not 'imprisonment' nor are they 'long-term detention'.

It is important to read s. 25 in the context of the pre-existing law, a perusal of which shows that the change made by s. 25 is a relatively small one. Part I of sch. 1 to the Bail Act 1976 provides that where a person is charged with or convicted of any offence punishable with imprisonment, the normal 'presumption of bail' contained in s. 4(1) of the Bail Act 1976 still applies, but he or she need not be granted bail if the court is satisfied that there are substantial grounds for believing that the defendant, if released on bail, would (by para. 2):

    (a)   fail to surrender to custody, or
    (b)   commit an offence while on bail, or
    (c)   interfere with witnesses or otherwise obstruct the course of justice, whether in relation to himself or any other person.

Paragraph 3 establishes, further, that if the court is satisfied that the defendant should be kept in custody for his or her own protection or welfare then bail need not be granted. Under para. 9, in making its decision over whether to grant bail, the court is bound to have regard, *inter alia*, to the nature and seriousness of the offence (and the likely sentence), and the person's character, record and associations. Most pertinently, by para. 9A, where a defendant is charged with murder, manslaughter, rape, attempted murder or attempted rape (the same range of offences covered by the new s. 25 of the CJPOA 1994), and the prosecution raise one or more of considerations (a) to (c) above, and the court decides to grant bail, the court must state the reasons for its decision and enter those reasons in the record of the proceedings.

There are no figures available for the number of cases in which persons charged or convicted of such very serious offences are granted bail, but this must surely be a very rare occurrence. The pre-existing legislation clearly contemplates that there are some such cases, and according to *Blackstone's Criminal Practice*, D5.26, 'It is still unusual for bail to be granted in murder cases, but not as exceptional as it once was'. The Bail Act 1976 suggests that where a court grants bail to an accused charged with murder it should normally impose as a condition of that bail a requirement that he or she attend hospital to undergo examination by doctors (Bail Act 1976, s. 3(6A) and (6B), inserted by CJA 1988).

The bail decision is one which involves a difficult balancing of risks. Although the seriousness of the current offence is a crucial matter, the bail decision does not translate directly into offence seriousness. As Robert Maclennan MP (*Hansard*, Commons, 11 January 1994, col. 60) pointed out, those accused of serious crimes of violence who already have a record for the same offence, are amongst the *least* likely to offend while on bail: 'Those most likely to do so have a recent history of burglary and car theft, and the Bill will not prevent their crimes.' In the circumstances outlined in s. 25 of the CJPOA 1994, where the person is charged or convicted with a grave offence *and* has a previous conviction for another grave offence, it seems unlikely that he or she would *ever* have been granted bail under the old law. During the passage of the Bill through Parliament Mr Blair, then shadow Home Secretary, criticised the provision as a 'gimmick' for that reason, and challenged the government to provide details of any case in which a person falling within the prohibition of s. 25 had previously been granted bail. Reference was then made by the government to the case of *Hagans* (1991, unreported), where the offender who was convicted of the rape and murder of Anna McGurk, 'had been arrested for rape and let out on bail' (see *Hansard*, Commons, 11 January 1994, col. 33). It is not clear, however, that this case would fall within s. 25 in any event. The offender did not have a relevant previous conviction, and so bail would have been a matter for consideration by the court in accordance with the normal provisions of Bail Act 1976 and, in particular, para. 9A of part I of sch. 1.

2.2 Alleged Offence Committed on Bail: Removal of Presumption of Bail

By s. 26 of the 1994 Act, where a person has been charged with any offence which is not a purely summary offence, and it appears to the court that at the date of the alleged offence *the person was on bail, the normal presumption in favour of granting bail is removed*. According to Michael Shersby (*Hansard*, Commons, 11 January 1994, col. 76), as a result of this change:

... the scandal of the so-called bail bandits is to come to an end. The Bill rightly removes the right to bail for someone charged with an offence allegedly committed on bail. That should stop the so-called revolving door, by which persons are arrested, charged with an offence and granted bail and then offend again and again.

The section does not, however, appear to make such a dramatic difference. Magistrates, when considering bail, have always been required to take account of the fact that the person was on bail when the alleged offence was committed. Paragraph 2 of part I of sch. 1 of the Bail Act 1976 lists among the 'exceptions to the right to bail' cases where the court is satisfied that there are substantial grounds for believing that the defendant would commit an offence while on bail, and para. 9 already provides that when considering whether to grant bail to a person charged or convicted with an imprisonable offence, where relevant 'the defendant's record as respects the fulfilment of his obligations under previous grants of bail in criminal proceedings' should be taken into account.

Section 26 does certainly provide a shift of emphasis, by providing an additional ground upon which the magistrates' court may refuse bail, further to the well established grounds set out in part I of sch. 1 to the 1976 Act, and outlined above. The court will certainly *not*, however, be *bound* to refuse bail to a defendant in a case where it appears that the alleged offence occurred while he or she was on bail. The same familiar factors provided for in para. 9 of part I of sch. 1 (such as the relative seriousness of the alleged offence, the defendant's character, antecedents and community ties, and the strength of the evidence against the defendant) must still be weighed in making the decision whether to grant bail or not.

2.3   Conditional Bail by the Police

The third change, brought about by s. 27 of the 1994 Act, relates to the *granting of conditional bail by the police*. Currently, the police may grant bail either:

(a)   to a suspect during an investigation but before charge, subject to a duty to attend back at the police station, or

(b)   to an arrestee after charge, subject to a duty to appear before the relevant magistrates' court at an appointed time to answer the charge.

In either case, the discretion to grant bail is in the hands of the custody officer at the police station. The custody officer must hold at least the rank of sergeant, and must be unconnected with the relevant investigation (PACE 1984, s. 36). There must always be at least one such officer present at the police station (*Vince v Chief Constable of Dorset Police* [1992] 1 WLR 47). The central provision on police bail is s. 38(1) of PACE, which provides that '... the custody officer *shall* order' (emphasis added) the arrestee's release from police detention, either on bail or without bail, unless the officer reasonably fears that to grant bail would have one or more of a number of undesirable consequences (such as the arrestee absconding, or interfering with witnesses). Prior to the 1994 Act, powers of the courts to grant bail were more flexible than those of the police. The courts can grant bail subject to a range of specified conditions whereas the police, when granting bail to a person charged, could only require a surety or sureties in addition to the standard condition that the person bailed attend at the appropriate time. According to *Emmins on Criminal Procedure*, 5th ed. (1992), p. 398, there is a growing practice of granting 'extended bail', with a period in the order of a fortnight elapsing between bail from the police station and the first court appearance.

The Royal Commission on Criminal Justice in its *Report* (Cm 2263, 1993) expressed the view that the police's lack of power to grant bail subject to conditions meant that many suspects were brought before the court unnecessarily. The Commission said (at para. 22):

> In many cases suspects are brought before the courts to make applications for bail even though the police might be willing to grant bail themselves. This is because the police have power to release a suspect on bail but not to release him subject to conditions. We recommend that they should have the additional power of releasing on bail subject to conditions, since this would reduce the suspect's liability to attend court. A person bailed by the police in this way whom it was later decided not to charge or prosecute would thus be able to avoid a court appearance and any attendant publicity altogether.

Section 27 of the CJPOA 1994 implements this proposal. The effect of s. 27(1) is, in general, to allow the 'normal powers to impose conditions of bail' to apply where a custody officer releases a person on bail under s. 38(1) of PACE (person arrested and charged: see above) or s. 40(10) of PACE (a person whose detention is under review, but who has now been charged). This has been achieved by extending the application of s. 3 of the Bail Act 1976 to police bail, but with a number of modifications explained below. The law now is that a person released on police bail, in addition to the standard duty to surrender to custody and the power to require that person to provide a surety or sureties,

> ... may be required to comply, before release on bail or later, with such requirements as appear *to the court* to be necessary to secure that—
>
> (a)   he surrenders to custody,
>
> (b)   he does not commit an offence while on bail,
>
> (c)   he does not interfere with witnesses or otherwise obstruct the course of justice whether in relation to himself or any other person.

No conditions should be imposed on a grant of bail by the police unless it appears to the custody officer that they are necessary for the purposes of (a), (b), or (c) above (Bail Act 1976, s. 3A(5), inserted by CJPOA 1994, s. 27(3)). The phrase in italics 'to the court', should surely be read as 'to the custody officer' in the context of police bail, but the 1994 Act fails to make this clear. How do these conditions (a) to (c) differ from those which may be inserted by a court? One difference is that a court, by s. 3(6)(d) and s. 3(6A) of the Bail Act 1976, may order reports to be compiled on the person granted bail. This power is clearly not appropriate in respect of police bail and is inapplicable in that context (Bail Act 1976, s. 3A(2) and (3), as inserted by CJPOA 1994, s. 27(3)). A second difference is that the police may not require the person to live in a bail hostel. Thirdly, where a custody officer, rather than the court, has granted bail, that officer (or another custody officer serving at the same police station) may, at the request of the person bailed, vary the conditions of the bail (Bail Act 1976,

s. 3A(4), as inserted by the CJPOA 1994, s. 27(3)). In such a case it is possible for the custody officer to impose new conditions or more onerous conditions. This possibility is designed, presumably, to discourage those bailed from asking to have their conditions of bail varied. In addition, para. 3 of sch. 3 to the CJPOA 1994 inserts a new s. 43B into the Magistrates' Courts Act 1980, which permits a person given police bail to make an application to a magistrates' court to vary the bail conditions. That court may do so but, again, it has power to insert more onerous conditions. Indeed, it is further open to the court to respond to such an application by withholding bail altogether and remanding the person in custody. Again, this seems to provide a powerful disincentive to making a less than well-founded application to the court. Custody officers imposing or varying bail conditions must always give reasons for their decisions, inform the person bailed of those reasons, and record them in the custody record (1994 Act, sch. 3).

The courts make extensive use of their powers to insert conditions on the grant of bail. According to *Blackstone's Criminal Practice*, D5.23, conditions frequently imposed in reliance on paras (a) to (c) above include:

(a)   a condition of residence, frequently expressed as a condition that the person is to live and sleep at a specified address;

(b)   a condition that the person is to notify any changes of address to the police;

(c)   a condition of reporting (whether daily, weekly or at other intervals) to a local police station;

(d)   a curfew (i.e., the person must be indoors between certain hours);

(e)   a condition that the person is not to enter a certain area or building, or go within a specified distance of a certain address;

(f)   a condition that the person is not to contact (whether directly or indirectly) the victim of the alleged offence and/or any other probable witnesses; and

(g)   a condition that the person's passport is to be surrendered to the police.

The appellate courts have construed widely the judicial power to insert conditions on the grant of bail. In *Mansfield Justices, ex parte Sharkey* [1985] QB 613, the Court of Appeal held that magistrates had been entitled to impose in respect of defendants arrested for public order offences allegedly committed by them while on duty as 'flying pickets' during the miners' strike of 1984–5, conditions of bail that they should not picket otherwise than peacefully at their own pits. It was stressed by the court, however, that magistrates were under a duty to act judicially when imposing conditions and so it would not be appropriate to adopt a blanket policy of imposing the same conditions in all such cases. In *Bournemouth Magistrates' Court, ex parte Cross* [1989] Crim LR 207 it was established that conditions could be imposed on bail for non-imprisonable offences. It is far from clear that a similarly broad discretion should be vested in the custody officer at the police station.

2.4   Bail following Charge

Section 28 of the 1994 Act amends s. 38 of PACE, which deals with bail following charge. When a person arrested has been charged at the police station, the custody officer must decide whether to keep the accused in custody until he or she can be brought before a magistrate, or release the accused on bail with a requirement to attend the magistrates' court on a specified date. Section 38 requires the officer to order the person's release unless one of the specified grounds (i) to (iii) exists. Section 28(2) of the 1994 Act replaces sub-paragraphs (ii) and (iii) with five new sub-paragraphs (ii) to (vi). The changes are, in fact, relatively minor, but they bring the criteria for refusing police bail more closely into line with the criteria for refusing bail by a court.

First, the new sub-paragraph (iii) provides that the custody officer may not order release where (in the case of a person arrested for an imprisonable offence) 'the custody officer has reasonable grounds for believing that the detention of the person arrested is necessary to prevent him from committing an offence'. Fear of commission of a further offence was not, surprisingly, a relevant ground under s. 38(1) prior to its amendment. Second, the new sub-paragraph (iv) retains the pre-existing ground for refusing release where 'the detention of the person arrested is necessary to prevent him from causing physical injury to any other person or from causing loss of or damage to property', but restricts this ground to cases where the person has been arrested for a *non*-imprisonable offence. Section 28(3) of the 1994 Act further amends s. 38 of PACE by inserting a new subsection (2A). This creates a general requirement that the custody officer, when reaching a decision under the section, should have regard to the same considerations as those to which a court is required to have regard under para. 2 of part I of sch. 1 to the Bail Act 1976 (exceptions to the right to bail).

2.5 Breach of Police Bail: Power of Arrest

The law relating to police bail is further amended by s. 29 of the 1994 Act, which creates a new power of *arrest, without warrant, in respect of an individual who breaches police bail*. Prior to the 1994 Act, where a person who was bailed from a police station on condition that he or she attend at the police station at a later date, but failed to do so, it seems that the police would have had power to arrest the person without warrant in only two circumstances. The first would be where new evidence came to light which justified a further arrest (this possibility is catered for by PACE, s. 47(2), and remains in place after the 1994 Act). The second would be where the police rearrested the person in reliance upon whichever power justified the original arrest. The legality of the rearrest would depend upon whether the relevant arrest power was still operative at the later date (see *Blackstone's Criminal Practice*, D5.44).

The police have long sought a clear general power to arrest immediately a person granted police bail who fails to appear at the police station, and the government promised in their election manifesto to provide one. The relevant law is amended by s. 29(2) of the CJPOA 1994, which inserts a new s. 46A into PACE. A further amendment, by s. 29(3) of the 1994 Act, inserts a new subsection (7) into s. 34 of PACE. This subsection makes it clear that the arrest of a person following failure to appear at the police station would be an arrest for an *offence*, namely the offence in respect of which the person was originally granted police bail. A number of consequential amendments are made to ss. 37, 41, 42, 43 and 47 of PACE by s. 29 of the CJPOA 1994.

Section 29(5) states that these changes apply whether the person released on bail was granted bail before or after the commencement of s. 28.

2.6 Reconsideration of Decision to Grant Bail

Finally on bail, s. 30 of the CJPOA 1994 allows for the possibility of a *magistrates' court being asked by the prosecutor to reconsider a decision to grant bail* for a non-summary offence, on the basis of fresh information which has come into the possession of the prosecutor. Section 30 creates this new power by insertion of a new s. 5B into the Bail Act 1976. The power is available in any case where bail was originally granted by a magistrates' court, or by the police. On application by the prosecutor the relevant magistrates' court may:

(a) vary the conditions of the bail, or

(b) impose conditions of bail where bail had previously been granted unconditionally, or

(c) withhold bail.

The new s. 5B(2) states that the magistrates' court's power to reconsider is available in respect of offences triable on indictment (the subsection should read 'triable *only* on indictment') and offences triable either way, and the new s. 5B(3) makes it clear that no such application may be considered by the court 'unless it is based on information which was not available to the court or constable when the decision [to grant bail] was taken'. The magistrates' court will have to consider any representations made by the defendant before making its decision (s. 5B(9)).

JURIES

2.7 Person on Bail: Disqualification from Jury Service

Continuing with the general theme of the 'crackdown' on bail, s. 40 of the CJPOA 1994 disqualifies from jury service in the Crown Court any person who is at the relevant time on bail in criminal proceedings. 'Bail in criminal proceedings' has the same meaning as in the Bail Act 1976, which includes both bail by a court and police bail (Bail Act 1976, s. 1). While the effect of s. 40 is perfectly clear, it might perhaps have been better for the change to have been made by amendment to the Juries Act 1974, where the general law on disqualification from jury service is to be found. The effect of a change to the law made in this area by a single section in a compendious Criminal Justice Act might easily be overlooked. The change is in line with Recommendation 219 made by the Royal Commission on Criminal Justice (*Report*, 1993, Cm 2263).

The law governing qualification for jury service is complex. Certain persons are ineligible for jury service, such as lawyers, JPs, prison officers, police officers, the clergy and mentally disordered persons. Incidentally, the Royal Commission proposed that the clergy should be removed from this list, but the proposal has not been acted upon. Certain other persons are disqualified from jury service. By part II of sch. 1 to the Juries Act 1974, a person who has served at any time a custodial sentence of five years or more, or within the last 10 years has served a custodial sentence of any length, or within the last 10 years has received a suspended prison sentence or a community service order, or within the last five years has been placed on probation, is disqualified from jury service. The effect of s. 40 of the 1994 Act is to add persons on bail to the list of those disqualified. Whilst many people would regard this change in the law as a sensible extension, the obvious problem of principle, of course, is that those who are on bail awaiting trial are presumed by the law to be innocent of the charges against them.

2.8 Jury Service: Disabled Persons

By insertion of a new s. 9B into the Juries Act 1974, s. 41 of the CJPOA 1994 deals with the difficult issue of the suitability of persons who are physically disabled for jury service. There is no problem in a case where the person, because of their disability, would prefer not to serve, since the judge has a discretion under s. 9 of the Juries Act to excuse from service. See also *Practice Direction (Jury Service: Excusal)* [1988] 1 WLR 1162. If the disabled person wishes to serve, the issue is more complex. This question came to recent public attention when Elaine Heath, a deaf person, was discharged from jury service at King's Lynn Crown Court because the judge doubted her ability to follow the proceedings (various press reports, 21 January 1994). In that case the judge was, no doubt, acting in pursuance of powers in s. 10 of the Juries Act 1976 which (prior to the 1994 Act change) permitted a judge to discharge a potential juror '... on account of physical disability or insufficient understanding of English'. The new s. 9B provides that where there is doubt over whether a person suffering from physical disability will be able effectively to act as a juror, the relevant court officer should bring the person before the judge, who has the responsibility of deciding whether that person shall act as a juror. In making this decision, s. 9B(2) requires the judge to operate a *presumption* that the person is suitable to serve unless the person is not, on account of disability, capable of acting effectively as a juror. No similar presumption operates in respect of persons who have insufficient understanding of English, who will continue to be dealt with in the judge's discretion under s. 10.

This new provision brings additional guidance to the law, but still leaves the decision squarely with the judge. It seems clear now, if it was not clear before, that a person should not be regarded as unsuitable to act as a juror merely because of difficulties involving, say, wheelchair access to the court building or to the courtroom. More difficult cases arise where the potential juror is, for example, significantly impaired in sight or hearing. In a letter to *The Times* on 5 August 1994, Lord Ashley of Stoke, the former MP who is now President of the Royal National Institute for Deaf People, pointed out that 'with computer systems which can "hear" the spoken word, such as court proceedings, and instantly transcribe them on to a screen in front of a juror, there is little reason why deaf people should not serve as jurors'. While this is clearly true in principle, there is no suggestion in the Act that public funds might be made available to equip all Crown Courts with such facilities. Notwithstanding s. 9B(2), judges will still have to decide when the additional expense and delay required by accommodating a juror with a physical disability can outweigh the obligation upon all eligible citizens to serve on a jury when called upon.

2.9 Jury Service: Excusal on Religious Grounds

Section 42 of the 1994 Act creates a new category of persons who, while eligible for jury service, may be 'excusable as of right' under part III of sch. 1 to the Juries Act 1974. The section adds 'members of certain religious bodies' to this category, which currently includes persons over 65 years of age, Parliamentary members and officers, full-time serving members of the armed forces, doctors, dentists, nurses, midwives, vets and pharmacists. The change is broadly in line with that proposed by the Royal Commission on Criminal Justice, *Report* (Cm 2263, 1993), recommendation 217.

The section may do little more than confirm the common law. In *Guildford Crown Court, ex parte Siderfin* [1990] 2 QB 683 the potential juror was a member of the Plymouth brethren, who took the view that serving on a jury was contrary to her religious beliefs, such that she would have to reach her verdict alone without discussion with other members of the jury. The Divisional Court held that a potential juror's religious belief was not *in itself* sufficient reason for excusal, but that the issue (to be determined by the appropriate officer of the court, rather than by the judge) was whether the person's belief was such that it would interfere with carrying out the duties of a juror 'properly, honestly and responsibly'. The refusal to excuse was quashed. Section 42 may be more narrowly drawn than the decision in *Siderfin*, since the new statutory category extends only to 'A practising member of a religious society or order the tenets or beliefs of which are incompatible with jury service'. There might still be a case of a juror who did not come strictly within the terms of this provision, but in respect of whom the appropriate officer (considering *Siderfin*) might be prepared to exercise his or her discretion to excuse under s. 9(2) of the 1974 Act. There is a right of appeal against a refusal to excuse: see generally *Practice Direction (Jury Service: Excusal)* [1988] 1 WLR 1162.

2.10   Separation of Jury during Consideration of Verdict

Section 43 substitutes a new s. 13 in the Juries Act 1974. This section deals with the circumstances in which a jury may, with the permission of the court, be allowed to separate at any time. For obvious reasons it is normal to permit such separations during lunch adjournments, and overnight where trials last for more than one day. When the jurors separate the judge should warn them that they should not speak about the case to anyone else (*Prime* (1973) 57 Cr App R 632). Before the 1994 Act the law did not permit the jury to separate once they had been directed to consider their verdict. They should not separate or leave the place appointed for the deliberations without express leave of the court, and only for reasons of evident necessity (*Neal* [1949] 2 KB 590). It has long been recognised that an overnight stay for a jury in a hotel is preferable to their continuing to deliberate late into the evening. Generally, the judge should make a decision about the need to secure overnight accommodation for the jury no later than 5.00 p.m. of that day (*Akano, The Times*, 3 April 1992). Members of the jury should not continue their deliberations at the hotel, but should await their return to court the following day (*Tharakan, The Times*, 10 November 1994).

Occasionally, however, a departure from the strict rules about jury separation has been permitted. In *Alexander* [1974] 1 WLR 422, for example, the Court of Appeal held that where a juror had left court with the others and the bailiffs, had walked a short way, but had then returned to court alone to collect exhibits, there had been no irregularity serious enough to justify quashing the conviction. A case which fell on the other side of the line was *Goodson* [1975] 1 WLR 549. After the jury had retired, one juror, with the jury bailiff's permission, left the room and made a telephone call from a nearby booth. Although the judge discharged the juror and prevented him from communicating with the other jurors, the Court of Appeal quashed the conviction and held that in the circumstances the entire jury should have been discharged.

The new s. 13 extends the discretion to allow the jury to separate. Where the court thinks fit, the jury may now also be permitted to separate at a time *after* they have been directed to consider their verdict. The new section recognises the increasing frequency with which juries, particularly in complex cases such as fraud trials, are unable to reach their decision speedily and may find themselves subject to the strain of enforced confinement for many hours, and sometimes even for a few days. The section also no doubt recognises the financial savings to be made by permitting jurors to separate and return to their homes, rather than accommodating them all in a hotel. It is estimated by the government that this provision could yield annual savings in the order of £0.2 million for the Lord Chancellor's Department.

ABOLITION OF COMMITTAL PROCEEDINGS

Section 44(1) of the 1994 Act abolishes 'the functions of a magistrates' court as examining justices'. By s. 44(2), the present provisions contained in ss. 4 to 8 of the Magistrates' Courts Act 1980 are replaced by new provisions set out in part I of sch. 4 to the 1994 Act. These create a new procedure of 'transfer for trial', which allows cases to be transferred to Crown Court administratively, but with a procedure enabling the defence to argue that there is no case to answer in advance of the trial at Crown Court. Section 44(3) and part II of sch. 4 make numerous minor and consequential amendments to the law, for the purpose of bringing about these changes. Section 44(4) explains that the new arrangements will not apply in any case where a magistrates' court has begun to inquire into a case as examining justices before the commencement of the section.

2.11 Background to the Abolition of Committal Proceedings

The impetus for change in this area was provided by the Royal Commission on Criminal Justice (*Report*, Cm 2263, 1993).

According to the Commission (at p. 89) committal proceedings are intended to enable the sufficiency of the evidence against a defendant to be examined by a magistrates' court so that weak cases are weeded out before they receive a full trial in Crown Court. The Commission, expressing agreement with the Royal Commission on Criminal Procedure (1981, Cmnd 8092) and the Fraud Trials Committee Report (1986), stated that while this was a laudable objective, there were more efficient ways of securing it. As the Commission points out, the great majority of committals have in practice been a formality. Under the present s. 6(2) of the Magistrates' Courts Act 1980 the magistrates may commit the defendant to Crown Court on the basis solely of written statements: a so-called 'paper committal'. This form of committal takes place without consideration of the contents of the documents by the court, unless the defendant is unrepresented or the defence submit that the statements disclose insufficient evidence to put the defendant on trial. In either of these cases the magistrates must hold a full committal, under s. 6(1) of the 1980 Act. Evidence obtained by the Commission indicated that full committals represented only some 7 per cent of all committals. The Commission, after noting some criticisms of the way in which full committal arrangements were currently working (such as their cumbersome procedure, including the laborious process of putting into writing by the clerk of oral evidence given by witnesses, and the unacceptable pressure upon some vulnerable witnesses of having to tell their stories in open court twice over), concluded that committal proceedings in their present form should be abolished.

The Commission also considered whether there should be abolition of the procedure for submitting before trial that there is no case to answer. There is no such arrangement in Scotland, and the Commission felt that appropriate safeguards could perhaps be provided by more rigorous scrutiny of potentially weak cases by the Crown Prosecution Service and greater clarification of issues through pre-trial procedures. On balance, however, the Commission was persuaded that '... in the interests of stopping a demonstrably inadequate case against a defendant at the earliest possible stage, there should remain some opportunity for the defence to take the initiative' (p. 90). Accordingly, the Commission's recommendations Nos. 116–19 were as follows:

> Committal proceedings in their present form should be abolished. Where the defendant makes a submission of no case to answer, it should be considered on the papers, although the defence should be able to advance oral argument in support of the submission and the prosecution should be able to reply. Witnesses should not be called. In indictable-only cases submissions of no case to answer should be decided by the Crown Court. In either-way cases the responsibility should fall to the magistrates' courts, where stipendiary magistrates should preside over the hearings. There should be time limits. starting from the moment the defence receive the prosecution's case, for the making of submissions of no case to answer.

These recommendations may be compared with the detailed provisions of the 1994 Act, which are described next. They may also be compared with the 'notice of transfer' arrangements already in existence, in respect of (a) cases of serious or complex fraud (CJA 1987, s. 4), (b) cases where a child will be a witness at the trial of an offence to which CJA 1988, s. 32(2), applies, namely, sexual offences and offences of violence or cruelty (CJA 1991, s. 53), and (c) war crimes (War Crimes Act 1991, s. 1). See further on these, *Blackstone's Criminal Practice*, D7.6. In many ways the new arrangements can be seen as the full flowering of these originally rather specialised notice of transfer schemes (each of which were specifically introduced to avoid various disadvantages of committal for trial by the magistrates' court).

2.12 The New Transfer for Trial Arrangements

The detailed provisions are set out in sch. 4 to the CJPOA 1994. New provisions are substituted for ss. 4 to 8 of the Magistrates' Courts Act 1980.

By the new s. 4 of the 1980 Act, where a person is charged with an indictable-only offence, or a triable-either-way offence which the magistrates' court has decided is more suitable for Crown Court trial or for which the defendant has not consented to summary trial, then the court and prosecutor must proceed with a view to transferring the proceedings to Crown Court for trial. Notwithstanding the mandatory nature of this provision, the prosecutor still retains the option of discontinuing or withdrawing the proceedings (s. 4(2)(a)), and the magistrates' court may at any stage adjourn the proceedings and remand the defendant (s. 4(4)). Other exceptional cases are those where notice of transfer under CJA 1987, s. 4, or CJA 1991, s. 53, has been served on the court. It may be noted here that the government has not adopted the suggestion that for indictable-only cases submissions of no case should be heard by the Crown Court, nor has it adopted the proposal that in triable-either-way cases the matter should be heard by a stipendiary (rather than a lay) magistrate.

By the new s. 5(1) the prosecutor is required, within the prescribed period to serve on the court, and on each of the defendants, a 'notice of the prosecution case', which must (by s. 5(2)) specify the charge(s) and include a set of documents containing the evidence upon which the charge(s) are based. This prescribed period is not given in the Act. The defence are given an opportunity to oppose this in writing within a specified period (s. 5(3), although again the period is not given in the Act), and may make 'an application for dismissal' (new s. 6(1)), sending copies to the court, the prosecutor and any co-accused (s. 6(2)). The prosecutor may oppose the application for dismissal (s. 6(3)). Oral representations may be made by the accused if he or she is unrepresented (s. 6(5)). Oral representations may be made on behalf of an accused who is represented if a request to do so is included in the application for dismissal on the basis of the complexity of the case (s. 6(6)). If oral representations are made by or on behalf of the accused then the prosecutor may make oral representations in response (s. 6(8)). The court, after considering the evidence and representations, shall dismiss a charge against the defendant 'if it appears to the court that there is not sufficient evidence against the accused to put him on trial by jury for the offence charged' (s. 6(10)). Dismissal of the charge has the effect of barring any further proceedings on that charge on the same evidence other than by preferring a voluntary bill of indictment (s. 6(13)). For the procedure for obtaining a voluntary bill see *Practice Direction (Crime: Voluntary Bills)* [1990] 1 WLR 1633 and *Blackstone's Criminal Practice*, D7.3.

The new s. 7 of the Magistrates' Courts Act 1980 deals with the arrangements for transfer to the appropriate Crown Court. The new s. 8 deals with arrangements for bail or remand in custody awaiting trial at Crown Court. The new s. 8A deals with reporting restrictions in respect of applications for dismissal. By the new s. 8B, where a notice of the prosecution case has been given before a magistrates' court, the court must 'have regard to the desirability of avoiding prejudice to the welfare of any witness that may be occasioned by unnecessary delay in transferring the proceedings for trial'.

OTHER PROCEDURAL CHANGES

2.13 Pleading Guilty: Non-attendance in Court

Section 45 of, and sch. 5 to, the 1994 Act will reform and extend the procedures under s. 12 of the Magistrates' Courts Act 1980, which enable magistrates' courts to deal with cases in which the accused pleads guilty and does not wish to make a personal appearance before the court: 'non-appearance of accused: plea of guilty'.

Paragraph 1 of sch. 5 to the 1994 Act substitutes a new s. 12 in the 1980 Act. There are a number of differences in drafting and layout between the old and new sections, but the import has been very little affected. However, para. 2 of sch. 5 inserts a new s. 12A into the 1980 Act, which deals with the application of the s. 12 procedure in the situation where the accused actually appears in court. This does not appear to have been catered for under the 1980 Act's original provisions. Two situations may arise. The first is where the clerk of the court has received notification from the accused, or the accused's legal adviser, that the accused intends to plead guilty without appearing in court, but then the accused turns up anyway. Section 12A(1) gives the court power, with the consent of the accused, to proceed to hear and dispose of the case as if the accused were not there in court. Secondly, and more significantly in practice, is the case where the clerk receives no such notification, but the accused appears and informs the court of an intention to plead guilty. Now, by s. 12A(2), the court may, with the consent of the accused, proceed to deal with the case as if such notification had been given and the accused was absent. In either of these two cases the court must, before accepting the plea of guilty and convicting the accused, give the accused the opportunity to make an oral submission in mitigation (s. 12A(3), (4) and (5)).

2.14   Criminal Damage and Aggravated Vehicle Taking: Relevant Sum for Summary Trial

Section 46 of the CJPOA 1994 amends s. 22(1) of the Magistrates' Courts Act 1980, with the effect that the offence of *criminal damage* must now be tried summarily whenever the value of the property alleged to have been damaged or destroyed is £5,000 or less (rather than £2,000 or less, as in the previous law).

In consequence of this change, criminal damage is an offence triable either way, except that where the value of the property alleged to have been destroyed, or the extent of the alleged damage, is not more than £5,000 (and provided that the damage was not occasioned by fire and thus constitutes arson, which is triable either way or, in the case of aggravated arson, triable only on indictment), criminal damage is treated as if it were triable only summarily.

The mode of trial guidelines suggested that even where the value was more than £2,000 the offence of criminal damage should, in general, be tried summarily unless the magistrates' court considers that one or more of the following features is present and that its sentencing powers are insufficient: (a) deliberate fire-raising, (b) committed by a group, (c) damage of a high value (at least £10,000), (d) the offence has a clear racial motivation (*Practice Note (Mode of Trial: Guidelines)* [1990] 1 WLR 1439). This change seems to raise the threshold so that more criminal damage cases will be heard in the magistrates' courts.

Section 46 also has an impact on the offence of aggravated vehicle taking, under s. 12A of the Theft Act 1968 (offence created by the Aggravated Vehicle Taking Act 1992). That offence requires the prosecution to prove that the defendant committed an offence under s. 12 of the Theft Act 1968 (taking conveyance without authority) and that the case is aggravated by one or more circumstances: (a) that the vehicle was driven dangerously on a road or other public place, (b) that owing to the driving of the vehicle an accident occurred by which injury was caused to any person, (c) that owing to the driving of the vehicle an accident occurred by which damage was caused to any property, other than the vehicle, and (d) that damage was caused to the vehicle. Aggravated vehicle taking is an offence triable either way, unless the s. 12A offence involves no prosecution allegation other than damage to the vehicle or other property or both and where the total value of the damage alleged to have been caused is less than £2,000, in which case the offence is triable only summarily. By s. 46 of the 1994 Act, that sum of £2,000 is also raised to £5,000.

Neither in respect of criminal damage nor aggravated vehicle taking does this change apply to an offence charged in respect of an act done before this section comes into force (s. 46(2)).

2.15 Recovery of Fines etc. by Deduction from Income Support

The CJA 1991, s. 24, made provision for the deduction from income support payment monies levied against the offender by way of fine or compensation order. This was subsequently augmented by the Fines (Deduction from Income Support) Regulations 1992 (SI 1992/2182) and Home Office Circular 74 of 1992. Courts have been able to use the new power since 1 October 1992. In outline the system is that, after the court has held an inquiry into the offender's means, the justices' clerk of the magistrates' court responsible for enforcement of the fine or compensation order may apply to the head of the appropriate district office of the Department of Social Security (DSS) to make deductions at source from income support paid to the offender. The DSS must determine whether there is sufficient income support to allow the deduction to be made and, where other deductions are being made from income support, the priority of those deductions. Deductions should not be made unless the offender is aged 18 or over at the time when the application is made. If the DSS accepts the application the court will be informed that deductions at a standard rate have started. The DSS will provide an account and make payments quarterly.

The provisions of the 1991 Act were slightly defective in permitting application only by the magistrates' court which imposed the fine or compensation order (or where the court had remitted to it a fine or compensation order imposed by the Crown Court). It did not allow for the possibility that the fine or compensation order might have been transferred from one magistrates' court to another, by transfer of fine order under the Magistrates' Courts Act 1980, s. 89. Transfer of fine is appropriate under s. 89 where the offender is residing in a petty sessions area different from that for which the court imposing the fine was acting. Section 47 of the CJPOA 1994 proceeds by inserting a new subsection (2A) into s. 89, which permits that where a transfer of fine order has been made this shall be deemed to include power to deduct payment from income support where this would be otherwise appropriate. Section 47 also amends the relevant provisions in CJA 1991, s. 24, by adding a new paragraph (c) to s. 24(3), and by amending s. 90 of the Magistrates' Courts Act 1980, which gave magistrates power to transfer a fine to Scotland.

2.16 Criminal Division of Court of Appeal: Circuit Judges

The effect of s. 52 of the 1994 Act is to permit, in certain circumstances, circuit judges to act as judges of the Criminal Division of the Court of Appeal. Circuit judges approved by the Lord Chancellor may sit in appeals specified as suitable by the Lord Chancellor, save where the appeal is from a decision of a High Court judge. The changes to the existing law are effected by amendment to the Supreme Court Act 1981.

The office of circuit judge was created by the Courts Act 1971. The minimum qualification for a circuit judge is to be (a) a barrister of at least 10 years' standing or (b) a recorder who has held that office for at least three years (Courts Act 1971, s. 16(3)). The appointment is full time (s. 17(6)).

This section is to be brought into force on a day to be appointed by the Lord Chancellor (s. 172(2)).

2.17   Police Powers: Cross-Border Enforcement

Section 136 of the CJPOA 1994 provides for a warrant issued in England and Wales or in Northern Ireland, for the arrest of a person charged with an offence, to be executed in Scotland. It also provides for a warrant issued in Scotland or in Northern Ireland, for the arrest of a person charged with an offence, to be executed in England and Wales.

Section 137 provides that, subject to certain conditions, an officer of a police force in England and Wales who has reasonable grounds for suspecting that an offence has been committed or attempted in England and Wales, and that the person responsible is in Scotland or Northern Ireland, may arrest without warrant the suspected person wherever he or she is in Scotland or Northern Ireland. Equivalent powers are conferred by this section on police officers in Scotland and in Northern Ireland. The main condition precedent to the operation of these powers is that the relevant suspected offence must be an arrestable offence.

Sections 138 and 139 provide supplementary powers of arrest and search to those provided in ss. 136 and 137.

2.18   Police Powers: Aid and Assistance between Police Forces

Section 141 of the CJPOA 1994 provides for the possibility of aid and assistance (such as the provision of additional manpower) being given to a police force in England and Wales, or in Scotland, or in Northern Ireland, by a police force elsewhere in the United Kingdom.

2.19   Police Powers: Extension to United Kingdom Waters

Section 160(1) amends s. 19 of the Police Act 1964 (area within which a police officer's powers and privileges are exercisable) so as to include waters adjacent to the United Kingdom. By the new s. 19(5A), 'United Kingdom waters' means 'the sea and other waters within the seaward limits of the territorial sea'. Section 17 of the equivalent Police (Scotland) Act 1967 is correspondingly amended by s. 160(2).

Chapter Three
Evidence and Related Provisions

This chapter deals with the provisions of part III of the CJPOA 1994 dealing with the law of evidence (ss. 31 to 39 and s. 50) and the sections in part IV of the Act dealing with the powers of the police to take body samples (ss. 54 to 59). Section 32 abolishes the requirements of corroboration warnings in respect of the evidence of complainants in sexual offences and in respect of accomplices and s. 33 removes the requirements of actual corroboration in the case of offences of procuration and others in the Sexual Offences Act 1956. Sections 34 to 39 controversially modify the accused's right to remain silent when questioned under caution or charged by the police or when able to give evidence at his or her trial. Although in all these situations the accused still has the right to remain silent, adverse inferences may be drawn if that right is exercised and the prosecution will no longer be barred from commenting on the accused's silence. Section 31 provides for the accused to lose the shield provided by s. 1(f) of the Criminal Evidence Act 1898 if he or she casts imputations on the character of the deceased victim. Section 50 clarifies and slightly liberalises the provisions for examination-in-chief of child witnesses whose testimony is primarily given by means of a video recording under s. 32A of the CJA 1988, whilst sch. 9, para. 33 makes it clear that there is no special test of competence for child witnesses.

Sections 54 to 59 reflect the growing importance of DNA profiles as identification evidence and extend the powers of the police to take body samples and to retain and consult the information derived from them in databases. They also facilitate the taking of saliva and mouth swabs by reclassifying them as non-intimate samples and remove searches of the mouth from the category of intimate searches and expressly permit such a search to be made on arrest.

3.1 Introduction

The centre-pieces of the changes to the law of evidence in the CJPOA 1994 are the provisions relating to corroboration and to the so-called right to silence. Discussion on both these topics can be traced back at least as far as the 1972 Report of the Criminal Law Revision Committee (CLRC) on Evidence (Eleventh Report, Cmnd 4991). The Act broadly follows the CLRC proposals, which were highly controversial even then, to remove or restrict the right to silence but goes in the opposite direction to the Committee in abrogating the requirement of a corroboration warning in sexual cases which the Committee had thought should be retained in a part of their Report which attracted much less critical comment in those less self-consciously egalitarian times. This chapter will first look at the provisions of the Act relating to corroboration and then at the right-to-silence provisions before dealing with the other assorted provisions concerned with the law of evidence and the taking of body samples.

CORROBORATION

3.2 Background

Until relatively recently, there were three main situations where the judge was required to give a warning to the jury about the dangers of convicting on uncorroborated evidence. These were in relation to:

(a) the evidence of children,
(b) the evidence of an accomplice giving evidence for the prosecution, and
(c) the evidence of the complainant in a sexual offence.

The requirement in the first of these situations was abolished by s. 34 of the CJA 1988 (which also removed any requirement of *actual* corroboration as a matter of law on the grounds of it being the *unsworn* evidence of children) and, as a result of the CJA 1991, evidence of children is always given unsworn and no corroboration warning is required on that ground. However, if the child witness was the complainant in a sexual offence, a corroboration warning still had to be given for that reason. The 1989 report of the Pigot Committee (Home Office Advisory Group on Video Evidence), on which the children's evidence reforms of the 1991 Act were based, pointed out at para. 5.17 that 'unless the rule [requiring a corroboration warning about the evidence of a sexual complainant] is altered, our proposals for facilitating the testimony of children and other vulnerable witnesses may, at any rate in so far as sexual offences are concerned, have a much more limited effect than we intend'.

The Law Commision then issued a Working Paper (No. 115, 1990) on corroboration. This review, like that of the Pigot Committee had been instigated partly as a result of the public concern about child abuse and the practical difficulties involved in securing convictions of those responsible. It was not surprising that the Working Paper heeded the warning so clearly given in Pigot and came down in favour of abolishing the requirement of a warning in relation to the evidence of a complainants generally in sexual offences (see Birch [1990] Crim LR 667 for a thorough and penetrating review of the Working Paper). The Law Commission had no difficulty, however, in finding plenty of other reasons for recommending the abolition of the warning requirement (whether for the evidence of sexual complain-ants or accomplices). The rules on what constituted corroboration were very technical and likely to lead to appeals in which, if there was found to be a misdirection, the Court of Appeal would only rarely apply the proviso in order to uphold the conviction (see *Birchall* (1985) 82 Cr App R 208; *Trigg* [1963] 1 WLR 305). The judge might not only have to warn the jury about the dangers of convicting without corroboration but also have to point out whether there was anything capable of amounting to corroboration and what evidence the jury could treat as corroboration if they so wished and what evidence was incapable of amounting to corroboration. At the same time, the judge was entitled to make it clear that the jury could still convict even if they concluded that there was no corroboration if they were satisfied that the witness was telling the truth.

Whether all this complexity in any way furthered its intended purpose of protecting the accused from evidence likely to be unreliable or fabricated is open to doubt and there was a school of thought that the warning could actually operate to the detriment rather than to the benefit of the accused (see *Director of Public Prosecutions* v *Hester* [1973] AC 296 at p. 328; Working Paper, para. 4.23; Report paras 2.9 and 2.18). Research with mock juries in the early 1970s suggested that the jury were more likely to convict if a corroboration warning was given (see [1973] Crim LR 208) which may be explicable on the basis that the corroboration warning served to emphasise potentially prejudicial evidence by repeating it and reminding the jury of it (see *Vetrovec* v *R* (1982) 136 DLR (3d) 89 at p. 95).

Quite apart from the issues of complexity, effectiveness and the impact on cases involving children, there was also the issue of whether it was appropriate to treat members of a class of witnesses differently on that account rather than emphasising the issue of the credibility and reliability of the individual witness. Branding all members of a class as being prone to give unreliable or false testimony was a type of discrimination which sat increasingly uneasily with contemporary notions of equal treatment and respect for the individual, particularly in respect of sexual complainants who tend more frequently to be women rather than men. Although the rule applies equally to male as well as female complainants, it was perceived in some quarters as an insult to women and as an unholy relic of the bygone days when it could be intellectually respectable to argue that women were less objective, accurate or honest witnesses than men. It was also subject to criticism as providing one of the disincentives to the reporting of sexual offences by victims. This point is possible to overplay since it is debatable how many potential complainants were actually aware of the rule but no doubt it contributed as one of the factors productive of the negative expectations of the experience that such complainants could anticipate and undergo.

3.3 Abrogation of Warnings Requirement

The combined weight of all the above reasons led the Law Commission to confirm in its final report (1991, Law Com. No. 202, Cm 1620) the conclusion in its earlier working paper that the mandatory requirement to give a warning in relation to the evidence of accomplices and sexual complainants should be abolished. This recommendation was endorsed by the Royal Commission on Criminal Justice (Cm 2263) and is put into effect by s. 32(1) of the CJPOA 1994 which reproduces the provision contained in the draft Bill attached to the Law Commission report. Under s. 32(1) the requirement to give a warning is only abrogated where it is required 'merely' because the witness is an alleged accomplice or a complainant in a sexual offence. Given the previous abolition of the requirement to give a corroboration warning in respect of children's evidence in s. 32 of the CJA 1988 that would seem to leave no other possible reasons for requiring a corroboration warning in criminal cases. It should be remembered, however, that warnings, though not strictly corroboration warnings, may need to be given in relation to certain other types of evidence on other grounds, notably identification evidence which requires a *Turnbull* ([1977] QB 224) direction or the caution authorised under *Beck* [1982] 1 WLR 461 and *Spencer* [1987] AC 128 where a witness has a purpose of his or her own to serve in giving evidence against the accused even though not technically an accomplice. These types of warning are not afflicted by the same technicalities which plagued the corroboration warnings and are generally considered to be working reasonably well.

The question which arises therefore is whether there remains the possibility for the judge to give some form of warning to the jury in the accomplice and sexual complainant cases now that the requirement of a full corroboration warning has been abolished. The Act itself gives no specific guidance on this matter but the issue was fully canvassed in the debates in the House of Lords as a result of amendments put forward by Baroness Mallalieu and others which would, *inter alia*, have required a practice direction of the sort suggested by the Law Commission in their Report No. 202 at para. 4.30. This would have involved the judge discussing with counsel at the conclusion of evidence and in the absence of the jury the possible need for and the type of warning required on the particular facts (a procedure that could have applied not only to accomplice and sexual complainant cases but any case where some sort of warning might be thought to be advisable on the facts). The government rejected this suggestion at the report stage (see *Hansard*, Lords, 5 July 1994, cols 1249–68) on the grounds that it was not appropriate or necessary to require the Lord Chief Justice to issue a practice direction especially as it had already consulted him and had been advised that his current view was that a practice direction was not necessary at this stage and that if further guidance did prove to be necessary, the Court of Appeal would provide it. Nevertheless, Baroness Mallalieu came back with a further amendment at third reading which would have inserted a new subsection (5) into s. 32 as follows:

Nothing in this section shall prevent the court from warning the jury of a special need for caution in relation to a witness where the court considers such a warning to be necessary in the interests of justice

Earl Ferrers for the government again resisted this amendment on the grounds that it was merely declaratory of a discretion which a judge in any event has under the existing law but he did at least partially placate the Baroness by assuring her that he endorsed the Law Commssion recommendation 'that a judge should not be prohibited from giving a warning in any particular terms about the evidence of any type or category of witness'. This assurance was welcomed as going 'some way at least to enable counsel, when trying to persuade a judge as to whether he should or should not give a warning in a particular case, to have resort to *Hansard* for a clear expression of what the government intend in enacting these clauses'. (*Hansard*, Lords, 19 July 1994, cols 162–3).

The upshot of all this seems likely to be as follows:

(a) Judges are no longer required to and will in fact no longer give the full corroboration warning in all cases involving evidence of accomplices or sexual complainants.

(b)   Judges still have a residual discretion to give a warning tailored to the particular witness and facts of the case whether it be a case that formerly would have attracted a full corroboration warning or not.

(c)   Such a warning may, in an appropriate case, be as strongly worded as the full corroboration warning and talk about the danger of convicting solely on the evidence of the witness in question but equally it may take a milder form and speak only of being cautious or of the need to take care. In any event, it will be unnecessary (see Law Com. No. 202, paras 4.10–4.18) to reintroduce the technical complications of what is strictly corroboration implicating the accused and what is merely supportive evidence restoring trust in the witness (cf. *Baskerville* [1916] 2 KB 658 and *Beck* [1982] 1 WLR 461 and compare *Vetrovec* v *R* (1982) 136 DLR (3d) 89 at p. 103. 'The overriding rule', as Lord Ackner put it in *Spencer* [1987] AC 128, is that the judge must put the defence fairly and adequately to the jury.

(d)   It would be contrary to the spirit of the abrogation of the mandatory warning to decide to give any sort of warning merely because of the fact that the witness is an accomplice or a complainant in a sexual offence but an appropriately tailored warning may still be necessary because of the circumstances or history (cf. *Spencer* [1987] AC 128) of the particular witness or because of the nature of the witness's testimony. It will probably be easier to justify some sort of cautionary statement in the case of accomplices who will quite often fall under the formula of a witness who has some interest of his or her own to serve whereas this might be less frequently the case in relation to sexual complainants. So too where the only evidence against the accused is that of an accomplice or a complainant and there is no other evidence supporting it. The difficulty of making even these types of generalisations, when the whole point of the current reforms is to get away from generalisations, perhaps explains the Lord Chief Justice's reluctance to draw up a practice statement and also his preference for leaving it to the discretion of trial judges in relation to the particular facts before them, the Court of Appeal being there as a backstop should the judge take a wholly unreasonable approach.

It has already been mentioned that the requirement of corroboration warning solely on the grounds that the witness is a child was abrogated in s. 34 of the CJA 1988. Section 30(2) of the CJPOA 1994 now deletes the concluding words of s. 34 of the 1988 Act to remove the restriction that the corroboration warning was *only* required on the grounds of the witness being a child in order to make it clear that a corroboration warning *stricto sensu* is now not required in relation to a child's evidence on *any* ground whether it be as a child, an accomplice or a sexual complainant. In other words, the abrogation of the compulsory warnings for accomplices and sexual complainants applies to child as well as to adult accomplices and complainants. Equally, it should be said, discretionary warnings tailored to the facts and circumstances of the particular case can be given in relation to children as much as to adults although again it would presumably be wrong to give any form of warning *merely* on the grounds that the witness is a child. See *Pryce* [1991] Crim LR 379 where the argument that a *warning* should have been given on the grounds that the witness was a child was rejected although the Court of Appeal seemed to approve of the judge telling the jury to *take account* of the fact that the witness was a child.

Corroboration warnings can have little direct impact where one does not have a jury to warn but s. 30(3) removes any theoretical requirement that magistrates should direct themselves to be wary of the dangers of convicting on uncorroborated evidence of accomplices, children or sexual complainants.

3.4 Commencement

By s. 32(4), corroboration warnings will still be required and be relevant for the evidence of accomplices and sexual complainants in trials or magistrates' court proceedings beginning before commencement of the section. For the propriety of adjourning the start of a trial for a few days in order to avoid the application of the corroboration rules see *Walsall Justices, ex parte W* [1990] 1 QB 253. It should also be noted that even once brought into force, s. 32 only expressly affects criminal proceedings. Corroboration warnings or 'self-directions' by the judge may still be appropriate in civil cases (cf. *M.* v *Cain* (1989) *The Times*, 15 December 1989).

3.5 Abolition of Corroboration Requirements under the Sexual Offences Act 1956

Quite apart from the cases where a coroboration warning has been required, there are still a number of situations where statute has required actual corroboration before a person can be convicted of an offence. These include s. 13 of the Perjury Act 1911 in relation to the issue of the falsity of a statement and s. 89 of the Road Traffic Regulation Act 1984 in relation to speeding. Although such statutory requirements are generally left untouched by the 1994 Act, the requirements of corroboration set out in the Sexual Offences Act 1956 (which are closely related to the corroboration warning formerly required for complainants in sexual offences) in relation to offences of procuring unlawful sexual intercourse and prostitution are repealed by s. 33(1). Unless this had been done, the abolition in s. 32 of the general requirement of a corroboration warning would have been meaningless in the case of these particular sexual offences.

Prior to the commencement of ss. 32 and 33, actual corroboration was a prerequisite to a conviction for any of the following offences under the Sexual Offences Act 1956:

    (a)   procurement of a woman by threats (s. 2),
    (b)   procurement of a woman by false pretences (s. 3),
    (c)   administering drugs to obtain or facilitate intercourse (s. 4),
    (d)   causing prostitution of women (s. 22),
    (e)   procuration of a girl under 21 (s. 23).

In future, not only will it be *possible* to convict in the absence of corroboration it will not even be necessary (although it will be permissible) for the judge to give any warning of any dangers involved in convicting in the absence of such corroboration.

As with s. 32, the abolition of the corroboration requirement under s. 33 does not apply to any trial or magistrates' court proceedings begun before the commencement of the section (s. 33(2)).

'THE RIGHT TO SILENCE':
INFERENCES FROM THE ACCUSED'S SILENCE

3.6 Introduction and Background

Notwithstanding the fact that similar provisions were introduced in Northern Ireland in 1988 (Criminal Evidence (Northern Ireland) Order 1988, SI 1988/1987) the provisions in ss. 34 to 39 of the CJPOA 1994 are amongst the most controversial in this or any other piece of criminal justice legislation of recent years. The main argument of the many advanced against them, particularly relevant to silence under police questioning, is that accused persons are often weak, vulnerable or of below average intelligence and that they need the protection of the right to remain silent or else they are likely to confuse or contradict themselves and be too easily led, not necessarily deliberately, to falsely incriminate themselves.

On the other side of the debate are those who believe that protecting the accused's right to remain silent under police questioning or in court is a protection which disproportionately benefits guilty persons and 'professional criminals' and is of little practical benefit to the innocent who are normally keen and willing to proclaim that innocence. This is a view that can be traced back at least as far as Bentham who famously said (of silence at trial rather than under police questioning) in his *Treatise on Evidence*: 'If all criminals of every class had assembled, and framed a system after their own wishes, is not this rule the very first which they would have established for their security? Innocence never takes advantage of it. Innocence claims the right of speaking, as guilt invokes the privilege of silence.' The theme was picked up in 1972 by the Criminal Law Revision Committee (*Eleventh Report*, Cmnd 4991) who made recommendations to the effect that adverse inferences could be drawn by a court or jury from an accused's failure to answer police questions and furthermore that an accused should be formally called in court to give evidence and, although the accused could not be compelled to do so, adverse inferences could again be drawn from failure to give evidence. These proposals were too controversial for the time (see Cross (a member of the Committee), 'A very wicked animal defends the 11th Report of the Criminal Law Revision Committee' [1973] Crim LR 329) and a majority of the Royal Commission on Criminal Procedure in 1981 (Cmnd 8092) was against modifying the right to silence.

Following the introduction in PACE 1984 of more protection for suspects under questioning, however, the government started asking itself whether the balance had not now shifted in some respects too far and in 1988 Douglas Hurd as Home Secretary announced the setting up of a Home Office working group on the right to silence which reported in July 1989 on how rather than whether the right to silence could be modified (see *Zuckerman* [1989] Crim LR 855). In the meantime, the government had already effected changes in Northern Ireland based on the CLRC Report of 1972 but no such change was included in the 1991 Criminal Justice Act, the government being content to await the outcome of the Royal Commission on Criminal Justice which reported in 1993 (Cm 2263). Somewhat inconveniently for the government, a majority of the Commission, like its predecessor 12 years earlier, were not in favour of modifying the right of silence but that did not prevent the Home Secretary, Michael Howard, announcing on 6 October 1993 that the government intended to abolish the 'right to silence' and ss. 34 to 39 of the Act were included pursuant to that commitment.

The debate about the current provisions is more often obscured rather than helped by talk about a general right to silence and from failure to differentiate between silence at trial and silence under police questioning. It is also not helped by the emotive but well-established language of the right to silence and talk of its abolition since the current provisions do not purport to compel an accused to speak or answer questions but rather they permit adverse inferences to be drawn if he or she does not.

This should be contrasted, for example, with the existing powers in relation to serious fraud under s. 2 of the Criminal Justice Act 1987 whereby a person can be compelled to answer questions put by the Serious Fraud Office in the sense that refusal to answer those questions itself constitutes an imprisonable offence (see also the powers of DTI inspectors under companies legislation and the adverse opinion of the European Commission of Human Rights in relation to the case of Ernest Saunders in September 1994 (see various news items in *The Times*, 19–21 September 1994). Contrast the decision of the House of Lords in *In re Arrows (No. 4)* [1994] 3 WLR 656 (concerned with liquidators' powers under the Insolvency Act 1986 rather than DTI Inspectors). The provisions of the 1994 Act do not remove the right to remain silent in this sense but rather permit adverse inferences to be drawn in certain situations which will now be examined in turn.

3.7 Permissible Inferences from Failure to Mention Facts when Questioned or Charged

Although this is in the eyes of many the most controversial of the modifications to the right to silence and its actual effects on the behaviour of police suspects are potentially wide-ranging and difficult to predict, it is important to note the restricted nature of the legal changes authorised by s. 34. Lord Taylor of Gosforth CJ underlined many of these restrictions in a speech at Committee stage in the House of Lords that was influential in shaping the eventual form of s. 34 as enacted (*Hansard*, Lords, 23 May 1994, cols 519–23).

First, the fact which the accused failed to mention must be one on which the accused subsequently relies in his or her defence in court (s. 34(1)(a). If the fact is not one subsequently relied on in the defence, no matter how reasonable or helpful to the police it might have been for the accused to mention it, no adverse comment can be made concerning failure to mention it. Thus if the accused merely contends that the prosecution have not made out their case and does not rely on any particular facts by way of defence, or relies only on facts which he or she could not have been expected to mention under police questioning, s. 34 is of no relevance even if the accused did not mention facts which might have saved the police a lot of time and trouble. (Equally, s. 34 is of no relevance if an accused fails to mention a fact which is relied on by a co-accused in court if it is not relied on by the first accused even though the first accused may have been interviewed much earlier than the co-accused and may have been in as good as or better position than the co-ccused to know of facts relevant to the subsequent defence put forward by the co-accused.)

Secondly, the fact must be one 'which in the circumstances existing at the time the accused could reasonably have been expected to mention'. If the accused was ill, tired or confused at the time or failed to mention something which would compromise his personal or professional life (e. g., being with a prostitute at the time of the offence) or which creates a danger of reprisals against his or her family, then it will be arguable that the accused could not 'reasonably have been expected to mention that fact' even though it is subsequently relied on in court when perhaps the danger of compromise or reprisals has disappeared or become irrelevant. Even if the court takes the view that the accused could still have been expected to mention the fact under questioning despite factors such as these, the same factors may still be relevant under the next paragraph.

The third limitation is that the court, judge or jury may draw such inferences as appear 'proper'. Possible explanations as to why an accused may have been reluctant or unable to mention a particular fact will affect the strength and nature of the inference that it is permissible to draw from failure to mention it. The natural inference from failure to mention a fact later relied on by way of defence is that the defence has been concocted subsequently (and this may also affect the accused's general credibility) but this inference will be weakened to the extent that there are other credible explanations of why the accused initially failed to mention the fact. The correct inference for the court or jury to draw in some cases might be that the accused was more afraid of his or her spouse (or more concerned for his or her safety) than of being tried and convicted of a criminal offence!

Fourthly, silence cannot of itself establish a prima facie case. Since the natural potential adverse inference to be drawn is that the subsequent defence based on the unmentioned fact is concocted, s. 34 cannot logically on its own positively establish a prima facie case as opposed to undermining a defence to or denial of a prima facie case supported by other evidence. The matter is expressly dealt with anyway in s. 38(3) whereby 'A person shall not have the proceedings against him transferred to the Crown Court for trial, have a case to answer or be convicted of an offence solely on an inference drawn fom such a failure or refusal as is mentioned in s. 34(2) ...'. Section 38(4) is to similar effect in relation to applications for dismissal in relation to notices of transfer under CJA 1987 (serious fraud) or CJA 1991 (violent or sexual offences against children).

However, the very fact that paras (a), (b) and (c) of s. 34(2) make the accused's silence relevant to various situations where the issue is whether there is a prima facie case or a case to answer demonstrates that silence under police questioning can contribute to the establishment of a prima facie case even though it cannot on its own establish one. This should be contrasted with the accused's silence at trial under s. 35 where existing case law under the Northern Ireland Order makes it clear that the prosecution have to establish a case to answer without the help of any adverse inferences that might be drawn if the accused fails to testify. This must be logically correct in any event since the issue of whether a case to answer has been established arises before the accused has to make a decision whether to testify. Silence under police questioning comes in advance of the decision whether there is a case to answer and can apparently be used to help to establish a prima facie case together with other evidence even if without the inferences drawn from the failure to answer there may not be a sufficient case to answer.

The help that this may give to the prosecution may be more apparent than real. Inferences can arise only if the accused fails to mention a fact which he or she later relies on in the criminal proceedings. Challenging whether the prosecution have established a prima facie case does not normally amount to relying on any fact in defence. Indeed it will not normally involve raising any 'defence' as such at all. The accused will merely be saying that the prosecution have not provided sufficient evidence of the essential ingredients of the offence. The fact that the accused has failed to mention any facts under police questioning is not relevant under s. 34 until the fact is actually relied on, which by definition will not normally be until *after* the challenge to the prima facie case. Provided the accused's defence is reserved until the trial and until after the close of the prosecution case, which is perfectly proper, the question of inferences drawn from failure to mention facts later relied on in defence simply cannot arise. Such inferences could only possibly arise in relation to the establishment of a prima facie case if the accused is actually challenging the existence of such a case by reference to the strength of the defence he or she is disclosing in advance such as an alibi (but which was not disclosed under police questioning) which is not the typical case at all.

3.8 Accused Must Have Been Under Caution

A fifth and most important limitation on s. 34 is that it applies to silence before charge (under s. 34(1)(a)) only if the accused is being questioned 'under caution'. (Under s. 34(1)(b) 'on being charged' a caution will be administered or have recently been administered anyway.) The insertion of the two words 'under caution' (which were absent from the virtually identically worded art. 3(1) of the Northern Ireland Order but which are now also inserted in that Order by sch. 10, para. 61(2)) was an important amendment to the Bill finally secured at report stage in the House of Lords (*Hansard*, Lords, 7 July 1994, cols 1386–1418). It was designed to answer the concerns expressed about the stage at which an accused's failure to answer questions would become relevant evidence should proceedings subsequently be brought. There were two principal threads to these concerns, (a) that the clause might apply at too early a stage of police enquiries where a person is being questioned merely as a potential witness and with no clear indication that he or she is suspected of being responsible for the offence or on what grounds, and (b) that unless the section was restricted to questioning in a police station in a tape-recorded interview with a right to a legal adviser present, the old problem of police 'verbals' would be resurrected in the shape of 'non-verbals', i.e., the police alleging that the accused did not mention a fact to them under questioning and the accused alleging that it was mentioned right from the start.

Requiring the questioning to be under caution before s. 34 can apply at least partially meets these concerns although it falls short of limiting adverse inferences to where the accused has failed to mention facts when being formally interviewed in a police station. (It was pointed out that there was no equivalent rule automatically excluding admissions made before reaching the police station.) It certainly prevents the prosecution using against an accused the fact that he or she was silent before being told that he or she is a suspect in relation to an offence but it does not go as far as some would have preferred in requiring the purpose and the reasoning behind a particular question to be put to an interviewee. Presumably, though, if a suspect asked why a particular question was being asked or in what sense it was relevant and the police officer unreasonably declined to explain, that might be a factor influencing a court subsequently to say that the accused was acting reasonably in not mentioning a particular fact at that stage, e.g., because the accused did not realise its relevance. The report of the Home Office Working Group had been in favour of statutory guidance to cater for these sorts of factors whereby the judge would have invited the jury to consider, *inter alia*, whether it was reasonable to have expected the accused to disclose a fact in all the circumstances *including the extent of his knowledge of the case against him*. Although the Act does not specifically provide these sorts of guidelines, this will surely be a factor that juries will and should consider.

The caution given will of course be quite different from that required under the previous law which despite being a well-known and almost routine formula is reasonably short and clearly puts an accused on notice that he or she need not say anything. Compare the old caution, 'You do not have to say anything unless you wish to do so, but what you say may be given in evidence' with the new version which has been used in Northern Ireland:

> You do not have to say anything unless you wish to do so but I must warn you that if you fail to mention any fact which you rely on in your defence in court, your failure to take this opportunity to mention it may be treated in court as supporting any relevant evidence against you. If you do wish to say anything, what you say may be given in evidence against you.

The caution proposed to be given in England and Wales following the Act is slightly different:

> You do not have to say anything. But if you do not mention now something which you later use in your defence the court may decide that your failure to mention it now strengthens the case against you. A record will be made of of anything you say and it may be given in evidence if you are brought to trial.

Opponents of s. 34 maintain that such a caution is so complicated and daunting to a person being questioned in relation to an offence that the theoretical right to remain silent with which it opens is completely lost sight of and the acccused receives an impression that he will be in trouble in court if he does not make a statement or answer the questions asked of him. The fact that if the accused remained silent, only limited inferences could be drawn against him and only if he relied on a fact which he could have mentioned earlier becomes irrelevant if the caution has the effect of encouraging him to make all sorts of statements which he could safely have refrained from without any adverse consequences being drawn. The effect on most accused will probably be to encourage them to talk rather than to remain silent and this effect will be much more common than that of a court being in a position to draw proper inferences from silence – silence which the form of caution makes less likely – in relation to facts which are subsequently relied on. The safeguard built in therefore of requiring a caution pointing to the inferences that can be drawn will often operate not so much as a safeguard but more as an encouragement to incriminate oneself perhaps unnecessarily and, more importantly, in some cases inaccurately and unjustly. The fact that the accused made a statement that he need not have made and that no inference could have been drawn from failure to make it does not provide any grounds for excluding the statement. Some would say this is all well and good if it leads to more convictions of the guilty but the unanswerable question is how many convictions of the innocent will it lead to? The traditional view was that the prospect of many more convictions of the guilty were necessary to outweigh the risk of just one wrongful conviction of the innocent but the balance seems to be shifting somewhat in the mind of the government as evidenced from the remark of Lord Ferrers for the government (*Hansard*, Lords, 7 July 1994, col. 1417) that 'it is just as much a miscarriage of justice when guilty people go free and untried as when innocent people are convicted'. See also the criticism by Lee and Bridges of the approach of the Royal Commission in (1994) 57 MLR 75 and the response by Zander at 264 and their rejoinder at 267.

In any event, the ability to draw inferences from silence once a caution has been administered and the effect on many accused of the wording of the caution may well have the effect of encouraging police officers to form the view that a caution is required earlier than might be the case under the previous law. Formerly, the potential disincentive effect of the caution on the suspect's willingness to answer questions provided a temptation for the police to delay coming to the conclusion that there were grounds for suspecting a person to have committed an offence.

An interesting conflict arises where a constable cautions a suspect before questioning but is not yet at the stage where the suspect is being arrested. The new caution must warn the suspect of the consequences of failing to mention any fact later relied on but at the same time under current PACE Code of Practice C, para. 10.2, the suspect must also be told that he or she is not under arrest and is not obliged to remain with the officer. The smart suspect will tell the officer that although there are lots of things he would like to tell him he has not got the time as he has urgent appointments elsewhere and must leave immediately! Under the previous law, the suspect may have been content to remain, safe in the knowledge that questions need not be answered. Under the new situation, remaining plus silence can give rise to adverse inferences whereas leaving on some pretext would make the inferencees harder to draw although the court would probably still draw them if the pretext for leaving was a flimsy one. In any event, the consequence of this tactic may well be that the constable decides an arrest is called for immediately. It is to be hoped that the amended versions of the Codes will deal with such potential conflicts in any event.

3.9   Verbals and Non-verbals

Whatever the effects of limiting s. 34 to questioning following a caution and whatever the effects of administering the new-style caution, the caution itself cannot deal with the potential problem of 'non-verbals'.

The government resisted varous amendments to restrict the application of s. 34 to silence in interviews at the police station by promising to adopt certain amendments to the PACE Codes of Practice. These would introduce a new procedure, based on proposals in the report of the Royal Commission on Criminal Justice (ch. 3, paras 7–15) whereby any exchange taking place between the police and a suspect before the formal interview in the police station would be put on record at the start of that formal interview and the accused given the opportunity to comment on it and to confirm or deny whether it took place. The Commission was concerned with actual statements by the accused including in particular admissions but the government intends to widen this to include failures to mention facts so as to ensure that any disputes about non-verbals are at least identified early on as soon as the formal interview stage is reached. Furthermore, a suspect will be put on notice and the fact recorded that he or she has failed to answer a question so as to avoid allegations much later that there was a failure or refusal to answer a particular question. The adoption of these proposals was instrumental in securing the support of Lord Taylor of Gosforth CJ for the final form of s. 34 (see *Hansard*, Lords, 7 July, cols 1399–1401) and they seem sensible enough as far as answers or failures to answer specific questions put to the accused. Where they will perhaps not be terribly effective is where the accused relies on a fact at trial which the prosecution allege the accused has never previously mentioned and the accused claims that he or she did in fact mention it on the way to the police station though not in response to any specifc question. There may well be no record of the fact being mentioned at the start of the formal interview since it is unlikely to be possible to record every statement made by the accused – what will be recorded are any admissions or questions to which the accused failed to respond. It will be difficult for the police to record the negative that certain statements were not made unless they are unusually prescient and can foresee what facts the accused may subsequently rely on at trial that would not have arisen naturally in response to the questions recorded as having been asked.

3.10 Ambush Defences

One of the justifications put forward for s. 34 is that it will reduce the effectiveness of ambush defences where the accused does not disclose his or her defence or the facts on which it is based until the actual trial and 'ambushes' the prosecution with it at a point where it is too late for the prosecution to check it out or show that it is unfounded. It was to counter one particular type of ambush defence that the CJA 1967 required advance notice of alibi defences. The Royal Commisson on Criminal Justice recommended a general duty to disclose defences once the details of the prosecution case have been disclosed (this procedure would in the view of the majority have made the modification of the right to silence at the interview stage unnecessary) and the opposition unsuccessfully pressed amendments in Parliament to replace s. 34 with such a procedure. It is significant to note though that Lord Taylor CJ (*Hansard*, Lords, 23 May 1994, col. 522) considered that even with a disclosure requirement, once the prosecution papers have been delivered, the possibility of drawing inferences from silence at an earlier stage would still be needed. Conversely, even with the enactment of the current provisions relating to silence during police questioning, Lord Taylor expressed the hope that a future Bill would provide for defence disclosure more generally. This prompts the observation that s. 34 only expressly refers to the inference to be drawn from silence when questioned or charged and does not refer to the relevance of continuing failure to mention any fact in the period between charge and trial. Presumably, though, where the accused does disclose the line of defence after charge but before trial the proper inference to be drawn will be less adverse than if the defence had been raised at the very last moment.

The more sophisticated defendants with good legal advice may well seek to delay disclosing their defence until they have received full details of the prosecution case against them and they have been able to consider this fully with their legal advisers. Such legal advisers may well advise them at the stage of interview under caution that they ought not to say anything until they have got full details of the prosecution case. The defence will subsequently argue that no adverse inference should be drawn from the failure to answer questions and this argument may be particularly cogent where the defence is subsequently disclosed well in advance of the trial and is not sprung on the prosecution as a last-minute ambush. The Royal Commission cited the probability that experienced professional criminals would justify their silence under police questioning by reference to the legal advice they had received as one of the reasons why it was not in favour of modifying the right to silence under such questioning (Report, ch. 4, para. 22 and see n. 9 to the effect that this is what routinely happens in Scotland where such accused are invited to comment on the charges at the judicial examination). On the other hand, this is not an issue which appears to have caused any particular problems in Northern Ireland and the government clearly thought that a reference to legal advice would not of itself prevent the court drawing an inference from silence even though it was exercised pursuant to such advice. The government seems to take the view that a court could merely rule that the accused had been badly advised but that poor legal advice was no more a ground for ignoring the inference from failure to mention a fact that could easily have been mentioned than if the accused had been badly advised that it was best to make a full and frank admission when it would in fact be virtually impossible to convict without such an admission. Nevertheless, the fact remains that an admission is unequivocal (though not conclusive) evidence in support of the accused's guilt whereas silence is much more equivocal. The fact that one has been advised by a lawyer to remain silent provides an alternative explanation of the silence to deflect the court or jury from the more natural inference that a fact was not mentioned because it was concocted later. The courts may well have to start speculating on why an accused was advised to stay silent on a particular occasion or inroads might have to be made into the privileged status of communications between solicitor and client.

Even if (which seems unlikely) the courts were to adopt a blanket rule that legal advice to remain silent should not be treated as weakening any inference from the silence that would otherwise be drawn, experienced criminals accused of serious crimes may well still be correctly advised in many situations that on balance it is better to say nothing at the interview stage and reserve any defence to a later stage when the full prosecution case is disclosed, particularly given the limited circumstances in which an adverse inference can be drawn. Indeed there is nothing to stop juries actually drawing such inferences at the moment since in most cases they become aware of the accused's silence in any event and they no doubt draw impermissible inferences that would not be permissible even under s. 34, e.g., from the accused's silence in relation to facts which he or she does not subsequently rely on. Section 34 will lead to juries being told what inferences are permissible and therefore by implication, or possibly expressly, what inferences should not be drawn from silence. The net result may be that in many cases, defendants who remain silent may not be subject to any more adverse inferences than the jury actually draw at the present time and they may in fact be better off. The confident experienced offender with a good lawyer will probably continue to refuse to answer questions whereas the less well-advised and the less streetwise may well feel intimidated into saying things which were unnecessary and which in some cases may point misleadingly to their guilt.

If an accused can legitimately point to the fact that he did subsequently, in advance of trial, disclose the factual basis of a defence which he did not mention under police questioning, the converse ought to be true that a person who not only fails to mention a fact under questioning but fails to mention it until the trial itself should have a stronger adverse inference drawn against him. However, s. 34 does not appear to allow for the continued failure up to trial to disclose facts to be specifically mentioned. Unless the jury recognise that the fact continued not to be mentioned right up to trial, it is difficult to see how such a continuation of silence will have any effect other than in the negative sense that the accused is not able to mitigate any inference drawn from his initial silence by reference to the fact that he did subsequently disclose it in advance of trial.

3.11 Evidence of the Failure to Mention the Fact Relied On

Where the accused is known to be relying on a fact which he or she could have mentioned under questioning, it seems that the prosecution will be entitled to give the evidence of the failure to mention it during the presentation of the rest of their evidence. It is in this less common type of case that the accused's silence may be relevant in helping to establish a prima facie case. It would seem to follow that if the defence subsequently choose not to rely on the particular fact, the jury would then have to be told not to draw any inferences from the evidence already given of the failure to mention it. However, where the fact that the defence are relying on the particular fact and hence making it relevant is only disclosed during the presentation of the defence evidence, the prosecution may thereafter, subject to any directions of the court, give the evidence of the accused's previous failure to mention the fact even though the prosecution case has otherwise closed (see s. 34(3)).

3.12 Questioning by Persons Other Than Constables

Although s. 34(1)(a) refers to questioning by constables, s. 34(4) extends the application of the section to an accused's silence when question by 'persons (other than constables) charged with the duty of investigating offences or charging offenders'. Thus the section applies equally not only to persons questioned (under caution) by persons such as customs and excise officers, trading standards officers etc. but also private individuals charged with such duties, for example, store detectives (cf. *Bayliss* (1993) 157 JP 1062). (Contrast the position of the Bank of England official in *Smith (Wallace)* [1994] 1 WLR 1396.) Such persons of course also have to follow the provisions of the PACE codes of practice (PACE, s. 67(9) which uses the same form of words as CJPOA 1994, s. 34(4)).

3.13 Other Inferences from Silence

CJPOA 1994, s. 34(5), makes it clear that the inferences permssible under s. 34 are in addition to and in no way prejudice any other inferences which may be drawn from the accused's silence or reaction in the face of anything said in the accused's presence relating to the conduct in respect of which he or she is charged and s. 34 does not prejudice the admissibility of any such evidence. Thus the rule is preserved whereby an accused's reaction to a statement made in his or her presence is capable of amounting to an acknowledgement of the truth of the statement (see *Christie* [1914] AC 545 and *Blackstone's Criminal Practice*, F17.50). Such an acknowledgement may be constituted by silence in appropriate circumstances where a denial would normally be expected even if it takes place in the presence of a police officer – see, e.g., *Horne* [1990] Crim LR 188. The authorities conflict on whether silence in the face of an allegation from a police officer can ever be treated as evidence of the truth of the allegation – compare *Hall* v *The Queen* [1971] 1 WLR 298 with *Chandler* [1976] 1 WLR 585.

3.14 Inferences from Failure or Refusal to Account for Objects, Substances, Marks or Presence at Scene of Crime

Sections 36 and 37 of the CJPOA 1994 are modelled on provisions enacted in the Republic of Ireland in ss. 18 and 19 of the Irish Criminal Justice Act 1984. Although they are of similar effect to s. 34 in that they permit inferences to be drawn from silence out of court, they are more specific in their application. Section 36 deals with incriminating objects, substances or marks and s. 37 with presence at the scene of the alleged offence but both sections only apply once a person has actually been arrested. If a constable (not necessarily the arresting constable) reasonably believes that the presence of the object, substance or mark or the presence of the accused is attributable to the accused's participation in the offence and so informs the accused, then the court in subsequent criminal proceedings for that offence may draw such inferences as appear proper from the refusal or failure.

Although the sections are similar to s. 34 in permitting inferences to be drawn from silence, the type of inference drawn may be different in some important respects. Section 34 is limited to failure to mention facts which subsequently form part of the accused's defence in court. It is concerned, partly at least, as we have seen, to prevent ambush defences and the inference drawn will be that the defence may be concocted or false. Sections 36 and 37 are in contrast concerned with facts which point to the accused's involvement with the offence rather than with defences. It is not so much the accused's failure to mention facts which could help him in his defence which is in issue but his failure to explain facts already known to the police and which point to his guilt. The inference from failure to explain is therefore relevant not so much to undermining the accused's defence but more in that it points directly to his guilt. Nevertheless, subsections (3) and (4) of s. 38 still apply so as to make it clear that an inference under s. 36 or s. 37 shall not be sufficient on its own for conviction or establishment of a case to answer etc. However, this provision may be of less utility to the accused in relation to ss. 36 and 37 since there will by definition be other evidence incriminating the accused quite apart from any inference drawn under the section, i.e., the incriminating object, substance or mark or presence itself. Furthermore, the inference under s. 36 or s. 37 may clearly help in establishing the prima facie case or the case to answer since it does not depend on the accused subsequently relying on any fact in his or her defence and can therefore operate even though the accused's defence has not yet been disclosed.

Having said all that, there may often be substantial overlap between s. 34 on the one hand and ss. 36 and 37 on the other. If the accused is asked about the presence of a certain type of clay on his boots which was found also at the scene of the crime and he gives no explanation but at trial claims that he had been fishing in a different area of the country where the same type of clay is found, both ss. 34 and 36 may be applicable. Section 34 applies because he failed to mention a fact which now is relied on in his defence (i.e., that the apparently incriminating clay was picked up elsewhere) and the inference which may be drawn is that that defence is concocted. Section 36 applies (and it does even before any defences are raised) because he failed to explain when asked originally about the presence of the clay on his boots and the inference is that the clay is indeed due to his participation in the offence. If the accused never puts forward, even at trial, the claim that the clay was due to some other cause than his having been at the scene of the crime then no inference would be permissible under s. 34 but the inference under s. 36 could still be drawn since it does not require the accused to subsequently rely on any fact. Section 36 applies merely because the accused has failed to explain the object, substance or mark and the inference that may be drawn is that the presence of the object, substance or mark is indeed due to the accused's participation in the offence.

Sections 36 and 37 have a number of subsections which mirror subsections of s. 34, in particular, s. 34(2) dealing with the types of proceedings in which the relevant inference may subsequently be drawn and s. 34(5)(b) to the effect that the section should not preclude the drawing of an inference which may be permissible apart from the section. However, ss. 36 and 37 are narrower than s. 34 in that they apply only where a person is actually arrested and, possibly as a consequence, they are extended beyond constables only to officers of customs and excise (as with many of the powers under PACE) rather than as with s. 34(4) to other 'persons charged with the duty of investigating offences or charging offenders'. Since the sections only apply if there has been an arrest, a caution will have been administered in any event but this may not have been immediately prior to the request to account for the object, substance, mark or presence etc. Therefore ss. 36(4) and 37(3) preclude the drawing of any inference unless the accused is told in ordinary language by the constable when making the request what the effect of the section would be if there is a failure or refusal to comply. A standard form of caution is being developed to guide constables in their choice of ordinary language but it will presumably not be sufficient to have given the normal caution on arrest even if this is immediately prior to the request to account.

A potentially significant difference between the sections is that s. 36 applies to requests to account in relation to 'an offence specified by the constable' (see s. 36(1)(b)), not necessarily, therefore, the offence for which the accused is arrested, whereas s. 37 applies only in relation to 'the offence for which he is arrested' (s. 37(1)(a)). The effect of s. 38(2) is to broaden this somewhat so that the inference can still be drawn (whether under s. 36 or s. 37, or indeed s. 34 or s. 35) in relation to alternative-verdict offences but the fact remains that if a person is arrested for an alleged robbery and is asked to account for his presence at the scene of the alleged robbery, then his failure to answer that question is not admissible under s. 37 in relation to an indictment charging, say, unlawful wounding rather than robbery. It could apply to charges other than the one originally arrested for only if the accused had been rearrested for the subsequent offence (see s. 31 of PACE) and even then only if the accused were asked again to account and failed to do so, a procedure which becomes more and more pointless the closer one gets to the actual trial since part of the purpose of s. 37 is to encourage suspects who have genuine exculpatory explanations of apparently incriminating circumstances to state them at an early stage and thereby avoid the waste of their own time and valuable police time.

The width of s. 36 by contrast is also apparent from s. 36(1)(a) under which it applies to any object, substance or mark, or any mark on any object which is:

(a)   on his person; or
(b)   in or on his clothing or footwear; or
(c)   otherwise in his possession; or
(d)   in any place in which he is at the time of his arrest.

Alternative (d) is particularly wide in its potential as literally it could apply to a mark on an object found in a football ground in which the accused was one of 30,000 spectators. However, this width is more apparent than real since it would be unlikely that any 'proper' adverse inference could be drawn in such extreme circumstances. But this *reductio ad absurdum* illustrates the general point that the sections only permit the drawing of proper inferences and the strength or weakness of them will depend on the precise circumstances. As has already been noted, the Home Office Working Group actually recommended guidelines to juries on this sort of point but the Act says nothing specific and leaves guidance of this sort to the judge's discretion, as with many other issues.

3.15 Commencement

The ability to draw inferences from silence only applies to silence occurring after the commencement of the relevant section (see ss. 34(6), 36(7) and 37(6)). It may thus occur that a person is questioned under caution and fails to answer questions before the commencement of the relevant section but is then subsequently arrested and questioned again after commencement in relation to the same offence. The silence at the earlier stage cannot be commented on under s. 34 but the silence at the later stage after commencement can.

3.16 Permissible Inferences from Failure to Testify in Court

Expressly permitting inferences to be drawn from the accused's silence at trial is generally regarded as slightly less contentious than the modification of the right to silence under police questioning. After all, the accused does now know the full prosecution case against him, there has been time to compose and reflect on his situation and any facts relevant to his defence and he has had ample time to take full legal advice and to secure adequate legal representation. It has to be remembered that, until 1898, the accused was not even permitted to give evidence and when the accused was made a comptetent witness in the Criminal Evidence Act of that year, comment by the prosecution on any failure of the accused to take up this new right was expressly forbidden by proviso (b) to s. 1 of that Act. However, the Act said nothing about the power of the judge to comment and the case law recognised that a limited form of comment from the judge was permissible and advisable. The latest in a long line of leading cases on the nature of such comment by the judge is *Martinez-Tobon* [1994] 1 WLR 388 where the Court of Appeal said that the following principles apply where the accused does not testify:

(a) The judge should give the jury a direction along the lines of the Judicial Studies Board specimen direction based on *Bathurst* [1968] 2 QB 99 at p. 107.

(b) The essentials of that direction are that the defendant is under no obligation to testify and the jury should not assume he is guilty because he has not given evidence.

(c) Provided those essentials are complied with, the judge may think it appropriate to make a stronger comment where the defence case involves alleged facts which (i) are at variance with prosecution evidence or additional to it and exculpatory and (ii) must, if true, be within the knowledge of the defendant.

(d) The nature and strength of such comment must be a matter for the discretion of the judge and will depend on the circumstances of the individual case. However, it must not be such as to contradict or nullify the essentials of the conventional direction.

The conventional direction referred to above and recommended by the Judicial Studies Board is as follows:

The defendant does not have to give evidence. He is entitled to sit in the dock and require the prosecution to prove its case. You must not assume that he is guilty because he has not given evidence. The fact that he has not given evidence proves nothing one way or the other. It does nothing to establish his guilt. On the other hand, it means that there is no evidence from the defendant to undermine, contradict, or explain the evidence put before you by the prosecution.

As can be seen, the above comment is partly in favour of the accused rather than being wholly adverse to him. It limits the significance which the jury might otherwise wrongly attach to a failure to testify if the judge made no comment at all. The CJPOA 1994 now changes the situation in a number of significant respects.

First of all, and this is not immediately apparent from s. 35 itself, the prosecution are permitted to comment on the accused's failure to testify. This is the effect of s. 168(3) and sch. 11 which repeal proviso (b) to s. 1 of the Criminal Appeal Act 1898.

Secondly, the court or jury may 'draw such inferences as appear proper from [the accused's] failure to give evidence or his refusal, without good cause, to answer any question'.

It is possible to argue that this is merely declaratory of the common law position permitting inferences to be drawn from failure to testify in so-called cases of confession and avoidance – point (c) in the principles described in *Martinez-Tobon* listed above. As has been seen, stronger comment by the judge was permissible in those cases to the effect that the alleged defence is seriously weakened by the failure to support it in the witness box. Thus in a case like *Martinez-Tobon* where it was suggested by the defence that the accused thought it was emeralds not drugs that he was carrying through customs, it was appropriate to comment that 'if in fact the accused thought it was emeralds not drugs, one might have thought that he would be very anxious to say so'. Such a comment was permissible on such facts provided it did not 'contradict or nullify the essentials of the conventional direction'. The essentials of the conventional direction are that the defendant is under no obligation to testify and the jury should not assume he is guilty because he has not given evidence. In the words of the Judicial Studies Board specimen: 'The fact that he has not given evidence proves nothing one way or another. It does nothing to establish his guilt.'

Such a limited interpretation of s. 35 is unlikely because it was clearly intended to change the current law and practice, and indeed for this reason the House of Lords has already rejected such a limited sort of interpretation in *Murray* v *Director of Public Prosecutions* [1994] 1 WLR 1 in respect of the very similarly worded art. 4 of the Northern Ireland Order introduced in 1988 (see Jackson (1993) 44 NILQ 103). The trial judge (Kelly LJ) in that case (sitting without a jury) said that it was remarkable that the accused, in the light of the cumulative strength of the circumstantial and forensic evidence against him, had not given evidence and it was only common sense to infer 'that he was not prepared to assert his innocence on oath because that was not the case'. This approach effectively uses the silence of the accused as direct evidence of guilt as opposed to merely undermining a possible defence although some would argue that this is a distinction without a difference (see

Zuckerman [1989] Crim LR 855). The House of Lords at any rate upheld the conviction for atempted murder which followed the inference drawn by the trial judge and said that in appropriate circumstances the inference that the defendant was guilty of the offence with which he was charged was permissible. In this case, the prosecution had established a clear prima facie case against the defendant which he had failed to answer and the judge had beeen entitled in all the circumstances of the case to infer that there could have been no innocent explanation of the prima facie case and that the defendant was guilty.

It is submitted that the above decision should be treated circumspectly and although it clearly authorises an important inference being drawn, it is not simply a direct inference that because the accused failed to give evidence he is guilty. The important point is that there is a prima facie case which points already towards guilt and the failure to testify justifies the inference that there is nothing to call that prima facie case into question and so *leads to the further conclusion* that the accused is guilty. The failure to testify is conclusive but only because the evidence is already on the threshold of proof beyond reasonable doubt and the extra inference cumulatively with the other evidence produces the weight of evidence necessary to convict.

Although the main judgment with which the other Law Lords agreed was given by Lord Slynn of Hadley, the significance of the existence of a prima facie case was more fully discussed in the judgment of Lord Mustill. The draft Bill proposed by the Criminal Law Revision Committee in 1972 expressly stated the negative condition that there shall not have been held to be no case to answer. This is not expressly provided for in s. 35 (or in the Northern Ireland Order) but Lord Mustill held (surely correctly) that the need to establish a prima facie case or a case to answer independently and in advance of the accused's failure to testify was so obviously still required that it was felt unnecessary to mention it expressly in the legislation. (Unlike ss. 34, 36 and 37, s. 35 does not provide for failure to testify to be relevant to the establishment of a case to answer or a prima facie case but merely makes it relevant for the court or jury in determining guilt.)

If a prima facie case has been established, Lord Mustill's judgment helpfully sets out the effect that the accused's failure to testify may or may not have in converting that prima facie case into one proved beyond reasonable doubt:

The fact-finder waits to see whether in relation to each essential ingredient of the offence the direct evidence, which it is at least possible to believe, should in the event be believed, and whether inferences that might be drawn from such evidence should actually be drawn. Usually, the most important of the events for which the fact-finder is keeping his judgment in suspense will be the evidence of the accused himself, for most prosecutions depend upon witnesses who speak directly to the participation of the defendant, who knows very well where the truth lies. So also with many of the inferences which the prosecutor seeks to draw from facts which are directly proved. If in such circumstances the defendant does not go on oath to say that the witnesses who have spoken to his actions are untruthful or unreliable, or that an inference which appears on its face to be plausible is in reality unsound for reasons within his personal knowledge, the fact-finder may suspect that the defendant does not tell his story because he has no story to tell, or none which will stand up to scrutiny; and this suspicion may be sufficient to convert a provable prosecution case into one which is actually proved. This is not of course because a silent defendant is presumed to be guilty, or because silence converts a case which is too weak to call for an answer into one which justifies a conviction. Rather the fact-finder is entitled as a matter of common sense to draw his own conclusions if a defendant who is faced with evidence which does call for an answer fails to come forward and provide it.

So also if the defendant seeks to outflank the case for the prosecution by means of a 'positive' defence – as for example where he replies in relation to a charge of murder that although he did kill the deceased he acted under provocation. If he does not give evidence in support of this allegation there will in very many cases be a legitimate inference that the defence is untrue.

It is, however, equally a matter of common sense that even where the prosecution has established a prima facie case in the sense indicated above, it is not in every situation that an adverse inference can be drawn from silence, the more so because in all but the simplest case the permissible inferences may have to be considered separately in relation to each individual issue. Everything depends on the nature of the issue, the weight of the evidence adduced by the prosecution upon it (see para. 110 of the [CLRC] report) and the extent to which the defendant should in the nature of things be able to give his own account of the particular matter in question. It is impossible to generalise, for dependent upon circumstances the failure of the defendant to give evidence may found no inference at all, or one which is for all practical purposes fatal.

It is submitted that the above passage summarises very well how s. 35 should be and will be applied. Its merit is that it avoids any artificial distinction between undermining defences raised by the accused and supporting the proof of the prosecution case. It gives an effect to the new provision without permitting the silence of the accused to create a prima facie case to answer where none existed before or without the accused's silence. It is sufficiently flexible to allow courts and juries to apply common sense whilst reserving power for the judge to point out that on the particular facts the silence of the accused is equivocal and capable of innocent explanation or in no way relevant to the credibility of the prosecution evidence (e.g., the only issue realistically in dispute in a murder trial might be whether the death was caused by the accused's admitted assault on the victim or some other cause and this might largely turn on medical evidence – the accused's failure to go into the witness-box is likely to be completely irrelevant to the issue of whether the prosecution evidence on causation has proved that issue beyond reasonable doubt as it will normally be extremely unlikely that any evidence the accused might have given, even had he chosen to testify, would be relevant to that issue).

Whether s. 35 interpreted along the lines suggested above really goes much beyond the effect of the comments permissible already at common law is open to debate. In *Haw Tua Tau* v *Public Prosecutor* [1982] AC 136 Lord Diplock thought that the enactment of the CLRC provisions in Singapore did not permit any adverse inferences to be drawn from failure to testify that would not have been permissible anyway under English common law. This may be an unduly optimistic view for those unhappy about the enactment of s. 35 particularly if the reasoning of the trial judge in *Murray* v *Director of Public Prosecutions* is followed since that seemed to go beyond inferring that a particular line of defence is not true and beyond noting that the accused has not taken the opportunity personally to contradict any of the prosecution evidence to actually inferring that the accused was not prepared to assert his innocence on oath because he was not innocent – in other words, a direct inference of guilt because of the accused's failure to testify. This is not contrary to s. 38(3) prohibiting conviction solely on the basis of an inference drawn from such failure because there is also the evidence establishing the prima facie case. The difference seems to be that whereas under the old law the failure to testify merely permitted the prima facie case to go undiminished but unaugmented, the inference drawn by the trial judge in *Murray* v *Director of Public Prosecutions* is actually added to the prima facie case which already exists and which on its own may or may not have been accepted by the jury as proof beyond reasonable doubt.

Whether the extra inference which the judge may now allow the jury to add to the scales will itself be decisive will depend ultimately on the overall view that the jury take of all the evidence and it may be questioned whether in practice juries will come to different verdicts than they would previously have done under the old law. The most important difference may well be the ability of the prosecution now to comment on the accused's failure to testify but the prosecution will have to be wary of making a stronger comment than the circumstances call for and thus rendering any conviction vulnerable to appeal. There is precious little evidence from either Singapore or Northern Ireland that the changes there have made much practical difference either way, although it has to be remembered that no juries were involved in Singapore nor in many of the Northern Ireland cases and therefore the effects of expressly permitting adverse inferences in trials on indictment before a jury in England and Wales may turn out to be rather different. Trial judges are likely to be cautious initially at least in the inferences that they leave it open for juries to draw. A direction based on the judgment of Lord Mustill in *Murray* v *Director of Public Prosecutions* (stressing the strength of the prima facie case) would in effect attach less significance to the failure to testify than is apparent from the form of words expressed by the trial judge in that case (referring simply to the accused being not prepared to assert his innocence on oath because that was not in fact the case) even though the House of Lords was happy to uphold the conviction based on that expression.

3.17   Procedure under s. 35

Section 35(2) lays down the procedure that is to apply before an inference under s. 35 is to be drawn from the accused's failure to give evidence. The procedure recommended by the Criminal Law Revision Committee and enshrined in the Northern Ireland Order whereby the accused is actually called on by the court to give evidence was also originally incorporated in the Bill as it was first presented to Parliament. This procedure met with considerable opposition from the judiciary and in particular from Lord Taylor of Gosforth CJ who in the Tom Sargant Memorial Lecture in January 1994 publicly criticised the proposal as likely to:

> produce undesirable and unfair results. . . . To speak of the defendant being 'called upon' to give evidence does not lie easily with the principle still intact . . . that the defendant has a free choice whether to give evidence.

Furthermore such a procedure whereby the accused would actually be called by the judge into the box even if it was clear that the accused had no intention of giving evidence would make it seem as though the judge was adopting an inquisitorial role and the defendant's refusal to testify might seem in those circumstances to be a form of defiance of the judge. It was, argued Lord Taylor, 'an unnecessary piece of ritual procedure'.

The result of this criticism was that the procedure was amended at report stage in the Commons (13 April) and the much watered-down version now contained in s. 35(2) substituted in its place (see sch. 10, para. 61 for consistent amendments to the Northern Ireland Order). It is not entirely clear precisely what is now required by s. 35(2) but it does still seem to contain a degree of ritual in that the court must, at the conclusion of the evidence for the prosecution, 'satisfy itself (in the case of proceedings on indictment, in the presence of the jury)' that the stage has been reached when the accused can if he or she wishes give evidence and that inferences may be drawn from any refusal to do so. The reference to 'in the presence of the jury' shows that the legislation is still concerned to highlight publicly the accused's competence to give evidence and to underline any reluctance or refusal by the accused to take advantage of this opportunity. If the concern was merely to ensure that the accused understands his or her rights, it would be possible to do this in the absence of the jury but the whole point seems to be to ensure that the jury are well aware of the fact that the accused could give evidence but is choosing not to do so. Despite the fact that s. 35(2) says 'at the conclusion of the evidence for the prosecution', in the light of the comments noted above by Lord Mustill in *Murray* v *Director of Public Prosecutions* [1994] 1 WLR 1 concerning the right to submit that there is no case to answer, the defence must be able to make a submission of this nature before the judge publicly explains to the accused his or her right to testify and that adverse inferences may be drawn from a failure to do so.

The procedure does not apply if the accused's guilt is not in issue, i.e., if the accused is pleading guilty, or if the accused's physical or mental condition makes it undesirable for him or her to give evidence or if the accused is under 14 years old. Neither does it apply if the accused's legal representative informs the court that the accused will give evidence or if the court ascertains from an unrepresented accused that he or she will give evidence.

The procedure under s. 35(2) not only requires the court to explain that inferences may be drawn from a failure to give evidence but also that they may be drawn from a refusal, without good cause, to answer any question having once been sworn. Again this explanation appears to be as much for the benefit of the jury as for the accused because if the accused indicates that he or she will give evidence and then refuses to do so or refuses to answer particular questions, adverse inferences may still be drawn under s. 35(3). In this case there will have been no explanation to the accused that this may happen since it is only s. 35(2) (providing for the explanation to the accused) which does not apply if the accused or his or her representative indicates in advance that the accused will give evidence – see s. 35(1).

Despite these encouragemnts to testify and answer questions, the underlying principle that the accused is not compellable still remains, as is expressly pointed out in s. 35(4). Thus although adverse inferences may be drawn, the accused is within his or her rights to refuse to testify or to answer a particular question and is not guilty of contempt of court for such a refusal as would be the case with a compellable witness. The only sanction for refusal to answer a question without good cause is that adverse inferences may be drawn. The question of what is good cause for refusing to answer a particular question is not left at large but is restricted by s. 35(5). This provides that a refusal to answer a question is without good cause unless either the accused is entitled to refuse by virtue of any enactment or on the ground of privilege, or the court in the exercise of its general discretion excuses the accused from answering it. This should also be read in the light of s. 38(6) which states that nothing in ss. 34 to 37 prejudices any power of a court to exclude evidence (whether by preventing questions being put or otherwise) at its discretion. Thus, for example, questions that must not be put tending to show an accused's previous convictions or bad character under proviso (f) to s. 1 of the Criminal Evidence Act 1898 are still not to be put (or required to be answered) and the judge still has a discretion not to allow such questions, even where the accused has thrown away the shield by casting imputations on the character of the prosecutor or the witnesses for the prosecution (see *Selvey* v *Director of Public Prosecutions* [1970] AC 304).

3.18   Imputations on the Character of a Deceased Victim

A long-standing anomaly in relation to the loss of the shield under s. 1(f)(ii) of the Criminal Evidence Act 1898 has been the fact that the shield is not lost where the imputations are cast not on the character of the prosecutor or a witness for the prosecution but on that of the deceased victim (who by definition cannot be a witness in the case) – see *Biggin* [1920] 1 KB 213, an early example of the so-called Portsmouth defence where the accused alleged that the deceased had made a violent and indecent homosexual attack on him. If the victim had not been killed but had been the chief prosecution witness in relation to a charge of a serious non-fatal offence, such an allegation would undoubtedly mean that the accused could be cross-examined (subject to the judge's discretion to prevent it) on his own record or bad character in order to allow the jury to assess the credibility of the accused in making such an allegation and to assess his credibility generally. The fact that such allegations can be made with impunity where the victim has actually been killed and is thus not available to be a witness is often a source of distress to the relatives of the deceased, particularly where the allegations are completely unfounded. Furthermore, it means that the accused may be in a better postion in this respect because of killing rather than merely injuring the victim.

   For these sorts of reasons, Lord Ackner introduced an amendment in the Lords at committee stage (*Hansard*, Lords, 17 May, col. 205) which ultimately became s. 31 of the Act and which adds 'the deceased victim of the alleged crime' to the list of persons whose character cannot be brought into the accused's defence without losing the accused the shield provided by the Criminal Evidence Act 1898, s. 1(f). The others in the list are the prosecutor and the witnesses for the prosecution. The government initially resisted the amendment on the grounds that the Law Commission has been asked to look more generally at the issue of the law governing evidence of previous misconduct and that it would be unwise to pre-empt the Law Commsion by piecemeal reform on the subject. However, the amendment was eventually accepted at the report stage (*Hansard*, Lords 5 July 1994, col. 1249).

   In initially resisting and also when eventually accepting the amendment, it was also pointed out that the amendment would sometimes inhibit the defence putting forward, perfectly properly, defences such as self-defence or provocation where the effect would be to open the accused up to cross-examination on his or her record which might be highly prejudicial and not particularly relevant to the credibility of the allegations being made against the deceased. The trial judge will have to consider carefully the discretion to refuse to permit questions in such cases even though the accused has lost the statutory shield by putting forward a defence which involves imputations on the character of the deceased victim. Furthermore, the guidelines, summarised, ironically by Ackner LJ, in *Burke* (1985) 82 Cr App R 156 at p. 161, on the exercise of the discretion to restrain cross-examination may need to be re-examined or modified for their application to cases where the imputation is on the deceased. For there is an important difference in that it is not a question of comparing the *credibility* of the deceased with that of the accused. What is in question is the credibility of the accused and of the attack made on the deceased's character as part of his or her defence. There is no question of the imputation undermining the credibilty of a prosecution *witness*, it is pure 'tit for tat' retaliation against an accused who attacks the character of the deceased and it is therefore submitted that unless the previous record of the accused is directly relevant to the credibility of the imputations being cast on the deceased, the courts should not be too slow to exercise their discretion to restrain the cross-examination of the accused on his or her record or character.

The amendment is peculiarly structured since it seems unnecessarily to add another semicolon followed by the word 'or' when in fact the more accurate way of achieving the desired effect would have been merely to insert the word 'or' before the phrase 'the deceased victim of the alleged offence'. As it stands the new version of s. 1(f) now provides that the accused shall retain his shield

unless—

(i)　the proof that he has committed or been convicted of such other offence is admissible evidence to show that he is guilty of the offence wherewith he is then charged; or

(ii)　he has personally or by his advocate asked questions of the witnesses for the prosecution with a view to establish his own good character, or has given evidence of his good character, or the nature or conduct of the defence is such as to involve imputations on the character of the prosecutor or the witnesses for the prosecution; or the deceased victim of the alleged crime; or

(iii)　....

By tacking the amendment on after the existing '; or' in s. 1(f)(ii) and adding another '; or' at the end of the amendment, the new phrase is somehow suspended in mid-air on its own, detached from what precedes it. It is also somewhat inelegant that the new phrase refers to the 'alleged crime' whereas s. 1(f)(ii) refers throughout to an 'offence' rather than a 'crime'. It should also be noticed that the amendment applies only where the victim is deceased. If the victim is unavailable at the trial, e.g., because in a coma or for any other reason, and is not therefore a witness for the prosecution or the prosecutor then an attack on the victim's character will not of itself endanger the accused's shield.

3.19　Child Testimony: Examination-in-Chief

Section 54 of the CJA 1991 introduced a new procedure enabling the evidence of child witnesses of certain sexual and violent offences to be given by means of a video recording and for that purpose introduced a new s. 32A into the CJA of 1988 alongside the previous provision in s. 32 providing for evidence in such cases to be given by live television link. The new s. 32A provided in subsection (5) that where a video recording is admitted under the section, the child witness shall be called by the party who tendered the recording in evidence but the child shall not be examined in chief on any matter which in the opinion of the court has been dealt with in the recorded testimony. In the passage of that provision through Parliament in 1991, an amendment to insert the word 'adequately' in front of the words 'dealt with' was rejected on the grounds that it was already implicit. In the present authors' guide to the 1991 Act, it was queried whether this was absolutely clear and the view was expressed that it would be unfortunate if the prosecution were precluded from asking the child witness to expand on a particular matter because it had already been 'dealt with' in the video.

Section 51 of the CJPOA 1994 now puts the matter beyond doubt by adopting the amendment which was rejected in 1991 and expressly inserting the word 'adequately' in s. 32A(5)(b) of CJA 1988. The acceptance of this amendment (moved initially at committee stage in the Lords – *Hansard*, Lords, 23 May 1994, col. 581 – and accepted on report – *Hansard*, Lords, 7 July 1994, col. 1463) was partly due to a problem not foreseen at the time of the 1991 Act. This is the fact that even if the prosecution have no real need to ask the child to expand on any matters dealt with in the video recording, to present the video without asking the child to answer any friendly questions in effect would confine the child's experience in court to the potentially distressing and stressful experience of being cross-examined by the defence. This may adversely affect the child's ability to answer properly questions put in cross-examination. In practice, judges or counsel for the prosecution have tended to ask some friendly questions of the child before and/or after the showing of the video in order both to put the child at ease before any cross-examination of the child commences and also where necessary to enable the child to expand on any matters not fully dealt with in the video. However, in some cases judges have apparently taken the view that there should not be questioning of the child witness by the prosecution and the amendment was therefore accepted on this occasion by the government in order to make it plain that such questioning can be undertaken and to ratify existing practice where it has in fact been allowed. It should be stressed that the provision is not normally designed to lead to lengthy questioning in court by the party calling the child (normally the prosecution but it could be the defence) since the whole point of s. 32A is to remove the need for the child to give evidence-in-chief at the trial. The amendment is merely designed to make it clear, although the wording is perhaps not the best for these purposes, that some questioning of the child is permissible before the witness is exposed to cross-examination by the other side, in order to prevent the child feeling that the court is wholly against it or that the scepticism necessarily presented in cross-examination is automatically shared by everyone in court (but see the refusal to accept a broader amendment, which would more clearly have permitted this – *Hansard*, Commons, 19 October 1994, cols 335–342). If, of course, there are substantial matters not covered either adequately or at all in the video recording, then a more substantial examination-in-chief of the child will be permitted.

It is worth noting that the government continued to resist amendments, as it had done in 1991, designed to implement fully the proposals of the Pigot Committee whereby the whole of the child's evidence, including cross-examination, could be taken on video in advance of the trial with a view to rendering it unnecessary in most cases for the child to attend at the trial at all. This was despite the fact that a procedure of this sort has now been provided for Scotland in s. 33 of the Prisoners and Criminal Proceedings (Scotland) Act 1993. The government wished to see the results of the procedure introduced in the 1991 Act, of the different procedure introduced in Scotland in 1993 and the outcome of a report being prepared by Profesor Graham Davies for the government which is expected in 1995.

3.20 Competence of Children as Witnesses

Prior to the CJA 1991, the competence of children to give evidence partly depended on whether they were to give evidence sworn or unsworn. A child could give sworn evidence if he or she understood the nature of an oath and 'the added responsibility to tell the truth ... over and above the duty to tell the truth which is an ordinary duty of normal social conduct' (*Hayes* [1977] 1 WLR 234 at p. 237). If the child was not able to understand the nature of the oath, he could still give evidence unsworn if he was 'possessed of sufficient intelligence to justify the reception of the evidence, and understands the duty to speak the truth' (s. 38(1), CYPA 1933). Section 52 of the CJA 1991 was designed to sweep away both these tests of competence:

(a)   by providing in a new CJA 1988, s. 33A that a 'child's evidence in criminal proceedings shall be given unsworn' thus making the test of understanding the oath irrelevant; and

(b)   by providing in CJA 1991, s. 52(2) that CYPA 1933, s. 38(1) shall '... cease to have effect; and accordingly the power of the court in any criminal proceedings to determine that a particular person is not competent to give evidence shall apply to children of tender years as it applies to other persons' thus apparently treating children as equally competent witnesses as adults and removing any special test of competence for the reception of children's unsworn evidence.

As was pointed out at the time (see the discussion in our *Guide to the Criminal Justice Act 1991* at 6.5), the wording of s. 52(2) was not the most felicitous and left open the possible interpretation, quite contrary to Parliament's intention, that children were required to have the same appreciation of the nature of an oath (despite the fact that they no longer gave evidence on oath) as an adult, or at least that they should have the same understanding of the ordinary duty to tell the truth as would an adult. It was thus feared that s. 52(2), in trying to abolish the competence requirement, might inadvertently re-establish one because of its defective wording. The fears about the ambiguous wording of CJA 1991, s. 52(2) have proved to be well founded. In introducing an amendment to s. 52(2) into the CJPOA 1994 to rectify matters, the Minister said:

The drafting of [section 52(2) CJA 1991] has been criticised by some academics and, more significantly, it appears that some judges have made rulings that severely restrict its operation and usefulness. ... The criticism of section 52 has been that it created a new competence requirement similar to that which asks whether an adult is capable of understanding the nature of the oath. We do not think that section 52 has that effect but we are not prepared to take the risk that any more prosecutions may fail because it is misunderstood. We consider that this amendment puts beyond any doubt that the only power available to the court to rule a child incompetent to give evidence is on the ground that the child is incapable of giving an intelligible acount. (*Hansard*, Commons, Standing Committee B, 23rd sitting, 24 February 1994, col. 1021.)

The minister, in giving reasons for preferring the governments own amendment to a previously tabled amendment, continued at col. 1026:

... [the previously tabled amendment] would require the court to satisfy itself as to the child's intelligibility before receiving his evidence. I am afraid that that might become a matter for preliminary investigations. The child should give evidence and be stopped from giving evidence only if it becomes clear that he cannot give an intelligible account. I do not want the court to have to satisfy itself in advance that the child is capable of giving intelligible evidence.

In the end, a third amendment was accepted by the government in an effort to make the above intentions absolutely clear at committee stage in the Lords. This is now to be found in the CJPOA 1994, sch. 9, para. 33, which inserts a new subsection 2A into s. 33A of the CJA 1988 as follows:

A child's evidence shall be received unless it appears to the court that the child is incapable of giving intelligible testimony.

It is clear from the remarks of the minister quoted above that the words 'unless it appears' are meant to refer to unintelligibility appearing in the course of the child's evidence and that courts should not be holding preliminary investigations or questioning the child in advance to determine whether the child is capable of giving intelligible evidence. The child should be permitted to commence giving evidence and only if it then appears that the child is incapable of giving intelligible evidence should the court consider preventing the child from continuing. The question of whether the child understands the nature of an oath or the duty to tell the truth is now clearly irrelevant to whether his testimony shall be received. In an appropriate case, however, the latter question may be relevant as to whether the judge chooses in his discretion to give the jury a warning of some sort about treating the particular witness' evidence with caution (see above, 3.3).

INTIMATE AND NON-INTIMATE BODY SAMPLES

Most of the existing provisions in this area are contained in ss. 61 to 65 of PACE 1984. The development of DNA profiling since that date has meant that these existing provisions are in need of amendment in order to provide an appropriate framework for the new forensic technology. A number of recommendations were made in ch. 2 of the report of the Royal Commission on Criminal Justice at pp. 14–16, and ss. 54 to 59 of the CJPOA 1994 are based on those recommendations, although not all of the limitations and safeguards recommended by the Royal Commission have been included.

3.21 Powers of the Police to Take Intimate Samples

The power to take intimate samples has been regulated by s. 62 of PACE 1984 which provides a power to take a sample from a person in police detention provided the person (or the person's parent or guardian in certain cases) gives *written consent and* a police officer of at least the rank of superintendent authorises it, which the officer can do only if he or she has reasonable grounds for suspecting the person to be involved in a *serious arrestable offence* and for believing that the sample will tend to confirm or disprove that involvement. Thus intimate samples cannot be taken without consent under s. 62 and furthermore, except for urine or saliva, they have to be taken by a medical practitioner. However, if a person refuses without good cause to give consent for an intimate sample to be taken, s. 62(10) has allowed a court or jury to draw such inferences from the refusal as appear proper. The definition of an intimate sample is contained in s. 65.

Section 62 of PACE is amended in the following respects by s. 54 of the CJPOA

(1) Intimate samples from persons not in police detention A new subsection (1A) is inserted into s. 62 providing a power to take an intimate sample from a person who is *not* in police detention 'but from whom, in the course of the investigation of an offence, two or more non-intimate samples suitable for the same means of analysis have been taken which have proved insufficient' subject to the usual consent of the person and the authorisation of at least a superintendent. The intention here seems to be to provide for intimate samples to be taken from persons who are no longer in police detention (defined in s. 118(2) of PACE) and from whom non-intimate samples have repeatedly (i.e., at least twice) been taken but which have proved insufficient for the purposes of enabling information to be produced (e.g., a DNA profile) by the means of analysis used. The person may no longer be in police detention but on remand in prison or on bail. The addition of this new power removes any incentive that the police may have to request an intimate sample whilst the accused is in their detention in cases where a non-intimate sample may be just as likely to provide the necessary information and thus enables them to feel safe in the knowledge that an intimate sample can later be requested even though the suspect is no longer in police detention. In this respect the provisions of a new s. 63A of PACE inserted by CJPOA s. 56 (discussed further below) should be noted. Under s. 63A(3) provision is made for a sample to be taken in a prison in appropriate cases and under s. 63A(4) to (9) persons not in custody may be required to attend at a police station for the purpose of having a sample taken. An intimate sample can still be taken only if the person consents in writing although refusal does mean that inferences can be drawn under s. 62(10).

(2) Extension to recordable offences Under the original s. 62 of PACE the police only had power, even where there was consent, to take intimate samples from persons reasonably suspected to be involved in a serious arrestable offence but CJPOA s. 54(3)(b) now amends PACE s. 62(2)(a) so that the power is available, again subject to consent, in the much broader category of recordable offences. This category is defined in the National Police Records (Recordable Offences) Regulations 1985 (SI 1985/1941) and includes all offences punishable by imprisonment and a limited number of others. This puts the power to take intimate samples in this respect on a

par with the power to take fingerprints and will help to build up a database of DNA profiles of all those convicted of recordable offences although the fact that there is no compulsion to consent should be borne in mind, the only sanction being the authorisation of adverse inferences under s. 62(10).

(3)   Amended definition of intimate sample   Sections 54 and s. 58 of the CJPOA 1994 amend s. 62 and s. 65 of PACE so that saliva and swabs from the mouth are removed from the list of intimate samples and thus becomes non-intimate samples which can in certain circumstances be taken without consent under s. 63 of PACE. This change of status is motivated by the fact that saliva can be used to obtain a DNA profile and reflects a change that was made for Northern Ireland in the CJA 1988, sch. 14, para. 6, which the Royal Commission on Criminal Justice regarded as having worked satisfactorily there (see Report, ch. 2, para. 29).

On the other hand, a dental impression is now expressly defined as an intimate sample although it was already treated as such by PACE Code D, sect. 5. CJPOA 1994, s. 54(5) amends PACE, s. 62(9), in such a way that the only cases where an intimate sample can be taken other than by a medical practitioner are urine and dental impressions and in this latter case, the impression must be taken by a registered dentist.

3.22   Powers of the Police to Take Non-intimate Body Samples

PACE, s. 63, governs the taking of non-intimate samples which included under s. 65 such things as a sample of hair (other than pubic hair), a sample taken from a nail or from under a nail, swabs from a person's body other than a body orifice and footprints or other similar impressions from a person's body other than from part of the person's hand. As has been seen, the definition has now been amended by CJPOA 1994, s. 58, so that saliva and swabs taken from the 'mouth but not any other body orifice' are added to the list of non-intimate samples, having been removed from the category of intimate samples. Curiously, s. 58(3) does not expressly limit the phrase 'impression of any part of a person's body other than a part of his hand' in the definition of a non-intimate sample so as to exclude dental impressions even though dental impressions are now expressly classified by virtue of s. 58(2) as intimate samples. This is unimportant as far as dental impressions are concerned since it is clear that they are now defined (as they were previously treated) as intimate samples but it perhaps does have implications for what is regarded as an 'impression of any part of a person's body' which clearly must be meant in some more limited sense if it does not include dental impressions.

The most important difference between intimate and non-intimate samples is that the latter can under certain conditions be taken without consent. Under PACE s. 63, it was a precondition (s. 63(3)(a)) for the taking of a non-intimate sample without consent that the accused had to be in police detention (or held in custody by the police on the authority of a court i.e., having been remanded to such custody for up to three days under s. 128(7) Magistrates' Courts Act 1980). As with the taking of intimate samples with consent, there then had to be authorisation by an officer of at least the rank of superintendent having reasonable grounds for suspecting the person's involvement in a serious arrestable offence and for believing that the sample will tend to confirm or disprove that involvement. This existing power is now broadened, as we have already seen, for the taking of intimate samples by virtue of CJPOA 1994, s. 55(3), amending s. 63(4) so that it applies to recordable as opposed to serious arrestable offences.

In addition, two new powers to take non-intimate samples without consent are provided which effectively parallel the powers already provided in PACE, s. 61, for the taking of fingerprints without consent. As with the fingerprint powers but unlike the existing power to take non-intimate samples, these new powers are not limited to the investigation of the current offence in relation to which the suspect is being questioned. Section 55(2) inserts two new subsections (3A) and (3B) into PACE, s. 63, providing the new powers.

3.23 DNA Databases

The new s. 63(3A) of PACE applies where (a) a person has been charged with or informed that he will be reported for a recordable offence and (b) either he has not had a non-intimate sample taken from him in the course of the investigation or he has had a sample taken but it was not suitable for the same means of analysis or though suitable proved insufficient. Since this power applies after the police have charged the suspect or formed the view that there is enough evidence to charge, it is not concerned with obtaining evidence to use against the suspect in this offence but is concerned with building up a database of samples for use on future occasions and for linking previously convicted persons with such future offences, in the same way that fingerprints can be used in this way at present. The new s. 63(3A) was foreshadowed in ch. 2, para. 35 of the Royal Commission on Criminal Justice report:

> Because, however, DNA profiling is now so powerful a diagnostic technique and so helpful in establishing guilt or innocence, we believe that it is proper and desirable to allow the police to take non-intimate samples (e.g., saliva, plucked hair etc.) without consent from all those arrested for serious criminal offences, whether or not DNA evidence is relevant to the particular offence, and so recommend. The relevant DNA data or samples would be retained for subsequent use if the person is convicted, but not otherwise unless retained under the conditions recommended in the next paragraph for the purposes of a frequency database.

It will be seen that s. 63(3A) goes further than the Royal Commission proposal in that the power is not restricted to 'serious' offences but applies to all recordable offences. Although s. 63(3A) may lead to samples being taken from persons who subsequently are not convicted, there are provisions (discussed below) providing for their destruction and/or for limiting the use of any information derived from them in such cases.

Where a person is subsequently convicted of a recordable offence a separate power to take non-intimate samples without consent arises under s. 63(3B) (the conviction must not be before s. 63(3B) comes into force – see CJPOA 1994, s. 55(6) inserting PACE, s. 63(10)). These samples will certainly not need to be destroyed and will remain for use in the future for the purposes of investigation of another offence and in evidence against the person from whom they were taken. This use in investigation of other offences (defined as 'speculative search' in CJPOA 1994, s. 58(4) inserting the definition into PACE, s. 65) is explicitly spelled out in a new s. 63A(1) which is inserted into PACE by CJPOA 1994, s. 56. Paragraphs 56 to 58 of sch. 10 to the CJPOA 1994 inserts new subsections into PACE, ss 61 to 63, requiring a person to be told in advance of the taking of his or her fingerprints or samples that they may be the subject of a speculative search. It should be noted that a speculative search covers not only checking the sample or information derived from it against samples or information held in a database of known offenders but also against samples or information 'held in connection with or as a result of an investigation of an offence'. This effectively confirms the use made of a blood sample in the case of *Kelt* [1994] 1 WLR 765 which was taken for the purposes of a murder investigation but which was subsequently used to link K with a robbery where traces of the blood of one of the robbers had been found on a bag of money which had been left behind. (There was nothing particularly 'speculative' about this in the normal sense of the word since the police had by this stage been told by an informer that K had taken part in the robbery.) The Court of Appeal held that the use of the blood sample was not restricted to the murder enquiry in connection with which the sample was obtained and until such time as the sample had to be destroyed (once the suspect had been cleared of the original suspected offence, i.e., the murder) it could be used to link the suspect with other offences and could be admitted in evidence at his trial for robbery.

In relation to checking with 'other ... samples or the information derived form other samples contained in records held by or on behalf of the police' (as opposed to samples etc. held in connection with the investigation of an offence) rather alarmingly, the new s. 63(A)(1) has no express limitation to checking against material held respect of convicted persons. One has to rely on s. 64(3A) and (3B) which are inserted by CJPOA 1994, s. 57(3) to find both the authorisation to retain samples and information relating to persons not convicted and the limitations on the use of such samples and information. Chapter 2, para. 36, of the Royal Commission report explained some of the reasons why it may be desirable to retain samples of persons not subsequently convicted:

> The police service have argued that there should be clear legal provisions governing DNA samples kept on 'frequency databases' which are necessary for giving estimates of the likelihood of a DNA sample matching a sample in the database. (Similar databases are not necessary for fingerprints because it has long been accepted that each person's fingerprint is unique.) The police argue that DNA databases should not be confined to samples from convicted persons. We see no objection to the retention for database purposes of any DNA samples obtained by the police in the course of their investigations provided that these are kept by an independent body. Where however a defendant is acquitted or a person is not proceeded against, it should only be possible to keep the sample on the database for statistical purposes, as opposed to the purpose of assisting in further investigation, and there should be strong safeguards to ensure that such samples can no longer be linked by the police or prosecution to the persons from whom they were taken.

The new PACE, s. 64(3A), enacts the limitations but does not specify the strong safeguards or the independent organisation which will ensure that there is no misuse of the samples taken from persons subsequently not convicted. However, slightly different reasons for retaining samples of non-convicted persons were given at committee stage in the Commons which may explain the reluctance to spell out practical safeguards or to establish an independent body:

> It is easy to destroy police files and records on those who have not been convicted, but it is impossible, in many cases, to destroy the computer printout of the DNA analysis or the sample of those who have not been convicted without destroying that of those who have been convicted.
>
> In the same way, I am informed that when many samples from different police stations are taken for analysis, the technology is that a mass spectrometer that holds 36 vessels or test tubes will normally process all those samples at one time. When they are analysed, any number of people may be convicted and any number may be found innocent. The net result is that there is a combined computer analysis, printout, disc or record containing a multitude of samples some of which relate to innocent people and some to the convicted. It is not a matter of money or resources. It is not technically feasible to keep separate the records of those who have been convicted while destroying the records of the innocent. (David McLean, Home Office Minister, House of Commons Standing Committee B, 11th sitting, 3 February 1994, col. 524.)

If it is not technically feasible to separate the records of the convicted from the non-convicted as is stated above then one wonders how strong the safeguards can be to ensure that only the records of the convicted will be used in the investigation of other offences. To understand the new s. 64(3A) and (3B) properly it is necessary to make a distinction between the sample itself (whether it be intimate or non-intimate, e.g., blood (intimate) or saliva (non-intimate)) on the one hand and information derived from the sample on the other hand. Subsections (1), (2) and (3) of PACE, s. 64, provide for the destruction of fingerprints or samples once the person from whom they were taken is cleared or not proceeded against or the purpose for which they were taken has been fulfilled. Subsection (3A) now provides in the case of samples (but not fingerprints) that they need not be destroyed 'if they were taken for the purpose of the same investigation of an offence of which a person from whom one was taken has been convicted'. (This formulation is more complicated and also seems wider than the formulation in the Bill as originally presented which spoke of samples 'processed together with' the samples of a person convicted.) Thus if A, B and C are all suspects in relation to a particular offence and samples are taken from them in the course of investigating the offence and A is subsequently convicted but B and C are cleared, B and C would previously have been entitled to have their samples destroyed (as is still the case with their fingerprints) but under subsection 3A, they need not be destroyed (even apparently if they were not processed together with the convicted person's samples provided they were taken for the purpose of the same investigation). However, *the information derived from the sample* (e.g., the DNA profile) cannot be used for investigation of some other offence (e.g., in a 'speculative search' under PACE, s. 63A(1)) or in evidence against the person who would, but for s. 64(3A), have been entitled to the destruction of the sample, i.e., the person whose sample it is. The information can however be used as part of a frequency database.

Section 64(3B) deals with the situation were the sample itself *is* destroyed, i.e., where the sample was obtained for the purpose of an investigation in which a sample was not taken from anyone who has been convicted, and it is implicit in the subsection that the information derived from the sample will not be destroyed, but again that information cannot be used against the person from whose sample it was derived but only as part of the frequnecy database. Thus if in the above example A, B and C (and anybody else from whom a sample was taken) were all cleared, the samples would be destroyed and the information derived from the samples (the DNA profiles) could not be used in evidence subsequently against A, B or C respectively or for the purpose of investigation an offence, e.g., to link A, B or C with some other offence, but they could be used to form part of the statistical picture presented by a DNA frequency database.

This is probably not intended to affect the situation in *Kelt* [1994] 1 WLR 765 where the samples were used to link the suspect with another offence *before* the stage had been reached when they were required to be destroyed. The prohibition in the new s. 64(3B) is designed to protect abuse of the information permitted to be retained purely for the purposes of the frequency databases. The subsection read literally, however, could be taken to prohibit the use in evidence of information derived from the sample once the stage has been reached when it is required to be destroyed because the person from whom the sample was taken is no longer suspected of the offence in connection with which the sample was originally taken. In *Kelt* the accused was still suspected of the murder even by the time of the trial for robbery but difficulties might be caused in a similar case if by the time of the trial the samples were required to be destroyed because the accused had then been cleared of suspicion of the original offence. This problem would be avoided if a separate sample was taken for the purposes of the second offence which would not be affected by the clearing of the suspect in relation to the original offence. Of course, such a second sample can be taken only if PACE, s. 62(2), is satisfied and an officer of at least the rank of superintendent has reasonable ground for believing that the sample will tend to confirm or disprove the suspect's involvement in the offence. Whether providing further confirmation is within the section, where there is already a perfectly adequate sample in existence, is perhaps a moot point.

Quite apart from the above technical difficulties raised by the drafting of s. 64(3B), whether it is right for the police to be able to build up frequency databases containing the DNA profiles of persons who have been investigated in connection with, but subsequently cleared of, recordable offences, when they have no rights to compile such data on the general population, is open to debate. (One might also question whether such a database is as statistically valuable as one compiled from a random sample.) The Royal Commission thought that it was acceptable if suitable safeguards were in place such as the frequency databases being kept by an organisation independent of the police. In ch. 2, para. 38, the Commission said:

> We make no detailed proposals on these matters since it is not part of our terms of reference to devise a new records system. We recommend that the problem be addressed by the legislature taking into account the proposals that we have indicated that we would find acceptable if suitable safeguards were in place.

Unfortunately, there was very little discussion of these matters as the Bill progressed through Parliament, probably partly because there were so many other controversial issues and partly because the technicalities in this area are difficult to understand. The result is that the legislation says very little about practical safeguards and nothing about an independent body.

3.24 Procedure for Taking Samples from Persons not in Police Detention

The CJPOA 1994 extends the powers to take samples both intimate and non-intimate beyond cases where the accused is in police detention. To make these extensions effective, a procedure has to be provided to enable the police to require the attendance of a person to provide the sample. The new subsection (4) to (8) of s. 63A of PACE inserted by CJPOA 1994, s. 56 now provides that procedure and are based on the existing procedure under PACE, s. 27, providing for the taking of fingerprints of persons convicted of recordable offences although the new procedure is not limited to those who have already been convicted. Under s. 63A(4) the police can require a person's attendance in two different situations which equate to the two new situations under s. 63(3A) and (3B) where the police can require a non-intimate sample to be taken, i.e.:

(a)   The person has been charged etc. and no sample has been taken or the sample taken has not yielded the DNA profile or other information sought.
(b)   The person has been convicted of a recordable offence and no sample has been taken since the conviction or any sample taken from him has not yielded the DNA profile etc.

Although the procedure seems primarily to be directed at the new powers to take non-intimate samples without consent, there is nothing in the subsection to limit it to non-intimate samples so it would seem also that a person can be required to attend for the purposes of an intimate sample being taken under the new PACE, s. 62(1A) (where two or more non-intimate samples have proved insufficient). However, this power is exercisable only if the supect gives consent and this cannot be overridden by s. 63A but the power to require attendance may still be useful to the police since the suspect may in fact consent either because he hopes the sample will clear him or because his refusal permits inferences to be drawn against him under s. 62(10).

A requirement to attend a police station must in any event give the person required at least seven days within which to attend and the requirement must be made within one month of the date of the charge or conviction or one month of the date of the appropriate officer being informed that the original sample has proved unsuitable or insufficient. The 'appropriate officer' is defined in s. 63A(8) and subsection (7) provides a power of arrest without warrant where a person fails to comply with a requirement to attend a police station for these purposes (although again this cannot affect the right of a person to refuse to consent to the taking of intimate samples).

If the person from whom the sample is sought is in prison, there is of course no need to require attendance at a police station and s. 63A(3) provides for the sample to be taken in prison. (Although note that this, as with the rest of s. 63A, does not confer any additional power to take samples over and above the powers provided for in the amended ss. 62 and 63 of PACE. It merely provides for how and where those powers can be exercised.)

3.25 Samples of Hair by Plucking

The new section 63A of PACE also clarifies in subsection (2) that a sample of hair other than pubic hair (thus a non-intimate sample which can be taken without consent) may be taken either by cutting or by plucking 'so long as no more are plucked than the person taking the sample reasonably considers to be necessary for a sufficient sample'. The significance of this is that if hair is plucked as opposed to being cut, one also obtains the roots or inner sheaths form which it is possible to prepare a DNA profile. The Royal Commission noted (ch. 2, para. 28) that the right to take hair by plucking had been challenged in a number of cases but the Court of Appeal has more recently in *Cooke* (1994) *The Times*, 10 August 1994, held that even before the CJPOA 1994, it was permissible to take hair by plucking even if the objective was to get the sheath rather than the hair itself. Thus s. 63A(3) can be regarded as merely confirming the position that the courts had already arrived at.

3.26   Extension of Powers to Search Persons' Mouths

A search of a person's mouth was formerly classified as an intimate search and thus under s. 55 of PACE could be carried out only in restricted circumstances on particular premises such as a police station or hospital and normally had to be carried out by a registered medical practitioner or nurse. Having taken the step of authorising saliva and swabs to be taken from the mouth without consent as non-intimate samples, the CJPOA 1994 in s. 59 consistently redefines an intimate search so as to exclude a search which consists of the examination of a person's mouth. The new definition is also relocated from PACE, s. 118, where it formerly resided to s. 65 along with the other definitions relating to part V of PACE. Section 59(2) of the CJPOA 1994 amends PACE, s. 32(4), so as to permit the search of person's mouth upon arrest. The most obvious though by no means the only application of this liberalisation of the regime applicable to searches of person's mouths is in relation to drugs which may be concealed therein. In *Hughes* (1994) 99 Cr App R 160 the Court of Appeal found that there was no intimate search because the appellant had merely been caused to spit out the drug and there had been no physical intrusion into the body orifice, in this case the mouth. Such an interpretation will no longer be necessary on such facts since a search of the mouth will no longer be classified as intimate. (See also the recommendation in ch. 2, para. 30, of the report of the Royal Commission on Criminal Justice.)

3.27   Application to Persons Arrested or Detained under the Prevention of Terrorism (Temporary Provisions) Act 1989

Paragraph 62 of sch. 10 to the CJPOA 1994 contains detailed provisions for the application of modified forms of the amended provisions of PACE, ss. 62 and 63. to persons arrested or detained under the terrorism provisions. It should be noted that PACE, s. 64, providing for the destruction of fingerprints and samples does not apply to persons detained under these provisions. Nor does it appear that the new s. 63A has any application to the terrorism provisions including s. 63A(2) clarifying that non-pubic hair can be taken by plucking as well as by cutting but given the decision, referred to in 3.24 in *Cooke* (1994) *The Times*, 10 August 1994, this would not appear to make any significant difference.

Chapter Four
Public Order

This chapter is concerned with a range of amendments made by the 1994 Act to the area of public order law. Several of these changes have proved highly controversial. Coverage of the legal changes can be found in this chapter; for consideration of the (often heated) exchanges both within and outside Parliament on these matters see the introduction to this Guide. One example here will suffice. In the course of the Parliamentary debates, Lord McIntosh of Haringey referred to the Bill's provisions in this area as '... an open invitation for the police and for the authorities generally to interfere in the legitimate activities of people, and particularly of young people, in our country.... These are repulsive extensions of police power in our society and at some stage they will have to be removed' (Hansard, Lords, 7 July 1994, col. 1490).

The changes proceed by way of creation of new offences, or amendment and addition to the Public Order Act 1986 and, taken together, there is no doubt that they considerably increase police powers and restrict freedom of movement and assembly of citizens. The key change is the development of trespass from a wrong which, in the past, has been almost entirely civil in character to one in which the use of the criminal sanction is seen as increasingly appropriate. A move to a more general law of criminal trespass was canvassed by the Home Office in a consultation paper in 1983, after an incident when a man entered the Queen's bedroom at Buckingham Palace. A Criminal Trespass Bill was drafted, but did not become law. The creeping criminalisation of various forms of trespass in the 1994 Act has been greeted with enthusiasm by some landowners who, in a number of well-publicised incidents, have seen their land taken over without their consent by congregations of large numbers of 'new age travellers' and others. It has also been welcomed by local authorities who have encountered problems in the past in using the law to dislodge unauthorised campers and squatters from their land and from their housing stock. It has been vigorously opposed by those who fear that it will provide an inappropriate disincentive to legitimate group protest and may (although this seems much less likely) involve the inadvertent breach of the criminal law by those who use the countryside, such as ramblers.

4.1 Powers to Remove Trespassers on Land

Section 61 of the CJPOA 1994 grants new powers to the police to 'remove trespassers on land'. According to the Home Secretary (*Hansard*, Commons, 11 January 1994, col. 29):

Part V of the Bill contains important measures designed to tackle the destruction and distress caused mainly to rural communities by trespassers. Local communities should not have to put up with, or even fear the prospect of, mass invasions by those who selfishly gather, regardless of the rights of others.

It is clear from the context of the debate that the government had in mind, among other groups, so-called 'new age travellers'. In *Hansard*, Commons, 13 April 1994, col. 296, Mr Maclean, government spokesman, said that 'new age travellers are the main offenders' against which the provision was directed, but that 'there may be others invading land'. It is important to place s. 61 in the context of the earlier law and, in particular, the debate over the criminalising of trespass. Section 39 of the Public Order Act 1986, which contained very similar provisions, is repealed by the 1994 Act and its provisions replaced by s. 61. In commenting upon the enactment of s. 39 in 1986, Dr A.T.H. Smith noted that the impetus for the section had come from concern over 'incidents of mass trespass', including one which occurred while the Bill was before the Lords, in which a 'Peace Convoy trespassed on the Somerset farm of a Mr Attwell with over 100 buses, trucks, caravans and other assorted vehicles' (*Offences against Public Order*, 1987, para. 14-18). Dr Smith doubted then 'whether such an offence was really necessary', given the availability of civil proceedings to evict trespassers (though such remedy may be rather slow, and expensive) and the almost invariable commission of criminal offences in the course of the trespass (criminal damage, breach of the peace, offences under s. 5 of the Public Order Act 1986).

Section 61(1) of the CJPOA 1994 repeats much of what was in s. 39(1) of the Public Order Act 1986. Where a senior police officer present at the scene reasonably believes that two or more people are trespassing on land, and are present there with the common purpose of residing there for any period, and reasonable steps have been taken by the occupier of the land to ask them to leave, and either:

(a)   damage has been caused to the land or to property on the land, or threatening, abusive or insulting words or behaviour have been used by any of those people towards the occupier of the land, or
(b)   those persons have between them six or more vehicles on the land,

then the senior officer (or another officer acting on his behalf) may direct the persons to leave the land and remove their vehicles and other property.

There are several changes from the wording of s. 39(1), some more significant than others. The first change is that the test in s. 61(1) is now whether the persons present on the land are *in fact trespassing there*, rather than (as under the 1986 Act) whether they originally entered the land as trespassers. Section 61(2) states that where the persons on the land are reasonably believed to be persons who were not originally trespassers but have since become trespassers (i.e., by ignoring the landowner's subsequent request that they leave) the power to eject them arises only where there is reasonable belief that all the conditions set out in subsection (1) are satisfied at a time after those persons became trespassers.

The second is that s. 61(1)(a) now includes 'damage to the land' itself, as well as damage to 'property on the land' (see further below).

The third is the reduction (again by s. 61(1)) from 12 to six in the number of vehicles which need to be present before the power to direct the persons to leave becomes available.

The fourth change is the wider definition given in the 1994 Act to 'land'. This now includes 'common land' (as defined in the Commons Registration Act 1965, s. 22) and is extended to encompass certain forms of thoroughfare (footpaths, bridleways, byways, public paths and cycletracks). It may be noted that a proposed amendment to the Bill, which would have had the effect of extending these powers to certain parts of highways (lay-bys, and co-called 'oxbows' which result from the straightening out of a bend in a road) was defeated.

The fifth difference is that under the 1994 Act the relevant senior police officer may now direct removal of 'vehicles and other property' as well as the persons themselves, from the land. It was not entirely clear from the decision of the Divisional Court in *Krumpa* v *Director of Public Prosecutions* [1989] Crim LR 295 whether s. 39 of the 1986 Act included power to order removal of vehicles as well. In that case the trespassers were living in converted buses on land belonging to Tesco; many of the vehicles were not in working order and were incapable of being moved without towing.

In the course of the second reading of the Bill, Warren Hawksley MP (*Hansard*, Commons, 11 January col. 71) expressed concern that s. 39 of the 1986 Act had in the past been little used by the police, and he indeed claimed that chief constables had instructed their officers not to use it. He questioned, therefore, what grounds there were to believe that the new provisions would actually be used. The government spokesman, Mr Maclean, explained (*Hansard*, Commons, 13 April 1994, col. 295) that s. 61 'is a restatement and a strengthening of s. 39 of the Public Order Act 1986', the government having been concerned that s. 39 was not adequate to safeguard a landowner who had invited people on to land but whose hospitality had been abused. In response to an expression of opposition concern over the extension of these powers, the government's view was that the police would exercise their powers with 'care and discretion', particularly where there had been no mass trespass, or where there had been a genuine disagreement over the original terms of a permission which had since been withdrawn.

Section 61(4) substantially repeats the language of s. 39(2) of the 1986 Act. Once a police officer has directed someone to leave under the power in s. 61(1), and that person either:

(a) fails to leave the land as soon as reasonably practicable or
(b) leaves, but re-enters the land as a trespasser within three months,

then that person commits a summary offence punishable with up to three months' imprisonment, a fine not exceeding level 4, or both. This is unchanged from the earlier law. In *Krumpa* v *Director of Public Prosecutions* [1989] Crim LR 295 the Divisional Court held that the phrase 'as soon as reasonably practicable', which is also used in s. 61, means that the trespassers should leave as soon as they reasonably could in the circumstances. Thus the test is an objective one to be applied in the light of all the facts (such as the unroadworthiness of the vehicles in *Krumpa*) and it cannot be determined entirely by the relevant police officer's view of how soon the trespassers might be expected to leave.

Section 61(5) confers a power of arrest without warrant for this offence. Such power was also available under s. 39(3) of the 1986 Act. Section 61(6) substantially repeats the language of s. 39(4) of the 1986 Act, to the effect that it is a defence to a charge under s. 61 for the accused to show:

(a) that he was not trespassing on the land, or
(b) that he had a reasonable excuse for failing to leave as soon as reasonably practicable, or for returning within three months.

The only difference from the earlier law, reflecting the change outlined above, is that the relevant issue in (a) is now the person's *current status*, rather than their status when first entering upon the land. Section 61(9) is a definition section. From this it is clear that 'land' does *not* include buildings (apart from certain agricultural buildings and certain scheduled monuments) or land forming part of a metalled highway. Common land, and non-metalled roads are, however, now included: see above. 'Property', in relation to damage to property on land, includes damage within the meaning of the Criminal Damage Act 1971 and the deposit of any substance capable of polluting the land. It is clear, in any event, that grass can be damaged by trampling it down (*Gayford* v *Choulder* [1898] 1 QB 316) and that the dumping of rubbish on land constitutes criminal damage (*Henderson*, 29 November 1984, Court of Appeal, unreported). 'Vehicle' includes any vehicle, whether or not it is in a fit state for use on roads, and includes any chassis or body, with or without wheels, and a caravan as defined by s. 29(1) of the Caravan Sites and Control of Development Act 1960. Finally, again in line with the earlier law, s. 61(9) makes it clear that a person may be regarded as having a purpose of residing on the land in question notwithstanding that the person has a home elsewhere.

Section 62 of the CJPOA 1994 creates supplementary powers of seizure. Where a direction has been given under s. 61 and any person to whom that direction applies has failed to leave, failed to remove a vehicle or other property or has been arrested for an offence (including an offence under s. 61), the police may, after a reasonable time, seize and remove from the land any vehicle which was under the control of that person. This section seems to have been introduced in order to clarify and strengthen the earlier law since, as we have seen, there was some doubt from *Krumpa* v *Director of Public Prosecutions* [1989] Crim LR 295 whether a direction under s. 39 of the 1986 Act to persons to leave land also extended in law to a direction to remove their vehicles. By s. 67(1) of the CJPOA 1994, any vehicles which have been seized and removed may be retained by the police in accordance with regulations made by the Secretary of State under s. 67(3). These regulations may relate to the safe keeping, disposal and destruction of those vehicles. Costs incurred in the course of such safe keeping etc. may be recovered as a simple contract debt from the owner of the vehicle (s. 67(6)) and vehicles may be retained until any such costs have been reimbursed. It should not be forgotten that in many cases the vehicles involved will constitute the homes of the persons concerned. Their destruction will be the destruction of the place where they live.

Section 61 (but not s. 62 or s. 67) of the CJPOA 1994 came into force on the date of Royal Assent, 3 November 1994.

4.2 'Raves'

In replying for the government at the end of the debate on second reading of the Bill, Mr Maclean (*Hansard*, Commons, 11 January col. 116–17) explained that the purpose of the new provisions contained in ss. 63 to 67 of the CJPOA 1994 was to '... prevent the appalling distress caused by unlicensed night-time raves on open land. Their incessant noise can keep residents for miles around awake all night.' The drafting of these provisions owes much to the revised wording in s. 61: see 4.1 above.

Section 63 applies in relation to gatherings on land in the open air, or partly open to the air, of 100 or more persons, whether or not they are trespassers, at which amplified music is played during the night, which, by reason of its loudness and duration and the time at which it is played, is likely to cause serious distress to the inhabitants of the locality. 'Music', for these purposes 'includes sounds wholly or predominantly characterised by the emission of a succession of repetitive beats'(!). During the course of debates on the Bill, Lord McIntosh argued that 'rave' was defined much too broadly, and suggested that ordinary wedding receptions and barbecues might easily come within it (*Hansard*, Lords, 7 July 1994, col. 1489). With respect, however, it seems most unlikely that the holding of a wedding reception would be likely to occasion serious distress to local inhabitants. Section 63(2) states that if a police officer of at least the rank of superintendent reasonably believes that 10 or more persons are present on land in the open air making preparations for such an event, attending it, or waiting for it to happen, then that officer (or another officer acting on his or her behalf) may direct that those persons and any others who have come to attend the gathering must leave the land and remove any vehicles or other property which they have with them.

A person who knows that a direction which applies to him or her has been given and who:

(a)   fails to leave as soon as reasonably practicable or
(b)   leaves but returns within seven days,

commits a summary offence punishable with imprisonment for up to three months, a fine not exceeding level 4, or both (s. 63(6)). Section 63(8) creates a power of arrest without warrant for this offence. For the meaning of 'reasonably practicable' see *Krumpa* v *Director of Public Prosecutions* [1989] Crim LR 295 discussed in 4.1 above. By s. 63(7) it is a defence to a charge under s. 63 for the accused to show that he or she had a reasonable excuse for failing to leave the land as directed, or for returning there within three months. By s. 63(9) the section 'does not apply to a gathering licensed by an entertainment licence'. An entertainment licence in this context means a licence granted by a local authority under sch. 12 to the London Government Act 1963, s. 3 of the Private Places of Entertainment (Licensing) Act 1967 or sch. 1 to the Local Government (Miscellaneous Provisions) Act 1982. Presumably, in any proceedings it would be for the organiser of the gathering to show, on the balance of probability, that he or she had such licence (Magistrates' Courts Act 1980, s. 101). The occupier of the land, any member of the occupier's family and any employee or agent of the occupier and any person whose home is situated on the land is 'exempt' from the effects of an order made under this section (s. 63(10)). 'Vehicle' has the same meaning in this section as it has in s. 61 (see 4.1).

Section 64 provides supplementary powers of entry and seizure. If a police officer of at least the rank of superintendent reasonably believes that circumstances exist which would justify giving a direction under s. 63, he may authorise any constable to enter the land without a warrant to ascertain whether such circumstances exist. If it is discovered that they do exist, and a direction under s. 63 has been given, and the constable reasonably suspects that any person to whom that direction applies has:

(a) failed to leave or
(b) failed to remove any vehicle or other property or
(c) has been arrested for an offence including an offence under this section,

the constable may after a reasonable time seize and remove any vehicle or sound equipment connected with the gathering.

Section 65 provides a very considerable and controversial new power. A police officer, who reasonably believes that a person is travelling on the way to a gathering to which s. 63 applies, and in relation to which a direction under s. 63 is in force, may stop that person and direct him or her not to proceed in the direction of the gathering. This power can only be exercised at a place within five miles of the boundary of the site of the gathering. According to the government spokesman Earl Ferrers in the House of Lords (*Hansard*, Lords, 7 July 1994, col. 1488):

> ... when the police are trying to stop a rave from happening it is essential that they have the ability to turn people away before sufficient numbers gather to make the dispersal operation impractical. ... I believe that five miles is a reasonable distance, given that these powers are envisaged for use in rural areas.

Attempts by opposition peers in the Lords to amend this provision to a one-mile radius of the site were defeated.

Section 66 provides that where a person is convicted of an offence under s. 63 and the court is satisfied that any sound equipment which has been seized from the offender under s. 64, or which was in the offender's possession or under his or her control at the relevant time, has been used at the gathering then the court may make an order for forfeiture of that sound equipment. These powers of forfeiture are available to the sentencing court 'whether or not it also deals with the offender in respect of the offence in any other way' (s. 66(2)). This appears to contemplate that forfeiture might stand alone on sentence. When considering whether to make such an order on sentence, s. 66(3) requires the court to have regard to the value of the property and to the likely financial and other effects on the offender of the making of the order. This is in line with other provisions on forfeiture, the main one being that under the Powers of Criminal Courts Act 1973, s. 43.

Section 67 specifies the arrangements which are to apply in respect of retention and charges for property (vehicles and sound equipment) seized under the powers in s. 64. By s. 67(1), any vehicles which have been so seized and removed may be retained by the police in accordance with regulations made by the Secretary of State under s. 67(3). These regulations may relate to the safe keeping, disposal and destruction of those vehicles. Costs incurred in the course of such safe keeping etc. may be recovered as a simple contract debt from the owner of the vehicle (s. 67(6)) and vehicles may be retained until any such costs have been reimbursed. By s. 67(2) any sound equipment which has been seized and removed may be retained until the conclusion of the proceedings. The other provisions of s. 67 do not appear to apply to sound equipment, so at the conclusion of the proceedings it seems that the police must return that equipment to the owner. Nor is there a power under the section to recover any costs of storage etc. of sound equipment from the owner.

Sections 63 and 65 of the CJPOA 1994 (but not ss. 64, 66 or 67) came into force on the date of Royal Assent, 3 November 1994.

4.3 Disruptive Trespassers and Aggravated Trespass: 'Hunt Saboteurs'

Section 68(1) creates an offence of 'aggravated trespass', which is committed where a person trespasses on land in the open air and, in relation to any lawful activity which persons are engaging in or are about to engage in on that or adjoining land in the open air, does there anything which is intended by him to have the effect:

(a)   of intimidating those persons or any of them so as to deter them or any of them from engaging in that activity or
(b)   of obstructing that activity or
(c)   of disrupting that activity.

In the context of 'land in the open air', 'land' has broadly the same definition as that which appears in s. 61 (see 4.1). Thus, it does not include a metalled highway or road (s. 68(5)), but does extend to footpaths, bridleways or byways which are used as public paths (see further s. 61(9) of the 1994 Act). The definition of 'land' in s. 61(9) also specifically excludes *most* buildings. Section 68(5) does not refer to buildings, but it can be inferred from the reference to 'land in the open air' in s. 68(1) that the legislative intention is to exclude *all* buildings from the scope of s. 68. Activity on land seems to be 'lawful' for the purposes of s. 68(1) if the persons engaging in that activity are committing no offence or trespass (s. 68(2)), but this subsection is oddly worded. It says that such activity is lawful if the persons 'may engage in the activity on the land on that occasion' without committing an offence or trespassing on the land. This seems to cater for a landowner giving a limited permission for a person or group of people (such as a hunt) to use the land on a specific occasion for a specific purpose. If that (limited) permission has been given, then the activity is lawful.

In explaining the purpose of this new offence, the Home Secretary said (*Hansard*, Commons, 11 January 1994, col. 29):

In recent months, we have seen many examples of disruptive and threatening behaviour – at the Grand National, during country sports and even fishing. Those who dislike such activities have a perfect right to campaign to change the law, but they do not have the right to trespass, threaten or intimidate. The Bill will give the police powers to direct trespassers to leave land if they have reason to believe that they will seek to disrupt or prevent a lawful activity. Furthermore, such disruption itself will be made a criminal offence.

Peter Thornton, chairman of the Civil Liberties Trust, has argued strongly against the new provisions because he fears that the drafting is 'dangerously wide' and may catch, for example, 'peaceful but noisy protest on the steps of the town hall against the reduction of nursery facilities'. Opposition amendments were tabled during the passage of the Bill through Parliament designed, according to Mr Michael, to tighten up the wording of the clause so as to preserve 'freedom of access, as well as the rights to peaceful protest' (*Hansard*, Commons, 13 April 1994, col. 299). Legitimate peaceful demonstrations may well, of course, tend to obstruct or disrupt an activity against which people are protesting. Mr Michael suggested that the wording was wide enough to cover a case where a farmer was ploughing his field and had closed off a right of way, and where ramblers were protesting at, or obstructing, this activity. It was further argued that walkers could fall foul of the law by inadvertently walking across a shooting moor. The Ramblers Association, the British Mountaineering Council and canoeists, have all expressed concern that they might infringe the law in the course of their ordinary leisure pursuits. This seems most unlikely, given the requirement of proof of *intent* to intimidate, obstruct or disrupt. The government has insisted throughout that ordinary ramblers will not be caught by the new law, and that the law would apply even-handedly to the hunt (where there was deliberate trespass on private property) as well as to hunt saboteurs.

A constable may arrest for the offence under s. 68 without warrant (s. 68(3)), and a person found guilty of the offence is liable on summary conviction to imprisonment for a term not exceeding three months or a fine not exceeding level 4, or to both (s. 68(4)).

Section 69 creates powers to remove persons who are committing or participating in aggravated trespass. If a senior police officer present at the scene reasonably believes that:

(a)   a person is committing, has committed, or intends to commit the offence of aggravated trespass on land in the open air, or

(b)   that two or more persons are trespassing on land in the open air and are there with the common purpose of intimidating persons so as to deter them from engaging in a lawful activity, or of obstructing or disrupting a lawful activity,

he may direct that person to leave the land. By s. 69(3), a person who, knowing that such a direction has been given and applies to him or her, either fails to leave the land as soon as practicable or, having left returns as a trespasser within three months, commits an offence. A police officer who reasonably suspects that a person is committing this offence may arrest without warrant, and the punishment for the offence is similarly to that for the offence under s. 68 (above).

In proceedings for an offence under s. 69, it is a defence for the accused to show:

(a)   that he or she was not trespassing on the land or

(b)   that he or she had a reasonable excuse for failing to leave the land as soon as practicable, or for returning as a trespasser.

Sections 68 and 69 of the CJPOA 1994 came into force on the date of Royal Assent, 3 November 1994. The first prosecutions for the offence of aggravated trespass were reported in the press on 21 November. The charge followed disturbances at a fox-hunting protest in Essex.

4.4   Trespassory Assemblies

Section 70 of the CJPOA 1994 amends the Public Order Act 1986 by inserting a new s. 14A and s. 14B. Section 71 adds a new s. 14C. The original s. 14, which deals with the imposing of conditions on public assemblies, contains three offences which cater for the person who either organises a public assembly, or takes part in a public assembly, or incites another to take part in a public assembly, and in any of these cases knowingly fails to comply with conditions which have been imposed under s. 14 on that assembly by a senior police officer at the time or beforehand. The conditions which may be imposed relate to the place at which the assembly may be held, its duration and the maximum number of people who may be permitted to attend, and they can be imposed under s. 14 in any case where the senior police officer reasonably believes (a) that the proposed assembly may result in serious public disorder, serious damage to property or serious disruption to the life of the community, or (b) that the purpose of organisers of the proposed assembly is the intimidation of others.

Section 14A, which is created by s. 70 of the 1994 Act, creates a new power in the relevant chief police officer to apply to the local council for an order prohibiting for a specified period the holding of all *trespassory public assemblies* in a specified area. The granting of such an order by the council, with or without modifications, requires the consent of the Secretary of State (s. 14A(2)). The chief officer of police may make an application for such an order only if he reasonably believes that an assembly (for these purposes meaning an assembly of 20 or more persons: s. 14A(9)) is intended to be held at a place on land in the open air to which the public has no right of access or a limited right of access, and (by s. 14A(1)) that the assembly:

(a)   is likely to be held without the permission of the occupier, or to exceed that permission or to exceed the public's right of access; and

(b)   may result in serious disruption to the life of the community, or in significant damage to land, or to a building or monument upon that land, where the land, building or monument is of historical, architectural, archaeological or scientific importance.

If the order is made, it shall in no case prohibit the holding of such assemblies for a period exceeding four days, or prohibit their being held outside an area within a radius of five miles from a specified centre (s. 14A(6)). There appears to be no right of appeal against the imposition of such a ban, though judicial review of the decision would be a possibility.

Section 14B, which is also created by s. 70 of the 1994 Act, creates three new offences in relation to persons who organise trespassory assemblies, take part in trespassory assemblies, or incite another to take part in a trespassory assembly, the holding of which that person knows to be prohibited by an order under s. 14A. The structure of these offences is parallel to those in s. 14 (above). All three offences are arrestable without a warrant, and they are all summary offences. Organising such an assembly is punishable with imprisonment for a term not exceeding three months, a fine not exceeding level 4, or both (s. 14B(5)). Taking part in the trespassory assembly is not imprisonable, but is punishable by a fine not exceeding level 3 (s. 14B(6)). Inciting another to take part in such an assembly is subject to the same maximum punishment as organising the trespassory assembly (i.e., three months' imprisonment: s. 14B(7)). This last offence is an example of an incitement to commit a summary offence being subject to a higher maximum penalty than the offence itself. Normally such maximum penalties should be the same (Magistrates' Courts Act 1980, s. 45(3)), but the effect of that provision is specifically excluded by s. 14B(7). The same applies to the offences under s. 14 (see s. 14(10)).

Section 14C is created by s. 71 of the 1994 Act. It creates a very considerable and controversial new power, which is parallel to that in s. 65 of the 1994 Act, in relation to raves: see 4.2. A police officer in uniform, who reasonably believes that a person is on his or her way to a trespassory assembly within the area to which an order under s. 14A applies, is empowered by s. 14C to stop that person and direct him or her not to proceed in the direction of that assembly. This power may only be exercised within the area to which the order applies (i.e., within an area with a radius of five miles from the specified centre) (s. 14C(2)). In defending this provision in the House of Lords, Earl Ferrers said (*Hansard*, Lords, 7 July 1994, col. 1489):

> We are talking here about gatherings that sometimes attract tens of thousands of people. . . . The people will be overwhelming in their numbers and the police will be unable to turn them back, not least because the very roads on which they will turn them back will already be jammed with other people who are going to the assembly.
>
> These assemblies can be deeply offensive to the local community. . . . The real infringement of liberty is what happens to the individuals whose lives are disrupted. Directions can be given only where a police officer believes a person to be going to the gathering, not just to the place where it is for some unconnected purpose.

Proposed amendments which would have removed this power, or would have restricted its operation to an area of one mile's radius from the site, were defeated.

Sections 70 and 71 of the CJPOA 1994 came into force on the date of Royal Assent, 3 November 1994.

4.5   Amendment of Criminal Law Act 1977

Sections 72 to 74 of the 1994 Act make changes to ss. 6, 7 and 12 of the Criminal Law Act 1977. Section 6 of the 1977 Act made it a summary offence for any person without lawful authority to use or threaten violence for the purpose of securing entry into premises, where there is someone on the premises who is known by the person threatening the violence to be opposed to that entry. Section 6(3) of the Act provided that it was a defence for the accused to prove that at the time of the alleged offence he or she was (or was acting on behalf of: see *Forest Justices, ex parte Hartmann* [1991] Crim LR 641) a displaced residential occupier of those premises. The displaced residential occupier has always been exempted from liability for this offence since 'it was felt that no offence should be committed by a householder who, coming home from holiday, for example, discovered that his property had been made the subject of a squat' (A.T.H. Smith, *Offences against Public Order*, 1987, para. 14-07). For the definition of 'displaced residential occupier' see s. 12 of the 1977 Act. Section 72 of the 1994 Act adds a new subsection (1A), after subsection (1), of s. 6. This deals further with the case of the displaced residential occupier and extends the scope of the exemption in that case also to the 'protected intending occupier' of the premises. A definition of 'protected residential occupier' was contained in s. 7 of the 1977 Act, but that section is repealed by the 1994 Act. 'Protected intending occupier' is now more broadly defined in s. 12A of the 1977 Act (inserted by s. 74 of the 1994 Act) as a person who:

(a)   has a freehold interest, or a leasehold interest with not less than two years still to run, and

(b)   requires the premises for his or her own occupation as a residence, and

(c)   is excluded from occupation of those premises by a person who entered them as a trespasser, and

(d)   is in possession of a written statement setting out the above, signed by himself or herself and witnessed in writing by a justice of the peace or a commissioner for oaths.

Criteria (a) to (d) above are subject to further detailed requirements which are set out in s. 12A(2) to (11) of the 1977 Act, as inserted by s. 74 of the 1994 Act.

Section 72(4) of the 1994 Act repeals s. 6(3) of the 1977 Act, which had placed upon a defendant relying on the displaced residential occupier exemption the burden of proof (on the balance of probabilities) that he or she was indeed such a person. Section 6(1A) of the 1977 Act (created by s. 72 of the 1994 Act) now states that where a person 'adduces sufficient evidence' that he or she is either a displaced residential occupier or a protected intending occupier, then this raises a presumption that the person does indeed fall within one of those exceptions. Such presumption may be rebutted by the prosecution, where 'the contrary is proved' (s. 6(1A)). The purpose of this change must be to reduce the burden on a person of the kind to whom Dr Smith makes reference in the passage quoted above. Subsection (1A) is a curious evidential provision, however, since it is unclear how much evidence would amount to 'sufficient evidence'. It can perhaps be inferred that once the defendant has discharged his or her evidential burden on this matter the prosecution must disprove the defendant's rightful claim to take possession of the premises beyond reasonable doubt.

By s. 7 of the 1977 Act, it is a summary offence for a person who is on any premises as a trespasser, after having entered as such, to fail to leave those premises on being required to do so by, or on behalf of, a displaced residential occupier of the premises (as defined in s. 12 of the Act) or a protected intending occupier of the premises (as newly defined in s. 12A of the Act). Section 73 of the 1994 Act substitutes a new s. 7 of the 1977 Act, but this contains little that is new and is merely a tidying-up exercise, in consequence of the changes to s. 6 of the 1977 Act. The provisions of the former subsections (6) and (7), which provided defences to the offence under s. 7 (and in respect of which the accused bears the burden of proof), can now be found in the new subsections (2) and (3) respectively. The provision on burden of proof is unchanged. The original subsection (3) provided that falsely claiming to be a protected intending occupier is a summary offence. That offence is no longer in s. 7 but can now be found in s. 12A(8).

4.6   Squatters: Recovery of Possession

According to the Home Secretary (*Hansard*, Commons, 11 January 1994, col. 29–30):

> Part V [of the Bill] also deals with changes to the law to deal with squatters. We made a commitment in our election manifesto to improve the law in that respect. The Bill provides the teeth behind the new procedures introduced by the Lord Chancellor to give lawful owners and occupiers of property access to a quick and effective remedy against squatting. It will mean that the owner or occupier of a

property can go to court immediately and apply for an interim possession order *ex parte*. If the interim order is granted, the squatters will have 24 hours in which to leave the premises. Failure to do so will be an offence, and the police will have powers to enter property to enforce the order.

These changes have proved to be controversial. It is clear that by effectively criminalising adverse possession, the police will be expected to assume a more central role in this area, including carrying out the functions of bailiffs.

Towards the end of 1993 it was estimated that about 3,000 council houses were being occupied by squatters, with a far smaller number of shops, offices and privately owned houses also being occupied. One or two untypical cases, which achieved considerable press attention, involved squatters taking over more luxurious accommodation. In 1991, 60 squatters occupied a 10-bedroom house in Surrey, and a group of six squatters moved into a six-storey house in Kensington. There have also been press reports of squatters moving into empty properties and then demanding money from the owners before they would leave. It is clear, however, that these are very unusual cases. There may well be some public sympathy for those who are genuinely homeless moving into council accommodation which is at that time lying empty. Squatting is not in itself a criminal offence. It is, however, an offence for a person who is on any premises as a trespasser, after having entered as such, to fail to leave those premises on being required to do so by or on behalf of a displaced residential occupier of the premises or an individual who is a protected intending occupier of the premises: see the Criminal Law Act 1977, s. 7(1), and 4.5. That offence is punishable summarily with imprisonment for a term not exceeding six months or a fine not exceeding the statutory maximum, or both.

In two consultation papers, one issued in October 1991 and the other in March 1994, the government has declared its intention to speed up the eviction of squatters by introducing a new civil procedure backed up by criminal sanctions. The criminal sanctions are now contained in the CJPOA 1994, but it is necessary first to say something about the civil procedure. In order to recover possession from an alleged squatter the applicant must use summary proceedings in the High Court or county court (see Rules of the Supreme Court, ord. 113, and County Court Rules, ord. 24, part 1, introduced in 1970). These proceedings require a court hearing at which both parties have a right to be represented, and a period of time thereafter to enforce the court order (see Lord Chancellor's Department, *New Procedures to Combat Squatting in Houses, Shops and Other Buildings*, 1994). In the new civil procedure, in contrast, an interim possession order may be granted on an *ex parte* application to a circuit judge sitting in the county court, provided only that notice has been given to the alleged squatter. The applicant will attend before the judge, but the alleged squatter will not be given notice of the hearing. The court is expected to grant an interim possession order on the day of application, and will provide a written notice requiring the alleged squatter to leave within 24 hours. A further date for hearing will be fixed by the court. Unless the alleged squatter applies to have the interim order set aside, the order will be confirmed on that date. A squatter who fails to leave within 24 hours of an interim order being made, or re-enters as a trespasser within one year, will incur criminal liability (see below).

Sections 75 and 76 of the 1994 Act create two new offences in relation to interim possession orders. Section 75 creates an offence committed where a person knowingly or recklessly makes a false statement for the purpose of obtaining, or resisting the making of, an interim possession order. For these purposes 'statement' means any statement, oral or in writing, whether as to fact or belief, made in or for the purposes of the summary proceedings for possession of premises occupied by squatters (s. 75(4)). The offence is triable either way. It is punishable on indictment with up to two years' imprisonment, a fine or both. When dealt with summarily the maximum penalty is a term of imprisonment not exceeding six months, a fine not exceeding the statutory maximum, or both (s. 75(3)). Such an offence might be relevant in a case of a tenancy dispute, where the landlord is tempted to misuse the new procedure to eject the tenant. The March 1994 consultation paper from the Lord Chancellor's Department, *New Procedures to Combat Squatting in Houses, Shops and Other Buildings*, notes that if a judge has grounds for believing that an applicant has made a statement, which he knows to be false or misleading, for the purpose of obtaining an interim possession order, the judge may refer the matter to the Crown Prosecution Service.

Section 76 creates an offence where an interim possession order has been made in respect of particular premises and served in accordance with the relevant rules of court: any person subject to the order who fails to leave the premises within 24 hours or, having left, re-enters as a trespasser or attempts to do so within one year, commits an offence (s. 76(4)). During the course of passage of the Bill through Parliament, opposition amendments were tabled to change the relevant notice period from 24 hours to seven days (*Hansard*, Commons, 13 April 1994, col. 313), but these were defeated. A police officer may arrest without warrant a person who is, or whom the officer reasonably suspects to be, guilty of this offence. The offence is punishable on summary conviction to imprisonment for a term not exceeding six months or a fine not exceeding level 5, or both (s. 76(5)). For the purposes of ss. 75 and 76, the term 'premises' has the same meaning as it has in part II of the Criminal Law Act 1977, i.e., 'any building, or part of a building under separate occupation, and land ancillary to a building, the site comprising any building or buildings together with any land ancillary thereto' (s. 12 of the 1977 Act).

4.7 Unauthorised Campers

Section 77(1) creates a power in the appropriate local authority, where it appears that persons are for the time being residing in a vehicle or vehicles on a highway or any unoccupied land (in the open air), or on any occupied land (in the open air) without the occupier's consent, to give a direction that those persons must leave the land and take with them their vehicles and any other property they have with them. Notice of a direction must be served on those persons (s. 77(2) and s. 79).

If a person, knowing that he or she is subject to a direction under s. 77(1), either (a) fails, as soon as practicable, to leave the land or to remove any vehicle or other property or (b) re-enters the land within a period of three months, then he or she commits an offence punishable summarily by a fine not exceeding level 3 (s. 77(3)). Section 77(5) creates a defence, which the accused has the burden of proving, that the failure to leave, or failure to remove a vehicle or other property, 'was due to illness, mechanical breakdown or other immediate emergency'. For the purpose of s. 77, 'vehicle' includes (a) any vehicle, whether or not it is in a fit state for use on roads, and includes any body, with or without wheels, appearing to have formed part of such a vehicle, and any load carried by, and anything attached to, such a vehicle; and (b) a caravan as defined in s. 29(1) of the Caravan Sites and Control of Development Act 1960. A person may be regarded as residing on land despite having a home elsewhere (s. 77(6)).

Section 78 deals with enforcement of directions issued under s. 77. A magistrates' court if satisfied that persons and vehicles in which they are residing are present on land in contravention of a direction given under s. 77, may make an order requiring the removal of any such vehicle and any person residing in it. The order may be made on a complaint made by the local authority in whose area the land is situated. Such an order authorises the local authority 'to take such steps as are reasonably necessary to ensure that the order is complied with', which may include entry upon the land (provided that the owner of the land has been given 24 hours' notice of the entry), entry to the vehicles, rendering such vehicles suitable for removal, and their removal (s. 78(2)). Wilful obstruction of the exercise of these powers is an offence punishable on summary conviction by a fine not exceeding level 3.

Section 80(1) repeals part II of the Caravan Sites Act 1968. That Act required every county, metropolitan district and London borough to ensure that there was an adequate number of authorised camping sites in its area, and also to deal with the problem of unauthorised camping in 'designated areas'. The Secretary of State could designate an area only if there were adequate authorised camping sites or if sites were unnecessary. Section 6(1) of the 1968 Act provided that:

> ... it shall be the *duty* of every local authority ... to exercise their powers under section 24 of the Caravan Sites and Control of Development Act 1960 (provision of caravan sites) so far as may be necessary to provide adequate accommodation for gipsies residing in or resorting to their area. (Emphasis added.)

Section 6 has been repealed by the 1994 Act, but the definition of 'gipsies' contained in s. 16 of the 1968 Act is preserved. Section 80(2) of the 1994 Act amends s. 24 of the Caravan Sites and Control of Development Act 1960 by inserting a new para. (c) into s. 24(2). This amendment includes within the '*power* to provide sites for caravans' (emphasis added) in that section a *power* 'to provide, in or in connection with sites for the accommodation of gipsies, working space and facilities for the carrying on of such activities as are normally carried on by them'. Section 80(2) of the 1994 Act also amends s. 24(8) of the 1960 Act, inserting a definition of 'gipsies', which means:

> ... persons of nomadic habit of life, whatever their race or origin, but does not include members of an organised group of travelling showmen, or persons engaged in travelling circuses, travelling together as such.

This is identical to the definition which appeared in s. 16 of the 1968 Act and so the effect is that this definition is preserved in the new law. It has been held that this definition excludes 'new age travellers' (see further below).

The law, as amended in the 1994 Act, thus still empowers local authorities to provide sites for gipsies, but no longer requires them to do so. Since gipsies seem to be, to put it bluntly, a problem that no local authority wants, this must point inevitably to a local authority policy of 'moving on' gipsies, and thereby transferring the problem (temporarily) to another authority. Luke Clements, a solicitor writing in (1994) 2(6) *Parliamentary Brief* at p. 14, claims that the repeal of the duty to provide sites will rekindle the situation which existed before 1968, where local authorities employed 'caravan removal officers' to drive out gipsies from their areas. Much disquiet over the likely effect of these amendments was expressed in the debates on the Bill. Cranley Onslow MP (*Hansard*, Commons, 11 January 1994, col. 46) said that while there was no doubt that the 1968 Act had 'passed its use-by date', he asked the government to provide more details of the future arrangements for gipsy sites. He said that:

> Under [the clause] the number of genuine camping sites for gipsies will be reduced ... they will no longer receive any government grant towards their maintenance. That means that fewer sites will be available and that those who use them will lose their current stability. They will be found parking illegally because of the lack of legal sites, and will be moved on by the police. That often creates conditions that are distressing to local residents, and I am afraid that the incidence of such illegal parking is bound to increase, because those who have travelled for years will be unable to find a genuine site on which to stay.

He asked whether a target was to be set for the number of new sites to be opened, and who would have the responsibility for making sure that sites were made available. Who would own and manage the existing sites?

It seems that while local authorities have been under a statutory duty in the 1968 Act to provide sites for gipsies, 60 per cent of authorities have failed to provide sites as required, notwithstanding the availability of 100 per cent grants from central government to do so. No doubt this is partly explained by inertia on the part of local authorities, and partly by strong local opposition when the location of a proposed site is revealed by the local authority. There is some private site provision for gipsies, but this is very limited in scope. According to Earl Ferrers in the House of Lords debates on the Bill, the government is no longer prepared to accept that local authorities should be the bodies required to provide sites for gipsies. He suggests that gipsies should be encouraged to establish their own sites, through the normal planning mechanisms. A proposed amendment in the House of Lords to leave in place the local authority duty to provide camping sites (and for their continued receipt of 100 per cent grant for doing so) for a further five years, was defeated. See, for further discussion of these issues, P. A. Thomas, 'Housing gipsies' (1992) NLJ 1714.

The definition of 'gipsy' has recently been the subject of judicial decision in the Court of Appeal in the consolidated appeals of *South Hams District Council, ex parte Gibb, Gloucestershire County Council, ex parte Davies* and *Dorset County Council, ex parte Rolls, The Times*, 8 June 1994. The appeals all resulted from local authority decisions to issue proceedings for possession of land occupied by the appellants. The basis of the argument was that the appellants were not 'gipsies' within the definition. In *ex parte Rolls* they were described by the local authority as 'new age travellers', who had set up camp at Blackdown, Hardy's Monument. The Divisional Court dismissed an application for judicial review of the local authority decisions, and the Court of Appeal dismissed a further appeal against this refusal. In the Court of Appeal, Neill LJ accepted that the definition in s. 16 was not 'a particularly happy one' (see further *Mole Valley District Council v Smith* (1992) 24 HLR 442), but that the definition required that there must be some recognisable connection between the 'wandering or travelling' and the means whereby the persons concerned made or sought their livelihood. In the Divisional Court, Laws J had said that a 'nomadic habit of life' meant more than merely moving from place to place, and that the definition was meant to include 'that class of persons whose means of getting an independent living necessarily involved their wandering from place to place'. The notion of economic independence, or at least an aspiration to economic independence was, he said, inherent in the idea of a nomadic life. In holding that 'new age travellers' fell outside the statutory definition of gipsy, he said that the purpose of the Act had been to accord rights to gipsies, and that Parliament had not intended '... to confer the benefits of the Act on any person simply because he had no permanent home of his own'.

Sections 77–80 of the CJPOA 1994 came into force on the date of Royal Assent, 3 November 1994.

4.8 Terrorism: Stop and Search Powers

According to the Home Secretary (*Hansard*, Commons, 11 January 1994, col. 30):

> Part VI of the Bill gives the police new stop and search powers aimed against terrorism and creates two new offences against public security. There will be a power to stop and search vehicles and their occupants, and to stop pedestrians to search anything that they may be carrying. Those new powers will help to safeguard the public against the dual threats of vehicle bombs and small devices carried by individual terrorists....
>
> The Bill provides for very strict controls over how and when the new powers on terrorism can be used. Those new powers could help to save lives, and when lives can be saved Parliament has a duty to act.

These two offences already exist in Northern Ireland and, according to David Trimble MP (*Hansard*, Commons, 11 January 1994, col. 78), in the past, 'The police, particularly in London, have been fortunate that they have not had difficulties because of the lack of legal basis for some of their operations'. 'He argued that there ought to be uniform legislation on terrorism in the UK because it is a UK rather than a Northern Ireland problem.

Section 81(1) amends the Prevention of Terrorism (Temporary Provisions) Act 1989, by inserting a new s. 13A. That section provides for an authorisation to be made by a senior police officer (of or above the rank of commander or assistant chief constable) for powers to stop and search persons, vehicles, ships and aircraft, within a specified locality for a (renewable) period not exceeding 28 days, where to do so is expedient to prevent acts of terrorism (s. 13A(1)). The authorisation will allow police officers to search persons or vehicles in that vicinity for articles which could be used for the commission of acts of terrorism (s. 13A(3)). A person who fails to stop, or fails to stop his vehicle when required to do so by a constable acting in pursuance of these powers, or who wilfully obstructs a constable in the exercise of these powers, is guilty of an offence punishable on summary conviction with imprisonment not exceeding six months, a fine not exceeding level 5, or both (s. 13A(6) and (7)).

Section 82(1) also amends the Prevention of Terrorism (Temporary Provisions) Act 1989, by the insertion of new ss. 16A and 16B. Section 16A creates a new offence which is committed where a person has any article in his or her possession in circumstances which give rise to a reasonable suspicion that the article is in his or her possession for a purpose connected with terrorism. It is a defence for the accused to show that the article was not in his or her possession for such a purpose (s. 16A(3)). By s. 16A(4), where a person is charged with this offence and it is proved that either (a) at the relevant time the person and the article were both present in any premises (including a ship or aircraft), or (b) at the relevant time the article was in premises of which the person was the occupier, or which the person habitually used otherwise than as a member of the public, the court may presume that the person was in possession of that article unless it is further proved (by the accused) that he or she did not at the relevant time know that the article was there, or that he or she had no control over it. This offence is punishable on indictment with imprisonment for a term not exceeding 10 years, a fine or both, and summarily to imprisonment for a term not exceeding six months, a fine not exceeding the statutory maximum, or both.

The new offence under s. 16B applies where a person, without lawful authority or reasonable excuse (which the accused has the burden of paying) collects or records, whether by photography or any other means, or has in his or her possession, any information which is of such a nature as is likely to be useful to terrorists in planning or carrying out any act of violence. This offence is punishable on indictment by imprisonment for a term not exceeding 10 years, a fine or both, and summarily by imprisonment not exceeding six months, a fine not exceeding the statutory maximum, or both. An example of a situation which would be covered by this offence would be possession of a list of names and addresses of prominent politicians or other people in public life. In principle the offence would appear to cover possession of a copy of *Who's Who*, with the accused required to establish a defence of reasonable excuse on the balance of probability.

Section 81 of the CJPOA 1994 came into force on the date of Royal Assent, 3 November 1994. Section 82 will come into force two months after the date of Royal Assent (s. 82(3)).

4.9 Powers to Stop and Search for Offensive Weapons and Dangerous Instruments

During March 1994 it emerged that the Home Secretary was prepared to consider the adoption of new police powers to stop and search people on the street for guns or knives. The change in the law is thought to have come as a result of pressure from the police, who had been expressing concern over what they perceived to be increasing violence being shown towards their officers on the streets, and it followed a period of consultation with police associations, superintendents and rank-and-file police officers. It has been suggested that the police were also pressing for such a change because they felt that the previous law was too restrictive, making it difficult to carry out searches of members of the public because of the need to show reasonable grounds for suspicion.

The main powers to stop and search people and vehicles are to be found in s. 1 of PACE 1984. Section 1(3) of PACE restricts the use of these powers to cases where the police officer 'has reasonable grounds for suspecting that he will find stolen or prohibited articles'. This is further elaborated upon in PACE Code of Practice A. Courts have generally set high standards when assessing whether the policeman in question acted reasonably. It is now well established, for example, that the reasonable suspicion must relate strictly to the offence for which the arrest was made (*Chapman v Director of Public Prosecutions* (1988) 89 Cr App R 190).

Section 60 of the CJPOA 1994 empowers a police officer of or above the rank of superintendent (or an inspector, if no more senior officer is available) to issue a written and signed authorisation which will permit all uniformed police officers in a particular locality to stop any pedestrian and search him or her, or anything carried by him or her, for offensive weapons or dangerous instruments, and to stop any vehicle and search that vehicle, its driver and any passenger for offensive weapons or dangerous instruments. Such an authorisation can be given only if the officer reasonably believes that incidents involving serious violence may take place in the locality and that it is expedient to give the authorisation to prevent the occurrence of such incidents. When acting under such general authority, a constable may make such a search as he thinks fit, '*whether or not he has any grounds for suspecting that the person or vehicle is carrying weapons or articles of that kind*' (s. 60(5), emphasis added). This provides a remarkably broad new power.

The powers so conferred may be exercised at any place within the locality for a period not exceeding 24 hours. This period may be extended by the relevant senior officer in writing for a further six hours when expedient to do so, having regard to offences which have been, or are reasonably suspected to have been, committed in connection with any incident falling within the original authorisation period. Failure to stop when required to do so by a constable exercising these powers is an offence, punishable on summary conviction with imprisonment not exceeding one month, a fine not exceeding level 3 on the standard scale, or both (s. 60(8)). Where a pedestrian or the driver of a vehicle is stopped under the powers conferred by this section, the pedestrian or driver is entitled to obtain a written statement from the police that they were stopped under those powers, provided that he or she applies for such statement within 12 months.

4.10   Intentional Harassment, Alarm or Distress

A new offence of intentional harassment, alarm or distress was introduced into the Bill on a government amendment in the Lords on 16 July 1994. Much of the impetus for this development came from concern over the reported increase in incidents of racial violence and racial harassment, but the final version of the offence, though capable of being used in cases of racial harassment, is certainly not confined to such cases and, in fact, does not mention the factor of race at all (see further the letters to *The Times* of Mr John Monks, General Secretary of the TUC, Mr Julian Brazier MP and Mr Tariq Rafique, Chairman of the Commonwealth and Ethnic Barristers Association, on 11, 15 and 28 July 1994, respectively). It is appropriate to say something about the general background and then to focus on the likely scope of the new offence.

The Home Affairs Committee, in its Third Report, *Racial Attacks and Harassment*, HMSO, reported that the number of racial incidents had risen from 4,383 in 1988, to 7,734 in 1992, but that the British Crime Survey suggested that, because of considerable under-reporting, a more realistic figure was between 13,000 and 14,000 incidents. The Committee called on the Home Secretary, Mr Michael Howard, to reconsider his opposition to the creation of a new offence of racially motivated violence. Their suggestion was that, on conviction, a person would be liable to serve up to five years in prison in addition to the sentence he or she would receive for the offence were it not thus aggravated. Mr Howard had previously rejected calls for such an offence by the Commission for Racial Equality and others, arguing that racial motivation can, and properly should, be reflected in the sentencing level for existing offences. The Home Secretary also expressed doubts whether there was any advantage in creating an additional burden for the prosecution, in requiring them to prove in addition to the normal elements of the offence, that the offence was racially motivated. Proposals, during the passage of the Bill, that there should be a new offence of 'racially motivated violence', or that 'racial motivation' should be specified in statute as an aggravating factor in sentencing, were both defeated.

The new offence, created by s. 154 of the 1994 Act, is defined in terms of intentionally causing a person harassment, alarm or distress, and it takes its place as s. 4A of the Public Order Act 1986. Section 4A is clearly based upon the wording of s. 4 (fear or provocation of violence) and s. 5 (harassment, alarm or distress) of the 1986 Act. It is placed just above s. 5 in the hierarchy of public order offences since, unlike the offence under s. 5, the offence in s. 4A requires proof both of an *intent* on the part of the defendant to cause harassment, alarm or distress and proof that the victim *did suffer such consequence*. Neither such intent nor such consequence needs to be proved for the offence under s. 5. The prosecution must show that the defendant, with the requisite intent to cause a person harassment, alarm or distress:

(a)   used threatening, abusive or insulting words or behaviour, or disorderly behaviour, or

(b)   displayed any writing, sign or other visible representation which was threatening, abusive or insulting,

thereby causing that person, or another person, harassment, alarm or distress. It will be seen that it does not matter if the person who was affected in this way was a different person from the one whom the defendant intended should be affected. A proposal that this offence should be restricted to cases where the defendant had acted 'on racial grounds' was defeated. The offence of causing intentional harassment, alarm or distress will carry a maximum penalty of six months' imprisonment and/or a fine at level 5 on summary conviction (s. 4A(5)). This is the same maximum as the s. 4 offence (which requires proof that the defendant intended to cause the victim to believe that immediate unlawful violence would be used against him or another), while the s. 5 offence is punishable only by a fine, at level 3.

Since the wording of the offences under s. 4, s. 4A and s. 5 is so similar, it will be important when construing the new offence to have regard to the context of the 1986 Act as a whole, and to look at previous decisions on the meaning of terms. 'Threatening, abusive and insulting' are not, in fact, defined in the Public Order Act 1986, but it is clear from appellate decisions of high authority that these words must be given their ordinary meaning, and whether the conduct in issue so qualifies is a matter of fact for the court to determine (*Brutus* v *Cozens* [1973] AC 854 (decided in relation to the term 'insulting', as used in an earlier statutory provision)). See further *Director of Public Prosecutions* v *Clarke* (1991) 94 Cr App R 359, *Masterson* v *Holden* [1986] 1 WLR 101 and *Parkin* v *Norman* [1983] QB 92. In *Director of Public Prosecutions* v *Oram* [1989] 1 WLR 88 the Divisional Court held that where a police officer was a witness to an argument between the defendant and his girlfriend, the police officer was within the range of people who might be caused harassment, alarm or distress (see further *Ball* (1989) 90 Cr App R 378). The Court felt, however, that seasoned police officers were hardly likely to be caused harassment, alarm or distress by such behaviour. If, on these facts, the police officer is not discomfited, there can be no offence under s. 4A. In *Lodge* v *Director of Public Prosecutions* (1988) *The Times*, 26 October 1988 the Divisional Court held that whether a person was likely to be caused harassment, alarm or distress was a question of fact for the justices to determine. In the offence under s. 4A, however, it must be proved that the victim *did so suffer*, so that this would be a matter for proof beyond reasonable doubt. In *Atkin* v *Director of Public Prosecutions* (1989) 89 Cr App R 199 it was held that the offence under s. 4 could not be made out where the victim did not perceive the threat personally but was told about it by a third party. This decision turned on the words 'uses towards', which is found in s. 4. This phrase does not appear in s. 4A, so that *Atkin* may well not apply in respect of the new offence.

By s. 4A(2), an offence under s. 4A can be committed in a public place or in a private place, but no offence is committed where the words or behaviour are used, or the writing, sign etc. is displayed, by a person inside a dwelling and the person who is harassed, alarmed or distressed is also inside that or another dwelling. According to Earl Ferrers in the House of Lords, 'It is much more common for people to be abused or threatened by others outside the house or in the street'. Also, the terms of the new offence thereby reflect its basis in the law on public order. This provision on the place of commission is, indeed, virtually identical to provisions in s. 4(2) and s. 5(2) of the 1986 Act. For the definition of 'dwelling' see s. 8 of the 1986 Act ('any structure or part of a structure occupied as a person's home or as other living accommodation') and *Rukwira* v *Director of Public Prosecutions* [1993] Crim LR 882. There is a defence provided by s. 4A(3) for the defendant to show either (a) that at the relevant time he or she was inside a dwelling, had no reason to believe that the words or behaviour, or the writing, sign etc. would be heard or seen by a person outside the dwelling, or (b) that his or her conduct was reasonable. An identical defence is available in respect of s. 5, by s. 5(3) (on which see *Director of Public Prosecutions* v *Clarke* (1991) 94 Cr App R 359 and *Kwasi Poku* v *Director of Public Prosecutions* [1993] Crim LR 705), but there is no equivalent defence in respect of s. 4.

4.11   Racially Inflammatory Publication

Section 155 of the 1994 Act makes the offence under s. 19 of the Public Order Act 1986 (publishing or distributing written material which is threatening, abusive or insulting and which is either intended to stir up racial hatred, or likely to do so) an arrestable offence, by inserting a new para. (i) to s. 24(2) of PACE 1984. A new para. (h) to s. 24(2) is created by s. 166(4) of the 1994 Act.

Chapter Five
Sexual Offences, Obscenity and Videos

This chapter is concerned with a range of amendments to the law in the general areas of sexual offences and obscenity. Section 142 of the Act redefines the offence of rape in two ways: first, by confirming in statute the landmark decision of the House of Lords in R [1992] 1 AC 599 on 'rape within marriage' and, secondly, by extending the ambit of the offence of rape to include non-consensual anal intercourse, whether committed on a male or a female victim. By s. 145 the age of consent for homosexual acts in private is reduced from 21 to 18. Sections 84 to 87 of the Act extend the ambit of the Protection of Children Act 1978 and of s. 160 of the Criminal Justice Act 1988 so as to cover computer pornography relating to children and increase the penalties for an offence under the latter Act. Offences under the 1978 Act and under s. 2 of the Obscene Publications Act 1959 are made serious arrestable offences and the definition of publication in the 1959 Act is amended so as to cover transmission of electronic data. CJPOA 1994, s. 92, increases the penalties for improper use of public telecommunications systems under the Telecommunications Act 1984. Sections 88 to 91 increase the penalties for offences under the Video Recordings Act 1984, improve the powers of enforcement of trading standards officers and tighten up the controls on video recordings as applied under the 1984 Act by the British Board of Film Classification (the BBFC). Not covered in this chapter is the redefinition of 'sexual offence' for various purposes connected with the sentencing of offenders. This matter is considered in 1.19.

SEXUAL OFFENCES

5.1 Redefinition of Offence of Rape

Section 142 of the CJPOA 1994 makes two very significant changes to the definition of the crime of rape. It substitutes a new s. 1 of the Sexual Offences Act 1956. The new s. 1 states:

(1) It is an offence for a man to rape a woman or another man.
(2) A man commits rape if—
    (a) he has sexual intercourse with a person (whether vaginal or anal) who at the time of the intercourse does not consent to it; and
    (b) at the time he knows that the person does not consent to the intercourse or is reckless as to whether that person consents to it.

(3)   A man also commits rape if he induces a married woman to have sexual intercourse with him by impersonating her husband.

(4)   Subsection (2) applies for the purpose of any enactment.

The two changes are that, first, this new provision gives statutory effect to the decision of the House of Lords in *R* [1992] 1 AC 599 that the crime of rape applies within marriage in just the same way as it does outside marriage. Secondly, the definition extends the offence of rape to include non-consensual anal sexual intercourse with a woman, or with a man.

Section 142 of the CJPOA 1994 came into effect on the date of Royal Assent, 3 November 1994.

5.2   Rape within Marriage

The government, on 14 June 1994, accepted an amendment tabled by Lord Lester of Herne Hill, a Liberal Democrat peer, which placed on a statutory footing the effect of the House of Lords decision in *R* [1992] 1 AC 599, which was to the effect that the law of rape applies within marriage exactly as it does outside marriage. Previously, the common law took the view that the offence of rape could not be committed by a husband on his wife since the wife could not retract the consent to intercourse which she gave upon marriage. Prior to its repeal by the 1994 Act (see sch. 11), s. 1 of the Sexual Offences (Amendment) Act 1976 stated that '. . . a man commits rape if (a) he has *unlawful* sexual intercourse with a woman who at the time of the intercourse does not consent to it; and (b) at the time he knows that she does not consent to the intercourse or he is reckless as to whether she consents to it . . .' (emphasis added).

It had been generally assumed that the function of the word 'unlawful' in s. 1(1) of the 1976 Act was to confine the offence of rape to incidents which took place outside the bond of marriage (see *Chapman* [1959] 1 QB 100; *Jones* [1973] Crim LR 710). This interpretation was somewhat strained, given that extramarital sexual intercourse is not *per se* unlawful, but it was assumed by the courts and by most commentators that the non-applicability of the laws of rape within marriage was what had been intended by Parliament when it used that term in the legislation. The issue of whether the law should be changed, so as to permit a husband's conviction for the rape of his wife, was considered by the Criminal Law Revision Committee in 1976, but that committee was divided on the issue. When the matter came before the Court of Appeal in *R*, it held, in a decision that attracted much discussion at the time, that the law *did* so extend and that the word 'unlawful' in the definition of rape was 'mere surplusage'. The Court of Appeal's decision was upheld by the House of Lords. Immediately prior to the ruling of the Court of Appeal, the issue of marital rape had been the subject of consultation by the Law Commission, in its Working Paper No. 116, *Rape within Marriage*. The Law Commission ultimately recommended that the decision of the House of Lords in *R* be confirmed by legislation (see the final *Report*, Law Com. No. 116 (1992)). This has now been achieved by s. 142 of the 1994 Act, which simply omits the term 'unlawful' from the revised s. 1 of the Sexual Offences Act 1956. Further similar amendments to the law of sexual offences are made by the 1994 Act, so that the same word 'unlawful' is also omitted from s. 2(1) of the 1956 Act (procuring sexual intercourse by threats or intimidation) and s. 3(1) of that Act (procuring sexual intercourse by false pretences or false representations): see 1994

Act, sch. 9, para. 2. These offences can now be committed by a husband on his wife. Should not the word 'unlawful' also have been removed from the definition of the offence in s. 4(1) of the 1956 Act (applying or administering a drug so as to enable a man to have unlawful sexual intercourse with a woman)?

The Law Commission, in its Report, noted various practical problems of proof associated with establishing the offence of rape within marriage. These matters are not dealt with in the Act, and may still require attention (see J.C. Smith and B. Hogan, *Criminal Law*, 7th ed., 1992, p. 453). It may be noted that a wife is a compellable witness for the prosecution in a case where her husband has been indicted for rape committed upon her (PACE 1984, s. 80(3)(a)). On the other hand, the long-standing requirement in the law of evidence, that the judge must warn the jury of the dangers of relying upon the uncorroborated evidence of a complainant in a sexual offence, is repealed by s. 32(1)(b) of the 1994 Act (see further 3.3).

5.3   Extension of Rape to Include Non-consensual Anal Intercourse

As a result of an amendment to the Bill tabled in the House of Lords, by s. 142 of the 1994 Act the definition of the offence of rape has been extended to include non-consensual anal intercourse, whether the victim of that offence is a woman or a man. This conduct, as with rape as it was formerly defined, will carry a maximum penalty of life imprisonment.

Before the 1994 Act, non-consensual anal intercourse with a woman (whether this occurred within marriage or not) constituted the offence of buggery, and was punishable with life imprisonment. The effect of the 1994 Act amendment in respect of female victims, then, is simply to change the name of the offence committed from buggery to rape. This is not to suggest that the label to be attached to the offence is unimportant. Ten years ago the Criminal Law Revision Committee, in its Fifteenth Report, *Sexual Offences*, Cmnd 9213, 1984, was of the view that the offence of rape should continue to be restricted in law to the penetration by the penis of the vagina since 'the concept of rape, as a distinct form of criminal misconduct, is well established in popular thought, and corresponds to a distinctive form of wrongdoing' (para. 45). Apart from the argument from 'popular thought', the Committee suggested that the risk of pregnancy was a further and important distinguishing characteristic of rape'. It also thought that the crime of buggery should deal exclusively with acts of anal intercourse (para. 3.8).

Before the change to the law by s. 142 of the 1994 Act, acts of non-consensual anal intercourse with a male were punishable as follows. If the offence was committed on a boy or youth under the age of 16, the maximum penalty was life imprisonment (the maximum penalty for the attempted offence in these circumstances was 10 years). These maxima are *unchanged* by the 1994 Act, and the effect of the 1994 Act is simply to change the name of the offence from buggery to rape. If the offence was committed on a male aged over 16, the maximum penalty was 10 years. This is now (in effect, because of the subsuming of non-consensual buggery within rape) increased by the 1994 Act to life imprisonment. The effect of the 1994 Act change is, once again, to alter the name of the offence committed from buggery to rape, but the increase in the maximum sentence is likely to require some consequent changes to sentencing levels. In *Wall* (1989) 11 Cr App R (S) 111, the Court of Appeal observed that non-consensual buggery on a victim aged over 16 should be regarded as a somewhat less serious offence than rape, since the maximum sentence available for the offence was 10 years, rather than life. The amendment to the law now made by the 1994 Act will require that the Court of Appeal reconsiders this sentencing differential.

It should be noted that the new definition of rape, as substituted in s. 1 of the 1956 Act, does not extend to non-consensual oral sex, whether committed on a man or on a woman. Nor does it extend to the insertion into the vagina or anus of any other part of the human body, or any other object. While such conduct remains characterised in English law as indecent assault, and is thereby punishable with up to 10 years' imprisonment on indictment, rape definitions in other jurisdictions have been extended to include it. See, for example, the Crimes (Sexual Offences) Act 1980 of the State of Victoria in Australia, discussed in J. Temkin, *Rape and the Legal Process*, 1987, p. 30. Nor does the redefinition of rape affect the law on consensual buggery. For changes to maximum penalties where this is an offence see 5.6.

Subsection (4) of the new s. 1 of the Sexual Offences Act 1956 (set out above) states that the extension of the definition of rape to include anal intercourse in subsection (2) applies 'for the purpose of any enactment'. If, however, the word 'rape' appears in a statute qualified by the words 'of a woman', subsection (4) surely could not be taken to have the effect of repealing those qualifying words. Further specific statutory change would be necessary to achieve that effect. A number of such instances are picked up by the 1994 Act. Thus, in the offence of burglary with intent to commit rape, contained within s. 9(2) of the Theft Act 1968, the phrase 'raping any woman' is amended to read 'raping any person' (1994 Act, sch. 10, para. 26). The 1994 Act, sch. 10, para. 35 makes consequential amendments to the Sexual Offences (Amendment) Act 1976, s. 1(2) (jury considering whether a man believed that a woman *or a man* was consenting to sexual intercourse), s. 2(3) ('complainant' now means a woman *or a man* who is the victim of a rape) and s. 7(2) (sexual intercourse in the context of rape means intercourse *per anum* as well as *per vaginam*, so reversing the decision in *Gaston* (1981) 73 Cr App R 164).

Offences relating to sexual intercourse (other than rape) are *not* extended by the 1994 Act to include anal sexual intercourse with a woman, nor with a man. Thus the definitions of offences such as sexual intercourse with under-age females are unaffected by the 1994 Act. The offences of procurement of sexual intercourse by threats (Sexual Offences Act 1956, s. 2), procurement of sexual intercourse by false pretences (Sexual Offences Act 1956, s. 3) or administering drugs to obtain or facilitate sexual intercourse (Sexual Offences Act 1956, s. 4) remain confined to sexual intercourse *per vaginam*. These three offences thus continue to be possible alternative verdicts on a charge of rape (see Sexual Offences Act 1956, sch. 2) only where the alleged victim of the rape was a female.

5.4 Anonymity of Complainants

Another effect of the change to the law on rape is that it will extend to victims of non-consensual anal sexual intercourse the same treatment in relation to anonymity at trial which the victim of 'a rape offence' has received in the past, with their identity and address kept secret. 'Rape offence' means rape, attempted rape, aiding, abetting, counselling and procuring rape or attempted rape, incitement to commit rape, conspiracy to rape and burglary with intent to rape (Sexual Offences (Amendment)

Act 1976, s. 7(2), as amended by the CJA 1988, s. 158). The extension of victim anonymity is achieved by a number of amendments made by the 1994 Act to s. 4 of the Sexual Offences (Amendment) Act 1976, so as to include male as well as female complainants (for the details of these see sch. 10, para. 36 of the 1994 Act). Section 4 of the 1976 Act (as thus amended) forbids the publication of both the name and the address of the male or female complainant and also prohibits the publication within England and Wales of any still or moving picture of the complainant during his or her lifetime which is likely to lead members of the public to identify the complainant. The trial judge has a discretion to lift or relax these restrictions where it is in the public interest to do so (s. 4(3)). Section 6 of the 1976 Act originally made limited provision for anonymity of defendants charged with rape, but that section was repealed by the CJA 1988. See further on anonymity of victims para. 13 of sch. 9 to the 1994 Act.

It has been claimed that incidents of so-called 'male rape' are considerably under-reported. The extension of anonymity may encourage more men to admit that they have been attacked in that way, since their identity will not be revealed in court. This point should not be overstated, perhaps, given the fact that alleged victims of sexual offences are still likely to find themselves subjected to detailed and sometimes hostile cross-examination by the defence in court (see J. Temkin, 'Sexual history evidence' [1993] Crim LR 3). In line with the other changes brought about by the Act, the leave of the judge will be required before any question can be asked of the complainant (whether female *or male*) in a rape case regarding their sexual experience with any person other than the defendant (SOA 1976, s. 2(3), as amended by sch. 10, para. 35 of the 1994 Act).

5.5 Homosexuality: Age of Consent

Section 145(1) of the CJPOA 1994 amends s. 1(1) of the Sexual Offences Act 1967, by changing 'twenty-one' to 'eighteen'. Section 1(1) now has the effect that (subject to certain exceptions referred to in a moment) homosexual acts are not contrary to the criminal law provided that the acts take place in private, both parties consent thereto, and both parties have attained the age of 18 years. For these purposes homosexual acts are the acts of buggery, gross indecency, or being a party to the commission of either of these (Sexual Offences Act 1967, s. 1(7)).

The exceptions (which are unchanged from the earlier law) are where (a) more than two persons take part in the acts or are present at the time or (b) where the acts take place in a lavatory to which the public have access (s. 1(2)). The age of consent is also amended from 21 to 18 in Scotland, by s. 145(2), and in Northern Ireland, by s. 145(3).

For discussion of the background to the changes to the law on the age of consent to homosexual acts see the introduction to this *Guide*.

Section 145 came into force on 3 November 1994.

5.6 Buggery

Section 12(1) of the Sexual Offences Act 1956 (as amended by s. 143 of the CJPOA 1994) states that 'It is [an offence] for a person to commit buggery with another person otherwise than in the circumstances described in subsection (1A) below or with an animal'. Subsection (1A), as inserted by the 1994 Act, states that buggery between males, or between a male and a female, is not an offence provided that 'the act of buggery takes place in private and both parties have attained the age of 18'. The substantial change to the law here is the decriminalisation of anal sexual intercourse between an adult man and an adult woman conducted in private where both consent, 'an activity which is far from uncommon, which many of the general public are astonished to learn is a criminal offence, and yet more are dumbfounded to learn still attracts a maximum penalty of life imprisonment' (Baroness Mallalieu, *Hansard*, Lords, 20 June 1994, col. 75).

To escape liability for the offence of buggery, both parties must be aged at least 18 and the act must take place in private However, if there is no *consent* to an act of buggery then the offence of *rape* (as newly defined) will have been committed, whatever the age of the parties and whether or not the act takes place in private. It seems that an honest and reasonable mistake made by one party to an act of buggery as to the age of the other will be no defence (*Prince* (1875) LR 2 CCR 154). Where one of the parties is under 18, and the other is 18 or over, it appears that while the older party would be guilty of the offence of buggery, the younger party will not be implicated in the offence, since the law is designed to protect that person, as being the victim of the offence (*Tyrell* [1894] 1 QB 710).

'Private place' is not fully defined in the 1956 statute, and whether the place in which the act occurred is a private place or not will generally be a matter of fact to be determined by the court in all the circumstances (*Reakes* [1974] Crim LR 615). Section 12(1B) of the 1956 Act (as inserted by the 1994 Act) does state, however, that the act of buggery shall *not* be treated as being done in private (a) when more than two persons take part or are present or (b) when it takes place in a lavatory to which the public have access. It may be noted that s. 12(1B) refers to 'an act of buggery by one man with another', so that it does not apply to an act of buggery committed by a man with a woman. Section 12(1C) of the 1956 Act (as inserted by the 1994 Act) states that in any criminal proceedings for buggery 'it shall be for the prosecutor to prove that the act of buggery took place otherwise than in private or that one of the parties to it had not attained the age of 18'. This subsection makes it clear that these matters are elements of the offence which must be proved by the prosecution, rather than exceptions which have to be raised in evidence by the defence. A parallel provision can be found in s. 1(6) of the Sexual Offences Act 1967.

The effect of s. 146 of the 1994 Act is, by repealing s. 1(5) and s. 2 of the Sexual Offences Act 1967, to extend the operation of s. 1(1) (as now amended by s. 145 of and sch. 11 to the 1994 Act) to the armed forces and to the merchant navy. By s. 146 and s. 147, the exceptions which formerly related to homosexual acts in the armed services in Scotland and Northern Ireland are similarly repealed. In the House of Lords an amendment to the Bill was passed which was intended to confirm in law the right of the armed services to discipline and discharge homosexuals. The amendment, carried by 82 votes to 61, and now contained in s. 146(4), confirms the existing practice in the armed forces. The provision had been opposed in Parliament, on the basis that it was properly a matter for the individual services to decide how they should deal with this issue.

Sections 143 and 146 came into effect on 3 November 1994.

5.7 Buggery: Maximum Penalties

Section 144 makes several changes to the maximum penalties available for buggery committed in those circumstances in which it is an offence.

By s. 144(2)(a), buggery with a male or female under 16 (or buggery committed with an animal) attracts a life sentence. If committed by a person of 21 or over on a male or female person aged under 18, the maximum is five years. In other cases the maximum is two years. These changes remove various anomalies which existed under the pre-existing law, such as that buggery committed on a woman was formerly always punishable with life imprisonment. By s. 144(2)(b) the maximum penalties for attempts to commit these offences are in each case made the same as the maxima for the full offences. This is the normal rule in respect of penalties for attempted crimes.

By s. 144(3)(a), the penalties for the offence of indecency between men are varied to take account of the change in the age of consent for homosexual conduct. Indecency between a man of 21 and over with another man aged under 18 now attracts a sentence of five years; otherwise the maximum is two years. A similar change is effected by s. 144(3)(b) in respect of an attempt to procure the commission of an act of gross indecency with another man.

Section 144 came into effect on the date of Royal Assent, 3 November 1994.

OBSCENITY, PORNOGRAPHY AND VIDEOS

5.8   Problems Caused by Digital Technology

The problems of child abuse, paedophile sex rings and the circulation and distribution of obscene and pornographic material featuring children have all received much publicity in recent years. Some progress was made in the Criminal Justice Act of 1991 in making it easier to obtain convictions of persons guilty of offences of this nature against children by removing some of the difficulties inhibiting the giving of children's evidence in such cases. However, technological developments have been rapidly increasing the opportunities for the creation and distribution of child pornography which often is the first stage in the descent of susceptible adults into paedophile crime. Such pornography is also one of the devices used by child abusers and paedophiles to convince or reassure their child victims that the activities in which they are being persuaded or forced to participate are normal or acceptable. The Protection of Children Act 1978 deals with indecent photographs of children and makes it an imprisonable offence to do various acts in relation to indecent photographs of children such as to take or arrange to take them or to distribute or show them. Mere possession of such a photograph is not an offence under the 1978 Act but the CJA 1988, s. 160, made such possession a summary criminal offence punishable by a fine. Despite the existence of these offences, the police and those working with children have found that the availability of child pornography is rapidly increasing particularly through its creation and distribution via computer networks and on computer discs. Much child pornography has traditionally come from abroad and customs and border controls were one way of attempting to control the problem but with international computer networks and the ability to digitise images and send them down telephone lines to and from virtually anywhere in the world, this method is rapidly becoming obsolete or irrelevant. Furthermore, not only has computer technology facilitated the distribution of indecent and obscene material (whether or not featuring children), it has also aided its creation because once a photograph has been recorded digitally it can be manipulated and altered so as to become indecent or more indecent. In addition, the images displayed on computer screens can themselves be manipulated by the user so as to provide an interactive facility and enable the user to enter much more closely into the indecent or obscene fantasy world portrayed by the image or images.

Developments such as these do not fall neatly into the existing legislative provisions. Images which are produced or manipulated by computer do not appear to come within the definition of 'photograph' in the Protection of Children Act 1978, s. 7, although this does cover films and video recordings. A computer disc containing such an image or images would be an article under the Obscene Publications Act 1959 but much pornographic material would not qualify as obscene under the 1959 Act. Nor is the Obscene Publications Act 1959 of much use where there is no computer disc or other article being distributed but merely images available on an electronic bulletin board which may be controlled by a computer situated outside the jurisdiction from which individuals can obtain the images on their own computers. The nature and scale of the growing problem of computer pornography, whether it be images of children or images available to children, is also evident from a report of the Home Affairs Committee (1st Report, Session 93–94, *Computer Pornography*, HC No. 126, 9 February 1994).

5.9   Pseudo-photographs and Transmission of Data

To attempt to deal with such problems, s. 84 of the CJPOA 1994 makes various amendments to the Protection of Children Act 1978 and sch. 9, para. 3, amends the meaning of 'publication' in s. 1(3) of the Obscene Publications Act 1959. This latter amendment, which was not in the first version of the Bill but which broadly follows a recommendation of the Home Affairs Committee, can be dealt with quite briefly. Under s. 1(3) as it previously stood, a person publishes an article who:

   ...

   (b)   in the case of an article containing or embodying matter to be looked at or a record, shows play or projects it.

To this is now added the words:

   or, where the matter is data stored electronically, transmits that data.

This makes it clear that even though the article itself, the electronic database or disk, is not published in the sense of being physically distributed or circulated, the transmission of the data contained in the database or on the bulletin board or disk does amount to a publication of matter contained or embodied within an article. Amending the 1959 Act can only be a small part of the solution because the problem still remains that not all child pornography will easily come within the concept of obscenity in the 1959 Act. The Home Affairs Committee noted that the offence under s. 43 of the Telecommunications Act 1984 could be of some assistance here but a more direct response is to be found in the substantial amendments to the Protection of Children Act 1978 in the CJPOA 1994, s. 84.

These amendments are principally concerned to broaden the ambit of the Act beyond photographs in the traditional sense as envisaged in the 1978 Act by the addition of the concept of a pseudo-photograph which will include images made or manipulated by computer which are not technically photographs as defined above. Pseudo-photograph means 'an image, whether made by computer-graphics or otherwise howsoever, which appears to be a photograph' (Protection of Children Act 1978, s. 7(7) as substituted by the CJPOA 1994, s. 84(3)). The words 'or otherwise howsoever' are designed to cater for any new technologies for producing photo-like images in the future. Since such images are made rather than taken, Protection of Children Act 1978, s. 1(1)(a), is amended so as to make it an offence 'to make' as well as 'to take' a photograph or pseudo-photograph (CJPOA 1994, s. 84(2)(a)). The same subsection removes the limitation on the word 'child' in s. 1(1)(a) to a person under the age of 16 although a new s. 7(6) then defines a child again as a person under the age of 16 'subject to subsection (8)' which provides as follows:

If the impression conveyed by a pseudo-photograph is that the person shown is a child, the pseudo-photograph shall be treated for all purposes of this Act as showing a child and so shall a pseudo-photograph where the predominant impression conveyed is that the person shown is a child notwithstanding that some of the physical characteristics shown are those of an adult.

The reason for this convoluted extension to the meaning of a 'child' is that pornographic images may start off as a photograph of an adult which is then manipulated by computer techniques so as to have the face of a child (perhaps taken from another photograph) and then also in some cases the physical features such as breasts, genitalia etc. altered or reduced so as to look like those of a child. Subsection (8) pre-empts the argument that pseudo-photographs are not 'of a child' either because they do not accurately represent any particular individual or because the person on whom they are originally based was an adult rather than a child. It also reveals quite clearly that a principal aim of the amendments is to stem the making and circulation of material which encourages and facilitates paedophile activities as well as to protect children from becoming the subject of indecent photographs or pseudo-photographs. It does of course also deal with the distress that may be caused where a picture of a child's face has been superimposed on an indecent photograph and also where as a result an investigation takes place to see if an innocent child or family has been involved in child abuse.

The CJPOA 1994, s. 84(3), also substitutes a new partial definition of photograph in the Protection of Children Act 1978, s. 7(4), which adds 'data stored on a computer disc or by other electronic means which is capable of conversion into a photograph' to the original statement that 'the negative as well as the positive version' of a photograph is included. It also inserts a new partial definition of indecent pseudo-photograph in s. 7(9) which states:

References to an indecent pseudo-photograph include—
    (a)   a copy of an indecent pseudo photograph and
    (b)   data stored on a computer disc or by other electronic means which is capable of conversion into a pseudo-photograph.

The drafting of subsection (9) is slightly defective in that the word 'indecent' need not appear at all (as it does not in subsection (4)) but given that it does appear in the opening line and in para. (a)), it should also appear in para. (b). As it stands, para. (b), which has simply been taken from the new subsection (4) definition of photograph, literally means that any data stored on disc etc. capable of conversion into a pseudo-photograph is an indecent pseudo-photograph, irrespective of whether or not the data is capable of producing a pseudo-photograph which is actually indecent. It is, however, clear what is intended, i.e., that a pseudo-photograph of any description (even though only indecent ones portraying children are proscribed by the Act) includes electronically stored data capable of conversion into a pseudo-photograph even though a pseudo-photograph has not yet been created. Conversely, once a pseudo-photograph has been produced, if a subsequent copy of it is made, even though the copy may not itself appear to be a photograph and is therefore not a pseudo-photograph in that sense, then that copy is treated as a pseudo-photograph and therefore, for example, its distribution will be an offence.

It is perhaps convenient to set out s. 1(1) of the Protection of Children Act 1978 as amended by CJPOA 1994, s. 84:

It is an offence for a person—
(a)   to take, or permit to be taken or to make, any indecent photograph or pseudo-photograph of a child;
(b)   to distribute or show such indecent photographs or pseudo-photographs; or
(c)   to have in his possession such indecent photographs or pseudo-photographs, with a view to their being distributed or shown by himself or others; or
(d)   to publish or cause to be published any advertisement likely to be understood as conveying that the advertiser distributes or shows such indecent photographs or pseudo-photographs, or intends to do so.

Section 84(4) of the CJPOA 1994 similarly inserts the concept of a pseudo-photograph into the wording of CJA 1988, s. 160, which creates the offence of possession of an indecent photograph (and now also pseudo-photograph) of a child. Section 160 already incorporates a number of the ancillary provisions of the Protection of Children Act 1978 including the whole of s. 7 including, therefore, the new definitions and partial definitions referred to above.

CJPOA 1994, sch. 10 para. 37, also makes a number of consequential amendments to the Protection of Children Act 1978 which are largely concerned with adding the word 'pseudo-photograph' to provisions dealing with powers of entry, search, seizure and forfeiture.

Subsections (5) to (11) of s. 84 make amendments similar to all of the above in respect of the provisions in force in Scotland and Northern Ireland.

5.10   Offences under the Protection of Children Act 1978 and the Obscene Publications Act 1959 to Become Serious Arrestable Offences

The offences under the Protection of Children Act 1978 and the Obscene Publications Act 1959 were not previously classified as arrestable offences. Section 85 of the CJPOA 1994 now makes a significant change in order to improve the enforceability of these offences. Not only are they now made arrestable by s. 85(2), which adds them to the list in s. 24(2) of PACE 1984, but they are classified as serious arrestable offences by s. 85(3), which adds them to the list in PACE 1984, sch. 5, part II. Given the extensions elsewhere in the CJPOA 1994 to powers to take intimate samples in relation to all recordable offences, the most significant consequences of the offences coming into the serious arrestable category relate to the possibilities of detaining a suspect without charge for longer periods and for delaying the right to have someone informed about the arrest. This latter possibility seems to have been the main motivation behind the re-classification since if the police have picked up one member of a paedophile ring, they do not wish other members of the ring to be informed and have the opportunity to destroy photographs and other evidence before the police have had the time to act against them.

It should be noted that the less serious offence of mere possession of an indecent photograph or pseudo-photograph of a child under s. 160 of the Criminal Justice Act 1988 is not made an arrestable offence as a result of s. 85. However, s. 86(1) does make this offence an imprisonable one for the first time, although it remains a summary offence with the maximum penalty being six months. This is again a significant change for an offence which is exceptional in that it prohibits mere possession of indecent material as opposed to its creation or distribution, which perhaps indicates the seriousness with which the problems of indecent photographs and pseudo-photographs of children are now viewed. Section 86(2) makes a similar change for Northern Ireland. Section 87 makes a quite different sort of change for Scotland in bringing the maximum terms of imprisonment for the offences most closely corresponding to those in the Obscene Publications Act 1959 up to the equivalent level to those applying in England under the 1959 Act, i.e. three years on indictment or six months otherwise.

VIDEO RECORDINGS

5.11 Video Recordings Act 1984: Enforcement outside an Authority's Area

Sections 88 to 91 of the CJPOA 1994 make a number of amendments to the Video Recordings Act 1984, which regulates the distribution of video recordings particularly through the video rental industry. The 1984 Act creates various offences relating to the supply of videos which have not received a classification from the British Board of Film Classification (BBFC) or the supply of videos in breach of their classification (the classifications being 18R, 18, 15, PG, U and Uc). The Criminal Justice and Public Order Bill as originally introduced to Parliament in December 1993 contained only one clause dealing with video recordings, the clause which has now become s. 91. This section deals with the enforcement of the Video Recordings Act 1984, which was originally undertaken by the police but which became the responsibility of local weights and measures authorities (local trading standards departments) as a result of s. 162 of the CJA 1988 which inserted a new s. 16A into the 1984 Act. Because trading standards departments have jurisdiction only within their own local areas, some difficulties have been experienced where, as is often the case, there is a chain of supply which extends beyond one authority's area. Section 91 inserts new subsections into s. 16A of the 1984 Act which avoid these difficulties by extending the jurisdiction of any local weights and measures authority for these purposes outside its own area (provided it has the consent of the authority for the other area) in respect of offences 'linked' to its own area. According to the new subsection (4A), offences under the Act are linked to an authority's area if the illegal supply or possession of recordings in its area is 'likely to be or to have been the result of the supply or possession of those recordings in the other area' or if offences in the other area are likely to be or have been caused by illegal supply or possession in the authority's area – in other words where a chain of supply straddles two (or more) areas. By inserting a new s. 16B into the 1984 Act, s. 91(3) of the CJPOA 1994 also extends in a similar manner the jurisdiction of justices of the peace to issue summonses or warrants or to try offences which are linked to the supply or possession of video recordings within the area for which the justices act, i.e., where the offence outside the area is the cause or result of a supply or possession within the area.

Paragraph 22 of sch. 9 to the CJPOA 1994 amends the definitions of video work and video recordings in s. 1 of the 1984 Act so as to cover any new developments in the technology for producing a series of visual images.

5.12   Video Recordings: the Alton Amendments

The other three sections of the CJPOA 1994 relating to video recordings, ss. 88, 89 and 90, were added to the Bill during its passage through Parliament as a result of pressure brought to bear by David Alton MP and others who reflected the increased public concern about the viewing by children of unsuitable violent or sexually explicit videos in their own homes. Some of the increased public concern was due to speculation in the media that the killing of the toddler James Bulger by two young children, who were convicted of his murder in November 1993, was due in part to the boys having been able to watch violent videos at home. This speculation was itself partly due to comments by the trial judge in the case, Mr Justice Morland, who later made it clear that they were general contributions to the debate about videos and crime and were not based on any actual evidence in the case. Nevertheless, the influence of violent videos continued to be cited and highlighted in the press as a possible cause in other horrific murders such as that of Suzanne Capper in Manchester. Populist opinion was also given more considered support by the publication in March 1994 of a report on video violence and the protection of children by Elizabeth Newson, Professor of Developmental Psychology at Nottingham University, which was supported by a number of other leading child psychiatrists, to the effect that violent videos could indeed adversely affect the behaviour of children who were exposed to them. As against that there were other studies, e.g., by Hagell and Newburn for the Policy Studies Institute, *Young Offenders and the Media*, which found that the amount of video violence that young offenders watch is much the same as youngsters who do not offend. This sort of argument is itself open to the objection that the fact that videos have no effect on some juveniles does not prove that the videos are not part of the cause of offending in some of those juveniles who do offend. A virus may be no less the cause of illness in those who succumb to it merely because others who are immune to it or who are not as readily susceptible to it manage to escape unscathed.

Whatever the rights and wrongs of the debate about the effects of videos on children, David Alton had a substantial measure of cross-party support for amendments which he put forward at report stage in the Commons in April. The government initially resisted the amendments which were considered even by some of those prepared to support him to be too restrictive in their potential effects on some legitimate and important films portraying terrible events, such as *Schindler's List* to take a contemporary example, since the amendment talked about not presenting 'an inappropriate role model for children'. In order to head off an embarrassing defeat at a politically sensitive time in the run-up to the European elections, the government agreed to introduce its own amendments in the Lords which ultimately became ss. 88 to 90.

5.13   Video Recordings Act 1984: Increase in Maximum Penalties

Section 88 increases the maximum penalties for offences under the 1984 Act and for the first time makes some of them imprisonable. Previously all the offences in the Act were summary and the maximum penalty was a level 5 fine (£5,000) except that this maximum was £20,000 in the case of offences under ss. 9 and 10 of the Act (supplying videos of unclassified works and possessing such works for supply). In respect of these latter two offences, new sections 9(3) and 10(3) are now inserted into the 1984 Act by the CJPOA 1994, s. 88(2) and (3) making these two offences indictable for the first time with a maximum penalty of two years' imprisonment and also providing for a maximum term of six months on summary conviction in addition to the existing option of a maximum fine £20,000. As a result of s. 88(4), (5) and (6), the offences under ss. 11, 12 and 14 of the 1984 Act (supplying videos in breach of classification, supplying (other than in such a shop) videos classified only for supply in a licensed sex shop and supplying videos with false indication as to classification) remain summary but become punishable with a maximum term of six months' imprisonment. The penalty for the offence under s. 13 of supplying a video not complying with the requirements as to labelling (see s. 8 of the 1984 Act and the Video Recordings (Labelling) Regulations 1985, SI 1985/911) remains unaffected by s. 88 (but see sch. 10, para. 52, for consequential amendments affecting the internal organisation of the sections of the 1984 Act). Although the new penalties are of course not applicable to offences committed before the coming into force of s. 88 (s. 88(7)), once that section is in force the possibility of a prison sentence will constitute a greatly increased deterrent to serious breaches of the 1984 Act.

The above offences relate primarily to persons ignoring the system of classification set up by the 1984 Act or disregarding the classification given to a particular video by the BBFC. Sections 89 and 90 of the CJPOA 1994 seek to tighten up the actual system of control operated by the BBFC so that certain videos that were formerly exempt from the need for a classification certificate are no longer exempt and, perhaps more significantly, that when the BBFC do consider a non-exempt video, the criteria applied are stricter in terms of preventing unsuitable material becoming available to be seen by children, or indeed other viewers, to whom it may cause harm.

5.14   Restriction of Exemptions

Under s. 2(1) of the Video Recordings Act 1984 a video is an exempted work if:

taken as a whole—
  (a)   it is designed to inform, educate or instruct;
  (b)   it is concerned with sport, religion or music; or
  (c)   it is a video game.

Such an exempted work need not be submitted for classification to the BBFC and it is not an offence under s. 9 or s. 10 to supply or possess such a work for the purpose

of supplying it. Reasonable belief that a work is exempt is a defence to a charge of supplying it or possessing it for the purpose of supplying it contrary to s. 9 or s. 10.
However, s. 2(2) takes away this exemption from a video work if:

to any significant extent, it depicts—
    (a)   human sexual activity or acts of force or restraint associated with such activity;
    (b)   mutilation or torture of, or other acts of gross violence towards, humans or animals;
    (c)   human genital organs or human urinary or excretory functions;
or is designed to any significant extent to stimulate or encourage anything falling within paragraph (a) or, in the case of anything falling within para. (b), is designed to any extent to do so.

Section 89 of the CJPOA 1994 tightens up the above restrictions on exemptions in a number of ways. First it adds a para. (d) to the list of restrictions in s. 2(2) so that a video is not exempt:

if, to any significant extent, it depicts ... (d) techniques likely to be useful in the commission of offences.

This means that videos which give instructions on how to manufacture bombs or break into houses or cars or on how to engage in violent unarmed combat will no longer be exempt. An example of a previously exempt video which would now have to be submitted for classification was given by Lord Birkett (*Hansard*, Lords, 11 July 1994, col. 1587). This concerned an instructional video, *Deadly Explosives* which showed, *inter alia* how to concentrate explosives to blow a hole through armour plating using an empty wine bottle and three wooden stakes, and tips on how to blow apart an office colleague with a desktop bomb designed as a toy.
Secondly, the word 'designed' in s. 2(2) is replaced by the word 'likely' so that it is not the purpose of the maker of the video which matters so much as the likely effect of the video.
Thirdly, a new s. 2(3) is added which removes exempt status from any video which:

to any significant extent, ... depicts criminal activity which is likely to any significant extent to stimulate or encourage the commission of offences.

This differs from the new s. 2(2)(d) in that there is no need to show techniques for committing offences but rather it is the depiction of behaviour constituting offences which might encourage others to copy which deprives the video of exempt status. Thus pop videos showing illegal drug taking or high-speed car chases as desirable activities would no longer be exempt even though concerned with music and prima facie exempt under s. 2(1)(b).
It should be stressed that if the video is not exempt because of s. 2(2) or (3), it by no means automatically follows that cuts will be required in the video or that it will receive a restricted (or any) classification. It merely means that it requires classification and that the BBFC will decide what that classification will be and what cuts, if any, are necessary to allow it to receive that classification (or whether it can be distributed at all).

5.15 Statutory Criteria for the BBFC and Review of Earlier Classification

The BBFC started off its life and still remains a non-statutory and voluntary body funded by the fees from the film and video industry for whom it provides a *de facto* mechanism for protection from any liability for breach of obscenity or other similar laws. It existed long before the Video Recordings Act 1984 under which it was then designated by the Secretary of State by virtue of a power in s. 4 as the responsible authority, effectively expanding its previous voluntary role in relation to cinema screenings to cover the classification of video recordings distributed outside the cinema itself. The 1984 Act did not, however, lay down any detailed criteria for the 'designated authority' (the BBFC) other than to say that it was to have 'special regard to the likelihood of video works in respect of which . . . certificates have been issued being viewed in the home' (Video Recordings Act 1984, s. 4(1)(a)). The BBFC has certainly taken the view that the fact that videos are seen in the home where children may get to see them (even if an 18 classification is given) and where repeated or slow-motion playback is possible means that more restrictive cuts may be necessary to grant the same level of classification (e.g., 15) as may be applicable to the same film in the cinema.

However, the thrust of the amendments resulting from the pressure brought to bear by David Alton is that the BBFC is often not restrictive enough in the light of the opportunities for children to see such videos and the effects that unsuitable videos may have on them and indeed on susceptible adults. Section 90 of the CJPOA 1994 accordingly inserts a new s. 4A into the Video Recordings Act 1984 which requires the designated authority (the BBFC) to:

have special regard (among the other relevant factors) to any harm that may be caused to potential viewers or, through their behaviour, to society by the manner in which the work deals with—
  (a) criminal behaviour;
  (b) illegal drugs;
  (c) violent behaviour or incidents;
  (d) horrific behaviour or incidents; or
  (e) human sexual activity.

Section 4A(2) defines some of the key phrases including 'potential viewer' which means:

any person (including a child or young person) who is likely to view the video work in question if a classification certificate or a classification certificate of a particular description were issued

The new s. 4A raises a number of issues of interpretation for the BBFC (or for the courts if an application were to be made for judicial review of any of its decisions). It is clear that the section is talking about the effects on a number of viewers (not necessarily children) rather than just one but it is not clear how many. In relation to obscene publications where the test of obscenity is the tendency to deprave and corrupt persons who are likely to read see or hear the matter, the test appears to be whether a significant proportion of those persons would tend to be depraved or corrupted. This may be much less than 50 per cent but must not be numerically negligible (*Director of Public Prosecutions* v *Whyte* [1972] AC 849). A similar test would probably apply to s. 4A of the 1984 Act so that provided that a more than numerically negligible handful of persons would suffer harm, or cause harm to society by their behaviour, the BBFC ought to have special regard to that harm.

Another difficult issue is the relationship between the classification certificate issued and the likelihood of children of a particular age viewing the video. It is clear that the fact that, say, a 15 certificate is issued does not mean that the BBFC can ignore the likelihood that children under 15 may in fact view the film. However, unless the more restrictive classification certificates are deemed to have some effect on the likelihood of particular categories of viewers watching the video, there would be little point in having different types of classifications in the first place and indeed the definition of 'potential viewer' in s. 4A(2) refers to 'if a classification certificate or a classification certificate of a a particular description were issued'. Even an 18R certificate would not guarantee that children would not see the video and these are in any event very rare since distributors normally want at least an 18 classification to give them access to a meaningful market and will agree to cuts necessary to secure this. Other classifications such as 18 or 15, whilst prohibiting direct supply to children, would not prevent children in many homes seeing the video. Whatever the correct interpretation of s. 4A, it is clear that it will lead to a more restrictive approach on the part of the BBFC. At the time the Alton amendments were proposed, the director of the BBFC, James Ferman, was reported in *The Times* (13 April 1994) as acknowledging that too many children had access to videos which were classified only for adult viewing. 'From now on we are going to have to cut more and classify higher. Films that would previously have been 15 will be 18 and some of those which would have had an 18 certificate may not be given a video licence at all.'

Again, however, as with the exemption restrictions, it is important to remember that the factors mentioned in s. 4A(1) do not automatically lead to a video being banned or cut or given a restricted certification. The BBFC still has discretion to consider other (unspecified) factors (presumably both for and against the video) alongside any harm that may be caused under s. 4A. However, the harm is the factor to which it is required to give 'special regard' and the greater the harm and the larger the number of persons who may suffer it, the more restrictive the approach of the BBFC is likely to be.

Section 90 is one of the sections in the Act which came into force on Royal Assent (3 November 1994). Thus the new criteria in s. 4A of the 1984 Act apply to any classification decisions made by the BBFC from that date on. (Contrast s. 89, dealing with restrictions on exemptions, which applies only once that section is brought into force – presumably once it is brought into force some previously exempt videos will no longer be exempt and will have to be submitted for classification and in the meantime it will become an offence to supply them etc.). Videos which have already been given a classification in the past are unaffected by s. 4A even though there are quite a number of them which are of precisely the type which are aimed at by the new criteria. Right up to the very last stages of the Bill's passage through Parliament, the government took the view that, although desirable, it was not practical to do anything about videos already certified and in circulation. However, following another report of the Home Affairs Committee in June (4th Report, Session 1993-94, HC No. 514, *Video Violence and Young Offenders*) and also in the light of consultations with the

BBFC, it was decided that some limited review of previously certified videos was feasible and an amendment inserting a new s. 4B of the 1984 Act was introduced (*Hansard* Commons, 19 October 1994, col. 381). This does not spell out the details of how existing videos will be reviewed but empowers the Secretary of State to make provision by statutory instrument for such review by the designated authority (the BBFC). From s. 4B(2) it is evident that the BBFC will be able to select (presumably in the light of representations received) the videos which need review and, if appropriate, to amend or cancel the certificates already issued in relation to videos which it reviews. There is also likely to be a notice period before any alteration or cancellation of a certificate takes effect and special provisions made for labelling videos whose classifications have been altered. It is not envisaged that large numbers of the 25,000 or so videos with existing classifications will be subjected to reclassification or cancellation under this provision but much will depend on the details of the scheme, and its interpretation by the BBFC, once the scheme is established by statutory instrument.

In contrast to the concerns already discussed to keep children protected from unsuitable videos, s. 90(2) of the CJPOA 1994 makes an amendment to enable certain videos to be labelled as particularly suitable for young children by amending s. 7(2) of the 1984 Act. Previously, s. 7(2) authorised a certificate ('Uc') which advised the particular suitability of a video for viewing by children to which is now added the words 'or young children'. One aspect of the relatively innocuous problems with which this amendment is designed to deal had been that a parent might pick up a video marked Uc for a 10 or 11-year-old to watch and on arriving home and playing the video it might be found that the video was really intended for pre-school children. It will now be possible to put the words '*young* children' on such a video to avoid confusion of this sort. This important statutory provision is the essential stuff of Criminal Justice Acts and perhaps justifies them being so long and having them so often. It should be a major boon to those parents who do not have time to read the synopsis of the video usually provided on the packaging but it is at least consistent with the overall, and unfortunately realistic, approach of this part of the Act that many parents cannot be trusted to select or monitor and control suitable viewing for their children.

5.16 Obscene, Offensive or Annoying Telephone Calls

The offence of improper use of a public telecommunication system under s. 43(1) of the Telecommunications Act 1984 has been growing in importance recently with the increased potential that digital exchanges and equipment have provided for catching offensive, malicious or obscene callers. British Telecom has established a number of malicious and nuisance call bureaux to help and advise the victims of such calls and approximately 7,000, calls per year are traced for such purposes. One thousand two hundred offenders were cautioned or prosecuted in the year to June 1993 compared with about 200 in the previous year. Section 92 of the CJPOA 1994 increases the maximum fine for an offence under s. 43 to level 5 from level 3 and for the first time makes it imprisonable (though still summary) with a maximum term of six months. Besides dealing with indecent, obscene or offensive voice telephony, the s. 43 offence is also capable of application to the sending of indecent matter in digital format from one computer to another and so can be applicable to the distribution of computerised pornography over public telephone lines where such distribution falls outside the Obscene Publications Act 1959 because it is only indecent rather than obscene (see 5.8 above).

Chapter Six
Custodial Institutions

*Chapter I of part VIII of the CJPOA 1994 builds on the provisions of the CJA 1991
enabling the contracting out of prisons and prisoner escort arrangements in England
and Wales. The new provisions for England and Wales take effect by means of
amendments to the 1991 Act and can only really be understood in the context of those
existing provisions for which see M. Wasik and R. D. Taylor, Blackstone's Guide to the
Criminal Justice Act 1991. Chapters II and III by contrast introduce these
privatisation provisions for the first time in Scotland and Northern Ireland
respectively although the Northern Ireland provisions are limited to prisoner escort
arrangements (contracted-out prisons to be possibly authorised by means of an Order
in Council). Discussion of these provisions will also be linked with the similar
provisions found in ss. 5 to 14 of the CJPOA 1994 relating to the establishment and
running by the private sector of secure training centres for young offenders. Chapter
IV of part VIII is concerned mainly (though not exclusively) with the staff of directly
managed rather than contracted-out prisons. It regulates their employment rights and
the status of their trade unions, makes it illegal to induce industrial action by them and
provides for the establishment of regulations for the determination of their pay and
related terms and conditions of employment. Following discussion of the above
provisions, this chapter of this guide will also deal with some new powers created in
ss. 151 and 152 of the CJPOA 1994 enabling prison officers to test prisoners for drugs
and permitting other prison employees to search prisoners for unauthorised items.
Finally, the establishment of the Parole Board as a corporate body by s. 149 and some
minor amendments in respect of recall from parole licence are discussed.*

6.1 Prisoner Escorts

The task of escorting prisoners to and from courts, prisons and police stations has
traditionally been carried out by the police and the prison service. Section 80 of the
CJA 1991 empowered the Home Secretary to enable these tasks to be performed by
'prisoner custody officers' under 'prisoner escort arrangements' which could include
'entering into contracts with other persons for the provision by them of prisoner
custody officers'. (For the background to the introduction of the private sector to this
area see *Blackstone's Guide to the Criminal Justice Act 1991*, 7.8). Under these
provisions, one of the eight areas into which England and Wales has been divided for
these purposes was contracted out as from 5 April 1993 in a contract with Group 4

Court Services Ltd to cover the Humberside and East Midlands area (excluding category A prisoners). The contract is for a period of five years terminable by six months' notice or seven days in the case of default (including a failure to deliver 98 per cent of prisoners to court on time in any calendar month). The second area to be contracted out is the Metropolitan Police District which is being phased in five stages during 1994 and 1995 in a contract with Securicor which commenced in June 1994 in relation to Pentonville and Holloway prisons. It is believed that the next three areas to be contracted out will be East Anglia, Merseyside and North Wales, and the North of England after which the final three areas will be contracted out so that the whole of the court escort service is operated by the private sector.

The operation of the contract in the first area has not been without its problems or adverse publicity when prisoners have been able to escape or appear to have been treated badly, although the government takes the view that the general performance has been good and that the contract has operated to its satisfaction. Statistics on numbers of escapes are difficult to compare as figures for the state sector are kept separately for the police and the prison service respectively and not all police authorities have kept records of this matter. Nevertheless the following figures were given by the government minister (*Hansard*, Commons, Standing Committee B, 15 February 1994, col. 773–4):

> In the first nine months of the Group 4 contract . . . to December 1993, the company moved about 50,000 prisoners in Humberside and the East Midlands. There were 32 escapes. For the two years 1991 and 1992, the number of recorded escapes [in the same area] from escorts was 62 – 16 from Her Majesty's prison service and 46 from the police. That would tend to suggest . . . the State sector was marginally better. But of course the figure does not include escapes by prisoners who were being escorted by Nottingham police who, apparently, kept no records. . . . It is impossible to suggest from examining the figures that Group 4 is losing more prisoners than did the State sector.

Each side in the debate has used anecdotal evidence of good and bad practice in the privatised service according to the argument that they wished to support but the most serious incident which occurred in the contracted out area was the death of Ernest Hogg. Mr Hogg had drunk a litre of whisky unknown to his escorts and died of irreversible brain damage after choking on his own vomit in the back of a Group 4 van. The inquest on 15 February 1994 found that a lack of care had contributed to his death.

Of course things can and do go wrong in public sector controlled services and the government considers that there is nothing in the overall experience so far to make it slow down the planned extension of contracting out to other areas. Indeed the whole purpose of s. 93 of the CJPOA 1994 is to remove some of the technical restrictions in s. 80 of the CJA 1991 on what functions can be covered under 'prisoner escort arrangements'. The terms of s. 80(1) as enacted were very specific and covered:

(a) the *delivery* of prisoners *to* court premises,
(b) the *custody* of prisoners held *on* court premises,
(c) the *delivery* of prisoners *from* court *to* a prison or police station,
(d) the *delivery* of prisoners *from* one prison *to* another, and

(e)   the *custody* of prisoners while they are *outside* a prison for *temporary* purposes.

Inconveniently, the functions specified above did not cover a number of situations that can arise such as the transfer of prisoners from police stations to prison or from court to court, or from court to mental hospital. Neither did they cover custody *at* a central interchange prison in the course of inter-prison transfers. Furthermore the definition of a prisoner in s. 92(1) of the CJA 1991 meant that persons in police detention arrested *and charged* could be legally escorted to court, but *not* those arrested for non-payment of fines or non-appearance at court. The result was that the movement of some prisoners had to be effected by the police or prison service (which was inefficient for the relatively small number of cases, particularly as a contractor had been engaged specifically to free them from these sorts of duties) and there was inevitably confusion about the precise boundaries of the functions of prisoner escorts.

Section 93 of the CJPOA makes a number of amendments designed to rectify these difficulties. Section 80 of the CJA 1991 as a result is amended to read as follows:

(1) The Secretary of State may make arrangements for any of the following functions, namely—

(a)   the delivery of prisoners from one set of relevant premises to another;

(b)   the custody of prisoners held on the premises of any court (whether or not they would otherwise be in the custody of the court) and their production before the court;

(c)   the custody of prisoners held in a prison in the course of delivery from one prison to another; and

(d)   [repealed]

(e)   the custody of prisoners while they are outside a prison for temporary purposes,

to be performed in such cases as may be determined by or under the arrangements by prisoner custody officers who are authorised to perform such functions.

(1A)   In paragraph (a) of subsection (1) above 'relevant premises' means a court, prison, police station or hospital; and either (but not both) of the sets of premises mentioned in that paragraph may be situated in a part of the British Islands outside England and Wales.

This amended provision together with other amendments contained in s. 93 of the CJPOA, notably s. 93(5) amending and extending the definition of 'prisoner' in s. 92(1) of the CJA 1991, means that prisoner custody officers should be able to effect all movements of prisoners (and persons remanded or committed to hospital or local authority accommodation) without the inconvenient restrictions outlined above which previously applied under the original terms of the 1991 Act. Furthermore, the second part of the new s. 80(1A) of the CJA 1991 means that they can escort prisoners from Scotland or Northern Ireland (or the Channel Islands or Isle of Man) *to* England and Wales or vice versa. It should be noted in this context that ss. 102 and 118 of the CJPOA establish the power to set up prisoner escort arrangements in Scotland and Northern Ireland respectively in more or less identical terms including the function of escorting prisoners to and from other parts of the British Isles.

In addition to broadening the range of escort arrangements which can be made under the 1991 Act, ss. 94 and 95 of the CJPOA 1994 clarify and extend the powers and duties of prisoner custody officers. Section 84 of the CJA 1991 already provided a duty to search persons before the Crown Court on the orders of the Crown Court under s. 34A of the Powers of Criminal Courts Act 1973 but there was no similar power relating to the magistrates' court. Section 94(1) of the CJPOA now substitutes s. 82(4) of the CJA 1991 so as to add this duty under s. 80 of the Magistrates' Courts Act 1980 (which deals with searching for money found on fine defaulters).

Section 94(2) of the CJPOA 1994 deals with the quite separate issue of a person sentenced to prison where it is too late or otherwise not feasible to admit that person to prison that day and where under the Imprisonment (Temporary Provisions) Act 1980 such a person is now detained in police custody in a police cell. Section 6 of the 1980 Act is now amended to enable the detention to be in the custody of a prisoner custody officer rather than a police officer. It seems unlikely that this particular change will have much immediate impact until the operators of the contracted-out services have developed their own temporary holding centres. Section 95, of the CJPOA substitutes a new s. 83 in the CJA 1991 which deals with disciplinary offences committed by prisoners under escort. The main difference from the original s. 83 comes in s. 83(3) which now expressly provides that the prisoner custody officer is enabled to lay the charge against the prisoner, something that was not clear in the section as originally drafted. The charge would actually be investigated, however, by the governor of the prison to which the prisoner had been delivered. In the case of a contracted-out prison, even though s. 83 speaks of the prisoner being regarded as being in the custody of the director, the charge would be investigated by the controller (a Crown servant) not the director who is specifically precluded from this role by CJA 1991 s. 85(3)(a).

6.2 Contracting out Prisons

Section 84 of the CJA 1991 introduced the contracting out of prisons in what was at first a fairly limited fashion, only new remand prisons being at first eligible. However, the original s. 84(3) empowered the Secretary of State to amend s. 84 by statutory instrument in various ways to broaden the range of prisons which could be contracted out. This option was exercised twice, fairly rapidly after the opening of the first private-sector (Group 4) prison, the Wolds remand centre. SI 1992/1656 extended contracting out to any new prison (whether for remand or sentenced prisoners) which enabled Blakenhurst to be contracted out to UK Detention Services in May 1993 and Doncaster to Premier Prison Services in 1994. SI 1993/368 then broadened the scope of s. 84 still further to enable existing prisons to be contracted out which resulted in Manchester (Strangeways) Prison being 'market tested', i.e., put out to tender but with the prison service as being one of the bidders. In the event the 'in-house' bid was successful and Strangeways has not been contracted out although it operates on a slightly different basis to other public-sector prisons under a service-level agreement which provides the specification to which the prison is to be run in the same way that the contract would do in the case of a contracted-out prison. Buckley Hall prison near Rochdale was also market tested subsequently but the contract went to Group 4 although, unlike Strangeways, there was no existing staff already running the prison since it was a refurbishment of a former young offender institution.

Having been amended twice, s. 84 of the CJA 1991 is now completely rewritten by s. 96 of the CJPOA 1994 to enable the next step in the contracting-out process to be taken. What has been contracted out to date has been the running of prisons built and provided by the State. The new s. 84 enables the Secretary of State to contract 'with another person for the provision or running (or the provision and running) by him, or (if the contract so provides) for the running by subcontractors of his, of any prison or part of a prison'. This means that the contractor can now be given the job not only of running the prison but of designing and building it from scratch. Furthermore, the running of prisons can be subcontracted by the main contractor (provided the original contract provides for this) and the contract or subcontract may relate to the whole of a prison or for just part of it (e.g., a particular wing).

As far as designing and building a prison is concerned (these have come to be known as 'design, construct, manage and finance' or DCMF new prisons) the government will identify and provide the site which will then be leased to the contractor probably for a period of 25 years. The contractor will recoup the design and construction costs through the annual charges under the contract or, if the contract is terminated early for any reason, through a payment on termination. The new s. 84(3) excludes various provisions of the Landlord and Tenant Acts and the Law of Property Act 1925 to ensure that the government can get repossession in the event of such early termination. The first two DCMF prisons will be at Fazackerly (near Liverpool) and Bridgend and several more are planned as part of the government's initial aim to have 10 per cent of the total number of prison places provided by the private sector. The extension to design and build prisons is a significant development since it removes one of the difficulties and disincentives from the government's point of view in the way of further increasing the overall total of available prison places, i.e., the need to fund the capital expenditure which can now effectively be spread over the period of the lease of the prison as revenue expenditure under the management contract. It also, disturbingly for some, raises the spectre of the private, sector having a more direct interest in seeing a large and increasing prison population, something that was less likely when contracting-out was limited to existing prisons or those new prisons that were already being built.

Those who believe that private-sector prisons enable improved regimes and facilities for prisoners to be provided at lower cost than in the public sector will welcome the extensions to the contracting-out programme authorised by the new s. 84 (which have been well trailed in advance and on which much pre-contractual work has already been done). On the other hand, those opposed to the whole principle of contracting-out the State's exclusive right to punish offenders and to deprive them of their liberty see the new s. 84 as a further extension of a deplorable trend before any real hard information has been made available about the success or otherwise of the prisons already privatised or about their true costs. Requests for detailed information about the financial and other details of contracts are often met even in Parliament with the response that they cannot be disclosed because of commercial confidentiality. Ironically, it is easier in some cases to obtain such information relating to UK contracts from the Securities and Exchange Commission in the United States where the parent companies of some of the contractors are based (see, e.g., *Prison Report, The Prison Reform Trust Magazine*, Autumn 1994).

Doncaster prison, in particular, has attracted adverse media attention in its first few months of opening and has gained the nick-name 'Doncatraz'. Critics allege that a combination of inexperienced staff and reliance on modern technology (such as video surveillance) coupled with low staffing levels has led to a high level of violence and intimidation of prisoners. The official prison service view is that Doncaster is not experiencing any greater level of difficulties than is normally encountered in the first year of any new prison.

6.3   Temporary Attachment of Prison Officers

Prison officers at directly managed public-sector prisons have always been available to provide support and assistance to other prisons at times of crisis or special need. Contracted-out prisons have previously been unable legally to draw on such support from the staff of directly managed prisons since s. 85(1) of the CJA 1991 only authorises prisoner custody officers (i.e., staff employed by private contractors, not prison officers employed by the Prison Service) to perform custodial duties at a contracted-out prison. Section 97(1) of the CJPOA 1994 amends s. 85 of the CJA 1991 so as to add 'a prison officer who is temporarily attached to the prison' to the category of persons authorised to perform such custodial duties. The Act does not specifically provide for payment or recompense by the contractor to the public sector (as was pressed for unsuccessfully by the opposition) for the provision of prison officers but it is envisaged that arrangements will be made to deal with this point. It is also intended that the private sector should be able to provide aid to public-sector prisons although the opportunities for this will clearly be more limited given the much greater number of public-sector prisons at the moment. Section 99 inserts a new s. 88A into the CJA 1991 which will enable contractual arrangements to be made to allow for assistance from the private sector to the public sector and to give (private-sector) prisoner custody officers the necessary powers to act at directly managed prisons. This section of course goes beyond assistance in times of emergency or crisis and would allow the contracting out of the regular staffing of an otherwise directly managed prison.

In the same way that s. 93 of the CJPOA 1994 remedies some inconvenient restrictions on the functions that can be covered by privatised escort arrangements, s. 98 extends the duties of anyone (whether a prisoner custody officer or a prison officer temporarily attached to such a prison) carrying out custodial duties at a contracted-out prison so as to include duties in relation to a prisoner who is temporarily outside such a prison. This is designed simply to ensure that prisoner custody officers are acting within their duties in supervising prisoners temporarily outside the prison on home leave or on a local prison farm or in hospital, to take three examples given by the minister (*Hansard*, Commons, Standing Committee B, 17 February 1994, col. 803).

6.4   Floating Prisons

Although it had been hoped that the prison population would possibly decrease and certainly not rise as a result of the CJA 1991, since the amendments introduced by the CJA 1993, the prison population has been rising inexorably again toward the 50,000 mark. In case the prison building and privatisation programme should prove unable to cope with future increases in the prison population, thus causing the sort of overcrowding which is unacceptable on a number of grounds and which contributed to the Strangeways riot and other disturbances in 1990, the Home Office asked the prison service to look at contingency plans to deal with any sudden surges in the prison population. One of the options of last resort which could be used would be floating prisons or 'maritime detention facilities' which have been used in the United States. The nearest we have come to this in recent years in this country was in 1987 when the *Earl William* was used to house Tamil refugees off Harwich in 1987 and unfortunately broke loose during a storm and the use of the *Maidstone* as a prison ship in Belfast Lough in the 1970's. The government defended the provision in s. 100 CJPOA (which amends s. 33 of the Prison Act 1952) enabling the Secretary of State to declare to be a prison a 'floating structure or part of such a structure' on the basis that:

> ... the Prison Service intends to use floating structures solely as a contingency measure to relieve any overcrowding.... It is right to plan ahead for contingencies. We want to ensure that any structures which are used, built or hired meet the high standards set by the Prison Service. Those standards will need to ensure that the facilities are secure, that prisoners can be properly kept and that, in an emergency, there can be proper access and egress. Given those assurances, it is right to include the clause in the Bill, to put beyond doubt the status of any maritime detention facilities should they be needed. (*Hansard*, Commons, Standing Committee B, 17 February 1994, cols. 826 and 828.)

The director general of the Prison Service, Derek Lewis, is on record as saying that prison ships would be the last resort after exhausting police cells and army camps and it does not appear that there any imminent plans to commission the construction of prison ships. Should the prison population continue to rise, the statutory authority is clearly now in place.

6.5 Contracting out in Scotland and Northern Ireland

As far as England and Wales are concerned, the Act of Parliament governing contracting out of prisons and escort services is still the CJA 1991 as amended by the CJPOA 1994 provisions discussed above. The 1991 Act did not apply to Scotland or Northern Ireland but chapter II of Part VIII of the CJPOA (ss. 102 to 117) effectively reproduces the 1991 provisions as amended in a form that makes them effective for Scotland. Putting aside the differences in the legal framework that these provisions have to fit into (e.g., that references in Scotland are to the Prisons (Scotland) Act 1989 instead of to the Prison Act 1952) these provisions more clearly set out the statutory framework for privatisation than do the complex amendments to the 1991 Act applying to England and Wales. In that sense they may be of interest south of the Border as giving an idea of how the amended English provisions would look but detailed discussion of their application to Scotland is beyond the scope of this work. Progress on privatisation in Scotland appears likely to be at a somewhat slower pace than in England and Wales and it has apparently been agreed that at this stage there will not be market testing of existing prisons but that the private sector should be invited to tender for a new DCMF prison.

Northern Ireland is in a slightly different position. Chapter III of part VIII of the CJPOA 1994 (ss. 118 to 125) makes provision for the contracting out of prisoner escort arrangements on a similar basis to that applicable in England and Wales and Scotland. There are, however, no provisions authorising the contracting out of the running or provision of prisons themselves. It should not be supposed from this that the government has ruled out private prisons for Northern Ireland either on the grounds of the special security situation there or for any other reason. It was not necessary to legislate on this topic because it is possible to provide authority for prison privatisation under the Order in Council procedure by which much Northern Ireland legislation is made. No such Order in Council has yet been made and much may depend on the effect on the overall size of the prison population of the peace process currently underway.

6.6   Secure Training Centres

Part I of the CJPOA 1994 creates the new sentence of a secure training order for young offenders of 12, 13 or 14 (see chapter 1 of this Guide) and the period of detention under such an order will normally be served in a secure training centre. No such secure training centres currently exist and the intention is to provide five of them initially via the private sector. Sections 5 to 15 of the CJPOA 1994 accordingly provide the framework for the provision of such centres via the private sector in much the same way that the CJA 1991 as amended by part VII of the CJPOA 1994 provides the framework for the contracting out of the provision and/or running of prisons. The provisions are very similar except for details such as that secure training centres will have custody officers rather than prisoner custody officers (since it is children and young persons who are being detained and trained rather than 'prisoners'). Just as with privatised prisons, each centre will have a director appointed by the contractor rather than a governor, with a monitor appointed by the Secretary of State to keep the running of the centre under review and to report to the Secretary or State. Schedule 1 to the CJPOA 1994 provides for escort arrangements in relation to offenders detained at a secure training centre and sch. 2 provides for the training and certification of custody officers.

Although s. 11 envisages the possibility of directly managed secure training centres, the current plans are that they will all be contracted out to the private sector both in their construction and their running. Five potential 'preferred' sites have been identified on government-owned land for which planning permission is currently being sought, the locations being County Durham, Nottinghamshire, Northants, Oxfordshire and Kent although there are apparently reserve locations should any insuperable difficulties be experienced in relation to any one of these. Given the current state of progress it is difficult to see any of the sites being operational much before 1996 at the earliest. Each secure training centre will accommodate 40 children and the total cost per year once all five are up and running, including the cost of supervision in the community for the second half of the sentence, is estimated at around £30 million a year.

The unease that many people feel at the contracting out of prisons for adults is accentuated when the responsibility for keeping children in secure conditions is put in the hands of private enterprise. The Home Affairs Committee in its 1993 report on juvenile offenders (HC 441) was of the view (at para. 158) that the Home Office needed to learn from the lessons of privatisation of the Prison Service before granting any contracts for secure training centres. There are of course safeguards built in such as the role of the monitor and although the centres will not be visited by the Chief Inspector of Prisons, s. 6(3) of the CJPOA 1994 provides for rules to be made under the Prison Act 1952 for the inspection of centres and the appointment of independent visitors. The inspections will be carried out by Department of Health inspectors (who are already responsible for inspecting local authority secure accommodation) but they will report to the Home Office.

The specifications for the centres will require proper education and training to be provided consistent with the National Curriculum and will be designed to enable the trainees to re-integrate into school life on release. Earl Ferrers sought to reassure those concerned about the establishment of secure training centres (*Hansard*, Lords, 16 May 1994, cols. 52–4):

> ... secure training centres will not be part of the prison system. The staff will not wear prison uniforms. The staff in the centres will include trained teachers. They will be required to have the skills and experience to provide welfare and care work. The centres will be required to develop policies and systems to prevent bullying and self-harm. As part of the assessment procedure the centres will work with probation officers and social services staff who are involved with the offenders.
>
> Some noble lords said that units for 40 people were too large. There will be small living units of eight to 10 places, individual bedrooms and intensive staffing. Those will be vital components in ensuring that a subculture of bullying does not emerge among the children. Contractors will be required to assess offenders on arrival at a centre for the risk of suicide and self-harm and to operate a monitoring policy. The Home Office monitor will ensure that those requirements are met and satisfactorily carried out.
>
> In line with the principles of the Children Act, children in secure training centres will have free access to an independent complaints investigator....
>
> As regards education, the centres will provide 25 hours of education [per week]. Each youngster will be assessed on his educational attainment and will receive a broad and balanced curriculum appropriate to his needs. There will be liaison with the youngster's local education authority when he returns to mainstream education on release. The education staff will be trained and experienced in teaching this age group.

Despite these reassurances, critics remain unconvinced and point also to the difficulties caused by the fact that only five centres will mean that families and other visitors will have to travel a long way to keep in touch with children in the centres. To try to meet this point, it has been stated that the Assisted Visits Scheme will be further extended in relation to secure training centres to provide travelling expenses for weekly rather than fortnightly visits as would normally be the case. Nevertheless the practical and logistical difficulties involved in travelling substantial distances to visit will remain. The arguments for and against secure training centres and for and against them being provided by the private sector will not be fully resolved for some time until the first ones have been constructed and are up and running. Only time will tell whether they are an efficient, progressive and cost-effective solution to the problem of young offenders for whom the system has exhausted all other options or whether they will prove to be an expensive and temporary experiment with a group of vulnerable and disturbed children.

6.7   Employment Status of Prison Officers

Prison officers in England and Wales have the powers and duties of a constable under s. 8 of the Prison Act 1952. This status is useful to them in carrying out their duties and gives them also a certain amount of protection whilst so doing. However, it has also gradually been recognised that it means that they do not legally have the status of employees or 'workers' as far as employment rights are concerned because they are in 'police service' and furthermore that the organisation representing them, the Prison Officers Association (POA), is not legally a trade union enjoying the legal immunities normally available to such a body in respect of properly called industrial action. Not all these legal facts had been fully appreciated by either the POA or the Home Office until the Home Office successfully applied for an injunction to restrain threatened strike action in November 1993 (*Home Office* v *POA* (1993) *The Times*, 19 November 1993).

Sections 126 to 128 of the CJPOA 1994 are designed to clarify the situation following this case (which being a claim for an interlocutory injunction did not fully resolve all the legal issues). Section 126(1) effectively gives individual prison officers the status of an employee or worker for the purposes of the Employment Protection (Consolidation) Act 1978 and the Trade Union and Labour Relations (Consolidation) Act 1992. This ensures that prison officers will have the same rights as any other employee in relation to matters such as unfair dismissal, redundancy, maternity rights and gives them the right of access to Industrial Tribunals thus reversing the effect of *Home Office* v *Robinson & POA* [1981] IRLR 524. It also restores trade union status to bodies representing prison officers and, by virtue of s. 126(4), does so retrospectively 'except for the purpose of validating anything that would have been a contravention of section 127(1) below'. Section 127(1) provides that:

A person contravenes this section if he induces a prison officer—
    (a)   to withhold his services as such an officer; or
    (b)   to commit a breach of discipline.

The net result is that the status of the trade unions and the legality of all the contracts and other arrangements into which they might have entered over the years is fully restored except that any illegal strike calls remain illegal whether these be in the past or the future. The opposition pressed for past industrial action, which was taken in good faith in the belief that the POA was properly regarded as a trade union, to be retrospectively legalised and although the government was unwilling to concede this point it did give the following assurance (*Hansard*, Commons, Standing Committee B, 22 February 1994, col. 883):

The government have no intention of raking over earlier disputes, or of initiating proceedings in respect of anything which took place before the matters referred to in the injunctions, but previous calls to industrial action – some of which were serious and may have been unlawful at the time – should not be rendered lawful in retrospect.

As to the future, the government is clearly not going to allow industrial action by the unions to take place and s. 127(3) expressly confers on the Home Secretary the right to compensation for any loss or damage caused as result of any breach of s. 127(1). The newly clarified status of the POA and similar bodies as trade unions as a result of s. 126 provides no immunity from liability under s. 127 as is made clear by s. 127(8). It should be noted that the prohibition on inducing industrial action in s. 127 applies equally to private-sector prisoner custody officers (i.e., whether performing custodial duties at privatised or directly managed prisons or performing escort functions) and to custody officers within part I of the CJPOA 1994 (at secure training centres).

Having removed the right of the prison officer trade unions to take industrial action it is necessary to make some provision to take account of their reduced bargaining power in the determination of salaries and related terms and conditions Section 128 of the CJPOA 1994 addresses this point but merely provides authority for the Secretary of State to make regulations setting up a procedure (after consultation) but does not specify the detailed content of those regulations and whether, for example, they should include an independent pay review body. The regulations will apply to rates of pay etc. in the 'prison service' but this does not include custody officers or prisoner custody officers in the private sector (see s. 128(5)) despite the fact that s. 127 (making industrial action unlawful) does apply to them. This appears to put them in a particularly vulnerable position but the government appears not to be terribly sympathetic on this issue. The minister was quite frank:

> ... the government will not establish a pay review body for all the different companies that could be involved in the private sector. That would be nonsense. It is up to those companies to determine pay and conditions for their staff. We are creating powers to give a right of action against anyone who induces another to strike or to withhold his services or commit a breach of discipline. If a person joins the private sector knowing those conditions, and if he does not like them, I suggest that he gets a job somewhere else. (*Hansard*, Commons, Standing Committee B, 22 February 1994, col. 906.)

6.8   Powers of Testing for Drugs in Prisons and of Searching for Unauthorised Property

Sections 152 and 153 were both added to the Bill at committee stage in the House of Commons (*Hansard*, Commons, Standing Committee B, 1 March 1994, col. 1062) but they are quite different in their scope. Section 151 gives powers to *prison officers* to require a sample of urine in order to test for drugs. Section 152 by contrast is concerned to give an 'authorised employee' who is not a prison officer power to search prisoners for unauthorised property. By inserting a new s. 8A into the Prison Act 1952, it will give prison governors the power to authorise non-prison officer grades to carry out 'rub-down' searches for concealed items such as knives or sharp implements. It will be used, for example, where prisoners have been supervised in a workshop or kitchen by civilian grades and means that they can be searched when leaving the area without having to deploy prison officers who may be better deployed elsewhere. Staff authorised to conduct such searches will need training and the power to search does not extend to intimate or strip searches, see the new s. 8A(2)(a), although reasonable force may be used. The power to authorise this type of search will not apply in contracted out prisons – see CJPOA 1994, sch. 10, para. 68.

Section 151 inserts a new s. 16A into the Prison Act 1952 and only gives potential powers to prison officers (which for this purpose includes prisoner custody officers in the private sector). If an authorisation by the governor at the prison (or the director at a contracted-out prison – see CJPOA 1994, sch. 10, para. 69) is in force, a urine sample can be required under s. 16A(1). No power to compel the taking of the sample is given by the section and it would seem that the only sanction would be disciplinary action against the prisoner. Section 16A(2) permits the authorisation also to provide the power to require other sorts of samples (but not other intimate ones) instead of or in addition to urine but this would exclude the most obvious alternative sample that may be required, i.e., a sample of blood.

6.9   The Parole Board: Incorporation and Functions

The changes to the parole system in the CJA 1991 Act made the Parole Board less of an advisory body to the Home Secretary and gave it more power to make executive decisions of its own. Although the Home Secretary still has the final say in relation to mandatory lifers and those serving seven years or more, the Parole Board's decisions on the release of discretionary life sentence prisoners and on prisoners sentenced to between four and seven years are now binding. With the abolition of the local review committees it now has responsibility for around 5,500 interviews per year. Section 149 of the CJPOA 1994 accordingly marks the Board's increased independence from the Home Secretary by making it a body corporate and sch. 10, para. 70, substitutes a new sch. 5 in the CJA 1991 setting out the Board's new legal status. The provisions in the schedule governing the membership of the Board are, however, unchanged.

Section 50 of the CJA 1991 enabled certain amendments to be made by statutory instrument to various other sections of the Act so as to give the Parole Board the effective final say on matters which still remained under the primary legislation ultimately for the Home Secretary to decide. Under s. 50(2), SI 1992/1829 gave the Parole Board the final say under s. 35 on the release of long-term prisoners sentenced to less than seven years and this appears to have worked well. However, s. 50(4) which enabled the Parole Board similarly to have the final and exclusive right to recall the same category of prisoners (under s. 39 of the CJA 1991) from release on licence has caused difficulties especially where quick decisions needed to be taken out of office hours. The Parole Board has agreed that it would be preferable if this function should revert to the Home Office for all those serving long-term sentences and so s. 150 of the CJPOA 1994 repeals s. 50(4) of the CJA 1991 and makes a consequential amendment to s. 50(1). It should be remembered that under s. 39(5) of the CJA 1991, the Parole Board still retains the final say on whether an offender who has been recalled from release on licence by the Home Secretary should be immediately released again.

Chapter Seven
Miscellaneous Changes

This chapter deals with a number of issues covered in the CJPOA 1994 which do not fall neatly within the ambit of earlier chapters. This Act, like earlier Criminal Justice Acts, covers a great deal of ground and makes changes to many different areas of criminal justice. The Bill, on its passage through Parliament, was also subject to a range of small individual amendments on specific matters of current concern. Many of these changes, while of importance in their own context, are unlikely to make a significant impact upon the operation of the criminal justice system as a whole. Several of these miscellaneous matters are considered below, ranging from the introduction of new offences directed at the intimidation of jurors and witnesses and the obtaining of computer-held personal information, to the further regulation of the scientific use of cells taken from embryos or foetuses, to the creation of new offences relating to ticket touts and taxi touts.

7.1 Intimidation of Jurors and Witnesses

Section 51 creates two new offences of intimidating a juror or witness, and harming, or threatening to harm, a juror or witness. The maximum penalty for these offences is five years' imprisonment on indictment, a fine or both; six months' imprisonment summarily and/or a fine not exceeding the statutory maximum (s. 51(6)).

According to the Home Secretary (*Hansard*, Commons, 11 January 1994, col. 29):

> We need to make it clear that intimidating those who assist the criminal justice process will not be tolerated. The law already takes a serious view of such behaviour, but there is scope to do more, particularly in relation to activity before and after the period when a trial is in progress. That is why the Bill creates new offences which will make it easier to bring to justice those who intimidate or take revenge on people for assisting the police or acting as witnesses or jurors in a criminal trial.

There are two offences.

The first offence, under s. 51(1), is established where A does an act which intimidates (and which A intends to intimidate) B, knowing or believing that B is assisting in the investigation of an offence, or is a witness or potential witness, or a juror or potential juror, and A intends thereby to cause the investigation or the course of justice to be obstructed, perverted or interfered with. By s. 51(4) the intimidation may take the form of a physical threat to B, a threat to B's property, or a financial threat. Section 51(7) eases the burden on the prosecution by stating that where the fact of the intimidation is proved, and the requisite knowledge or belief is established, A is presumed, until the contrary is proved, to have done the act with the intention of interfering with the course of justice. Section 51(5) further provides that this intention need not have been the only or the predominating intention with which the intimidation was done. Thus, for example, the offence would be made out even though A had a profound belief in the innocence of the person on trial, and believed that B was intending to commit perjury to secure that person's conviction.

Section 51(1) seems to cover nothing which could not have been perfectly well dealt with under the earlier law, which is itself unaffected by the introduction of the new offence. Section 51(11) states that the new offence is in addition to, and not in derogation of, any offence subsisting at common law. Cases of intimidation of witnesses and jurors have routinely been prosecuted as conduct tending to pervert the course of justice (a common law offence triable only on indictment), or as contempt of court, though of course those offences also extend to conduct which falls well outside the scope of the new s. 51(1). Bribery of a juror, for example, would fall outside the scope of the new offences, but is covered by the common law offence of embracery, or may be dealt with as a contempt of court (*Owen* [1976] 1 WLR 840). The making of a payment to a witness to encourage that witness to commit perjury would not constitute intimidation and hence would fall outside s. 51(1), but would amount to a contempt of court (*Attorney-General v Hislop* [1991] 1 QB 514). More generally, in *Toney* (1993) 97 Cr App R 176, the Court of Appeal said that where A seeks to prevent B from giving evidence, or seeks to procure false evidence from B, A is guilty of tending to pervert the course of justice, even where no bribe, threat, undue pressure or unlawful means was used. Suppose that A claims that his motive for approaching B was to dissuade B from giving evidence which A knew or believed to be false. This issue was discussed by the Court of Appeal in *Kellett* [1976] QB 372 and considered further in *Toney*. It seems that a conviction may be obtained in such a case if A resorted to improper methods, but the use of mere persuasion might not constitute a perversion of the course of justice. Again s. 51(1) adds nothing to the law. In the absence of intimidation there is no offence, but where there is intimidation the presence of a motive to prevent B from committing perjury would not avail A (see the discussion of s. 51(5) above). In the context of the earlier law, as confirmed in *Toney*, it is difficult to see what useful purpose is achieved by placing the offence in s. 51(1) on the statute book.

The second offence, under s. 51(2), is established where A harms or threatens to harm (and intends to harm) B, knowing or believing that B, or some other person, has assisted in the investigation of an offence, or has given evidence, or has acted as a juror, and this is the motive for A's harming or threatening B. Such harm may be physical injury, damage to property, or financial harm (s. 51(4)). Section 51(8) eases the burden on the prosecution by stating that where the harmful act is proved, and the requisite knowledge or belief is established, A is presumed, until the contrary is proved, to have done the act with the motive required. Section 51(5) further provides that this motive need not have been the only or the predominating reason for which the act was done.

The offence under s. 51(2), being directed to the harming, or threatening to harm, a witness or juror *after the trial has come to an end*, may offer something new to the prosecutor. It must be doubted how far a prosecution for perverting the course of justice would lie when a juror or witness is harmed or threatened after the close of the trial. In *Attorney-General* v *Butterworth* [1963] 1 QB 696 it was said to be a contempt of court to assault a witness after he had given evidence, but contempt of court would not seem to be an appropriate charge in relation to incidents taking place once the trial itself is over. Recently, in *Attorney-General* v *Judd, The Times*, 15 August 1994, the Divisional Court held that a contempt of court was committed where the defendant, *two days* after being convicted at Croydon Crown Court, had sought out a member of the jury, intimidated her, and asked her to write to the trial judge to say that she had been mistaken about his guilt. Otherwise, the issue seems to have been little discussed in the cases, perhaps because where a witness or juror has been harmed or put in fear there is the obvious possibility of a prosecution for assault. Section 51(2) in principle sets *no limit* to the length of time which can elapse after the trial is concluded but within which a prosecution for this new offence may be brought. There is a curious provision in s. 51(8), which says that where A has been shown to have harmed, or to have threatened to harm, B within 'the relevant period' then A can be presumed, unless the contrary is proved, to have had the motive required by the subsection. 'The relevant period' for these purposes is defined in s. 51(9), and varies in accordance with whether B was (a) a witness or juror in the proceedings, or (b) a person who assisted in the investigation of the offence but did not appear as a witness, or (c) did both. The relevant periods are, for (a), from the institution of proceedings to a date 12 months after the trial (including any subsequent appeal) was concluded; for (b) a period of 12 months from date of the assistance given; and for (c) from the date of any assistance given until a date 12 months after the trial (including any subsequent appeal) was concluded. The effect of s. 51(8) and (9) is to ease the burden of proof for the prosecution in respect of an offence alleged under s. 51(2) which took place within that period. It is important to realise, however, that the offence under s. 51(2) is *not confined* to cases of harm or threatened harm which occurred within the relevant period. It is simply that where the alleged harm or threat occurred outside that period, the prosecution cannot rely upon the presumption in s. 51(8). It would be possible to gain a conviction for the offence under s. 51(2) in a case where A, having been convicted on the evidence of witness B, and having served a life sentence, sought out B on his release many years later, and assaulted him.

7.2 Obtaining Information Held on Computer

Pressure for the creation of a new offence in this area arose because of the existence of various commercial agencies in the country which offer to sell, at a price, confidential information about the private affairs of others. This whole matter originally came to light as a result of various investigations by the press. See, for example, 'Private lives for sale in illicit info-market', *Sunday Times*, 18 July 1993. In a commercial circular referred to in the House of Lords by Lord Brightman, who was pressing hard for the creation of a new offence in this area, the agency concerned was offering to obtain a person's bank balance for £245, a copy of his last bank statement for £1,000, his salary for £200, and his pension details for £200 (*Hansard*, Lords, 12 July 1994, col. 1668).

Confidential information of the kind described may be obtained by a number of different means. If the agency has obtained it by intentionally gaining unauthorised access to information held on a computer, there would be liability for the hacking offence under the Computer Misuse Act 1990, s. 1. If the agency obtained it by enlisting the help of a compliant insider at the bank, criminal liability could attach to that insider (and the bank) under the Data Protection Act 1984, s. 5(2) and (3). These subsections deal, *inter alia*, with the disclosure by a person or an organisation registered under the 1984 Act to hold personal data, to any person who is not listed in the relevant entry in the register (see further on s. 5, I. Lloyd, *Information Technology Law*, 1993). More generally, however, the dishonest obtaining of confidential information falls outside the scope of the offence of theft (see *Oxford* v *Moss* (1978) 68 Cr App R 183) and the various deception offences in the Theft Acts. Thus there would seem to be no offence committed where an outsider deceives an employee into thinking that the inquirer is entitled to the information he is asking for. The *Sunday Times* found cases where, for example, an agent obtained ex-directory telephone numbers by convincing BT office staff that he was a BT engineer. He did so by using identification numbers, and drivers' names, both of which are openly on display in BT service vehicles. Medical records have been obtained by an agent telephoning a GP or receptionist and pretending to be an official from the local health authority.

In light of the expressed view of the Director of Public Prosecutions that the obtaining of personal financial information and its sale for profit might well in these circumstances not be a criminal offence, an amendment was moved in the House of Lords to create a new offence designed to close the gap. The clause as drafted would have made it an offence, punishable with up to five years' imprisonment, 'for a person to sell or offer to sell information as to the financial affairs of another person' if that information was obtained dishonestly or by deception and without the consent of the person concerned. The government opposed this suggestion, preferring to move by way of amendment to the Data Protection Act 1984, so as to make the wrongful procurement of computer-held personal information an offence. This route to reform had already been suggested by Mr Eric Howe, then the Data Protection Registrar (see further the comments of Earl Ferrers, *Hansard*, Lords, 12 July 1994, col. 1670). Initially the Lords voted for Lord Brightman's offence, but when the Bill returned to the Commons the government's wishes prevailed. The Lords' offence was struck out, and replaced by s. 161 which inserts new subsections (6) to (11) into s. 5 of the Data Protection Act 1984. The new subsection (6) states that:

A person who procures the disclosure to him of personal data the disclosure of which to him is in contravention of subsection (2) or (3) above, knowing or having reason to believe that the disclosure constitutes such a contravention, shall be guilty of an offence.

This offence will cover procuring the disclosure of any kind of personal data held on a computer. Dishonestly gaining access to medical (or any other) records which are held manually, rather than on a computer, will still not be an offence. It may also be noted that while the Lords' offence would have attracted a maximum penalty of five years, the offence in subsection (6), in line with the other offences in s. 5 of the 1984 Act, is punishable only by way of a fine (Data Protection Act 1984, s. 19).

The offence is committed where the defendant 'knew or had reason to believe' that the disclosure constituted a contravention. This makes the offence one where negligence is sufficent fault for liability. Indeed, the standard for liability may be lower still, since subsection (11) states that a person's belief that he or she had 'reasonable grounds' for making the disclosure shall be disregarded. Institution of proceedings under s. 5 requires the consent of the DPP (s. 19(1)). Subsections (7) to (11), also inserted into s. 5 of the 1984 Act by s. 161 of the 1994 Act, extend liability to a person who sells, or offers to sell, personal data which has been *obtained by him* in contravention of subsection (6). This wording does not seem apt to cover the seller of personal data in a case where some other person has procured the disclosure of the data and then passed it on to him to sell.

In contrast to the new offence under subsection (6), the original Lords' proposal would not have been limited to personal data held on computer. On the other hand the Lords' offence was limited to information relating to 'financial' matters, so that it would not have covered the dishonest obtaining of a person's medical records, whether they were held on computer or not.

Section 162 of the 1994 Act makes a minor amendment to the Computer Misuse Act 1990, s. 10. Section 10 is a 'saving provision', which prevents certain investigative activities of the police and other law enforcement agencies amounting to offences under the 1990 Act. A number of enactments provide powers of access for law enforcement agencies to computer records (e.g., PACE 1984, s. 19 and s. 20; Children Act 1989, s. 63). Where the authorities gain access to computer records in pursuance of their statutory powers they, by virtue of s. 10, commit no offence. The amendment to s. 10 effected by s. 162 of the 1994 Act clarifies and strengthens that protection. A notice purporting to deny a police officer access to a computer system will not in itself render such an access unauthorised under the 1990 Act.

7.3 Copyright and Illicit Recordings

Section 107 of the Copyright, Designs and Patents Act 1988 creates various offences relating to commercial dealing in infringing copies of copyright works of which pirate video and sound recordings are important examples in this context. Section 198 creates very similar offences relating to illicit recordings of performances (bootleg recordings). No special provision was made for the enforcement of these offences, which was left in the hands of the police or private prosecutions. In practice, trading standards officers have been very active against those dealing in pirate and bootleg videos, using their powers under the Trade Descriptions Act 1968. This was possible because usually the pirate videos or records by their packaging (which itself would often infringe copyright) would be made to appear to be the authorised versions released by the record and film companies and this constituted a false trade description which enabled trading standards to intervene to protect consumers who were being misled into purchasing inferior-quality recordings believing they were buying authorised top-quality versions. However, in *Kent County Council* v *Price* (1993) 157 JP 1161, the Divisional Court held that there is no offence under the Trade Descriptions Act 1968 where a trader sells counterfeit goods under a well-known trade mark if an effective disclaimer is used. Although this was concerned with goods infringing trade marks (counterfeits) rather than goods infringing copyright (pirates) it was thought that the same principle would apply to take pirate copies of copyright works, including records and tapes, outside the Trade Descriptions Act 1968 where there was a similar disclaimer. Section 165 of the CJPOA 1994 therefore inserts new ss. 107A and 198A into the Copyright, Designs and Patents Act 1988 which confer on local weights and measures authorities (trading standards departments) the duties of enforcing s. 107 and s. 198 in their own areas. The new sections also confer on them relevant powers under the Trade Descriptions Act 1968 (e.g., to make test purchases and seize goods) to enable them to carry out these duties just as they did previously acting directly under the 1968 Act. A similar provision was enacted in s. 93 of the Trade Marks Act 1994 in relation to the enforcement of the offences under s. 92 of that Act thus reinstating the jurisdiction of trading standards officers in the very situation found in *Kent County Council* v *Price*.

7.4   Football Ticket Touts

It is made a new summary offence by s. 166 of the CJPOA 1994 for an unauthorised person to sell, or to offer to sell, a ticket for a designated football match, in any public place (or, if in the course of a trade or business, in any other place). The maximum penalty is a fine not exceeding level 5 (s. 166(3)).

The idea for this offence originated in the report by Lord Justice Taylor (as he then was) on the Hillsborough Stadium Disaster (Cm 962, 1990). Lord Justice Taylor noted that sometimes, before important matches, many fans travelled to the game without a ticket, in the hope of obtaining one from a tout outside the ground. Touts would, of course, sell to the highest bidder. This situation could lead to confrontation and violence and would also tend to frustrate the efforts of clubs to keep rival supporters in separate parts of the ground. His conclusion was that 'the presence and activities of touts have a grossly antisocial effect leading both directly and indirectly to disorder'. Proposal No. 70 in the report was that it should be made an offence to 'sell tickets for and on the day of a football match without authority from the home club to do so' (p. 82). Section 166 implements this proposal.

This new offence completes the legislative implementation of four new offences recommended in the Taylor Report. The other three (the throwing of missiles, the chanting of obscene or racist abuse, and going on to the playing area without reasonable excuse) were implemented by the Football (Offences) Act 1991. These offences, as well as the new ticket tout offence, extend to 'designated' football matches, a term which is defined in the Football Offences (Designation of Football Matches) Order 1991 (SI 1991/1565) as covering any UEFA club or national team competition played at either a sports ground designated under the Safety of Sports Grounds Act 1975 or the ground of a member of the Football League or the Football Association Premier League.

Section 166(2) states that a person is 'unauthorised' to sell tickets, unless he or she is authorised in writing to do so by the home club or by the organisers of the match. Section 166(4) makes this an offence for which the police may arrest without warrant. Section 166(5) gives the police power, on reasonable suspicion, to search persons, premises or vehicles for evidence relating to the offence. It should be noted that the offence is *not* restricted (as was the Taylor proposal) to sales on the day of the match.

In an amendment tabled in the House of Lords by Lord Donoghue (*Hansard*, Lords, 20 June 1994, col. 144), it was argued that the ambit of the new offence in s. 166 should be extended to all sporting events at which 6,000 or more tickets are issued for sale. Lord Donoghue accepted that while of course Lord Justice Taylor's recommendation was made in the context of football matches, public order concerns were not limited to such venues. Lord Donoghue said:

> We do not wish to burden the police and authorities with regulating smaller events where there is normally no problem. But 6,000 is a number which covers both the No. 1 Court and the Centre Court at Wimbledon. It also clearly involves Twickenham, Cardiff Arms Park, Lord's, top golf, horse-race and motor-race venues. So it is targeted just to the areas where the problems exist.

He argued that it was 'deeply mistaken' to assume that 'ticket touting is a problem only in football', and that there was 'much evidence that ticket touting has been taken over by professional criminals in other sports'.

In a Parliamentary answer given on 16 June 1993, Mr Maclean had explained that, while the government had considered trying to outlaw the practice of ticket touting more generally, the conclusion was that 'it would not be appropriate for the criminal law to prohibit people from reselling tickets which they have lawfully obtained, any more than it would be appropriate to forbid people to sell their other possessions. Such an offence would in any event be unenforceable.' In line with these more cautious remarks, then, the 1994 Act does not incorporate Lord Donoghue's amendment in its entirety: instead s. 166(6) gives the Secretary of State power to make an order by statutory instrument to apply the new offence, with such modifications as seem appropriate, 'to such sporting event or category of sporting event for which 6,000 or more tickets are issued for sale as he thinks fit'.

Section 166(6) makes it clear that such an order could only be made where 6,000 or more tickets have been issued for sale for the day on which the event, or part of the event, takes place. Thus, say, a cricket match scheduled to extend over several days could only come within the scope of subsection (6) where tickets issued for a particular day (rather than all the days together) totalled 6,000 or more. It should be noted that subsection (6) extends only to sporting events: ticket touting in respect of other events, such as theatrical performances, is not covered by the offence. This appears to be consistent with the underlying concern of the section, which is not ticket touting as such, but the public order problems which may be associated with it.

Section 166 came into force on the date of the passing of the Act (3 November 1994). No order can be made under subsection (6) unless a draft of the order has been laid before, and approved by a resolution of, each House of Parliament (s. 172(5)).

7.5 Taxi Touts

Section 167 of the Act creates a new summary offence of touting for hire car services. This section came about as a result of an amendment tabled in the Lords by Lord Rodger of Earlsferry (*Hansard*, Lords, 20 June 1994, col. 153). According to Lord Rodger the purpose of the offence is to allow the police to take effective action against people who tout for passengers in vehicles acting as unlicensed taxis. His lordship identified two aspects of what was perceived to be 'a serious problem, particularly in London'. The first was that of the tout who 'preys on strangers and tourists, especially at railway stations and at airports ... such people set out to fleece their victims and if they protest about the charges that are eventually levied, then the passengers are likely to lose their luggage, if nothing worse'. The second is where touts offer the services of minicabs or private hire vehicles in the street: 'in those circumstances the car is being used as an unlicensed taxi and there is always a risk that the driver may have no valid insurance'.

The offence under s. 167 is punishable by a fine not exceeding level 4 on the standard scale (s. 167(5)). By s. 167(7) this offence is made an offence for which the police may arrest without warrant. This is achieved by insertion of a new para. (j) in s. 24(2) of PACE 1984.

Section 167 came into force on the date of the passing of the Act (3 November 1994).

7.6   Offences Aggravated by Firearm Possession: Robbery

By para. 8 of sch. 9 to the CJPOA 1994, amendment is made to sch. 1 to the Firearms Act 1968, which specifies the offences to which s. 17(2) of that Act applies. Section 17(2) states that where a person committing a specified offence has in his or her possession at the time of committing the offence or being arrested for the offence a firearm or imitation firearm, he or she is guilty of an offence under the subsection, unless he or she shows that the weapon was carried for a lawful object. Paragraph 8 inserts 'robbery' into the list of offences specified in sch. 1 to the 1968 Act.

This rectifies an anomaly, since it seems that the offence of robbery was omitted from sch. 1 by oversight. This matter was drawn to the attention of Parliament by the Court of Appeal in *Guy* (1991) 93 Cr App R 108. The court in that case nonetheless managed to uphold a conviction under s. 17 since, although robbery did not appear in the schedule, the offence of theft did appear there, and robbery necessarily included theft. Also by para. 8, offences under the CJA 1991, s. 90(1) (assaulting a prisoner custody officer), and under the CJPOA 1994, s. 13(1) (assaulting a secure training centre custody officer), are to be included within sch. 1 to the 1968 Act. The offence under s. 90(1) had already been included within the scope of s. 17(2) of the 1968 Act, be virtue of s. 90(2) of the 1991 Act, but it seems that the government wanted to make the matter doubly clear by specific amendment to the text of sch. 1 to the 1968 Act, which had not been made by s. 90(2).

For changes to firearms penalties see 1.22.

7.7   Prohibition on use of Female Germ Cells from Human Embryos or Foetuses

Section 156 of the CJPOA 1994 amends the Human Fertilisation and Embryology Act 1990, by the insertion of a new s. 3A into that Act providing that:

(1)   No person shall, for the purposes of providing fertility services for any woman, use female germ cells taken or derived from an embryo or a foetus or use embryos created by using such cells.

The purpose of the provision is to prevent the use of eggs being taken from aborted female foetuses, for fertilisation in a test tube and insertion into women who wish to become pregnant. Such 'eggs for fertilisation' procedure is apparently not yet scientifically possible, though eggs drawn from aborted mice have been fertilised in this way and within a relatively short time span (estimates vary from two to 10 years) the process will become possible with human beings. To allow this procedure would clearly have very serious consequences for the child, since it would at some point have to be explained to it that its mother had not been allowed to be born. It was pointed out in the course of Parliamentary debate that the child could not know what its mother looked like, what her attributes were, or what her medical history might have been had she been allowed to live. There was also concern expressed that to allow the practice might start a lucrative market in aborted foetuses: becoming pregnant so that the aborted foetus could be used in this way might be a new way of making money. According to Dame Jill Knight, who sponsored this clause, the wording will:

> ... apply to all current and all expected future techniques for treating infertility, such as *in vitro* fertilisation and transplants of foetal ovarian tissue, or the use of early female germ cells from an embryo before the ovaries have developed. The new clause is a catch-all, intended to stop what I have described as an abhorrent practice.

The Health Secretary, Virginia Bottomley, said that the acceptance of the amendment showed the strength of feeling on the issue. She added that 'I share the widespread feeling of revulsion at the notion'.

Despite this 'widespread feeling' it may be objected, first, that a single provision on such a complex and emotive issue should have been inserted into a Bill dealing with entirely different matters and, second, that the amendment to the law has been made at the very time when the Human Fertilisation and Embryology Authority (a statutory body established by the government to consult public and scientific views on the appropriate use of foetal tissue) was involved in carrying out an extensive consultation exercise on this very issue at the government's request.

7.8 Closed-circuit Television Surveillance by Local Authorities

Section 163 of the CJPOA 1994 clarifies the legal position in relation to the use by local authorities outside London of closed-circuit television cameras in streets and other public places. The position in London is regulated by the London Local Authorities (No. 2) Act 1990, and s. 163 brings the powers of other councils into line by making it clear that a local authority may, after consultation with the relevant chief officer of police, incur expenditure by installing surveillance systems. When the clause which became s. 163 was introduced into the House of Lords by Baroness Flather (*Hansard*, Lords, 20 June 1994, col. 142) it proved to be uncontroversial since it was '... designed to help prevent crime and antisocial behaviour, and it should also reduce fear of crime'.

While these are certainly laudable objectives, and there are some recent figures to suggest that video surveillance can have a dramatic impact on the levels of vandalism and car theft (see, for example, the report 'Something to watch over you', *The Times*, 12 May 1994), there is concern over the 'Big Brother' element of public surveillance. In Birmingham in 1993, for example, councillors on the planning committee voted to prevent more surveillance cameras being installed in the city centre, because of 'intrusion into civil liberties' (news report, *The Times*, 2 June 1993). While it can be argued that surveillance in the street, in shopping centres and car parks, for example, does not infringe civil liberties, since these places are clearly in the public domain, the organisation Liberty has expressed concern over the unregulated spread of surveillance equipment, and has called for the introduction of clearer rules on how long the surveillance tapes can be kept, who has access to them and who can use them ('Pressure grows for controls on crime surveillance cameras', *The Times*, 3 June 1994). Nonetheless, in October 1994 the government announced an initiative whereby local authorities will be encouraged to bid for a share in a £2 million fund to install additional closed-circuit television systems.

7.9   Grants in Relation to Crime Prevention

Section 169 of the CJPOA 1994 gives the Home Secretary power to make, with the consent of the Treasury, and subject to such conditions as the Home Secretary or the Treasury think fit, payments or grants to such persons as the Home Secretary considers appropriate, in connection with measures intended to prevent crime or to reduce the fear of crime.

The government has stated that it does not expect this provision to have a significant financial effect.

7.10   Security Costs at Party Conferences

Section 170 of the CJPOA 1994 gives the Home Secretary power to pay, with the consent of the Treasury, grants towards expenditure incurred by any qualifying political party for the protection of persons or property in connection with a party conference held in Great Britain (but not in Northern Ireland), where those security measures have been certified by a chief police officer as having been appropriate. A political party qualifies for such a grant if at the last general election at least two of its members were elected to the House of Commons, or one member was so elected and not less than 150,000 votes were given to candidates of that party.

Prior to the implementation of s. 170, payments for security provisions at party conferences (outside Northern Ireland) have been made under a scheme which was announced by the then Prime Minister, Margaret Thatcher, in a Parliamentary written answer to Sir Ian Percival on 25 July 1986. Mrs Thatcher said:

> ... I am aware that since the bomb at the Grand Hotel, Brighton, in 1984, a number of heavy security costs, especially to do with searching, are now incurred by political parties in connection with their conferences. In the view of the Government, the continuation of party conferences is essential to the public interest and the cost of these exceptional precautions, which will not be necessary in every case, could not be borne entirely by the parties themselves. Following discussions through the usual channels, therefore, the Government propose that a contribution towards these expenses should be made from public funds.

In a written answer given to Mr Tony Banks on 23 November 1992, the Prime Minister set out the sums which had been claimed from central funds for security costs associated with conferences over the previous three years. The figures were, for the Conservative Party £274,500 (1989), £270,500 (1990) and £330,000 (1992), and for the Labour Party £70,500 (1989), £76,900 (1990) and £90,500 (1991). Figures recently released by the Home Office and reported in *The Times* on 21 October 1994, indicate rapidly escalating security costs for the Conservative conferences. In 1993 the figure was £1.5 million, and in 1994 it was £2.5 million (including the cost of a minesweeper cruising off the coast). The Labour Party conference cost £90,000 and the Liberal Democrat conference cost £3,500.

The government has stated, nonetheless, that it does not expect that this provision will have a significant financial effect.

Criminal Justice and Public Order Act 1994

CHAPTER 33

ARRANGEMENT OF SECTIONS

PART I   YOUNG OFFENDERS

Criminal Justice and Public Order Act 1994

An Act to make further provision in relation to criminal justice (including employment in the prison service); to amend or extend the criminal law and powers for preventing crime and enforcing that law; to amend the Video Recordings Act 1984; and for purposes connected with those purposes.

[3rd November 1994]

BE IT ENACTED by the Queen's most Excellent Majesty, by and with the advice and consent of the Lords Spiritual and Temporal, and Commons, in this present Parliament assembled, and by the authority of the same, as follows:—

PART I   YOUNG OFFENDERS

Secure training orders

1. Secure training orders

(1) Subject to section 8(1) of the Criminal Justice Act 1982 and section 53(1) of the Children and Young Persons Act 1933 (sentences of custody for life and long term detention), where—

(a) a person of not less than 12 but under 15 years of age is convicted of an imprisonable offence; and

(b) the court is satisfied of the matters specified in subsection (5) below, the court may make a secure training order.

(2) A secure training order is an order that the offender in respect of whom it is made shall be subject to a period of detention in a secure training centre followed by a period of supervision.

(3) The period of detention and supervision shall be such as the court determines and specifies in the order, being not less than six months nor more than two years.

(4) The period of detention which the offender is liable to serve under a secure training order shall be one half of the total period specified by the court in making the order.

(5) The court shall not make a secure training order unless it is satisfied—

(a) that the offender was not less than 12 years of age when the offence for which he is to be dealt with by the court was committed;

(b) that the offender has been convicted of three or more imprisonable offences; and

(c) that the offender, either on this or a previous occasion—

    (i)   has been found by a court to be in breach of a supervision order under the Children and Young Persons Act 1969, or

    (ii)   has been convicted of an imprisonable offence committed whilst he was subject to such a supervision order.

(6)   A secure training order is a custodial sentence for the purposes of sections 1 to 4 of the Criminal Justice Act 1991 (restrictions etc. as to custodial sentences).

(7)   Where a court makes a secure training order, it shall be its duty to state in open court that it is of the opinion that the conditions specified in subsection (5) above are satisfied.

(8)   In this section 'imprisonable offence' means an offence (not being one for which the sentence is fixed by law) which is punishable with imprisonment in the case of a person aged 21 or over.

(9)   For the purposes of this section, the age of a person shall be deemed to be that which it appears to the court to be after considering any available evidence.

(10)   This section shall have effect, as from the day appointed for each of the following paragraphs, with the substitution in subsections (1) and (5)—

    (a)   of '14' for '12';

    (b)   of '13' for '14';

    (c)   of '12' for '13';

but no substitution may be brought into force on more than one occasion.

2.   Secure training orders: supplementary provisions as to detention

(1)   The following provisions apply in relation to a person ('the offender') in respect of whom a secure training order ('the order') has been made under section 1.

(2)   Where accommodation for the offender at a secure training centre is not immediately available—

    (a)   the court may commit the offender to such place and on such conditions—

    (i)   as the Secretary of State may direct, or

    (ii)   as the Secretary of State may arrange with a person to whom this sub-paragraph applies,

and for such period (not exceeding 28 days) as the court may specify or until his transfer to a secure training centre, if earlier;

    (b)   if no such accommodation becomes or will become available before the expiry of the period of the committal the court may, on application, extend the period of committal (subject to the restriction referred to in paragraph (a) above); and

    (c)   the period of detention in the secure training centre under the order shall be reduced by the period spent by the offender in such a place.

(3)   The power conferred by subsection (2)(b) above may, subject to section 1(4), be exercised from time to time and the reference in subsection (2)(b) to the expiry of the period of the committal is, in the case of the initial extension, a reference to the expiry of the period of the committal under subsection (2)(a) above and, in the case of a further extension, a reference to the expiry of the period of the previous committal by virtue of this subsection.

(4)   Where the circumstances of the case require, the Secretary of State may transfer the offender from a secure training centre to such other place and on such conditions—

    (a)   as the Secretary of State may direct, or

    (b)   as the Secretary of State may arrange with a person to whom this paragraph applies;

and the period of detention in the secure training centre under the order shall be reduced by the period spent by the offender in such a place.

(5)   The persons to whom subsections (2)(a)(ii) and (4)(b) apply are local authorities, voluntary organisations and persons carrying on a registered children's home.

(6)   Where the Secretary of State is satisfied that exceptional circumstances exist which justify the offender's release on compassionate grounds he may release the offender from the secure training centre; and the offender shall, on his release, be subject to supervision for the remainder of the term of the order.

(7)   A person detained in pursuance of directions or arrangements made for his detention shall be deemed to be in legal custody.

(8)   In this section 'local authority', 'voluntary organisation' and 'registered children's home' have the same meaning as in the Children Act 1989.

3.   Supervision under secure training order

(1)   The following provisions apply as respects the period of supervision of a person ('the offender') subject to a secure training order.

(2)   The offender shall be under the supervision of a probation officer, a social worker of a local authority social services department or such other person as the Secretary of State may designate.

(3)   The category of person to supervise the offender shall be determined from time to time by the Secretary of State.

(4)   Where the supervision is to be provided by a social worker of a local authority social services department, the social worker shall be a social worker of the local authority within whose area the offender resides for the time being.

(5)   Where the supervision is to be provided by a probation officer, the probation officer shall be an officer appointed for or assigned to the petty sessions area within which the offender resides for the time being.

(6)   The probation committee or local authority shall be entitled to recover from the Secretary of State the expenses reasonably incurred by them in discharging their duty under this section.

(7)   The offender shall be given a notice from the Secretary of State specifying—

   (a)   the category of person for the time being responsible for his supervision; and

   (b)   any requirements with which he must for the time being comply.

(8)   A notice under subsection (7) above shall be given to the offender—

   (a)   before the commencement of the period of supervision; and

   (b)   before any alteration in the matters specified in subsection (7)(a) or (b) comes into effect.

(9)   The Secretary of State may by statutory instrument make rules for regulating the supervision of the offender.

(10)   The power to make rules under subsection (9) above includes power to make provision in the rules by the incorporation by reference of provisions contained in other documents.

(11)   A statutory instrument made under subsection (9) above shall be subject to annulment in pursuance of a resolution of either House of Parliament.

(12)   The sums required by the Secretary of State for making payments under subsection (6) shall be defrayed out of money provided by Parliament.

4. Breaches of requirements of supervision of persons subject to secure training orders

(1)   Where a secure training order has been made as respects an offender and it appears on information to a justice of the peace acting for a relevant petty sessions area that the offender has failed to comply with requirements under section 3(7)(b) the justice may issue a summons requiring the offender to appear at the place and time specified in the summons before a youth court acting for the area or, if the information is in writing and on oath, may issue a warrant for the offender's arrest requiring him to be brought before such a court.

(2)   For the purposes of this section a petty sessions area is a relevant petty sessions area in relation to a secure training order—

(a)   if the secure training centre is situated in it;

(b)   if the order was made by a youth court acting for it; or

(c)   if the offender resides in it for the time being.

(3)   If it is proved to the satisfaction of the youth court before which an offender appears or is brought under this section that he has failed to comply with requirements under section 3(7)(b) that court may—

(a)   order the offender to be detained in a secure training centre for such period, not exceeding the shorter of three months or the remainder of the period of the secure training order, as the court may specify, or

(b)   impose on the offender a fine not exceeding level 3 on the standard scale.

(4)   Where accommodation for an offender in relation to whom the court decides to exercise their powers under subsection (3)(a) above is not immediately available, paragraphs (a), (b) and (c) of subsection (2) and subsections (5), (7) and (8) of section 2 shall apply in relation to him as they apply in relation to an offender in respect of whom a secure training order is made.

(5)   For the purposes of this section references to a failure to comply include references to a contravention.

5. Provision etc. of secure training centres

(1)   Section 43 of the Prison Act 1952 (which enables certain institutions for young offenders to be provided and applies provisions of the Act to them) shall be amended as follows.

(2)   In subsection (1), after paragraph (c), there shall be inserted the following paragraph, preceded by the word 'and'—

'(d)   secure training centres, that is to say places in which offenders not less than 12 but under 17 years of age in respect of whom secure training orders have been made under section 1 of the Criminal Justice and Public Order Act 1994 may be detained and given training and education and prepared for their release'.

(3)   After subsection (4), there shall be inserted the following subsection—

'(4A)   Sections 16, 22 and 36 of this Act shall apply to secure training centres and to persons detained in them as they apply to prisons and prisoners.'.

(4)   In subsection (5), for the words 'such centres' there shall be substituted the words 'centres of the descriptions specified in subsection (4) above'.

(5)   After subsection (5), there shall be inserted the following subsection—

'(5A)   The other provisions of this Act preceding this section, except sections 5, 5A, 6(2) and (3), 12, 14, 19, 25, 28 and 37(2) and (3) above, shall apply to secure training centres and to persons detained in them as they apply to prisons and prisoners, but subject to such adaptations and modifications as may be specified in rules made by the Secretary of State.'.

6. Management of secure training centres

(1)   Section 47 of the Prison Act 1952 (rules for the regulation and management of prisons and certain institutions for young offenders) shall be amended as follows.

(2)   In subsection (1), for the words between 'remand centres' and 'respectively', there shall be substituted the words ', young offender institutions or secure training centres'.

(3)   After subsection (4), there shall be inserted the following subsection—

'(4A)   Rules made under this section shall provide for the inspection of secure training centres and the appointment of independent persons to visit secure training centres and to whom representations may be made by offenders detained in secure training centres.'.

(4)   In subsection (5), for the words between 'remand centre' and 'not' there shall be substituted the words ', young offender institution or secure training centre'.

7. Contracting out of secure training centres

(1)   The Secretary of State may enter into a contract with another person for the provision or running (or the provision and running) by him, or (if the contract so provides) for the running by sub-contractors of his, of any secure training centre or part of a secure training centre.

(2)   While a contract for the running of a secure training centre or part of a secure training centre is in force the centre or part shall be run subject to and in accordance with the Prison Act 1952 and in accordance with secure training centre rules subject to such adaptations and modifications as the Secretary of State may specify in relation to contracted out secure training centres.

(3)   Where the Secretary of State grants a lease or tenancy of land for the purposes of any contract under this section, none of the following enactments shall apply to it, namely—

(a)   Part II of the Landlord and Tenant Act 1954 (security of tenure);

(b)   section 146 of the Law of Property Act 1925 (restrictions on and relief against forfeiture); and

(c)   section 19 of the Landlord and Tenant Act 1927 and the Landlord and Tenant Act 1988 (covenants not to assign etc.).

In this subsection 'lease or tenancy' includes an underlease or sub-tenancy.

(4)   In this section—

(a)   the reference to the Prison Act 1952 is a reference to that Act as it applies to secure training centres by virtue of section 43 of that Act; and

(b)   the reference to secure training centre rules is a reference to rules made under section 47 of that Act for the regulation and management of secure training centres.

8. Officers of contracted out secure training centres

(1)   Instead of a governor, every contracted out secure training centre shall have—

(a)   a director, who shall be a custody officer appointed by the contractor and specially approved for the purposes of this section by the Secretary of State; and

(b)   a monitor, who shall be a Crown servant appointed by the Secretary of State;

and every officer of such a secure training centre who performs custodial duties shall be a custody officer who is authorised to perform such duties or an officer of a directly managed secure training centre who is temporarily attached to the secure training centre.

(2)   The director shall have such functions as are conferred on him by the Prison Act 1952 as it applies to secure training centres and as may be conferred on him by secure training centre rules.

(3)   The monitor shall have such functions as may be conferred on him by secure training centre rules and shall be under a duty—

(a)   to keep under review, and report to the Secretary of State on, the running of the secure training centre by or on behalf of the director; and

(b)   to investigate, and report to the Secretary of State on, any allegations made against custody officers performing custodial duties at the secure training centre or officers of directly managed secure training centres who are temporarily attached to the secure training centre.

(4)   The contractor and any sub-contractor of his shall each be under a duty to do all that he reasonably can (whether by giving directions to the officers of the secure training centre or otherwise) to facilitate the exercise by the monitor of all such functions as are mentioned in or imposed by subsection (3) above.

9.   Powers and duties of custody officers employed at contracted out secure training centres

(1)   A custody officer performing custodial duties at a contracted out secure training centre shall have the following powers, namely—

(a)   to search in accordance with secure training centre rules any offender who is detained in the secure training centre; and

(b)   to search any other person who is in or who is seeking to enter the secure training centre, and any article in the possession of such a person.

(2)   The powers conferred by subsection (1)(b) above to search a person shall not be construed as authorising a custody officer to require a person to remove any of his clothing other than an outer coat, headgear, jacket or gloves.

(3)   A custody officer performing custodial duties at a contracted out secure training centre shall have the following duties as respects offenders detained in the secure training centre, namely—

(a)   to prevent their escape from lawful custody;

(b)   to prevent, or detect and report on, the commission or attempted commission by them of other unlawful acts;

(c)   to ensure good order and discipline on their part; and

(d)   to attend to their wellbeing.

(4)   The powers conferred by subsection (1) above, and the powers arising by virtue of subsection (3) above, shall include power to use reasonable force where necessary.

10.   Intervention by Secretary of State in management of contracted out secure training centres

(1)   This section applies where, in the case of a contracted out secure training centre, it appears to the Secretary of State—

(a) that the director has lost, or is likely to lose, effective control of the secure training centre or any part of it; and

(b) that the making of an appointment under subsection (2) below is necessary in the interests of preserving the safety of any person, or of preventing serious damage to any property.

(2) The Secretary of State may appoint a Crown servant to act as governor of the secure training centre for the period—

(a) beginning with the time specified in the appointment; and

(b) ending with the time specified in the notice of termination under subsection (4) below.

(3) During that period—

(a) all the functions which would otherwise be exercisable by the director or monitor shall be exercisable by the governor;

(b) the contractor and any sub-contractor of his shall each do all that he reasonably can to facilitate the exercise by the governor of those functions; and

(c) the officers of the secure training centre shall comply with any directions given by the governor in the exercise of those functions.

(4) Where the Secretary of State is satisfied—

(a) that the governor has secured effective control of the secure training centre or, as the case may be, the relevant part of it; and

(b) that the governor's appointment is no longer necessary for the purpose mentioned in subsection (1)(b) above,

he shall, by a notice to the governor, terminate the appointment at a time specified in the notice.

(5) As soon as practicable after making or terminating an appointment under this section, the Secretary of State shall give a notice of the appointment, or a copy of the notice of termination, to the contractor, any sub-contractor of his, the director and the monitor.

11. Contracted out functions at directly managed secure training centres

(1) The Secretary of State may enter into a contract with another person for any functions at a directly managed secure training centre to be performed by custody officers who are provided by that person and are authorised to perform custodial duties.

(2) Section 9 shall apply in relation to a custody officer performing contracted out functions at a directly managed secure training centre as it applies in relation to such an officer performing custodial duties at a contracted out secure training centre.

(3) In relation to a directly managed secure training centre, the reference in section 13(2) of the Prison Act 1952 (legal custody of prisoners) as it applies to secure training centres to an officer of the prison shall be construed as including a reference to a custody officer performing custodial duties at the secure training centre in pursuance of a contract under this section.

(4) Any reference in subsections (1), (2) and (3) above to the performance of functions or custodial duties at a directly managed secure training centre includes a reference to the performance of functions or such duties for the purposes of, or for purposes connected with, such a secure training centre.

12. Escort arrangements and officers

(1) The provisions of Schedule 1 to this Act (which make provision for escort arrangements for offenders detained at a secure training centre) shall have effect.

(2)　The provisions of Schedule 2 to this Act shall have effect with respect to the certification of custody officers.

(3)　In this Part, 'custody officer' means a person in respect of whom a certificate is for the time being in force certifying—

(a)　that he has been approved by the Secretary of State for the purpose of performing escort functions or custodial duties or both in relation to offenders in respect of whom secure training orders have been made; and

(b)　that he is accordingly authorised to perform them.

13.　Protection of custody officers at secure training centres

(1)　Any person who assaults a custody officer—

(a)　acting in pursuance of escort arrangements;

(b)　performing custodial duties at a contracted out secure training centre; or

(c)　performing contracted out functions at a directly managed secure training centre,

shall be liable on summary conviction to a fine not exceeding level 5 on the standard scale or to imprisonment for a term not exceeding six months or to both.

(2)　Any person who resists or wilfully obstructs a custody officer—

(a)　acting in pursuance of escort arrangements;

(b)　performing custodial duties at a contracted out secure training centre; or

(c)　performing contracted out functions at a directly managed secure training centre,

shall be liable on summary conviction to a fine not exceeding level 3 on the standard scale.

(3)　For the purposes of this section, a custody officer shall not be regarded as acting in pursuance of escort arrangements at any time when he is not readily identifiable as such an officer (whether by means of a uniform or badge which he is wearing or otherwise).

14.　Wrongful disclosure of information relating to offenders detained at secure training centres

(1)　A person who—

(a)　is or has been employed (whether as a custody officer or otherwise) in pursuance of escort arrangements or at a contracted out secure training centre; or

(b)　is or has been employed to perform contracted out functions at a directly managed secure training centre,

commits an offence if he discloses, otherwise than in the course of his duty or as authorised by the Secretary of State, any information which he acquired in the course of his employment and which relates to a particular offender detained at a secure training centre.

(2)　A person guilty of an offence under subsection (1) above shall be liable—

(a)　on conviction on indictment, to imprisonment for a term not exceeding two years or a fine or both;

(b)　on summary conviction, to imprisonment for a term not exceeding six months or a fine not exceeding the statutory maximum or both.

15.　Interpretation of sections 7 to 14

In sections 7 to 14—

'contracted out functions' means any functions which, by virtue of a contract under section 11, fall to be performed by custody officers;

'contracted out secure training centre' means a secure training centre or part of a secure training centre in respect of which a contract under section 7(1) is for the time being in force;

'the contractor', in relation to a contracted out secure training centre, means the person who has contracted with the Secretary of State for the provision or running (or the provision and running) of it;

'custodial duties' means custodial duties at a secure training centre;

'directly managed secure training centre' means a secure training centre which is not a contracted out secure training centre;

'escort arrangements' means the arrangements specified in paragraph 1 of Schedule 1 to this Act;

'escort functions' means the functions specified in paragraph 1 of Schedule 1 to this Act;

'escort monitor' means a person appointed under paragraph 2(1)(a) of Schedule 1 to this Act;

'secure training centre rules' has the meaning given by section 7(4)(b); and

'sub-contractor', in relation to a contracted out secure training centre, means a person who has contracted with the contractor for the running of it or any part of it.

Custodial sentences for young offenders

16. Long term detention of young offenders

(1)   Section 53 of the Children and Young Persons Act 1933 (which provides for the long term detention of children and young persons for certain grave crimes) shall be amended as follows.

(2)   In subsection (1), for the words after 'conditions' there shall be substituted—
'—
   (a)   as the Secretary of State may direct, or
   (b)   as the Secretary of State may arrange with any person.'.

(3)   In subsection (2), for the words from the beginning to the words 'and the court' there shall be substituted the following—
'(2)   Subsection (3) below applies—
   (a)   where a person of at least 10 but not more than 17 years is convicted on indictment of—
      (i)   any offence punishable in the case of an adult with imprisonment for fourteen years or more, not being an offence the sentence for which is fixed by law, or
      (ii)   an offence under section 14 of the Sexual Offences Act 1956 (indecent assault on a woman);
   (b)   where a young person is convicted of—
      (i)   an offence under section 1 of the Road Traffic Act 1988 (causing death by dangerous driving), or
      (ii)   an offence under section 3A of the Road Traffic Act 1988 (causing death by careless driving while under influence of drink or drugs).
   (3)   Where this subsection applies, then, if the court'.

(4)   For the words from 'as the' in subsection (3) to the end of the section there shall be substituted—
   '—

(a)   as the Secretary of State may direct, or

(b)   as the Secretary of State may arrange with any person.

(4)   A person detained pursuant to the directions or arrangements made by the Secretary of State under this section shall, while so detained, be deemed to be in legal custody.'.

17.   Maximum length of detention for young offenders

(1)   Section 1B of the Criminal Justice Act 1982 (maximum length of detention in young offender institution for offenders aged 15, 16 or 17 years) shall be amended as follows.

(2)   In subsection (2)(b), for the words '12 months' there shall be substituted the words '24 months'.

(3)   In subsection (4), for the words '12 months' there shall be substituted the words '24 months'.

(4)   In subsection (5), for the words '12 months' in both places where they occur there shall be substituted the words '24 months'.

18.   Accommodation of young offenders sentenced to custody for life

(1)   In section 1C of the Criminal Justice Act 1982 (young offenders sentenced to detention in a young offender institution to be detained in such an institution unless the Secretary of State otherwise directs)—

(a)   in subsection (1), after the words 'young offender institution' there shall be inserted the words 'or to custody for life' and for the words 'such an institution' there shall be substituted the words 'a young offender institution'; and

(b)   in subsection (2), after the words 'in a young offender institution' there shall be inserted the words 'or to custody for life'.

(2)   Subsections (6) and (7) of section 12 of the Criminal Justice Act 1982 (which provide for the detention of young offenders sentenced to custody for life in a prison unless the Secretary of State otherwise directs) are hereby repealed.

(3)   In section 43(1) of the Prison Act 1952 (which relates to the institutions for the detention of young offenders which may be provided by the Secretary of State), in paragraph (aa), at the end, there shall be inserted the words 'or to custody for life'.

Secure accommodation for certain young persons

19.   Extension of kinds of secure accommodation

(1)   Section 23 of the Children and Young Persons Act 1969 (remands and committals to local authority accommodation) shall be amended by the insertion, in subsection (12), in the definition of 'secure accommodation', after the words 'community home', of the words ', a voluntary home or a registered children's home', and, at the end of that subsection, of the words 'but, for the purposes of the definition of "secure accommodation", "local authority accommodation" includes any accommodation falling within section 61(2) of the Criminal Justice Act 1991.'.

(2)   In the Children Act 1989, Schedules 5 and 6 (which provide for the regulation of voluntary homes and registered children's homes respectively) shall be amended as follows, that is to say—

(a)   in Schedule 5, in paragraph 7(2) (regulations as to conduct of voluntary homes)—

(i)   head (f) (power to prohibit provision of secure accommodation) shall be omitted; and

(ii)   after that head, there shall be inserted the following—

'(ff)   require the approval of the Secretary of State for the provision and use of accommodation for the purpose of restricting the liberty of children in such homes and impose other requirements (in addition to those imposed by section 25) as to the placing of a child in accommodation provided for that purpose, including a requirement to obtain the permission of any local authority who are looking after the child;'; and

(b)   in Schedule 6, in paragraph 10(2) (regulations as to conduct, etc. of registered children's homes)—

(i)   head (j) (power to prohibit use of accommodation as secure accommodation) shall be omitted; and

(ii)   after that head, there shall be inserted the following—

'(jj)   require the approval of the Secretary of State for the provision and use of accommodation for the purpose of restricting the liberty of children in such homes and impose other requirements (in addition to those imposed by section 25) as to the placing of a child in accommodation provided for that purpose, including a requirement to obtain the permission of any local authority who are looking after the child.'.

(3) In section 61 of the Criminal Justice Act 1991 (provision by local authorities of secure accommodation)—

(a)   in subsection (2), at the end, there shall be inserted the words 'or by making arrangements with voluntary organisations or persons carrying on a registered children's home for the provision or use by them of such accommodation or by making arrangements with the Secretary of State for the use by them of a home provided by him under section 82(5) of the Children Act 1989'; and

(b)   in subsection (5), at the end, there shall be inserted the words 'and expressions, other than ''local authority'', used in the Children Act 1989 have the same meanings as in that Act.'.

20.   Secure remands for young offenders

In section 23(5) of the Children and Young Persons Act 1969 (as substituted by section 60 of the Criminal Justice Act 1991) (conditions for imposing a security requirement in case of young persons remanded to local authority accommodation), for the words 'young person who has attained the age of fifteen' there shall be substituted the words—

(a)   'person who has attained the age of fourteen':

(b)   'person who has attained the age of thirteen'; or

(c)   'person who has attained the age of twelve';

but no substitution may be brought into force on more than one occasion.

21.   Cost of secure accommodation

After section 61 of the Criminal Justice Act 1991 there shall be inserted the following section—

'61A.   Cost of secure accommodation

(1)   The Secretary of State may, in relation to any costs incurred by a local authority in discharging their duty under section 61(1) above—

(a)   defray such costs to such extent as he considers appropriate in any particular case;

(b)   defray a proportion to be determined by him from time to time of such costs; and

(c) defray or contribute to such costs in accordance with a tariff to be determined by him from time to time.

(2) The Secretary of State may require any person providing secure accommodation to transmit to him, at such times and in such form as he may direct, such particulars as he may require with respect to any costs to which this section applies.

(3) Payments under this section shall be made out of money provided by Parliament.'.

22. Management of secure accommodation

(1) The Children Act 1989 shall be amended as follows.

(2) In section 53 (provision and management of community homes)—

(a) in subsection (3) (homes which may be community homes)—

(i) in paragraph (a), for the words 'managed, equipped and maintained' there shall be substituted the words 'equipped, maintained and (subject to subsection (3A)) managed'; and

(ii) in paragraph (b)(i), for the words 'management, equipment and maintenance' there shall be substituted the words 'equipment, maintenance and (subject to subsection (3B)) management'; and

(b) after subsection (3) there shall be inserted the following subsections—

'(3A) A local authority may make arrangements for the management by another person of accommodation provided by the local authority for the purpose of restricting the liberty of children.

(3B) Where a local authority are to be responsible for the management of a community home provided by a voluntary organisation, the local authority may, with the consent of the body of managers constituted by the instrument of management for the home, make arrangements for the management by another person of accommodation provided for the purpose of restricting the liberty of children.'.

(3) In Part II of Schedule 4 (management of controlled and assisted community homes)—

(a) in paragraph 3(4), after the word 'managers' there shall be inserted the words ', except in so far as, under section 53(3B), any of the accommodation is to be managed by another person.'; and

(b) in paragraph 3(5), after the word 'body' there shall be inserted the words '; and similarly, to the extent that a contract so provides, as respects anything done, liability incurred or property acquired by a person by whom, under section 53(3B), any of the accommodation is to be managed'.

Arrest of young persons in breach of conditions of remand

23. Liability of young persons to arrest for breaking conditions of remand

After section 23 of the Children and Young Persons Act 1969 there shall be inserted the following section—

'**23A. Liability to arrest for breaking conditions of remand**

(1) A person who has been remanded or committed to local authority accommodation and in respect of whom conditions under subsection (7) or (10) of section 23 of this Act have been imposed may be arrested without warrant by

a constable if the constable has reasonable grounds for suspecting that that person has broken any of those conditions.

(2) A person arrested under subsection (1) above—

(a) shall, except where he was arrested within 24 hours of the time appointed for him to appear before the court in pursuance of the remand or committal, be brought as soon as practicable and in any event within 24 hours after his arrest before a justice of the peace for the petty sessions area in which he was arrested; and

(b) in the said excepted case shall be brought before the court before which he was to have appeared.

In reckoning for the purposes of this subsection any period of 24 hours, no account shall be taken of Christmas Day, Good Friday or any Sunday.

(3) A justice of the peace before whom a person is brought under subsection (2) above—

(a) if of the opinion that that person has broken any condition imposed on him under subsection (7) or (10) of section 23 of this Act shall remand him; and that section shall apply as if he was then charged with or convicted of the offence for which he had been remanded or committed;

(b) if not of that opinion shall remand him to the place to which he had been remanded or committed at the time of his arrest subject to the same conditions as those which had been imposed on him at that time.'.

Police detention of young persons

24. Detention of arrested juveniles after charge

In section 38(6) of the Police and Criminal Evidence Act 1984 (detention of arrested juveniles after charge), in paragraph (b), for the words 'age of 15 years' there shall be substituted the words 'age of 12 years'.

PART II   BAIL

25. No bail for defendants charged with or convicted of homicide or rape after previous conviction of such offences

(1) A person who in any proceedings has been charged with or convicted of an offence to which this section applies in circumstances to which it applies shall not be granted bail in those proceedings.

(2) This section applies, subject to subsection (3) below, to the following offences, that is to say—

(a) murder;

(b) attempted murder;

(c) manslaughter;

(d) rape; or

(e) attempted rape.

(3) This section applies to a person charged with or convicted of any such offence only if he has been previously convicted by or before a court in any part of the United Kingdom of any such offence or of culpable homicide and, in the case of a previous conviction of manslaughter or of culpable homicide, if he was then sentenced to imprisonment or, if he was then a child or young person, to long-term detention under any of the relevant enactments.

(4)   This section applies whether or not an appeal is pending against conviction or sentence.

(5)   In this section—

'conviction' includes—

(a)   a finding that a person is not guilty by reason of insanity;

(b)   a finding under section 4A(3) of the Criminal Procedure (Insanity) Act 1964 (cases of unfitness to plead) that a person did the act or made the omission charged against him; and

(c)   a conviction of an offence for which an order is made placing the offender on probation or discharging him absolutely or conditionally;

and 'convicted' shall be construed accordingly; and

'the relevant enactments' means—

(a)   as respects England and Wales, section 53(2) of the Children and Young Persons Act 1933;

(b)   as respects Scotland, sections 205 and 206 of the Criminal Procedure (Scotland) Act 1975;

(c)   as respects Northern Ireland, section 73(2) of the Children and Young Persons Act (Northern Ireland) 1968.

(6)   This section does not apply in relation to proceedings instituted before its commencement.

26.   No right to bail for persons accused or convicted of committing offence while on bail

In Part I of Schedule 1 to the Bail Act 1976 (exceptions to right to bail for imprisonable offences)—

(a)   after paragraph 2, there shall be inserted the following paragraph—

'2A.   The defendant need not be granted bail if—

(a)   the offence is an indictable offence or an offence triable either way; and

(b)   it appears to the court that he was on bail in criminal proceedings on the date of the offence.'; and

(b)   in paragraph 9, after the words 'paragraph 2' there shall be inserted the words 'or 2A'.

27.   Power for police to grant conditional bail to persons charged

(1)   Part IV of the Police and Criminal Evidence Act 1984 (detention of persons, including powers of police to grant bail) shall have effect with the following amendments, that is to say, in section 47 (bail after arrest)—

(a)   in subsection (1), for the words after 'in accordance with' there shall be substituted the words 'sections 3, 3A, 5 and 5A of the Bail Act 1976 as they apply to bail granted by a constable'; and

(b)   after subsection (1) there shall be inserted the following subsection—

'(1A) The normal powers to impose conditions of bail shall be available to him where a custody officer releases a person on bail under section 38(1) above (including that subsection as applied by section 40(10) above) but not in any other cases.

In this subsection, "the normal powers to impose conditions of bail" has the meaning given in section 3(6) of the Bail Act 1976.'.

(2)   Section 3 of the Bail Act 1976 (incidents including conditions of bail in criminal proceedings) shall be amended as follows—
  (a)   in subsection (6), the words '(but only by a court)' shall be omitted;
  (b)   at the end of subsection (6) there shall be inserted—
    'and, in any Act, "the normal powers to impose conditions of bail" means the powers to impose conditions under paragraph (a), (b) or (c) above';
  (c)   after subsection (9), there shall be inserted the following subsection—
    '(10)   This section is subject, in its application to bail granted by a constable, to section 3A of this Act.'.
(3)   After section 3 of the Bail Act 1976 there shall be inserted the following section—
  '**3A.   Conditions of bail in case of police bail**
  (1)   Section 3 of this Act applies, in relation to ball granted by a custody officer under Part IV of the Police and Criminal Evidence Act 1984 in cases where the normal powers to impose conditions of bail are available to him, subject to the following modifications.
  (2)   Subsection (6) does not authorise the imposition of a requirement to reside in a bail hostel or any requirement under paragraph (d).
  (3)   Subsections (6ZA), (6A) and (6B) shall be omitted.
  (4)   For subsection (8), substitute the following—
    "(8)   Where a custody officer has granted bail in criminal proceedings he or another custody officer serving at the same police station may, at the request of the person to whom it was granted, vary the conditions of bail; and in doing so he may impose conditions or more onerous conditions.".
  (5)   Where a constable grants bail to a person no conditions shall be imposed under subsections (4), (5), (6) or (7) of section 3 of this Act unless it appears to the constable that it is necessary to do so for the purpose of preventing that person from—
    (a)   failing to surrender to custody, or
    (b)   committing an offence while on bail, or
    (c)   interfering with witnesses or otherwise obstructing the course of justice, whether in relation to himself or any other person.
  (6)   Subsection (5) above also applies on any request to a custody officer under subsection (8) of section 3 of this Act to vary the conditions of bail.'.
(4)   The further amendments contained in Schedule 3 to this Act shall have effect.

28.   Police detention after charge
(1)   Section 38 of the Police and Criminal Evidence Act 1984 (which requires an arrested person charged with an offence to be released except in specified circumstances) shall be amended as follows.
(2)   In subsection (1)(a), for sub-paragraphs (ii) and (iii) there shall be substituted the following sub-paragraphs—
    '(ii)   the custody officer has reasonable grounds for believing that the person arrested will fail to appear in court to answer to bail;
    (iii)   in the case of a person arrested for an imprisonable offence, the custody officer has reasonable grounds for believing that the detention of the person arrested is necessary to prevent him from committing an offence;

(iv)   in the case of a person arrested for an offence which is not an imprisonable offence, the custody officer has reasonable grounds for believing that the detention of the person arrested is necessary to prevent him from causing physical injury to any other person or from causing loss of or damage to property;

(v)   the custody officer has reasonable grounds for believing that the detention of the person arrested is necessary to prevent him from interfering with the administration of justice or with the investigation of offences or of a particular offence; or

(vi)   the custody officer has reasonable grounds for believing that the detention of the person arrested is necessary for his own protection;'.

(3)   After subsection (2), there shall be inserted the following subsection—

'(2A)   The custody officer, in taking the decisions required by subsection (1)(a) and (b) above (except (a)(i) and (vi) and (b)(ii)), shall have regard to the same considerations as those which a court is required to have regard to in taking the corresponding decisions under paragraph 2 of Part I of Schedule 1 to the Bail Act 1976.'.

(4)   After subsection (7), there shall be inserted the following subsection—

'(7A)   In this section "imprisonable offence" has the same meaning as in Schedule 1 to the Bail Act 1976.'.

29.   Powers for police to arrest for failure to answer to police bail

(1)   Part IV of the Police and Criminal Evidence Act 1984 (detention of persons, including powers of police to grant bail) shall be amended as follows.

(2)   After section 46 there shall be inserted the following section—

'**46A.   Power of arrest for failure to answer to police bail**

(1)   A constable may arrest without a warrant any person who, having been released on bail under this Part of this Act subject to a duty to attend at a police station, fails to attend at that police station at the time appointed for him to do so.

(2)   A person who is arrested under this section shall be taken to the police station appointed as the place at which he is to surrender to custody as soon as practicable after the arrest.

(3)   For the purposes of—

(a)   section 30 above (subject to the obligation in subsection (2) above), and

(b)   section 31 above,

an arrest under this section shall be treated as an arrest for an offence.'.

(3)   In section 34 after subsection (6), there shall be inserted the following subsection—

'(7)   For the purposes of this Part of this Act a person who returns to a police station to answer to bail or is arrested under section 46A below shall be treated as arrested for an offence and the offence in connection with which he was granted bail shall be deemed to be that offence.'.

(4)   In consequence of the foregoing amendments—

(a)   in section 37(1), paragraph (b) shall be omitted;

(b)   in sections 41(9), 42(11) and 43(19), at the end, there shall be inserted the words '; but this subsection does not prevent an arrest under section 46A below.';

(c)   in section 47, subsection (5) shall be omitted;

(d)   in section 47(6), for the words 'is detained under subsection (5) above' there shall be substituted the words 'who has been granted bail and either has attended at the police station in accordance with the grant of bail or has been arrested under section 46A above is detained at a police station'; and

(e)   in section 47(7), at the end, there shall be inserted the words '; but this subsection does not apply to a person who is arrested under section 46A above or has attended a police station in accordance with the grant of bail (and who accordingly is deemed by section 34(7) above to have been arrested for an offence).'.

(5)   This section applies whether the person released on bail was granted bail before or after the commencement of this section.

30.   Reconsideration of decisions granting bail

After the section 5A of the Bail Act 1976 inserted by Schedule 3 to this Act there shall be inserted the following section—

'**5B.   Reconsideration of decisions granting bail**

(1)   Where a magistrates' court has granted bail in criminal proceedings in connection with an offence, or proceedings for an offence, to which this section applies or a constable has granted bail in criminal proceedings in connection with proceedings for such an offence, that court or the appropriate court in relation to the constable may, on application by the prosecutor for the decision to be reconsidered,—

(a)   vary the conditions of bail,

(b)   impose conditions in respect of bail which has been granted unconditionally, or

(c)   withhold bail.

(2)   The offences to which this section applies are offences triable on indictment and offences triable either way.

(3)   No application for the reconsideration of a decision under this section shall be made unless it is based on information which was not available to the court or constable when the decision was taken.

(4)   Whether or not the person to whom the application relates appears before it, the magistrates' court shall take the decision in accordance with section 4(1) (and Schedule 1) of this Act.

(5)   Where the decision of the court on a reconsideration under this section is to withhold bail from the person to whom it was originally granted the court shall—

(a)   if that person is before the court, remand him in custody, and

(b)   if that person is not before the court, order him to surrender himself forthwith into the custody of the court.

(6)   Where a person surrenders himself into the custody of the court in compliance with an order under subsection (5) above, the court shall remand him in custody.

(7)   A person who has been ordered to surrender to custody under subsection (5) above may be arrested without warrant by a constable if he fails without reasonable cause to surrender to custody in accordance with the order.

(8)   A person arrested in pursuance of subsection (7) above shall be brought as soon as practicable, and in any event within 24 hours after his arrest, before

a justice of the peace for the petty sessions area in which he was arrested and the justice shall remand him in custody.

In reckoning for the purposes of this subsection any period of 24 hours, no account shall be taken of Christmas Day, Good Friday or any Sunday.

(9) Magistrates' court rules shall include provision—

(a) requiring notice of an application under this section and of the grounds for it to be given to the person affected, including notice of the powers available to the court under it;

(b) for securing that any representations made by the person affected (whether in writing or orally) are considered by the court before making its decision; and

(c) designating the court which is the appropriate court in relation to the decision of any constable to grant bail.'.

PART III   COURSE OF JUSTICE: EVIDENCE, PROCEDURE, ETC.

Imputations on character

31. Imputations on character

In section 1 of the Criminal Evidence Act 1898 there shall be inserted at the end of sub-paragraph (ii) of paragraph (f) the words 'the deceased victim of the alleged crime; or'.

Corroboration

32. Abolition of corroboration rules

(1) Any requirement whereby at a trial on indictment it is obligatory for the court to give the jury a warning about convicting the accused on the uncorroborated evidence of a person merely because that person is—

(a) an alleged accomplice of the accused, or

(b) where the offence charged is a sexual offence, the person in respect of whom it is alleged to have been committed, is hereby abrogated.

(2) In section 34(2) of the Criminal Justice Act 1988 (abolition of requirement of corroboration warning in respect of evidence of a child) the words from 'in relation to' to the end shall be omitted.

(3) Any requirement that—

(a) is applicable at the summary trial of a person for an offence, and

(b) corresponds to the requirement mentioned in subsection (1) above or that mentioned in section 34(2) of the Criminal Justice Act 1988,

is hereby abrogated.

(4) Nothing in this section applies in relation to—

(a) any trial, or

(b) any proceedings before a magistrates' court as examining justices,

which began before the commencement of this section.

33. Abolition of corroboration requirements under Sexual Offences Act 1956

(1) The following provisions of the Sexual Offences Act 1956 (which provide that a person shall not be convicted of the offence concerned on the evidence of one witness only unless the witness is corroborated) are hereby repealed—

(a) section 2(2) (procurement of woman by threats),

    (b)   section 3(2) (procurement of woman by false pretences),
    (c)   section 4(2) (administering drugs to obtain or facilitate intercourse),
    (d)   section 22(2) (causing prostitution of women), and
    (e)   section 23(2) (procuration of girl under twenty-one).
  (2)   Nothing in this section applies in relation to—
    (a)   any trial, or
    (b)   any proceedings before a magistrates' court as examining justices,
which began before the commencement of this section.

Inferences from accused's silence

34.   Effect of accused's failure to mention facts when questioned or charged.
  (1)   Where, in any proceedings against a person for an offence, evidence is given that the accused—
    (a)   at any time before he was charged with the offence, on being questioned under caution by a constable trying to discover whether or by whom the offence had been committed, failed to mention any fact relied on in his defence in those proceedings; or
    (b)   on being charged with the offence or officially informed that he might be prosecuted for it, failed to mention any such fact,
being a fact which in the circumstances existing at the time the accused could reasonably have been expected to mention when so questioned, charged or informed, as the case may be, subsection (2) below applies.
  (2)   Where this subsection applies—
    (a)   a magistrates' court, in deciding whether to grant an application for dismissal made by the accused under section 6 of the Magistrates' Courts Act 1980 (application for dismissal of charge in course of proceedings with a view to transfer for trial);
    (b)   a judge, in deciding whether to grant an application made by the accused under—
       (i)   section 6 of the Criminal Justice Act 1987 (application for dismissal of charge of serious fraud in respect of which notice of transfer has been given under section 4 of that Act); or
       (ii)   paragraph 5 of Schedule 6 to the Criminal Justice Act 1991 (application for dismissal of charge of violent or sexual offence involving child in respect of which notice of transfer has been given under section 53 of that Act);
    (c)   the court, in determining whether there is a case to answer; and
    (d)   the court or jury, in determining whether the accused is guilty of the offence charged,
may draw such inferences from the failure as appear proper.
  (3)   Subject to any directions by the court, evidence tending to establish the failure may be given before or after evidence tending to establish the fact which the accused is alleged to have failed to mention.
  (4)   This section applies in relation to questioning by persons (other than constables) charged with the duty of investigating offences or charging offenders as it applies in relation to questioning by constables; and in subsection (1) above 'officially informed' means informed by a constable or any such person.
  (5)   This section does not—
    (a)   prejudice the admissibility in evidence of the silence or other reaction of the accused in the face of anything said in his presence relating to the conduct in

respect of which he is charged, in so far as evidence thereof would be admissible apart from this section; or

(b)   preclude the drawing of any inference from any such silence or other reaction of the accused which could properly be drawn apart from this section.

(6)   This section does not apply in relation to a failure to mention a fact if the failure occurred before the commencement of this section.

(7)   In relation to any time before the commencement of section 44 of this Act, this section shall have effect as if the reference in subsection (2)(a) to the grant of an application for dismissal was a reference to the committal of the accused for trial.

35.   Effect of accused's silence at trial

(1)   At the trial of any person who has attained the age of fourteen years for an offence, subsections (2) and (3) below apply unless—

(a)   the accused's guilt is not in issue; or

(b)   it appears to the court that the physical or mental condition of the accused makes it undesirable for him to give evidence;

but subsection (2) below does not apply if, at the conclusion of the evidence for the prosecution, his legal representative informs the court that the accused will give evidence or, where he is unrepresented, the court ascertains from him that he will give evidence.

(2)   Where this subsection applies, the court shall, at the conclusion of the evidence for the prosecution, satisfy itself (in the case of proceedings on indictment, in the presence of the jury) that the accused is aware that the stage has been reached at which evidence can be given for the defence and that he can, if he wishes, give evidence and that, if he chooses not to give evidence, or having been sworn, without good cause refuses to answer any question, it will be permissible for the court or jury to draw such inferences as appear proper from his failure to give evidence or his refusal, without good cause, to answer any question.

(3)   Where this subsection applies, the court or jury, in determining whether the accused is guilty of the offence charged, may draw such inferences as appear proper from the failure of the accused to give evidence or his refusal, without good cause, to answer any question.

(4)   This section does not render the accused compellable to give evidence on his own behalf, and he shall accordingly not be guilty of contempt of court by reason of a failure to do so.

(5)   For the purposes of this section a person who, having been sworn, refuses to answer any question shall be taken to do so without good cause unless—

(a)   he is entitled to refuse to answer the question by virtue of any enactment, whenever passed or made, or on the ground of privilege; or

(b)   the court in the exercise of its general discretion excuses him from answering it.

(6)   Where the age of any person is material for the purposes of subsection (1) above, his age shall for those purposes be taken to be that which appears to the court to be his age.

(7)   This section applies—

(a)   in relation to proceedings on indictment for an offence, only if the person charged with the offence is arraigned on or after the commencement of this section;

(b)   in relation to proceedings in a magistrates' court, only if the time when the court begins to receive evidence in the proceedings falls after the commencement of this section.

36. Effect of accused's failure or refusal to account for objects, substances or marks

(1) Where—

(a) a person is arrested by a constable, and there is—

(i) on his person; or

(ii) in or on his clothing or footwear; or

(iii) otherwise in his possession; or

(iv) in any place in which he is at the time of his arrest,

any object, substance or mark, or there is any mark on any such object; and

(b) that or another constable investigating the case reasonably believes that the presence of the object, substance or mark may be attributable to the participation of the person arrested in the commission of an offence specified by the constable; and

(c) the constable informs the person arrested that he so believes, and requests him to account for the presence of the object, substance or mark; and

(d) the person fails or refuses to do so,

then if, in any proceedings against the person for the offence so specified, evidence of those matters is given, subsection (2) below applies.

(2) Where this subsection applies—

(a) a magistrates' court, in deciding whether to grant an application for dismissal made by the accused under section 6 of the Magistrates' Courts Act 1980 (application for dismissal of charge in course of proceedings with a view to transfer for trial);

(b) a judge, in deciding whether to grant an application made by the accused under—

(i) section 6 of the Criminal Justice Act 1987 (application for dismissal of charge of serious fraud in respect of which notice of transfer has been given under section 4 of that Act); or

(ii) paragraph 5 of Schedule 6 to the Criminal Justice Act 1991 (application for dismissal of charge of violent or sexual offence involving child in respect of which notice of transfer has been given under section 53 of that Act);

(c) the court, in determining whether there is a case to answer; and

(d) the court or jury, in determining whether the accused is guilty of the offence charged,

may draw such inferences from the failure or refusal as appear proper.

(3) Subsections (1) and (2) above apply to the condition of clothing or footwear as they apply to a substance or mark thereon.

(4) Subsections (1) and (2) above do not apply unless the accused was told in ordinary language by the constable when making the request mentioned in subsection (1)(c) above what the effect of this section would be if he failed or refused to comply with the request.

(5) This section applies in relation to officers of customs and excise as it applies in relation to constables.

(6) This section does not preclude the drawing of any inference from a failure or refusal of the accused to account for the presence of an object, substance or mark or from the condition of clothing or footwear which could properly be drawn apart from this section.

(7) This section does not apply in relation to a failure or refusal which occurred before the commencement of this section.

(8) In relation to any time before the commencement of section 44 of this Act, this section shall have effect as if the reference in subsection (2)(a) to the grant of an application for dismissal was a reference to the committal of the accused for trial.

37. Effect of accused's failure or refusal to account for presence at a particular place

(1) Where—

    (a) a person arrested by a constable was found by him at a place at or about the time the offence for which he was arrested is alleged to have been committed; and

    (b) that or another constable investigating the offence reasonably believes that the presence of the person at that place and at that time may be attributable to his participation in the commission of the offence; and

    (c) the constable informs the person that he so believes, and requests him to account for that presence; and

    (d) the person fails or refuses to do so,

then if, in any proceedings against the person for the offence, evidence of those matters is given, subsection (2) below applies.

(2) Where this subsection applies—

    (a) a magistrates' court, in deciding whether to grant an application for dismissal made by the accused under section 6 of the Magistrates' Courts Act 1980 (application for dismissal of charge in course of proceedings with a view to transfer for trial);

    (b) a judge, in deciding whether to grant an application made by the accused under—

        (i) section 6 of the Criminal Justice Act 1987 (application for dismissal of charge of serious fraud in respect of which notice of transfer has been given under section 4 of that Act); or

        (ii) paragraph 5 of Schedule 6 to the Criminal Justice Act 1991 (application for dismissal of charge of violent or sexual offence involving child in respect of which notice of transfer has been given under section 53 of that Act);

    (c) the court, in determining whether there is a case to answer; and

    (d) the court or jury, in determining whether the accused is guilty of the offence charged,

may draw such inferences from the failure or refusal as appear proper.

(3) Subsections (1) and (2) do not apply unless the accused was told in ordinary language by the constable when making the request mentioned in subsection (1)(c) above what the effect of this section would be if he failed or refused to comply with the request.

(4) This section applies in relation to officers of customs and excise as it applies in relation to constables.

(5) This section does not preclude the drawing of any inference from a failure or refusal of the accused to account for his presence at a place which could properly be drawn apart from this section.

(6) This section does not apply in relation to a failure or refusal which occurred before the commencement of this section.

(7) In relation to any time before the commencement of section 44 of this Act, this section shall have effect as if the reference in subsection (2)(a) to the grant of an application for dismissal was a reference to the committal of the accused for trial.

38.   Interpretation and savings for sections 34, 35, 36 and 37

(1)   In sections 34, 35, 36 and 37 of this Act—

'legal representative' means an authorised advocate or authorised litigator, as defined by section 119(1) of the Courts and Legal Services Act 1990; and

'place' includes any building or part of a building, any vehicle, vessel, aircraft or hovercraft and any other place whatsoever.

(2)   In sections 34(2), 35(3), 36(2) and 37(2), references to an offence charged include references to any other offence of which the accused could lawfully be convicted on that charge.

(3)   A person shall not have the proceedings against him transferred to the Crown Court for trial, have a case to answer or be convicted of an offence solely on an inference drawn from such a failure or refusal as is mentioned in section 34(2), 35(3), 36(2) or 37(2).

(4)   A judge shall not refuse to grant such an application as is mentioned in section 34(2)(b), 36(2)(b) and 37(2)(b) solely on an inference drawn from such a failure as is mentioned in section 34(2), 36(2) or 37(2).

(5)   Nothing in sections 34, 35, 36 or 37 prejudices the operation of a provision of any enactment which provides (in whatever words) that any answer or evidence given by a person in specified circumstances shall not be admissible in evidence against him or some other person in any proceedings or class of proceedings (however described, and whether civil or criminal).

In this subsection, the reference to giving evidence is a reference to giving evidence in any manner, whether by furnishing information, making discovery, producing documents or otherwise.

(6)   Nothing in sections 34, 35, 36 or 37 prejudices any power of a court, in any proceedings, to exclude evidence (whether by preventing questions being put or otherwise) at its discretion.

39.   Power to apply sections 34 to 38 to armed forces

(1)   The Secretary of State may by order direct that any provision of sections 34 to 38 of this Act shall apply, subject to such modifications as he may specify, to any proceedings to which this section applies.

(2)   This section applies—

(a)   to proceedings whereby a charge is dealt with summarily under Part II of the Army Act 1955;

(b)   to proceedings whereby a charge is dealt with summarily under Part II of the Air Force Act 1955;

(c)   to proceedings whereby a charge is summarily tried under Part II of the Naval Discipline Act 1957;

(d)   to proceedings before a court martial constituted under the Army Act 1955;

(e)   to proceedings before a court martial constituted under the Air Force Act 1955;

(f)   to proceedings before a court martial constituted under the Naval Discipline Act 1957;

(g)   to proceedings before a disciplinary court constituted under section 50 of the Naval Discipline Act 1957;

(h)   to proceedings before the Courts-Martial Appeal Court;

(i)   to proceedings before a Standing Civilian Court;

and it applies wherever the proceedings take place.

(3)   An order under this section shall be made by statutory instrument and shall be subject to annulment in pursuance of a resolution of either House of Parliament.

Juries

40.   Disqualification for jury service of persons on bail in criminal proceedings
(1)   A person who is on bail in criminal proceedings shall not be qualified to serve as a juror in the Crown Court.

(2)   In this section 'bail in criminal proceedings' has the same meaning as in the Bail Act 1976.

41.   Jury service: disabled persons
After section 9A of the Juries Act 1974 there shall be inserted the following section—
'**9B.   Discharge of summonses to disabled persons only if incapable of acting effectively as a juror**
(1)   Where it appears to the appropriate officer, in the case of a person attending in pursuance of a summons under this Act, that on account of physical disability there is doubt as to his capacity to act effectively as a juror, the person may be brought before the judge.

(2)   The judge shall determine whether or not the person should act as a juror; but he shall affirm the summons unless he is of the opinion that the person will not, on account of his disability, be capable of acting effectively as a juror, in which case he shall discharge the summons.

(3)   In this section ''the judge'' means any judge of the High Court or any Circuit judge or Recorder.'.

42.   Jury service: excusal on religious grounds
In Schedule 1 to the Juries Act 1974, in Part III (Persons excusable as of right), after the entry entitled *Medical and other similar professions,* there shall be inserted the following—

'Members of certain religious bodies

A practising member of a religious society or order the tenets or beliefs of which are incompatible with jury service.'.

43.   Separation of jury during consideration of verdict
(1)   For section 13 of the Juries Act 1974 (under which a jury may be allowed to separate at any time before they consider their verdict) there shall be substituted—
'**13.   Separation**
If, on the trial of any person for an offence on indictment, the court thinks fit, it may at any time (whether before or after the jury have been directed to consider their verdict) permit the jury to separate.'.

(2)   The amendment made by subsection (1) above shall not have effect in relation to a trial where a direction to the jury to consider their verdict has been given before the commencement of this section.

Procedure, jurisdiction and powers of magistrates' courts

44.   Transfer for trial instead of committal proceedings
(1)   The functions of a magistrates' court as examining justices are hereby abolished.

(2)   The provisions set out in Part I of Schedule 4 to this Act as sections 4 to 8C of the Magistrates' Courts Act 1980 shall be substituted for sections 4 to 8 of that Act (which provide for the functions of magistrates' courts as examining justices).

(3)   The amendments specified in Part II of that Schedule shall also have effect.

(4)   Subsections (1) and (2) above do not apply in relation to proceedings in which a magistrates' court has begun to inquire into a case as examining justices before the commencement of this section.

45. Extension of procedures enabling magistrates' courts to deal with cases in which accused pleads guilty

The amendments to the Magistrates' Courts Act 1980 specified in Schedule 5 (being amendments designed principally to extend the procedures applicable in magistrates' courts when the accused pleads guilty) shall have effect.

46. Criminal damage, etc. as summary offence: relevant sum

(1)   In subsection (1) of section 22 of the Magistrates' Courts Act 1980 (under which, where an offence of or related to criminal damage or, in certain circumstances, an offence of aggravated vehicle-taking, is charged and it appears clear to the magistrates' court that the value involved does not exceed the relevant sum, the court is to proceed as if the offence were triable only summarily) in the second paragraph (which states the relevant sum), for '£2,000' there shall be substituted '£5,000'.

(2)   Subsection (1) above does not apply to an offence charged in respect of an act done before this section comes into force.

47. Recovery of fines, etc. by deduction from income support

(1)   In section 89 of the Magistrates' Courts Act 1980 (which gives a magistrates' court power to make a transfer of fine order), after subsection (2) there shall be inserted the following subsection—

'(2A) The functions of the court to which subsection (2) above relates shall be deemed to include the court's power to apply to the Secretary of State under any regulations made by him under section 24(1)(a) of the Criminal Justice Act 1991 (power to deduct fines etc. from income support).'.

(2)   In section 90 of the Magistrates' Courts Act 1980 (which gives a magistrates' court power to transfer a fine to Scotland), after subsection (3) there shall be inserted the following subsection—

'(3A) The functions of the court which shall cease to be exercisable by virtue of subsection (3) above shall be deemed to include the court's power to apply to the Secretary of State under regulations made by him under section 24(1)(a) of the Criminal Justice Act 1991 (power to deduct fines from income support).'.

(3)   In section 24(3) of the Criminal Justice Act 1991 (which relates to the Secretary of State's power to authorise deduction of fines etc. from income support), after paragraph (b) there shall be inserted the following paragraph—

'(c) the reference in paragraph (a) to "the court" includes a reference to a court to which the function in that paragraph has been transferred by virtue of a transfer of fine order under section 89(1) or (3) or 90(1)(a) of the 1980 Act (power of magistrates' court to make transfer of fine order) or under section 403(1)(a) or (b) of the Criminal Procedure (Scotland) Act 1975 (analogous provision as respects Scotland) and a reference to a court to which that function has been remitted by virtue of section 196(2) of the said Act of 1975 (enforcement of fine imposed by High Court of Justiciary).'.

(4) In section 403 of the Criminal Procedure (Scotland) Act 1975 (which gives a court of summary jurisdiction in Scotland power to make a transfer of fine order), after subsection (4) there shall be inserted the following subsection—

'(4A) The functions of the court to which subsection (4) above relates shall be deemed to include the court's power to apply to the Secretary of State under any regulations made by him under section 24(1)(a) of the Criminal Justice Act 1991 (power to deduct fines etc. from income support).'.

Sentencing: guilty pleas

48. Reduction in sentences for guilty pleas

(1) In determining what sentence to pass on an offender who has pleaded guilty to an offence in proceedings before that or another court a court shall take into account—

(a) the stage in the proceedings for the offence at which the offender indicated his intention to plead guilty, and

(b) the circumstances in which this indication was given.

(2) If, as a result of taking into account any matter referred to in subsection (1) above, the court imposes a punishment on the offender which is less severe than the punishment it would otherwise have imposed, it shall state in open court that it has done so.

Publication of reports in young offender cases

49. Restrictions on reports of proceedings in which children or young persons are concerned

For section 49 of the Children and Young Persons Act 1933 (restrictions on reports of proceedings in which children or young persons are concerned) there shall be substituted—

'**49. Restrictions on reports of proceedings in which children or young persons are concerned**

(1) The following prohibitions apply (subject to subsection (5) below) in relation to any proceedings to which this section applies, that is to say—

(a) no report shall be published which reveals the name, address or school of any child or young person concerned in the proceedings or includes any particulars likely to lead to the identification of any child or young person concerned in the proceedings; and

(b) no picture shall be published or included in a programme service as being or including a picture of any child or young person concerned in the proceedings.

(2) The proceedings to which this section applies are—

(a) proceedings in a youth court;

(b) proceedings on appeal from a youth court (including proceedings by way of case stated);

(c) proceedings under section 15 or 16 of the Children and Young Persons Act 1969 (proceedings for varying or revoking supervision orders); and

(d) proceedings on appeal from a magistrates' court arising out of proceedings under section 15 or 16 of that Act (including proceedings by way of case stated).

(3) The reports to which this section applies are reports in a newspaper and reports included in a programme service; and similarly as respects pictures.

(4)   For the purposes of this section a child or young person is 'concerned' in any proceedings whether as being the person against or in respect of whom the proceedings are taken or as being a witness in the proceedings.

(5)   Subject to subsection (7) below, a court may, in relation to proceedings before it to which this section applies, by order dispense to any specified extent with the requirements of this section in relation to a child or young person who is concerned in the proceedings if it is satisfied—

(a)   that it is appropriate to do so for the purpose of avoiding injustice to the child or young person; or

(b)   that, as respects a child or young person to whom this paragraph applies who is unlawfully at large, it is necessary to dispense with those requirements for the purpose of apprehending him and bringing him before a court or returning him to the place in which he was in custody.

(6)   Paragraph (b) of subsection (5) above applies to any child or young person who is charged with or has been convicted of—

(a)   a violent offence,

(b)   a sexual offence, or

(c)   an offence punishable in the case of a person aged 21 or over with imprisonment for fourteen years or more.

(7) The court shall not exercise its power under subsection (5)(b) above—

(a)   except in pursuance of an application by or on behalf of the Director of Public Prosecutions; and

(b)   unless notice of the application has been given by the Director of Public Prosecutions to any legal representative of the child or young person.

(8)   The court's power under subsection (5) above may be exercised by a single justice.

(9)   If a report or picture is published or included in a programme service in contravention of subsection (1) above, the following persons, that is to say—

(a)   in the case of publication of a written report or a picture as part of a newspaper, any proprietor, editor or publisher of the newspaper;

(b)   in the case of the inclusion of a report or picture in a programme service, any body corporate which provides the service and any person having functions in relation to the programme corresponding to those of an editor of a newspaper,

shall be liable on summary conviction to a fine not exceeding level 5 on the standard scale.

(10)   In any proceedings under section 15 or 16 of the Children and Young Persons Act 1969 (proceedings for varying or revoking supervision orders) before a magistrates' court other than a youth court or on appeal from such a court it shall be the duty of the magistrates' court or the appellate court to announce in the course of the proceedings that this section applies to the proceedings; and if the court fails to do so this section shall not apply to the proceedings.

(11)   In this section—

"legal representative" means an authorised advocate or authorised litigator, as defined by section 119(1) of the Courts and Legal Services Act 1990.

"programme" and "programme service" have the same meaning as in the Broadcasting Act 1990;

"sexual offence" has the same meaning as in section 31(1) of the Criminal Justice Act 1991;

"specified" means specified in an order under this section;

"violent offence" has the same meaning as in section 31(1) of the Criminal Justice Act 1991;

and a person who, having been granted bail, is liable to arrest (whether with or without a warrant) shall be treated as unlawfully at large.'.

Child testimony

50. Video recordings of testimony from child witnesses
In section 32A of the Criminal Justice Act 1988, in subsection (5)(b), the word 'adequately' shall be inserted after the words 'dealt with'.

Intimidation, etc., of witnesses, jurors and others

51. Intimidation, etc., of witnesses, jurors and others
(1)   A person who does to another person—
(a)   an act which intimidates, and is intended to intimidate, that other person;
(b)   knowing or believing that the other person is assisting in the investigation of an offence or is a witness or potential witness or a juror or potential juror in proceedings for an offence; and
(c)   intending thereby to cause the investigation or the course of justice to be obstructed, perverted or interfered with,
commits an offence.

(2)   A person who does or threatens to do to another person—
(a)   an act which harms or would harm, and is intended to harm, that other person;
(b)   knowing or believing that the other person, or some other person, has assisted in an investigation into an offence or has given evidence or particular evidence in proceedings for an offence, or has acted as a juror or concurred in a particular verdict in proceedings for an offence; and
(c)   does or threatens to do the act because of what (within paragraph (b)) he knows or believes,
commits an offence.

(3)   A person does an act 'to' another person with the intention of intimidating, or (as the case may be) harming, that other person not only where the act is done in the presence of that other and directed at him directly but also where the act is done to a third person and is intended, in the circumstances, to intimidate or (as the case may be) harm the person at whom the act is directed.

(4)   The harm that may be done or threatened may be financial as well as physical (whether to the person or a person's property) and similarly as respects an intimidatory act which consists of threats.

(5)   The intention required by subsection (1)(c) and the motive required by subsection (2)(c) above need not be the only or the predominating intention or motive with which the act is done or, in the case of subsection (2), threatened.

(6)   A person guilty of an offence under this section shall be liable—
(a)   on conviction on indictment, to imprisonment for a term not exceeding five years or a fine or both;
(b)   on summary conviction, to imprisonment for a term not exceeding six months or a fine not exceeding the statutory maximum or both.

(7)   If, in proceedings against a person for an offence under subsection (1)   above, it is proved that he did an act falling within paragraph (a) with the knowledge or belief required by paragraph (b), he shall be presumed, unless the contrary is proved, to have done the act with the intention required by paragraph (c) of that subsection.

(8)   If, in proceedings against a person for an offence under subsection (2) above, it is proved that he did or threatened to do an act falling within paragraph (a) within the relevant period with the knowledge or belief required by paragraph (b), he shall be presumed, unless the contrary is proved, to have done the act with the motive required by paragraph (c) of that subsection.

(9)   In this section—

'investigation into an offence' means such an investigation by the police or other person charged with the duty of investigating offences or charging offenders;

'offence' includes an alleged or suspected offence;

'potential', in relation to a juror, means a person who has been summoned for jury service at the court at which proceedings for the offence are pending; and

'the relevant period'—

(a)   in relation to a witness or juror in any proceedings for an offence, means the period beginning with the institution of the proceedings and ending with the first anniversary of the conclusion of the trial or, if there is an appeal or reference under section 17 of the Criminal Appeal Act 1968, of the conclusion of the appeal;

(b)   in relation to a person who has, or is believed by the accused to have, assisted in an investigation into an offence, but was not also a witness in proceedings for an offence, means the period of one year beginning with any act of his, or any act believed by the accused to be an act of his, assisting in the investigation; and

(c)   in relation to a person who both has, or is believed by the accused to have, assisted in the investigation into an offence and was a witness in proceedings for the offence, means the period beginning with any act of his, or any act believed by the accused to be an act of his, assisting in the investigation and ending with the anniversary mentioned in paragraph (a) above.

(10)   For the purposes of the definition of the relevant period in subsection (9) above—

(a)   proceedings for an offence are instituted at the earliest of the following times—

(i)   when a justice of the peace issues a summons or warrant under section 1 of the Magistrates' Courts Act 1980 in respect of the offence;

(ii)   when a person is charged with the offence after being taken into custody without a warrant;

(iii)   when a bill of indictment is preferred by virtue of section 2(2)(b) of the Administration of Justice (Miscellaneous Provisions) Act 1933;

(b)   proceedings at a trial of an offence are concluded with the occurrence of any of the following, the discontinuance of the prosecution, the discharge of the jury without a finding, the acquittal of the accused or the sentencing of or other dealing with the accused for the offence of which he was convicted; and

(c)   proceedings on an appeal are concluded on the determination of the appeal or the abandonment of the appeal.

(11) This section is in addition to, and not in derogation of, any offence subsisting at common law.

Criminal appeals

52. Circuit judges to act as judges of criminal division of Court of Appeal

(1) Section 9 of the Supreme Court Act 1981 (which provides for certain judges to act on request in courts other than that to which they were appointed) shall have effect with the amendments specified in subsections (2) to (5) below.

(2) In subsection (1)—

(a) after the words 'Table may', there shall be inserted the words ', subject to the proviso at the end of that Table,';

(b) in the Table, in column 2, in the entry specifying the court relating to entry 5 in column 1 (Circuit judges), after the words 'High Court' there shall be inserted the words 'and the Court of Appeal'; and

(c) at the end of the Table there shall be inserted the following—

'The entry in column 2 specifying the Court of Appeal in relation to a Circuit judge only authorises such a judge to act as a judge of a court in the criminal division of the Court of Appeal.'.

(3) In subsection (2)—

(a) in the definition of 'the appropriate authority' after the words 'High Court' there shall be inserted the words 'or a Circuit judge'; and

(b) at the end, there shall be inserted the following—

'but no request shall be made to a Circuit judge to act as a judge of a court in the criminal division of the Court of Appeal unless he is approved for the time being by the Lord Chancellor for the purpose of acting as a judge of that division.'.

(4) In subsection (5), for the words 'subsection (6)' there shall be substituted the words 'subsections (6) and (6A)'.

(5) After subsection (6) there shall be inserted the following subsection—

'(6A) A Circuit judge or Recorder shall not by virtue of subsection (5) exercise any of the powers conferred on a single judge by sections 31 and 44 of the Criminal Appeal Act 1968 (powers of single judge in connection with appeals to the Court of Appeal and appeals from the Court of Appeal to the House of Lords).'.

(6) The further amendments specified in subsections (7) to (9) below (which supplement the foregoing amendments) shall have effect.

(7) In section 55 of the Supreme Court Act 1981 (composition of criminal division of Court of Appeal)—

(a) in subsections (2) and (4), at the beginning, there shall be inserted the words 'Subject to subsection (6),'; and

(b) after subsection (5), there shall be inserted the following subsection—

'(6) A court shall not be duly constituted if it includes more than one Circuit judge acting as a judge of the court under section 9.'.

(8) After section 56 of the Supreme Court Act 1981 there shall be inserted the following section—

'**56A. Circuit judges not to sit on certain appeals**

No Circuit judge shall act in the criminal division of the Court of Appeal as a judge of that court under section 9 on the hearing of, or shall determine any application in proceedings incidental or preliminary to, an appeal against—

(a)   a conviction before a judge of the High Court; or

(b)   a sentence passed by a judge of the High Court.'.

(9)   After the section 56A of the Supreme Court Act 1981 inserted by subsection (8) above there shall be inserted the following section—

'**56B.   Allocation of cases in criminal division**

(1)   The appeals or classes of appeals suitable for allocation to a court of the criminal division of the Court of Appeal in which a Circuit judge is acting under section 9 shall be determined in accordance with directions given by or on behalf of the Lord Chief Justice with the concurrence of the Lord Chancellor.

(2)   In subsection (1) "appeal" includes the hearing of, or any application in proceedings incidental or preliminary to, an appeal.'.

53.   Expenses in criminal appeals in Northern Ireland Court of Appeal

(1)   After section 28(2) of the Criminal Appeal (Northern Ireland) Act 1980 (certain expenses to be defrayed up to amount allowed by the Master (Taxing Office)) there shall be inserted the following subsections—

'(2A)   Where a solicitor or counsel is dissatisfied with the amount of any expenses allowed by the Master (Taxing Office) under subsection (2)(a) above, he may apply to that Master to review his decision.

(2B)   On a review under subsection (2A) the Master (Taxing Office) may confirm or vary the amount of expenses allowed by him.

(2C)   An application under subsection (2A) shall be made, and a review under that subsection shall be conducted, in accordance with rules of court.

(2D)   Where a solicitor or counsel is dissatisfied with the decision of the Master (Taxing Office) on a review under subsection (2A) above, he may appeal against that decision to the High Court and the Lord Chancellor may appear and be represented on any such appeal.

(2E)   Where the Lord Chancellor is dissatisfied with the decision of the Master (Taxing Office) on a review under subsection (2A) above in relation to the expenses of a solicitor or counsel, he may appeal against that decision to the High Court and the solicitor or barrister may appear or be represented on any such appeal.

(2F)   On any appeal under subsection (2D) or (2E) above the High Court may confirm or vary the amount of expenses allowed by the Master (Taxing Office) and the decision of the High Court shall be final.

(2G)   The power of the Master (Taxing Office) or the High Court to vary the amount of expenses allowed under subsection (2)(a) above includes power to increase or reduce that amount to such extent as the Master or (as the case may be) the High Court thinks fit; and the reference in subsection (2) above to the amount allowed by the Master (Taxing Office) shall, in a case where that amount has been so varied, be construed as a reference to that amount as so varied.'.

(2)   Subsection (1) above does not have effect in relation to expenses allowed by the Master (Taxing Office) under section 28(2)(a) of the Criminal Appeal (Northern Ireland) Act 1980 before the date on which that subsection comes into force.

PART IV   POLICE POWERS

Powers of police to take body samples

54.   Powers of police to take intimate body samples

(1)   Section 62 of the Police and Criminal Evidence Act 1984 (regulation of taking of intimate samples) shall be amended as follows.

(2)   After subsection (1) there shall be inserted the following subsection—

'(1A)   An intimate sample may be taken from a person who is not in police detention but from whom, in the course of the investigation of an offence, two or more non-intimate samples suitable for the same means of analysis have been taken which have proved insufficient—

(a)   if a police officer of at least the rank of superintendent authorises it to be taken; and

(b)   if the appropriate consent is given.'.

(3)   In subsection (2)—

(a)   after the word 'authorisation' there shall be inserted the words 'under subsection (1) or (1A) above'; and

(b)   in paragraph (a), for the words 'serious arrestable offence' there shall be substituted the words 'recordable offence'.

(4)   In subsection (3), after the words 'subsection (1)' there shall be inserted the words 'or (1A)'.

(5)   In subsection (9)—

(a)   for the words 'or saliva' there shall be substituted the words 'or a dental impression'; and

(b)   at the end there shall be inserted the words 'and a dental impression may only be taken by a registered dentist'.

55.   Powers of police to take non-intimate body samples

(1)   Section 63 of the Police and Criminal Evidence Act 1984 (regulation of taking of non-intimate samples) shall be amended as follows.

(2)   After subsection (3), there shall be inserted the following subsections—

'(3A) A non-intimate sample may be taken from a person (whether or not he falls within subsection (3)(a) above) without the appropriate consent if—

(a)   he has been charged with a recordable offence or informed that he will be reported for such an offence; and

(b)   either he has not had a non-intimate sample taken from him in the course of the investigation of the offence by the police or he has had a non-intimate sample taken from him but either it was not suitable for the same means of analysis or, though so suitable, the sample proved insufficient.

(3B)   A non-intimate sample may be taken from a person without the appropriate consent if he has been convicted of a recordable offence.'.

(3)   In subsection (4), in paragraph (a), for the words 'serious arrestable offence' there shall be substituted the words 'recordable offence'.

(4)   After subsection (8), there shall be inserted the following subsection—

'(8A)   In a case where by virtue of subsection (3A) or (3B) a sample is taken from a person without the appropriate consent—

(a)   he shall be told the reason before the sample is taken; and

(b)   the reason shall be recorded as soon as practicable after the sample is taken.'.

(5)   In subsection (9), after the words 'subsection (8)' there shall be inserted the words 'or (8A)'.

(6)   After subsection (9) there shall be inserted the following subsection—

'(10)   Subsection (3B) above shall not apply to persons convicted before the date on which that subsection comes into force.'.

56. Fingerprints and samples: supplementary provisions

The following section shall be inserted after section 63 of the Police and Criminal Evidence Act 1984—

'**63A.** '**Fingerprints and samples: supplementary provisions**

(1) Fingerprints or samples or the information derived from samples taken under any power conferred by this Part of this Act from a person who has been arrested on suspicion of being involved in a recordable offence may be checked against other fingerprints or samples or the information derived from other samples contained in records held by or on behalf of the police or held in connection with or as a result of an investigation of an offence.

(2) Where a sample of hair other than pubic hair is to be taken the sample may be taken either by cutting hairs or by plucking hairs with their roots so long as no more are plucked than the person taking the sample reasonably considers to be necessary for a sufficient sample.

(3) Where any power to take a sample is exercisable in relation to a person the sample may be taken in a prison or other institution to which the Prison Act 1952 applies.

(4) Any constable may, within the allowed period, require a person who is neither in police detention nor held in custody by the police on the authority of a court to attend a police station in order to have a sample taken where—

(a) the person has been charged with a recordable offence or informed that he will be reported for such an offence and either he has not had a sample taken from him in the course of the investigation of the offence by the police or he has had a sample so taken from him but either it was not suitable for the same means of analysis or, though so suitable, the sample proved insufficient; or

(b) the person has been convicted of a recordable offence and either he has not had a sample taken from him since the conviction or he has had a sample taken from him (before or after his conviction) but either it was not suitable for the same means of analysis or, though so suitable, the sample proved insufficient.

(5) The period allowed for requiring a person to attend a police station for the purpose specified in subsection (4) above is—

(a) in the case of a person falling within paragraph (a), one month beginning with the date of the charge or one month beginning with the date on which the appropriate officer is informed of the fact that the sample is not suitable for the same means of analysis or has proved insufficient, as the case may be;

(b) in the case of a person falling within paragraph (b), one month beginning with the date of the conviction or one month beginning with the date on which the appropriate officer is informed of the fact that the sample is not suitable for the same means of analysis or has proved insufficient, as the case may be.

(6) A requirement under subsection (4) above—

(a) shall give the person at least 7 days within which he must so attend; and

(b) may direct him to attend at a specified time of day or between specified times of day.

(7) Any constable may arrest without a warrant a person who has failed to comply with a requirement under subsection (4) above.

(8)   In this section "the appropriate officer" is—

(a)   in the case of a person falling within subsection (4)(a), the officer investigating the offence with which that person has been charged or as to which he was informed that he would be reported;

(b)   in the case of a person falling within subsection (4)(b), the officer in charge of the police station from which the investigation of the offence of which he was convicted was conducted.'.

57.   Retention of samples in certain cases

(1)   Section 64 of the Police and Criminal Evidence Act 1984 (which prescribes the situations in which fingerprints and samples must be destroyed) shall be amended as follows.

(2)   In subsections (1), (2) and (3), after the words 'they must' there shall be inserted the words ', except as provided in subsection (3A) below,'.

(3)   After subsection (3), there shall be inserted the following subsections—

'(3A)   Samples which are required to be destroyed under subsection (1), (2) or (3) above need not be destroyed if they were taken for the purpose of the same investigation of an offence of which a person from whom one was taken has been convicted, but the information derived from the sample of any person entitled (apart from this subsection) to its destruction under subsection (1), (2) or (3) above shall not be used—

(a)   in evidence against the person so entitled; or

(b)   for the purposes of any investigation of an offence.

(3B)   Where samples are required to be destroyed under subsections (1), (2) or (3) above, and subsection (3A) above does not apply, information derived from the sample of any person entitled to its destruction under subsection (1), (2) or (3) above shall not be used—

(a)   in evidence against the person so entitled; or

(b)   for the purposes of any investigation of an offence.'.

58.   Samples: intimate and non-intimate etc.

(1)   Section 65 of the Police and Criminal Evidence Act 1984 (which contains definitions of intimate and non-intimate samples and other relevant definitions) shall be amended as follows.

(2)   For the definition of 'intimate sample' there shall be substituted—

'"intimate sample" means—

(a)   a sample of blood, semen or any other tissue fluid, urine or pubic hair;

(b)   a dental impression;

(c)   a swab taken from a person's body orifice other than the mouth;'.

(3)   For the definition of 'non-intimate sample' there shall be substituted—

'"non-intimate sample" means—

(a)   a sample of hair other than pubic hair;

(b)   a sample taken from a nail or from under a nail;

(c)   a swab taken from any part of a person's body including the mouth but not any other body orifice;

(d)   saliva;

(e)   a footprint or a similar impression of any part of a person's body other than a part of his hand;'.

(4)　After the definition of 'non-intimate sample' there shall be inserted the following definitions—

'"registered dentist" has the same meaning as in the Dentists Act 1984;

"speculative search", in relation to a person's fingerprints or samples, means such a check against other fingerprints or samples or against information derived from other samples as is referred to in section 63A(1) above;

"sufficient" and "insufficient", in relation to a sample, means sufficient or insufficient (in point of quantity or quality) for the purpose of enabling information to be produced by the means of analysis used or to be used in relation to the sample.'.

59.　Extension of powers to search persons' mouths

(1)　In section 65 of the Police and Criminal Evidence Act 1984 (definitions for purposes of Part V: treatment of persons by police), after the definition of 'intimate sample' there shall be inserted the following definition—

'"intimate search" means a search which consists of the physical examination of a person's body orifices other than the mouth;'.

(2)　In section 32 of that Act (powers of search upon arrest), in subsection (4), at the end, there shall be inserted 'but they do authorise a search of a person's mouth'.

Powers of police to stop and search

60.　Powers to stop and search in anticipation of violence

(1)　Where a police officer of or above the rank of superintendent reasonably believes that—

(a)　incidents involving serious violence may take place in any locality in his area, and

(b)　it is expedient to do so to prevent their occurrence,

he may give an authorisation that the powers to stop and search persons and vehicles conferred by this section shall be exercisable at any place within that locality for a period not exceeding twenty four hours.

(2)　The power conferred by subsection (1) above may be exercised by a chief inspector or an inspector if he reasonably believes that incidents involving serious violence are imminent and no superintendent is available.

(3)　If it appears to the officer who gave the authorisation or to a superintendent that it is expedient to do so, having regard to offences which have, or are reasonably suspected to have, been committed in connection with any incident falling within the authorisation, he may direct that the authorisation shall continue in being for a further six hours.

(4)　This section confers on any constable in uniform power—

(a)　to stop any pedestrian and search him or anything carried by him for offensive weapons or dangerous instruments;

(b)　to stop any vehicle and search the vehicle, its driver and any passenger for offensive weapons or dangerous instruments.

(5)　A constable may, in the exercise of those powers, stop any person or vehicle and make any search he thinks fit whether or not he has any grounds for suspecting that the person or vehicle is carrying weapons or articles of that kind.

(6)　If in the course of a search under this section a constable discovers a dangerous instrument or an article which he has reasonable grounds for suspecting to be an offensive weapon, he may seize it.

(7)   This section applies (with the necessary modifications) to ships, aircraft and hovercraft as it applies to vehicles.

(8)   A person who fails to stop or (as the case may be) to stop the vehicle when required to do so by a constable in the exercise of his powers under this section shall be liable on summary conviction to imprisonment for a term not exceeding one month or to a fine not exceeding level 3 on the standard scale or both.

(9)   Any authorisation under this section shall be in writing signed by the officer giving it and shall specify the locality in which and the period during which the powers conferred by this section are exercisable and a direction under subsection (3) above shall also be given in writing or, where that is not practicable, recorded in writing as soon as it is practicable to do so.

(10)   Where a vehicle is stopped by a constable under this section, the driver shall be entitled to obtain a written statement that the vehicle was stopped under the powers conferred by this section if he applies for such a statement not later than the end of the period of twelve months from the day on which the vehicle was stopped and similarly as respects a pedestrian who is stopped and searched under this section.

(11)   In this section—

'dangerous instruments' means instruments which have a blade or are sharply pointed;

'offensive weapon' has the meaning given by section 1(9) of the Police and Criminal Evidence Act 1984; and

'vehicle' includes a caravan as defined in section 29(1) of the Caravan Sites and Control of Development Act 1960.

(12)   The powers conferred by this section are in addition to and not in derogation of, any power otherwise conferred.

PART V   PUBLIC ORDER: COLLECTIVE TRESPASS OR NUISANCE ON LAND

Powers to remove trespassers on land

61.   Power to remove trespassers on land

(1)   If the senior police officer present at the scene reasonably believes that two or more persons are trespassing on land and are present there with the common purpose of residing there for any period, that reasonable steps have been taken by or on behalf of the occupier to ask them to leave and—

(a)   that any of those persons has caused damage to the land or to property on the land or used threatening, abusive or insulting words or behaviour towards the occupier, a member of his family or an employee or agent of his, or

(b)   that those persons have between them six or more vehicles on the land,

he may direct those persons, or any of them, to leave the land and to remove any vehicles or other property they have with them on the land.

(2)   Where the persons in question are reasonably believed by the senior police officer to be persons who were not originally trespassers but have become trespassers on the land, the officer must reasonably believe that the other conditions specified in subsection (1) are satisfied after those persons became trespassers before he can exercise the power conferred by that subsection.

(3)   A direction under subsection (1) above, if not communicated to the persons referred to in subsection (1) by the police officer giving the direction, may be communicated to them by any constable at the scene.

(4)   If a person knowing that a direction under subsection (1) above has been given which applies to him—

(a)   fails to leave the land as soon as reasonably practicable, or

(b)   having left again enters the land as a trespasser within the period of three months beginning with the day on which the direction was given,

he commits an offence and is liable on summary conviction to imprisonment for a term not exceeding three months or a fine not exceeding level 4 on the standard scale, or both.

(5)   A constable in uniform who reasonably suspects that a person is committing an offence under this section may arrest him without a warrant.

(6)   In proceedings for an offence under this section it is a defence for the accused to show—

(a)   that he was not trespassing on the land, or

(b)   that he had a reasonable excuse for failing to leave the land as soon as reasonably practicable or, as the case may be, for again entering the land as a trespasser.

(7)   In its application in England and Wales to common land this section has effect as if in the preceding subsections of it—

(a)   references to trespassing or trespassers were references to acts and persons doing acts which constitute either a trespass as against the occupier or an infringement of the commoners' rights; and

(b)   references to 'the occupier' included the commoners or any of them or, in the case of common land to which the public has access, the local authority as well as any commoner.

(8)   Subsection (7) above does not—

(a)   require action by more than one occupier; or

(b)   constitute persons trespassers as against any commoner or the local authority if they are permitted to be there by the other occupier.

(9)   In this section—

'common land' means common land as defined in section 22 of the Commons Registration Act 1965;

'commoner' means a person with rights of common as defined in section 22 of the Commons Registration Act 1965;

'land' does not include—

(a)   buildings other than—

(i)   agricultural buildings within the meaning of, in England and Wales, paragraphs 3 to 8 of Schedule 5 to the Local Government Finance Act 1988 or, in Scotland, section 7(2) of the Valuation and Rating (Scotland) Act 1956, or

(ii)   scheduled monuments within the meaning of the Ancient Monuments and Archaeological Areas Act 1979;

(b)   land forming part of—

(i)   a highway unless it falls within the classifications in section 54 of the Wildlife and Countryside Act 1981 (footpath, bridleway or byway open to all traffic or road used as a public path) or is a cycle track under the Highways Act 1980 or the Cycle Tracks Act 1984; or

(ii)   a road within the meaning of the Roads (Scotland) Act 1984 unless it falls within the definitions in section 151(2)(a)(ii) or (b) (footpaths and cycle tracks) of that Act or is a bridleway within the meaning of section 47 of the Countryside (Scotland) Act 1967;

'the local authority', in relation to common land, means any local authority which has powers in relation to the land under section 9 of the Commons Registration Act 1965;

'occupier' (and in subsection (8) 'the other occupier') means—

(a)   in England and Wales, the person entitled to possession of the land by virtue of an estate or interest held by him; and

(b)   in Scotland, the person lawfully entitled to natural possession of the land;

'property', in relation to damage to property on land, means—

(a)   in England and Wales, property within the meaning of section 10(1) of the Criminal Damage Act 1971; and

(b)   in Scotland, either—

(i)   heritable property other than land; or

(ii)   corporeal moveable property,

and 'damage' includes the deposit of any substance capable of polluting the land;

'trespass' means, in the application of this section—

(a)   in England and Wales, subject to the extensions effected by subsection (7) above, trespass as against the occupier of the land;

(b)   in Scotland, entering, or as the case may be remaining on, land without lawful authority and without the occupier's consent; and

'trespassing' and 'trespasser' shall be construed accordingly;

'vehicle' includes—

(a)   any vehicle, whether or not it is in a fit state for use on roads, and includes any chassis or body, with or without wheels, appearing to have formed part of such a vehicle, and any load carried by, and anything attached to, such a vehicle; and

(b)   a caravan as defined in section 29(1) of the Caravan Sites and Control of Development Act 1960;

and a person may be regarded for the purposes of this section as having a purpose of residing in a place notwithstanding that he has a home elsewhere.

62.   Supplementary powers of seizure

(1)   If a direction has been given under section 61 and a constable reasonably suspects that any person to whom the direction applies has, without reasonable excuse—

(a)   failed to remove any vehicle on the land which appears to the constable to belong to him or to be in his possession or under his control; or

(b)   entered the land as a trespasser with a vehicle within the period of three months beginning with the day on which the direction was given,

the constable may seize and remove that vehicle.

(2)   In this section, 'trespasser' and 'vehicle' have the same meaning as in section 61.

Powers in relation to raves

63.   Powers to remove persons attending or preparing for a rave
   (1)   This section applies to a gathering on land in the open air of 100 or more persons (whether or not trespassers) at which amplified music is played during the night (with or without intermissions) and is such as, by reason of its loudness and duration and the time at which it is played, is likely to cause serious distress to the inhabitants of the locality; and for this purpose—
   (a)   such a gathering continues during intermissions in the music and, where the gathering extends over several days, throughout the period during which amplified music is played at night (with or without intermissions); and
   (b)   'music' includes sounds wholly or predominantly characterised by the emission of a succession of repetitive beats.
   (2)   If, as respects any land in the open air, a police officer of at least the rank of superintendent reasonably believes that—
   (a)   two or more persons are making preparations for the holding there of a gathering to which this section applies,
   (b)   ten or more persons are waiting for such a gathering to begin there, or
   (c)   ten or more persons are attending such a gathering which is in progress,
he may give a direction that those persons and any other persons who come to prepare or wait for or to attend the gathering are to leave the land and remove any vehicles or other property which they have with them on the land.
   (3)   A direction under subsection (2) above, if not communicated to the persons referred to in subsection (2) by the police officer giving the direction, may be communicated to them by any constable at the scene.
   (4)   Persons shall be treated as having had a direction under subsection (2) above communicated to them if reasonable steps have been taken to bring it to their attention.
   (5)   A direction under subsection (2) above does not apply to an exempt person.
   (6)   If a person knowing that a direction has been given which applies to him—
   (a)   fails to leave the land as soon as reasonably practicable, or
   (b)   having left again enters the land within the period of 7 days beginning with the day on which the direction was given,
he commits an offence and is liable on summary conviction to imprisonment for a term not exceeding three months or a fine not exceeding level 4 on the standard scale, or both.
   (7)   In proceedings for an offence under this section it is a defence for the accused to show that he had a reasonable excuse for failing to leave the land as soon as reasonably practicable or, as the case may be, for again entering the land.
   (8)   A constable in uniform who reasonably suspects that a person is committing an offence under this section may arrest him without a warrant.
   (9)   This section does not apply—
   (a)   in England and Wales, to a gathering licensed by an entertainment licence; or
   (b)   in Scotland, to a gathering in premises which, by virtue of section 41 of the Civic Government (Scotland) Act 1982, are licensed to be used as a place of public entertainment.
   (10)   In this section—

'entertainment licence' means a licence granted by a local authority under—
(a)   Schedule 12 to the London Government Act 1963;
(b)   section 3 of the Private Places of Entertainment (Licensing) Act 1967; or
(c)   Schedule 1 to the Local Government (Miscellaneous Provisions) Act 1982;
'exempt person', in relation to land (or any gathering on land), means the occupier, any member of his family and any employee or agent of his and any person whose home is situated on the land;
'land in the open air' includes a place partly open to the air;
'local authority' means—
(a)   in Greater London, a London borough council or the Common Council of the City of London;
(b)   in England outside Greater London, a district council or the council of the Isles of Scilly;
(c)   in Wales, a county council or county borough council; and
'occupier', 'trespasser' and 'vehicle' have the same meaning as in section 61.
(11)   Until 1st April 1996, in this section 'local authority' means, in Wales, a district council.

64.   Supplementary powers of entry and seizure
(1)   If a police officer of at least the rank of superintendent reasonably believes that circumstances exist in relation to any land which would justify the giving of a direction under section 63 in relation to a gathering to which that section applies he may authorise any constable to enter the land for any of the purposes specified in subsection (2) below.
(2)   Those purposes are—
(a)   to ascertain whether such circumstances exist; and
(b)   to exercise any power conferred on a constable by section 63 or subsection (4) below.
(3)   A constable who is so authorised to enter land for any purpose may enter the land without a warrant.
(4)   If a direction has been given under section 63 and a constable reasonably suspects that any person to whom the direction applies has, without reasonable excuse—
(a)   failed to remove any vehicle or sound equipment on the land which appears to the constable to belong to him or to be in his possession or under his control; or
(b)   entered the land as a trespasser with a vehicle or sound equipment within the period of 7 days beginning with the day on which the direction was given,
the constable may seize and remove that vehicle or sound equipment.
(5)   Subsection (4) above does not authorise the seizure of any vehicle or sound equipment of an exempt person.
(6)   In this section—
'exempt person' has the same meaning as in section 63;
'sound equipment' means equipment designed or adapted for amplifying music and any equipment suitable for use in connection with such equipment, and 'music' has the same meaning as in section 63; and
'vehicle' has the same meaning as in section 61.

65. Raves: power to stop persons from proceeding

(1)   If a constable in uniform reasonably believes that a person is on his way to a gathering to which section 63 applies in relation to which a direction under section 63(2) is in force, he may, subject to subsections (2) and (3) below—

(a)   stop that person, and

(b)   direct him not to proceed in the direction of the gathering.

(2)   The power conferred by subsection (1) above may only be exercised at a place within 5 miles of the boundary of the site of the gathering.

(3)   No direction may be given under subsection (1) above to an exempt person.

(4)   If a person knowing that a direction under subsection (1) above has been given to him fails to comply with that direction, he commits an offence and is liable on summary conviction to a fine not exceeding level 3 on the standard scale.

(5)   A constable in uniform who reasonably suspects that a person is committing an offence under this section may arrest him without a warrant.

(6)   In this section, 'exempt person' has the same meaning as in section 63.

66. Power of court to forfeit sound equipment

(1)   Where a person is convicted of an offence under section 63 in relation to a gathering to which that section applies and the court is satisfied that any sound equipment which has been seized from him under section 64(4), or which was in his possession or under his control at the relevant time, has been used at the gathering the court may make an order for forfeiture under this subsection in respect of that property.

(2)   The court may make an order under subsection (1) above whether or not it also deals with the offender in respect of the offence in any other way and without regard to any restrictions on forfeiture in any enactment.

(3)   In considering whether to make an order under subsection (1) above in respect of any property a court shall have regard—

(a)   to the value of the property; and

(b)   to the likely financial and other effects on the offender of the making of the order (taken together with any other order that the court contemplates making).

(4)   An order under subsection (1) above shall operate to deprive the offender of his rights, if any, in the property to which it relates, and the property shall (if not already in their possession) be taken into the possession of the police.

(5)   Except in a case to which subsection (6) below applies, where any property has been forfeited under subsection (1) above, a magistrates' court may, on application by a claimant of the property, other than the offender from whom it was forfeited under subsection (1) above, make an order for delivery of the property to the applicant if it appears to the court that he is the owner of the property.

(6)   In a case where forfeiture under subsection (1) above has been by order of a Scottish court, a claimant such as is mentioned in subsection (5) above may, in such manner as may be prescribed by act of adjournal, apply to that court for an order for the return of the property in question.

(7)   No application shall be made under subsection (5), or by virtue of subsection (6), above by any claimant of the property after the expiration of 6 months from the date on which an order under subsection (1) above was made in respect of the property.

(8)   No such application shall succeed unless the claimant satisfies the court either that he had not consented to the offender having possession of the property or

that he did not know, and had no reason to suspect, that the property was likely to be used at a gathering to which section 63 applies.

(9)   An order under subsection (5), or by virtue of subsection (6), above shall not affect the right of any person to take, within the period of 6 months from the date of an order under subsection (5), or as the case may be by virtue of subsection (6), above, proceedings for the recovery of the property from the person in possession of it in pursuance of the order, but on the expiration of that period the right shall cease.

(10)   The Secretary of State may make regulations for the disposal of property, and for the application of the proceeds of sale of property, forfeited under subsection (1) above where no application by a claimant of the property under subsection (5), or by virtue of subsection (6), above has been made within the period specified in subsection (7) above or no such application has succeeded.

(11)   The regulations may also provide for the investment of money and for the audit of accounts.

(12)   The power to make regulations under subsection (10) above shall be exercisable by statutory instrument which shall be subject to annulment in pursuance of a resolution of either House of Parliament.

(13)   In this section—
'relevant time', in relation to a person—
(a)   convicted in England and Wales of an offence under section 63, means the time of his arrest for the offence or of the issue of a summons in respect of it;
(b)   so convicted in Scotland, means the time of his arrest for, or of his being cited as an accused in respect of, the offence;
'sound equipment' has the same meaning as in section 64.

Retention and charges for seized property

67.   Retention and charges for seized property

(1)   Any vehicles which have been seized and removed by a constable under section 62(1) or 64(4) may be retained in accordance with regulations made by the Secretary of State under subsection (3) below.

(2)   Any sound equipment which has been seized and removed by a constable under section 64(4) may be retained until the conclusion of proceedings against the person from whom it was seized for an offence under section 63.

(3)   The Secretary of State may make regulations—
(a)   regulating the retention and safe keeping and the disposal and the destruction in prescribed circumstances of vehicles; and
(b)   prescribing charges in respect of the removal, retention, disposal and destruction of vehicles.

(4)   Any authority shall be entitled to recover from a person from whom a vehicle has been seized such charges as may be prescribed in respect of the removal, retention, disposal and destruction of the vehicle by the authority.

(5)   Regulations under subsection (3) above may make different provisions for different classes of vehicles or for different circumstances.

(6)   Any charges under subsection (4) above shall be recoverable as a simple contract debt.

(7)   Any authority having custody of vehicles under regulations under subsection (3) above shall be entitled to retain custody until any charges under subsection (4) are paid.

(8) The power to make regulations under subsection (3) above shall be exercisable by statutory instrument which shall be subject to annulment in pursuance of a resolution of either House of Parliament.

(9) In this section—

'conclusion of proceedings' against a person means—

(a) his being sentenced or otherwise dealt with for the offence or his acquittal;

(b) the discontinuance of the proceedings; or

(c) the decision not to prosecute him,

whichever is the earlier;

'sound equipment' has the same meaning as in section 64; and

'vehicle' has the same meaning as in section 61.

Disruptive trespassers

68. Offence of aggravated trespass

(1) A person commits the offence of aggravated trespass if he trespasses on land in the open air and, in relation to any lawful activity which persons are engaging in or are about to engage in on that or adjoining land in the open air, does there anything which is intended by him to have the effect—

(a) of intimidating those persons or any of them so as to deter them or any of them from engaging in that activity,

(b) of obstructing that activity, or

(c) of disrupting that activity.

(2) Activity on any occasion on the part of a person or persons on land is 'lawful' for the purposes of this section if he or they may engage in the activity on the land on that occasion without committing an offence or trespassing on the land.

(3) A person guilty of an offence under this section is liable on summary conviction to imprisonment for a term not exceeding three months or a fine not exceeding level 4 on the standard scale, or both.

(4) A constable in uniform who reasonably suspects that a person is committing an offence under this section may arrest him without a warrant.

(5) In this section 'land' does not include—

(a) the highways and roads excluded from the application of section 61 by paragraph (b) of the definition of 'land' in subsection (9) of that section; or

(b) a road within the meaning of the Roads (Northern Ireland) Order 1993.

69. Powers to remove persons committing or participating in aggravated trespass

(1) If the senior police officer present at the scene reasonably believes—

(a) that a person is committing, has committed or intends to commit the offence of aggravated trespass on land in the open air; or

(b) that two or more persons are trespassing on land in the open air and are present there with the common purpose of intimidating persons so as to deter them from engaging in a lawful activity or of obstructing or disrupting a lawful activity,

he may direct that person or (as the case may be) those persons (or any of them) to leave the land.

(2) A direction under subsection (1) above, if not communicated to the persons referred to in subsection (1) by the police officer giving the direction, may be communicated to them by any constable at the scene.

(3)   If a person knowing that a direction under subsection (1) above has been given which applies to him—

(a)   fails to leave the land as soon as practicable, or

(b)   having left again enters the land as a trespasser within the period of three months beginning with the day on which the direction was given,

he commits an offence and is liable on summary conviction to imprisonment for a term not exceeding three months or a fine not exceeding level 4 on the standard scale, or both.

(4)   In proceedings for an offence under subsection (3) it is a defence for the accused to show—

(a)   that he was not trespassing on the land, or

(b)   that he had a reasonable excuse for failing to leave the land as soon as practicable or, as the case may be, for again entering the land as a trespasser.

(5)   A constable in uniform who reasonably suspects that a person is committing an offence under this section may arrest him without a warrant.

(6)   In this section 'lawful activity' and 'land' have the same meaning as in section 68.

Trespassory assemblies

70.   Trespassory assemblies

In Part II of the Public Order Act 1986 (processions and assemblies), after section 14, there shall be inserted the following sections—

'14A.   Prohibiting trespassory assemblies

(1)   If at any time the chief officer of police reasonably believes that an assembly is intended to be held in any district at a place on land to which the public has no right of access or only a limited right of access and that the assembly—

(a)   is likely to be held without the permission of the occupier of the land or to conduct itself in such a way as to exceed the limits of any permission of his or the limits of the public's right of access, and

(b)   may result—

(i)   in serious disruption to the life of the community, or

(ii)   where the land, or a building or monument on it, is of historical, architectural, archaeological or scientific importance, in significant damage to the land, building or monument,

he may apply to the council of the district for an order prohibiting for a specified period the holding of all trespassory assemblies in the district or a part of it, as specified.

(2)   On receiving such an application, a council may—

(a)   in England and Wales, with the consent of the Secretary of State make an order either in the terms of the application or with such modifications as may be approved by the Secretary of State; or

(b)   in Scotland, make an order in the terms of the application.

(3)   Subsection (1) does not apply in the City of London or the metropolitan police district.

(4)   If at any time the Commissioner of Police for the City of London or the Commissioner of Police of the Metropolis reasonably believes that an assembly is intended to be held at a place on land to which the public has no right of access or only a limited right of access in his police area and that the assembly—

(a)   is likely to be held without the permission of the occupier of the land or to conduct itself in such a way as to exceed the limits of any permission of his or the limits of the public's right of access, and

(b)   may result—
(i)   in serious disruption to the life of the community, or
(ii)   where the land, or a building or monument on it, is of historical, architectural, archaeological or scientific importance, in significant damage to the land, building or monument,
he may with the consent of the Secretary of State make an order prohibiting for a specified period the holding of all trespassory assemblies in the area or a part of it, as specified.

(5)   An order prohibiting the holding of trespassory assemblies operates to prohibit any assembly which—

(a)   is held on land to which the public has no right of access or only a limited right of access, and

(b)   takes place in the prohibited circumstances, that is to say, without the permission of the occupier of the land or so as to exceed the limits of any permission of his or the limits of the public's right of access.

(6)   No order under this section shall prohibit the holding of assemblies for a period exceeding 4 days or in an area exceeding an area represented by a circle with a radius of 5 miles from a specified centre.

(7)   An order made under this section may be revoked or varied by a subsequent order made in the same way, that is, in accordance with subsection (1) and (2) or subsection (4), as the case may be.

(8)   Any order under this section shall, if not made in writing, be recorded in writing as soon as practicable after being made.

(9)   In this section and sections 14B and 14C—
"assembly" means an assembly of 20 or more persons;
"land" means land in the open air;
"limited", in relation to a right of access by the public to land, means that their use of it is restricted to use for a particular purpose (as in the case of a highway or road) or is subject to other restrictions;
"occupier" means—
(a)   in England and Wales, the person entitled to possession of the land by virtue of an estate or interest held by him; or
(b)   in Scotland, the person lawfully entitled to natural possession of the land,
and in subsections (1) and (4) includes the person reasonably believed by the authority applying for or making the order to be the occupier;
"public" includes a section of the public; and
"specified" means specified in an order under this section.

(10)   In relation to Scotland, the references in subsection (1) above to a district and to the council of the district shall be construed—

(a)   as respects applications before 1st April 1996, as references to the area of a regional or islands authority and to the authority in question; and

(b)   as respects applications on and after that date, as references to a local government area and to the council for that area.

(11)   In relation to Wales, the references in subsection (1) above to a district and to the council of the district shall be construed, as respects applications on and after 1st April 1996, as references to a county or county borough and to the council for that county or county borough.

14B.   Offences in connection with trespassory assemblies and arrest therefor

(1)   A person who organises an assembly the holding of which he knows is prohibited by an order under section 14A is guilty of an offence.

(2)   A person who takes part in an assembly which he knows is prohibited by an order under section 14A is guilty of an offence.

(3)   In England and Wales, a person who incites another to commit an offence under subsection (2) is guilty of an offence.

(4)   A constable in uniform may arrest without a warrant anyone he reasonably suspects to be committing an offence under this section.

(5)   A person guilty of an offence under subsection (1) is liable on summary conviction to imprisonment for a term not exceeding 3 months or a fine not exceeding level 4 on the standard scale or both.

(6)   A person guilty of an offence under subsection (2) is liable on summary conviction to a fine not exceeding level 3 on the standard scale.

(7)   A person guilty of an offence under subsection (3) is liable on summary conviction to imprisonment for a term not exceeding 3 months or a fine not exceeding level 4 on the standard scale or both, notwithstanding section 45(3) of the Magistrates' Courts Act 1980.

(8)   Subsection (3) above is without prejudice to the application of any principle of Scots Law as respects art and part guilt to such incitement as is mentioned in that subsection.'.

71.   Trespassory assemblies: power to stop persons from proceeding
After the section 14B inserted by section 70 in the Public Order Act 1986 there shall be inserted the following section—
'**14C.   Stopping persons from proceeding to trespassory assemblies**

(1)   If a constable in uniform reasonably believes that a person is on his way to an assembly within the area to which an order under section 14A applies which the constable reasonably believes is likely to be an assembly which is prohibited by that order, he may, subject to subsection (2) below—
    (a)   stop that person, and
    (b)   direct him not to proceed in the direction of the assembly.

(2)   The power conferred by subsection (1) may only be exercised within the area to which the order applies.

(3)   A person who fails to comply with a direction under subsection (1) which he knows has been given to him is guilty of an offence.

(4)   A constable in uniform may arrest without a warrant anyone he reasonably suspects to be committing an offence under this section.

(5)   A person guilty of an offence under subsection (3) is liable on summary conviction to a fine not exceeding level 3 on the standard scale.'.

Squatters

72. Violent entry to premises: special position of displaced residential occupiers and intending occupiers

(1)   Section 6 of the Criminal Law Act 1977 (which penalises violence by a person for securing entry into premises where a person on the premises is opposed and is known to be opposed to entry) shall be amended as follows.

(2)   After subsection (1), there shall be inserted the following subsection—

'(1A) Subsection (1) above does not apply to a person who is a displaced residential occupier or a protected intending occupier of the premises in question or who is acting on behalf of such an occupier; and if the accused adduces sufficient evidence that he was, or was acting on behalf of, such an occupier he shall be presumed to be, or to be acting on behalf of, such an occupier unless the contrary is proved by the prosecution.'.

(3)   In subsection (2), at the beginning, there shall be inserted the words 'Subject to subsection (1A) above,'.

(4)   Subsection (3) (which is superseded by the provision made by subsection (2) above) shall be omitted.

(5)   In subsection (7), at the end, there shall be inserted the words 'and section 12A below contains provisions which apply for determining when any person is to be regarded for the purposes of this Part of this Act as a protected intending occupier of any premises or of any access to any premises.'.

73. Adverse occupation of residential premises

For section 7 of the Criminal Law Act 1977 (trespassers failing to leave premises after being requested to do so by specified persons to be guilty of an offence) there shall be substituted the following section—

'7. Adverse occupation of resiential premises

(1)   Subject to the following provisions of this section and to section 12A(9) below, any person who is on any premises as a trespasser after having entered as such is guilty of an offence if he fails to leave those premises on being required to do so by or on behalf of—

(a)   a displaced residential occupier of the premises; or

(b)   an individual who is a protected intending occupier of the premises.

(2)   In any proceedings for an offence under this section it shall be a defence for the accused to prove that he believed that the person requiring him to leave the premises was not a displaced residential occupier or protected intending occupier of the premises or a person acting on behalf of a displaced residential occupier or protected intending occupier.

(3)   In any proceedings for an offence under this section it shall be a defence for the accused to prove—

(a)   that the premises in question are or form part of premises used mainly for non-residential purposes; and

(b)   that he was not on any part of the premises used wholly or mainly for residential purposes.

(4)   Any reference in the preceding provisions of this section to any premises includes a reference to any access to them, whether or not any such access itself constitutes premises, within the meaning of this Part of this Act.

(5)   A person guilty of an offence under this section shall be liable on summary conviction to imprisonment for a term not exceeding six months or to a fine not exceeding level 5 on the standard scale or to both.

(6)   A constable in uniform may arrest without warrant anyone who is, or whom he, with reasonable cause, suspects to be, guilty of an offence under this section.

(7)   Section 12 below contains provisions which apply for determining when any person is to be regarded for the purposes of this Part of this Act as a displaced residential occupier of any premises or of any access to any premises and section 12A below contains provisions which apply for determining when any person is to be regarded for the purposes of this Part of this Act as a protected intending occupier of any premises or of any access to any premises.'.

74.   Protected intending occupiers: supplementary provisions

After section 12 of the Criminal Law Act 1977 there shall be inserted the following section—

'12A.   **Protected intending occupiers: supplementary provisions**

(1)   For the purposes of this Part of this Act an individual is a protected intending occupier of any premises at any time if at that time he falls within subsection (2), (4) or (6) below.

(2)   An individual is a protected intending occupier of any premises if—

(a)   he has in those premises a freehold interest or a leasehold interest with not less than two years still to run;

(b)   he requires the premises for his own occupation as a residence;

(c)   he is excluded from occupation of the premises by a person who entered them, or any access to them, as a trespasser; and

(d)   he or a person acting on his behalf holds a written statement—

(i)   which specifies his interest in the premises;

(ii)   which states that he requires the premises for occupation as a residence for himself, and

(iii)   with respect to which the requirements in subsection (3) below are fulfilled.

(3)   The requirements referred to in subsection (2)(d)(iii) above are—

(a)   that the statement is signed by the person whose interest is specified in it in the presence of a justice of the peace or commissioner for oaths; and

(b)   that the justice of the peace or commissioner for oaths has subscribed his name as a witness to the signature.

(4)   An individual is also a protected intending occupier of any premises if—

(a)   he has a tenancy of those premises (other than a tenancy falling within subsection (2)(a) above or (6)(a) below) or a licence to occupy those premises granted by a person with a freehold interest or a leasehold interest with not less than two years still to run in the premises;

(b)   he requires the premises for his own occupation as a residence;

(c)   he is excluded from occupation of the premises by a person who entered them, or any access to them, as a trespasser; and

(d)   he or a person acting on his behalf holds a written statement—

(i)   which states that he has been granted a tenancy of those premises or a licence to occupy those premises;

(ii)   which specifies the interest in the premises of the person who granted that tenancy or licence to occupy ('the landlord');

(iii)   which states that he requires the premises for occupation as a residence for himself, and

(iv)   with respect to which the requirements in subsection (5) below are fulfilled.

(5)   The requirements referred to in subsection (4)(d)(iv) above are—

(a)   that the statement is signed by the landlord and by the tenant or licensee in the presence of a justice of the peace or commissioner for oaths;

(b)   that the justice of the peace or commissioner for oaths has subscribed his name as a witness to the signatures.

(6)   An individual is also a protected intending occupier of any premises if—

(a)   he has a tenancy of those premises (other than a tenancy falling within subsection (2)(a) or (4)(a) above) or a licence to occupy those premises granted by an authority to which this subsection applies;

(b)   he requires the premises for his own occupation as a residence;

(c)   he is excluded from occupation of the premises by a person who entered the premises, or any access to them, as a trespasser; and

(d)   there has been issued to him by or on behalf of the authority referred to in paragraph (a) above a certificate stating that—

(i)   he has been granted a tenancy of those premises or a licence to occupy those premises as a residence by the authority; and

(ii)   the authority which granted that tenancy or licence to occupy is one to which this subsection applies, being of a description specified in the certificate.

(7)   Subsection (6) above applies to the following authorities—

(a)   any body mentioned in section 14 of the Rent Act 1977 (landlord's interest belonging to local authority etc.);

(b)   the Housing Corporation;

(c)   Housing for Wales; and

(d)   a registered housing association within the meaning of the Housing Associations Act 1985.

(8)   A person is guilty of an offence if he makes a statement for the purposes of subsection (2)(d) or (4)(d) above which he knows to be false in a material particular or if he recklessly makes such a statement which is false in a material particular.

(9)   In any proceedings for an offence under section 7 of this Act where the accused was requested to leave the premises by a person claiming to be or to act on behalf of a protected intending occupier of the premises—

(a)   it shall be a defence for the accused to prove that, although asked to do so by the accused at the time the accused was requested to leave, that person failed at that time to produce to the accused such a statement as is referred to in subsection (2)(d) or (4)(d) above or such a certificate as is referred to in subsection (6)(d) above; and

(b)   any document purporting to be a certificate under subsection (6)(d) above shall be received in evidence and, unless the contrary is proved, shall be deemed to have been issued by or on behalf of the authority stated in the certificate.

(10)   A person guilty of an offence under subsection (8) above shall be liable on summary conviction to imprisonment for a term not exceeding six months or to a fine not exceeding level 5 on the standard scale or to both.

(11)   A person who is a protected intending occupier of any premises shall be regarded for the purposes of this Part of this Act as a protected intending occupier also of any access to those premises.'.

75.   Interim possession orders: false or misleading statements

(1)   A person commits an offence if, for the purpose of obtaining an interim possession order, he—

(a)   makes a statement which he knows to be false or misleading in a material particular; or

(b)   recklessly makes a statement which is false or misleading in a material particular.

(2)   A person commits an offence if, for the purpose of resisting the making of an interim possession order, he—

(a)   makes a statement which he knows to be false or misleading in a material particular; or

(b)   recklessly makes a statement which is false or misleading in a material particular.

(3)   A person guilty of an offence under this section shall be liable—

(a)   on conviction on indictment, to imprisonment for a term not exceeding two years or a fine or both;

(b)   on summary conviction, to imprisonment for a term not exceeding six months or a fine not exceeding the statutory maximum or both.

(4)   In this section—

'interim possession order' means an interim possession order (so entitled) made under rules of court for the bringing of summary proceedings for possession of premises which are occupied by trespassers;

'premises' has the same meaning as in Part II of the Criminal Law Act 1977 (offences relating to entering and remaining on property); and

'statement', in relation to an interim possession order, means any statement, in writing or oral and whether as to fact or belief, made in or for the purposes of the proceedings.

76.   Interim possession orders: trespassing during currency of order

(1)   This section applies where an interim possession order has been made in respect of any premises and served in accordance with rules of court; and references to 'the order' and 'the premises' shall be construed accordingly.

(2)   Subject to subsection (3), a person who is present on the premises as a trespasser at any time during the currency of the order commits an offence.

(3)   No offence under subsection (2) is committed by a person if—

(a)   he leaves the premises within 24 hours of the time of service of the order and does not return; or

(b)   a copy of the order was not fixed to the premises in accordance with rules of court.

(4)   A person who was in occupation of the premises at the time of service of the order but leaves them commits an offence if he re-enters the premises as a trespasser

or attempts to do so after the expiry of the order but within the period of one year beginning with the day on which it was served.

(5) A person guilty of an offence under this section shall be liable on summary conviction to imprisonment for a term not exceeding six months or a fine not exceeding level 5 on the standard scale or both.

(6) A person who is in occupation of the premises at the time of service of the order shall be treated for the purposes of this section as being present as a trespasser.

(7) A constable in uniform may arrest without a warrant anyone who is, or whom he reasonably suspects to be, guilty of an offence under this section.

(8) In this section—
'interim possession order' has the same meaning as in section 75 above and 'rules of court' is to be construed accordingly; and
'premises' has the same meaning as in that section, that is to say, the same meaning as in Part II of the Criminal Law Act 1977 (offences relating to entering and remaining on property).

Powers to remove unauthorised campers

77. Power of local authority to direct unauthorised campers to leave land

(1) If it appears to a local authority that persons are for the time being residing in a vehicle or vehicles within that authority's area—
(a) on any land forming part of a highway;
(b) on any other unoccupied land; or
(c) on any occupied land without the consent of the occupier,
the authority may give a direction that those persons and any others with them are to leave the land and remove the vehicle or vehicles and any other property they have with them on the land.

(2) Notice of a direction under subsection (1) must be served on the persons to whom the direction applies, but it shall be sufficient for this purpose for the direction to specify the land and (except where the direction applies to only one person) to be addressed to all occupants of the vehicles on the land, without naming them.

(3) If a person knowing that a direction under subsection (1) above has been given which applies to him—
(a) fails, as soon as practicable, to leave the land or remove from the land any vehicle or other property which is the subject of the direction, or
(b) having removed any such vehicle or property again enters the land with a vehicle within the period of three months beginning with the day on which the direction was given,
he commits an offence and is liable on summary conviction to a fine not exceeding level 3 on the standard scale.

(4) A direction under subsection (1) operates to require persons who re-enter the land within the said period with vehicles or other property to leave and remove the vehicles or other property as it operates in relation to the persons and vehicles or other property on the land when the direction was given.

(5) In proceedings for an offence under this section it is a defence for the accused to show that his failure to leave or to remove the vehicle or other property as soon as practicable or his re-entry with a vehicle was due to illness, mechanical breakdown or other immediate emergency.

(6) In this section—

'land' means land in the open air; 'local authority' means—

(a) in Greater London, a London borough or the Common Council of the City of London;

(b) in England outside Greater London, a county council, a district council or the Council of the Isles of Scilly;

(c) in Wales, a county council or a county borough council;

'occupier' means the person entitled to possession of the land by virtue of an estate or interest held by him;

'vehicle' includes—

(a) any vehicle, whether or not it is in a fit state for use on roads, and includes any body, with or without wheels, appearing to have formed part of such a vehicle, and any load carried by, and anything attached to, such a vehicle; and

(b) a caravan as defined in section 29(1) of the Caravan Sites and Control of Development Act 1960;

and a person may be regarded for the purposes of this section as residing on any land notwithstanding that he has a home elsewhere.

(7) Until 1st April 1996, in this section 'local authority' means, in Wales, a county council or a district council.

78. Orders for removal of persons and their vehicles unlawfully on land

(1) A magistrates' court may, on a complaint made by a local authority, if satisfied that persons and vehicles in which they are residing are present on land within that authority's area in contravention of a direction given under section 77, make an order requiring the removal of any vehicle or other property which is so present on the land and any person residing in it.

(2) An order under this section may authorise the local authority to take such steps as are reasonably necessary to ensure that the order is complied with and, in particular, may authorise the authority, by its officers and servants—

(a) to enter upon the land specified in the order; and

(b) to take, in relation to any vehicle or property to be removed in pursuance of the order, such steps for securing entry and rendering it suitable for removal as may be so specified.

(3) The local authority shall not enter upon any occupied land unless they have given to the owner and occupier at least 24 hours notice of their intention to do so, or unless after reasonable inquiries they are unable to ascertain their names and addresses.

(4) A person who wilfully obstructs any person in the exercise of any power conferred on him by an order under this section commits an offence and is liable on summary conviction to a fine not exceeding level 3 on the standard scale.

(5) Where a complaint is made under this section, a summons issued by the court requiring the person or persons to whom it is directed to appear before the court to answer to the complaint may be directed—

(a) to the occupant of a particular vehicle on the land in question; or

(b) to all occupants of vehicles on the land in question, without naming him or them.

(6) Section 55(2) of the Magistrates' Courts Act 1980 (warrant for arrest of defendant failing to appear) does not apply to proceedings on a complaint made under this section.

(7) Section 77(6) of this Act applies also for the interpretation of this section.

79. Provisions as to directions under s. 77 and orders under s. 78

(1) The following provisions apply in relation to the service of notice of a direction under section 77 and of a summons under section 78, referred to in those provisions as a 'relevant document'.

(2) Where it is impracticable to serve a relevant document on a person named in it, the document shall be treated as duly served on him if a copy of it is fixed in a prominent place to the vehicle concerned; and where a relevant document is directed to the unnamed occupants of vehicles, it shall be treated as duly served on those occupants if a copy of it is fixed in a prominent place to every vehicle on the land in question at the time when service is thus effected.

(3) A local authority shall take such steps as may be reasonably practicable to secure that a copy of any relevant document is displayed on the land in question (otherwise than by being fixed to a vehicle) in a manner designed to ensure that it is likely to be seen by any person camping on the land.

(4) Notice of any relevant document shall be given by the local authority to the owner of the land in question and to any occupier of that land unless, after reasonable inquiries, the authority is unable to ascertain the name and address of the owner or occupier; and the owner of any such land and any occupier of such land shall be entitled to appear and to be heard in the proceedings.

(5) Section 77(6) applies also for the interpretation of this section.

80. Repeal of certain provisions relating to gipsy sites

(1) Part II of the Caravan Sites Act 1968 (duty of local authorities to provide sites for gipsies and control of unauthorised encampments) together with the definition in section 16 of that Act of 'gipsies' is hereby repealed.

(2) In section 24 of the Caravan Sites and Control of Development Act 1960 (power to provide sites for caravans)—

(a) in subsection (2), after paragraph (b) there shall be inserted the following—
', or

(c) to provide, in or in connection with sites for the accommodation of gipsies, working space and facilities for the carrying on of such activities as are normally carried on by them,'; and

(b) in subsection (8), at the end, there shall be inserted the words 'and "gipsies" means persons of nomadic habit of life, whatever their race or origin, but does not include members of an organised group of travelling showmen, or persons engaged in travelling circuses, travelling together as such.'.

(3) The repeal by subsection (1) above of section 8 of the said Act of 1968 shall not affect the validity of directions given under subsection (3)(a) of that section; and in the case of directions under subsection (3)(c), the council may elect either to withdraw the application or request the Secretary of State to determine the application and if they so request the application shall be treated as referred to him under section 77 of the Town and Country Planning Act 1990.

(4) The repeal by subsection (1) above of the definition of 'gipsies' in section 16 of the said Act of 1968 shall not affect the interpretation of that word in the definition of 'protected site' in section 5(1) of the Mobile Homes Act 1983 or in any document embodying the terms of any planning permission granted under the Town and Country Planning Act 1990 before the commencement of this section.

(5)   Section 70 of the Local Government, Planning and Land Act 1980 (power to pay grant to local authorities in respect of capital expenditure in providing gipsy caravan sites) is hereby repealed so far as it extends to England and Wales except for the purposes of applications for grant received by the Secretary of State before the commencement of this section.

PART VI   PREVENTION OF TERRORISM

81.   Powers to stop and search vehicles, etc. and persons
   (1)   In Part IV of the Prevention of Terrorism (Temporary Provisions) Act 1989 (powers of arrest, detention and control of entry) there shall be inserted, before section 14, the following section—
   '**13A.   Powers to stop and search vehicles etc. and persons**
      (1)   Where it appears to—
         (a)   any officer of police of or above the rank of commander of the metropolitan police, as respects the metropolitan police area;
         (b)   any officer of police of or above the rank of commander of the City of London police, as respects the City of London; or
         (c)   any officer of police of or above the rank of assistant chief constable for any other police area,
      that it is expedient to do so in order to prevent acts of terrorism to which this section applies he may give an authorisation that the powers to stop and search vehicles and persons conferred by this section shall be exercisable at any place within his area or a specified locality in his area for a specified period not exceeding twenty eight days.
      (2)   The acts of terrorism to which this section applies are—
         (a)   acts of terrorism connected with the affairs of Northern Ireland; and
         (b)   acts of terrorism of any other description except acts connected solely with the affairs of the United Kingdom or any part of the United Kingdom other than Northern Ireland.
      (3)   This section confers on any constable in uniform power—
         (a)   to stop any vehicle;
         (b)   to search any vehicle, its driver or any passenger for articles of a kind which could be used for a purpose connected with the commission, preparation or instigation of acts of terrorism to which this section applies;
         (c)   to stop any pedestrian and search any thing carried by him for articles of a kind which could be used for a purpose connected with the commission, preparation or instigation of acts of terrorism to which this section applies.
      (4)   A constable may, in the exercise of those powers, stop any vehicle or person and make any search he thinks fit whether or not he has any grounds for suspecting that the vehicle or person is carrying articles of that kind.
      (5)   This section applies (with the necessary modifications) to ships and aircraft as it applies to vehicles.
      (6)   A person is guilty of an offence if he—
         (a)   fails to stop or (as the case may be) to stop the vehicle when required to do so by a constable in the exercise of his powers under this section; or
         (b)   wilfully obstructs a constable in the exercise of those powers.

(7) A person guilty of an offence under subsection (6) above shall be liable on summary conviction to imprisonment for a term not exceeding six months or a fine not exceeding level 5 on the standard scale or both.

(8) If it appears to a police officer of the rank specified in subsection (1)(a), (b) or (c) (as the case may be) that the exercise of the powers conferred by this section ought to continue beyond the period for which their exercise has been authorised under this section he may, from time to time, authorise the exercise of those powers for a further period, not exceeding twenty eight days.

(9) Where a vehicle is stopped by a constable under this section, the driver shall be entitled to obtain a written statement that the vehicle was stopped under the powers conferred by this section if he applies for such a statement not later than the end of the period of twelve months from the day on which the vehicle was stopped; and similarly as respects a pedestrian who is stopped under this section for a search of anything carried by him.

(10) In this section—

"authorise" and "authorisation" mean authorise or an authorisation in writing signed by the officer giving it; and

"specified" means specified in an authorisation under this section.

(11) Nothing in this section affects the exercise by constables of any power to stop vehicles for purposes other than those specified in subsection (1) above.'.

(2) In consequence of the insertion in Part IV of the Prevention of Terrorism (Temporary Provisions) Act 1989 of section 13A, for the title to that Part, there shall be substituted the following title—

'POWERS OF ARREST, STOP AND SEARCH, DETENTION AND CONTROL OF ENTRY'.

(3) For the purposes of section 27 of the Prevention of Terrorism (Temporary Provisions) Act 1989 (temporary provisions), the provisions inserted in that Act by this section shall be treated, as from the time when this section comes into force, as having been continued in force by the order under subsection (6) of that section which has effect at that time.

82. Offences relating to terrorism

(1) The Prevention of Terrorism (Temporary Provisions) Act 1989 shall be amended by the insertion, as Part IVA of that Act, of the following provisions—

'PART IVA   OFFENCES AGAINST PUBLIC SECURITY

16A.   Possession of articles for suspected terrorist purposes

(1) A person is guilty of an offence if he has any article in his possession in circumstances giving rise to a reasonable suspicion that the article is in his possession for a purpose connected with the commission, preparation or instigation of acts of terrorism to which this section applies.

(2) The acts of terrorism to which this section applies are—

(a) acts of terrorism connected with the affairs of Northern Ireland; and

(b) acts of terrorism of any other description except acts connected solely with the affairs of the United Kingdom or any part of the United Kingdom other than Northern Ireland.

(3) It is a defence for a person charged with an offence under this section to prove that at the time of the alleged offence the article in question was not in his possession for such a purpose as is mentioned in subsection (1) above.

(4) Where a person is charged with an offence under this section and it is proved that at the time of the alleged offence—

(a)   he and that article were both present in any premises; or

(b)   the article was in premises of which he was the occupier or which he habitually used otherwise than as a member of the public,

the court may accept the fact proved as sufficient evidence of his possessing that article at that time unless it is further proved that he did not at that time know of its presence in the premises in question, or, if he did know, that he had no control over it.

(5) A person guilty of an offence under this section is liable—

(a)   on conviction on indictment, to imprisonment for a term not exceeding ten years or a fine or both;

(b)   on summary conviction, to imprisonment for a term not exceeding six months or a fine not exceeding the statutory maximum or both.

(6) This section applies to vessels, aircraft and vehicles as it applies to premises.

16B.   Unlawful collection, etc. of information

(1) No person shall, without lawful authority or reasonable excuse (the proof of which lies on him)—

(a)   collect or record any information which is of such a nature as is likely to be useful to terrorists in planning or carrying out any act of terrorism to which this section applies; or

(b)   have in his possession any record or document containing any such information as is mentioned in paragraph (a) above.

(2) The acts of terrorism to which this section applies are—

(a)   acts of terrorism connected with the affairs of Northern Ireland; and

(b)   acts of terrorism of any other description except acts connected solely with the affairs of the United Kingdom or any part of the United Kingdom other than Northern Ireland.

(3) In subsection (1) above the reference to recording information includes a reference to recording it by means of photography or by any other means.

(4) Any person who contravenes this section is guilty of an offence and liable—

(a)   on conviction on indictment, to imprisonment for a term not exceeding ten years or a fine or both;

(b)   on summary conviction, to imprisonment for a term not exceeding six months or a fine not exceeding the statutory maximum or both.

(5) The court by or before which a person is convicted of an offence under this section may order the forfeiture of any record or document mentioned in subsection (1) above which is found in his possession.'.

(2) For the purposes of section 27 of the Prevention of Terrorism (Temporary Provisions) Act 1989 (temporary provisions), the provisions constituting Part IVA of that Act inserted by this section shall be treated, as from the time when those provisions come into force, as having been continued in force by the order under subsection (6) of that section which has effect at that time.

(3) This section shall come into force at the end of the period of two months beginning with the date on which this Act is passed.

83. Investigations into activities and financial resources of terrorist organisations

(1) In Schedule 7 to the Prevention of Terrorism (Temporary Provisions) Act 1989, in Part I (England, Wales and Northern Ireland)—

(a) in paragraph 3 (orders for production of excluded or special procedure material)—

(i) in sub-paragraph (2) for the words from 'he may make' to 'shall' there shall be substituted the words 'he may order a person who appears to him to have in his possession, custody or power any of the material to which the application relates, to—' and after the word 'possession' where it subsequently appears in that sub-paragraph there shall be inserted in both places the words ', custody or power'; and

(ii) in sub-paragraph (5)(b)(ii), for the words from 'in possession' to the end there shall be substituted the words 'has the material in his possession, custody or power';

(b) in paragraph 4(6) (order for production made to government department)—

(i) after the word 'possession' where it first appears there shall be inserted the words ', custody or power'; and

(ii) for the words 'be in possession of' there shall be substituted the words 'have in his possession, custody or power'; and

(c) in paragraph 8(1) (orders of Secretary of State authorising searches for certain investigations), at the end, there shall be inserted the words 'or an offence under section 27 of the Northern Ireland (Emergency Provisions) Act 1991'.

(2) In Schedule 7 to the Prevention of Terrorism (Temporary Provisions) Act 1989, in Part II (Scotland)—

(a) in paragraph 12 (order for production of material)—

(i) in sub-paragraph (2) for the words from 'he may make' to 'shall' there shall be substituted the words 'he may order a person who appears to him to have in his possession, custody or power any of the material to which the application relates, to—' and after the word 'possession' where it subsequently appears in that sub-paragraph there shall be inserted in both places the words ', custody or power';

(ii) in sub-paragraph (5)(b)(ii), for the words from 'in possession' to the end there shall be substituted the words 'has the material in his possession, custody or power'; and

(b) in paragraph 13(5) (order for production made to government department)—

(i) after the word 'possession' where it first appears there shall be inserted the words ', custody or power'; and

(ii) for the words 'be in possession of' there shall be substituted the words 'have in his possession, custody or power'.

(3) In Schedule 5 to the Northern Ireland (Emergency Provisions) Act 1991, in paragraph 2 (investigative powers of authorised investigators), after sub-paragraph (1), there shall be inserted the following sub-paragraph—

'(1A) An authorised investigator may by notice in writing require any such person to furnish specified information relevant to the investigation within a specified time or such further time as the investigator may allow and in a specified manner or in such other manner as the investigator may allow.'.

(4) For the purposes of section 27 of the Prevention of Terrorism (Temporary Provisions) Act 1989 (temporary provisions) the amendments made in that Act by subsections (1) and (2) above shall be treated, as from the time when those subsections come into force, as having been continued in force by the order under subsection (6) of that section which has effect at that time.

(5) For the purposes of section 69 of the Northern Ireland (Emergency Provisions) Act 1991 (temporary provisions) the amendments made in that Act by subsection (3) above shall be treated, as from the time when that subsection comes into force, as having been continued in force by the order under subsection (3) of that section which has effect at that time.

PART VII   OBSCENITY AND PORNOGRAPHY AND VIDEOS

Obscene publications and indecent photographs of children

84.   Indecent pseudo-photographs of children

(1) The Protection of Children Act 1978 shall be amended as provided in subsections (2) and (3) below.

(2) In section 1 (which penalises the taking and distribution of indecent photographs of children and related acts)

(a)   in paragraph (a) of subsection (1)—

(i)   after the word 'taken' there shall be inserted the words 'or to make', and the words following 'child' shall be omitted;

(ii)   after the word 'photograph' there shall be inserted the words 'or pseudo-photograph';

(b)   in paragraphs (b), (c) and (d) of subsection (1), after the word 'photographs' there shall be inserted the words 'or pseudo-photographs';

(c)   in subsection (2), after the word 'photograph' there shall be inserted the words 'or pseudo-photograph'; and

(d)   in paragraphs (a) and (b) of subsection (4), after the word 'photographs' there shall be inserted the words 'or pseudo-photographs'.

(3) In section 7 (interpretation)—

(a)   in subsection (3), at the end, there shall be inserted the words 'and so as respects pseudo-photographs'; and

(b)   for subsection (4) there shall be substituted the following subsection—

'(4)   References to a photograph include—

(a)   the negative as well as the positive version; and

(b)   data stored on a computer disc or by other electronic means which is capable of conversion into a photograph.'.

(c)   after subsection (5) there shall be inserted the following subsections—

'(6)   ''Child'', subject to subsection (8), means a person under the age of 16.

(7)   ''Pseudo-photograph'' means an image, whether made by computer-graphics or otherwise howsoever, which appears to be a photograph.

(8)   If the impression conveyed by a pseudo-photograph is that the person shown is a child, the pseudo-photograph shall be treated for all purposes of this Act as showing a child and so shall a pseudo-photograph where the predominant impression conveyed is that the person shown is a child notwithstanding that some of the physical characteristics shown are those of an adult.

(9)   References to an indecent pseudo-photograph include—
    (a)   a copy of an indecent pseudo-photograph; and
    (b)   data stored on a computer disc or by other electronic means which is capable of conversion into a pseudo-photograph.'.

(4)   Section 160 of the Criminal Justice Act 1988 (which penalises the possession of indecent photographs of children) shall be amended as follows—
    (a)   in subsection (1), after the word 'photograph' there shall be inserted the words 'or pseudo-photograph' and the words from '(meaning' to '16)' shall be omitted; and
    (b)   in paragraphs (a), (b) and (c) of subsection (2), after the word 'photograph' there shall be inserted the words 'or pseudo-photograph'; and
    (c)   in subsection (5), the reference to the coming into force of that section shall be construed, for the purposes of the amendments made by this subsection, as a reference to the coming into force of this subsection.

(5)   The Civic Government (Scotland) Act 1982 shall be amended as provided in subsections (6) and (7) below.

(6)   In section 52 (which, for Scotland, penalises the taking and distribution of indecent photographs of children and related acts)—
    (a)   in paragraph (a) of subsection (1)—
        (i)   after the word 'taken' there shall be inserted the words 'or makes'; and
        (ii)   for the words from 'of a' to the end there shall be substituted the words 'or pseudo-photograph of a child';
    (b)   in paragraphs (b), (c) and (d) of subsection (1), after the word 'photograph' there shall be inserted the words 'or pseudo-photograph'; and
    (c)   in subsection (2), at the beginning there shall be inserted 'In subsection (1) above 'child' means, subject to subsection (2B) below, a person under the age of 16; and';
    (d)   after subsection (2), there shall be added—

'(2A)   In this section, ''pseudo-photograph'' means an image, whether produced by computer-graphics or otherwise howsoever, which appears to be a photograph.

(2B)   If the impression conveyed by a pseudo-photograph is that the person shown is a child, the pseudo-photograph shall be treated for all purposes of this Act as showing a child and so shall a pseudo-photograph where the predominant impression conveyed is that the person shown is a child notwithstanding that some of the physical characteristics shown are those of an adult.

(2C)   In this section, references to an indecent pseudo-photograph include—
    (a)   a copy of an indecent pseudo-photograph;
    (b)   data stored on a computer disc or by other electronic means which is capable of conversion into a pseudo-photograph.'.
    (e)   in subsection (3)—
        (i)   in paragraph (a), for the words '3 months' there shall be substituted the words '6 months'; and
        (ii)   in paragraph (b), for the words 'two years' there shall be substituted the words '3 years';
    (f)   in subsection (4), and in paragraphs (a) and (b) of subsection (5), after the word 'photograph' there shall be inserted the words 'or pseudo-photograph'; and
    (g)   for subsection (8)(c) there shall be substituted—

'(c)   references to a photograph include—
  (i)   the negative as well as the positive version; and
  (ii)   data stored on a computer disc or by other electronic means which is capable of conversion into a photograph.'.

(7)   In section 52A (which, for Scotland, penalises the possession of indecent photographs of children)—

(a)   in subsection (1), for the words from 'of a' to '16)' there shall be substituted the words 'or pseudo-photograph of a child';

(b)   in subsection (2), in each of paragraphs (a) to (c), after the word 'photograph' there shall be inserted the words 'or pseudo-photograph';

(c)   in subsection (3)—
  (i)   after the word 'to' there shall be inserted the words 'imprisonment for a period not exceeding 6 months or to'; and
  (ii)   at the end there shall be added the words 'or to both.';

(d)   in subsection (4), after the word '(2)' there shall be inserted the words 'to (2C)'.

(8)   The Protection of Children (Northern Ireland) Order 1978 shall be amended as provided in subsections (9) and (10) below.

(9)   In Article 2 (interpretation)—

(a)   in paragraph (2)—
  (i)   in the definition of 'child', after 'child' there shall be inserted the words 'subject to paragraph (3)(c)';
  (ii)   for the definition of 'photograph' there shall be substituted the following definitions—

'"indecent pseudo-photograph" includes—
  (a)   a copy of an indecent pseudo-photograph; and
  (b)   data stored on a computer disc or by other electronic means which is capable of conversion into a pseudo-photograph;

"photograph" includes—
  (a)   the negative as well as the positive version; and
  (b)   data stored on a computer disc or by other electronic means which is capable of conversion into a photograph;

"pseudo-photograph" means an image, whether made by computer-graphics or otherwise howsoever, which appears to be a photograph;';

(b)   in paragraph (3)
  (i)   in sub-paragraph (a), after the word 'photograph' there shall be inserted the words 'or pseudo-photograph';
  (ii)   in sub-paragraph (b), at the end, there shall be inserted the words 'and so as respects pseudo-photographs; and';
  (iii)   after sub-paragraph (b) there shall be inserted the following sub-paragraph—

'(c)   if the impression conveyed by a pseudo-photograph is that the person shown is a child, the pseudo-photograph shall be treated as showing a child and so shall a pseudo-photograph where the predominant impression conveyed is that the person shown is a child notwithstanding that some of the physical characteristics shown are those of an adult.'.

(10)   In Article 3 (which, for Northern Ireland, penalises the taking and distribution of indecent photographs of children and related acts)—

(a)   in sub-paragraph (a) of paragraph (1)—
    (i)   after the word 'taken' there shall be inserted the words 'or to make';
    (ii) after the word 'photograph' there shall be inserted the words 'or pseudo-photograph';
(b)   in sub-paragraphs (b), (c) and (d) of paragraph (1), after the word 'photographs' there shall be inserted the words 'or pseudo-photographs';
(c)   in sub-paragraphs (a) and (b) of paragraph (3), after the word 'photographs' there shall be inserted the words 'or pseudo-photographs'.
(11)   Article 15 of the Criminal Justice (Evidence, etc.) (Northern Ireland) Order 1988 (which, for Northern Ireland, penalises the possession of indecent photographs of children) shall be amended as follows—
(a)   in paragraph (1), after the word 'photograph' there shall be inserted the words 'or pseudo-photograph' and the words from '(meaning' to '16)' shall be omitted;
(b)   in sub-paragraphs (a), (b) and (c) of paragraph (2), after the word 'photograph' there shall be inserted the words 'or pseudo-photograph'; and
(c)   in paragraph (6), the reference to the coming into operation of that Article shall be construed, for the purposes of the amendments made by this subsection, as a reference to the coming into force of this subsection.

85.   Arrestable offences to include certain offences relating to obscenity or indecency
(1)   The Police and Criminal Evidence Act 1984 shall be amended as follows.
(2)   In section 24(2) (arrestable offences), after paragraph (e), there shall be inserted the following paragraphs—
    '(f)   an offence under section 2 of the Obscene Publications Act 1959 (publication of obscene matter);
    (g)   an offence under section 1 of the Protection of Children Act 1978 (indecent photographs and pseudo-photographs of children);'.
(3)   At the end of Part II of Schedule 5 (serious arrestable offences mentioned in section 116(2)(b)) there shall be inserted the following paragraphs—
    'Protection of Children Act 1978 (c. 37.)
14.   Section 1 (indecent photographs and pseudo-photographs of children).
    Obscene Publications Act 1959 (c. 66.)
15.   Section 2 (publication of obscene matter).'.
(4)   The Police and Criminal Evidence (Northern Ireland) Order 1989 shall be amended as provided in subsections (5) and (6) below.
(5)   In Article 26(2) (arrestable offences), after sub-paragraph (e), there shall be inserted the following sub-paragraph—
    '(f)   an offence under Article 3 of the Protection of Children (Northern Ireland) Order 1978 (indecent photographs and pseudo-photographs of children).'.
(6)   At the end of Part II of Schedule 5 (serious arrestable offences mentioned in Article 87(2)(b)) there shall be inserted the following paragraph—
    'Protection of Children (Northern Ireland) Order 1978 (1978 N.I.17)
13.   Article 3 (indecent photographs and pseudo-photographs of children).'.

86.   Indecent photographs of children: sentence of imprisonment
(1)   In section 160(3) of the Criminal Justice Act 1988 (which makes a person convicted of certain offences relating to indecent photographs of children liable to a

fine not exceeding level 5 on the standard scale) there shall be inserted after the word 'to' the words 'imprisonment for a term not exceeding six months or' and at the end the words ', or both'.

(2) In Article 15(3) of the Criminal Justice (Evidence, etc.) (Northern Ireland) Order 1988 (which makes a person convicted in Northern Ireland of certain offences relating to indecent photographs of children liable to a fine not exceeding level 5 on the standard scale) there shall be inserted after the word 'to' the words 'imprisonment for a term not exceeding 6 months or' and at the end the words ', or both'.

87. Publishing, displaying, selling or distributing etc. obscene material in Scotland: sentence of imprisonment

In section 51(3) of the Civic Government (Scotland) Act 1982 (which makes persons convicted in summary proceedings in Scotland of certain offences relating to obscene material liable, among other penalties, to imprisonment for a period not exceeding 3 months and persons convicted there on indictment of such offences liable, among other penalties, to imprisonment for a period not exceeding 2 years), for the words '3 months' there shall be substituted the words '6 months' and for the words 'two years' there shall be substituted the words '3 years'.

Video recordings

88. Video recordings: increase in penalties

(1) The following provisions of the Video Recordings Act 1984 (which create offences for which section 15(1) and (3) prescribe maximum fines of, in the case of sections 9 and 10, £20,000 and, in the case of other offences, level 5) shall be amended as follows.

(2) In section 9 (supplying videos of unclassified work), after subsection (2), there shall be inserted the following subsection—

'(3) A person guilty of an offence under this section shall be liable—

(a) on conviction on indictment, to imprisonment for a term not exceeding two years or a fine or both,

(b) on summary conviction, to imprisonment for a term not exceeding six months or a fine not exceeding £20,000 or both.'.

(3) In section 10 (possessing videos of unclassified work for supply), after subsection (2), there shall be inserted the following subsection—

'(3) A person guilty of an offence under this section shall be liable—

(a) on conviction on indictment, to imprisonment for a term not exceeding two years or a fine or both,

(b) on summary conviction, to imprisonment for a term not exceeding six months or a fine not exceeding £20,000 or both.'.

(4) In section 11 (supplying videos in breach of classification), after subsection (2), there shall be inserted the following subsection—

'(3) A person guilty of an offence under this section shall be liable, on summary conviction, to imprisonment for a term not exceeding six months or a fine not exceeding level 5 on the standard scale or both.'.

(5) In section 12 (supplying videos in places other than licensed sex shops), after subsection (4), there shall be inserted the following subsection—

'(4A) A person guilty of an offence under subsection (1) or (3) above shall be liable, on summary conviction, to imprisonment for a term not exceeding six months or a fine not exceeding level 5 on the standard scale or both.'.

(6) In section 14 (supplying videos with false indication as to classification), after subsection (4), there shall be inserted the following subsection—

'(5) A person guilty of an offence under subsection (1) or (3) above shall be liable, on summary conviction, to imprisonment for a term not exceeding six months or a fine not exceeding level 5 on the standard scale or both.'.

(7) The amendments made by this section shall not apply to offences committed before this section comes into force.

89. Video recordings: restriction of exemptions

(1) Section 2 of the Video Recordings Act 1984 (exempted works) shall be amended as follows.

(2) In subsection (1), after the words 'subsection (2)' there shall be inserted the words 'or (3)'.

(3) In subsection (2)—

(a) after paragraph (c), there shall be inserted the following paragraph—

'(d) techniques likely to be useful in the commission of offences;'; and

(b) for the word 'designed' (in both places) there shall be substituted the word 'likely'.

(4) After subsection (2), there shall be inserted the following subsection—

'(3) A video work is not an exempted work for those purposes if, to any significant extent, it depicts criminal activity which is likely to any significant extent to stimulate or encourage the commission of offences.'.

90. Video recordings: suitability

(1) After section 4 of the Video Recordings Act 1984 there shall be inserted the following sections—

'4A. Criteria for suitability to which special regard to be had

(1) The designated authority shall, in making any determination as to the suitability of a video work, have special regard (among the other relevant factors) to any harm that may be caused to potential viewers or, through their behaviour, to society by the manner in which the work deals with—

(a) criminal behaviour;

(b) illegal drugs;

(c) violent behaviour or incidents;

(d) horrific behaviour or incidents; or

(e) human sexual activity.

(2) For the purposes of this section

"potential viewer" means any person (including a child or young person) who is likely to view the video work in question if a classification certificate or a classification certificate of a particular description were issued;

"suitability" means suitability for the issue of a classification certificate or suitability for the issue of a certificate of a particular description;

"violent behaviour" includes any act inflicting or likely to result in the infliction of injury;

and any behaviour or activity referred to in subsection (1)(a) to (e) above shall be taken to include behaviour or activity likely to stimulate or encourage it.

4B. Review of determinations as to suitability

(1) The Secretary of State may by order make provision enabling the

designated authority to review any determination made by them, before the coming into force of section 4A of this Act, as to the suitability of a video work.

(2)   The order may in particular provide—

(a)   for the authority's power of review to be exercisable in relation to such determinations as the authority think fit;

(b)   for the authority to determine, on any review, whether, if they were then determining the suitability of the video work to which the determination under review relates, they—

(i)   would issue a classification certificate, or

(ii)   would issue a different classification certificate;

(c)   for the cancellation of a classification certificate, where they determine that they would not issue a classification certificate;

(d)   for the cancellation of a classification certificate and issue of a new classification certificate, where they determine that they would issue a different classification certificate;

(e)   for any such cancellation or issue not to take effect until the end of such period as may be determined in accordance with the order;

(f)   for such persons as may appear to the authority to fall within a specified category of person to be notified of any such cancellation or issue in such manner as may be specified;

(g)   for treating a classification certificate, in relation to any act or omission occurring after its cancellation, as if it had not been issued;

(h)   for specified provisions of this Act to apply to determinations made on a review subject to such modifications (if any) as may be specified;

(i)   for specified regulations made under section 8 of this Act to apply to a video work in respect of which a new classification certificate has been issued subject to such modifications (if any) as may be specified.

(3)   In subsection (2) above "specified" means specified by an order made under this section.

(4)   The Secretary of State shall not make any order under this section unless he is satisfied that adequate arrangements will be made for an appeal against determinations made by the designated authority on a review.

(5)   The power to make an order under this section shall be exercisable by statutory instrument which shall be subject to annulment in pursuance of a resolution of either House of Parliament.

(6)   In this section "suitability" has the same meaning as in section 4A of this Act.'.

(2)   In section 7(2) of the Video Recordings Act 1984 (contents of classification certificates), in paragraph (a), after the words 'viewing by children', there shall be inserted the words 'or young children'.

91.   Enforcement by enforcing authorities outside their areas

(1)   The Video Recordings Act 1984 shall have effect with the following amendments.

(2)   In section 16A (enforcement)—

(a)   after subsection (1) there shall be inserted the following subsections—

'(1A)   Subject to subsection (1B) below, the functions of a local weights and measures authority shall also include the investigation and prosecution outside their area of offences under this Act suspected to be linked to their area as well as the investigation outside their area of offences suspected to have been committed within it.

(1B)   The functions available to an authority under subsection (1A) above shall not be exercisable in relation to any circumstances suspected to have arisen within the area of another local weights and measures authority without the consent of that authority.';

(b)   in subsection (4), for the words 'Subsection (1)' there shall be substituted the words 'Subsections (1) and (1A)';

(c)   after subsection (4), there shall be inserted the following subsection—

'(4A)   For the purposes of subsections (1A), (1B) and (2) above—

(a)   offences in another area are "linked" to the area of a local weights and measures authority if—

(i)   the supply or possession of video recordings in contravention of this Act within their area is likely to be or to have been the result of the supply or possession of those recordings in the other area; or

(ii)   the supply or possession of video recordings in contravention of this Act in the other area is likely to be or to have been the result of the supply or possession of those recordings in their area; and

(b)   "investigation" includes the exercise of the powers conferred by sections 27 and 28 of the Trade Descriptions Act 1968 as applied by subsection (2) above;

and sections 29 and 33 of that Act shall apply accordingly.'.

(3)   After section 16A there shall be inserted the following sections—

'16B.   Extension of jurisdiction of magistrates' courts in linked cases

(1)   A justice of the peace for an area to which section 1 of the Magistrates' Courts Act 1980 applies may issue a summons or warrant under and in accordance with that section as respects an offence under this Act committed or suspected of having been committed outside the area for which he acts if it appears to the justice that the offence is linked to the supply or possession of video recordings within the area for which he acts.

(2)   Where a person charged with an offence under this Act appears or is brought before a magistrates' court in answer to a summons issued by virtue of subsection (1) above, or under a warrant issued under subsection (1) above, the court shall have jurisdiction to try the offence.

(3)   For the purposes of this section an offence is "linked" to the supply or possession of video recordings within the area for which a justice acts if—

(a)   the supply or possession of video recordings within his area is likely to be or to have been the result of the offence; or

(b)   the offence is likely to be or to have been the result of the supply or possession of video recordings in his area.

16C.   Extension of jurisdiction of sheriff in linked cases

(1)   Subsection (4) of section 287 of the Criminal Procedure (Scotland) Act 1975 (Jurisdiction of sheriff as respects offences committed in more than one district) shall apply in respect of linked offences, whether or not alleged to have been committed by one and the same person, as that subsection applies in respect of offences alleged to have been committed by one person in more than

one sheriff court district which, if committed in one of those districts, could be tried under one complaint.

(2)   For the purposes of subsection (1) above, offences are linked if, being offences under this Act, they comprise the supply or possession of video recordings each within a different sheriff court district but such supply or possession within the one district is likely to be, or to have been, the result of such supply or possession within the other.

16D.   Extension of jurisdiction of magistrates' courts in Northern Ireland in linked cases

(1)   Paragraph (2) of Article 16 of the Magistrates' Courts (Northern Ireland) Order 1981 (Jurisdiction of magistrates' court as respects offences committed in another division) shall apply in respect of linked offences as that paragraph applies in respect of summary offences committed in other county court divisions.

(2)   For the purposes of subsection (1) above, an offence is a linked offence if the supply or possession of video recordings within one county court division is likely to be or to have been the result of the supply or possession of those recordings in another such division.'.

Obscene, offensive or annoying telephone calls

92.   Obscene, offensive or annoying telephone calls: increase in penalty

(1)   In section 43(1) of the Telecommunications Act 1984 (which makes a person convicted of certain offences relating to improper use of public telecommunication systems liable to a fine not exceeding level 3 on the standard scale), for the words 'a fine not exceeding level 3 on the standard scale' there shall be substituted the words 'imprisonment for a term not exceeding six months or a fine not exceeding level 5 on the standard scale or both'.

(2)   Subsection (1) above does not apply to an offence committed before this section comes into force.

PART VIII   PRISON SERVICES AND THE PRISON SERVICE
CHAPTER I   ENGLAND AND WALES

Prisoner escorts

93.   Arrangements for the provision of prisoner escorts

(1)   In subsection (1) of section 80 (arrangements for the provision of prisoner escorts) of the Criminal Justice Act 1991 ('the 1991 Act')—

(a)   for paragraph (a) there shall be substituted the following paragraph—

'(a)   the delivery of prisoners from one set of relevant premises to another;';

(b)   in paragraph (b), for the words 'such premises' there shall be substituted the words 'the premises of any court'; and

(c)   for paragraphs (c) and (d) there shall be substituted the following paragraph—

'(c)   the custody of prisoners temporarily held in a prison in the course of delivery from one prison to another; and'.

(2)   After that subsection there shall be inserted the following subsection—

'(1A)   In paragraph (a) of subsection (1) above "relevant premises" means a court, prison, police station or hospital; and either (but not both) of the sets of premises mentioned in that paragraph may be situated in a part of the British Islands outside England and Wales.'.

(3)   In subsection (3) of that section, for the words 'a warrant of commitment' there shall be substituted the words 'a warrant or a hospital order or remand' and for the words 'that warrant' there shall be substituted the words 'the warrant, order or remand'.

(4)   After that subsection there shall be inserted the following subsection—

'(4)   In this section—

"hospital" has the same meaning as in the Mental Health Act 1983;

"hospital order" means an order for a person's admission to hospital made under section 37, 38 or 44 of that Act, section 5 of the Criminal Procedure (Insanity) Act 1964 or section 6, 14 or 14A of the Criminal Appeal Act 1968;

"hospital remand" means a remand of a person to hospital under section 35 or 36 of the Mental Health Act 1983;

"warrant" means a warrant of commitment, a warrant of arrest or a warrant under section 46, 47, 48, 50 or 74 of that Act.'.

(5)   In subsection (1) of section 92 of that Act (interpretation of Part IV), for the definition of 'prisoner' there shall be substituted the following definition—

'"prisoner" means any person for the time being detained in legal custody as a result of a requirement imposed by a court or otherwise that he be so detained;'.

(6)   In subsection (3) of that section—

(a)   for the words from 'kept' to 'accommodation)' there shall be substituted the words 'remanded or committed to local authority accommodation under section 23 of the 1969 Act'; and

(b)   for the words 'section 80(1)(c) to (e)' there shall be substituted the words 'section 80(1)(c) or (e) or (1A)'.

(7)   After that subsection there shall be inserted the following subsection—

'(4)   In sections 80, 82 and 83 above, "prison"—

(a)   so far as relating to the delivery of prisoners to or from a prison situated in Scotland, includes a remand centre or young offenders institution within the meaning of section 19 of the Prisons (Scotland) Act 1989; and

(b)   so far as relating to the delivery of prisoners to or from a prison situated in Northern Ireland, includes a remand centre or young offenders centre.'.

94.   Powers and duties of prisoner custody officers acting in pursuance of such arrangements

(1)   For subsection (4) of section 82 of the 1991 Act (powers and duties of prisoner custody officers acting in pursuance of such arrangements) there shall be substituted the following subsection—

'(4)   Where a prisoner custody officer acting in pursuance of prisoner escort arrangements is on any premises in which the Crown Court or a magistrates' court is sitting, it shall be his duty to give effect to any order of that court made—

(a)   in the case of the Crown Court, under section 34A of the 1973 Act (power of Court to order search of persons before it); or

(b) in the case of a magistrates' court, under section 80 of the 1980 Act (application of money found on defaulter).'.

(2) After subsection (2) of section 6 of the Imprisonment (Temporary Provisions) Act 1980 (detention in the custody of a police constable) there shall be inserted the following subsection—

'(3) Any reference in this section to a constable includes a reference to a prisoner custody officer (within the meaning of Part IV of the Criminal Justice Act 1991) acting in pursuance of prisoner escort arrangements (within the meaning of that Part).'.

95. Breaches of discipline by prisoners under escort

For section 83 of the 1991 Act there shall be substituted the following section—

'83. Breaches of discipline by prisoners under escort

(1) This section applies where a prisoner for whose delivery or custody a prisoner custody officer has been responsible in pursuance of prisoner escort arrangements is delivered to a prison.

(2) For the purposes of such prison rules as relate to disciplinary offences, the prisoner shall be deemed to have been—

(a) in the custody of the governor of the prison; or

(b) in the case of a contracted out prison, in the custody of its director,

at all times during the period for which the prisoner custody officer was so responsible.

(3) In the case of any breach by the prisoner at any time during that period of such prison rules as so relate, a disciplinary charge may be laid against him by the prisoner custody officer.

(4) Nothing in this section shall enable a prisoner to be punished under prison rules for any act or omission of his for which he has already been punished by a court.

(5) In this section "prison rules", in relation to a prison situated in a part of the British Islands outside England and Wales, means rules made under any provision of the law of that part which corresponds to section 47 of the 1952 Act.'.

Contracted out prisons etc.

96. Contracted out parts of prisons, etc.

For section 84 of the 1991 Act there shall be substituted the following section—

'84. Contracting out prisons, etc.

(1) The Secretary of State may enter into a contract with another person for the provision or running (or the provision and running) by him, or (if the contract so provides) for the running by sub-contractors of his, of any prison or part of a prison.

(2) While a contract under this section for the running of a prison or part of a prison is in force—

(a) the prison or part shall be run subject to and in accordance with sections 85 and 86 below, the 1952 Act (as modified by section 87 below) and prison rules; and

(b)   in the case of a part, that part and the remaining part shall each be treated for the purposes of sections 85 to 88A below as if they were separate prisons.

(3)   Where the Secretary of State grants a lease or tenancy of land for the purposes of any contract under this section, none of the following enactments shall apply to it, namely—

(a)   Part II of the Landlord and Tenant Act 1954 (security of tenure);

(b)   section 146 of the Law of Property Act 1925 (restrictions on and relief against forfeiture);

(c)   section 19(1), (2) and (3) of the Landlord and Tenant Act 1927 and the Landlord and Tenant Act 1988 (covenants not to assign etc.); and

(d)   the Agricultural Holdings Act 1986.

In this subsection "lease or tenancy" includes an underlease or sub-tenancy.

(4)   In this Part—

"contracted out prison" means a prison or part of a prison for the running of which a contract under this section is for the time being in force;

"the contractor", in relation to a contracted out prison, means the person who has contracted with the Secretary of State for the running of it; and

"sub-contractor", in relation to a contracted out prison, means a person who has contracted with the contractor for the running of it or any part of it.'.

97.   Temporary attachment of prison officers

(1)   At the end of subsection (1) of section 85 of the 1991 Act (officers of contracted out prisons) there shall be inserted the words 'or a prison officer who is temporarily attached to the prison'.

(2)   At the end of paragraph (b) of subsection (4) of that section there shall be inserted the words 'or prison officers who are temporarily attached to the prison'.

(3)   For subsection (3) of section 87 of that Act (consequential modifications of 1952 Act) there shall be substituted the following subsection—

'(3)   Section 8 (powers of prison officers) shall not apply in relation to a prisoner custody officer performing custodial duties at the prison.'.

(4)   After subsection (4) of that section there shall be inserted the following subsection—

'(4A)   Section 11 (ejectment of prison officers and their families refusing to quit) shall not apply.'.

(5)   At the end of subsections (6) and (7) of that section there shall be inserted the words 'or a prison officer who is temporarily attached to the prison'.

98.   Prisoners temporarily out of prison

After subsection (1) of section 92 of the 1991 Act (interpretation of Part IV) there shall be inserted the following subsection—

'(1A)   Any reference in this Part to custodial duties at a contracted out prison includes a reference to custodial duties in relation to a prisoner who is outside such a prison for temporary purposes.'.

Miscellaneous

99.   Contracted out functions at directly managed prisons

After section 88 of the 1991 Act there shall be inserted the following section—

'Contracted out functions

88A.   Contracted out functions at directly managed prisons

(1)   The Secretary of State may enter into a contract with another person for any functions at a directly managed prison to be performed by prisoner custody officers who are provided by that person and are authorised to perform custodial duties.

(2)   Section 86 above shall apply in relation to a prisoner custody officer performing contracted out functions at a directly managed prison as it applies in relation to such an officer performing custodial duties at a contracted out prison.

(3)   In relation to a directly managed prison—

(a)   the reference in section 13(2) of the 1952 Act (legal custody of prisoners) to an officer of the prison; and

(b)   the reference in section 14(2) of that Act (cells) to a prison officer,

shall each be construed as including a reference to a prisoner custody officer performing custodial duties at the prison in pursuance of a contract under this section.

(4)   Any reference in subsections (1) to (3) above to the performance of functions or custodial duties at a directly managed prison includes a reference to the performance of functions or such duties for the purposes of, or for purposes connected with, such a prison.

(5)   In this Part—

"contracted out functions" means any functions which, by virtue of a contract under this section, fall to be performed by prisoner custody officers;

"directly managed prison" means a prison which is not a contracted out prison.'.

100.   Provision of prisons by contractors

(1)   For subsection (2) of section 33 of the Prison Act 1952 (power to declare buildings etc. to be prisons) there shall be substituted the following subsection—

'(2)   The Secretary of State may provide new prisons by declaring to be a prison—

(a)   any building or part of a building built for the purpose or vested in him or under his control; or

(b)   any floating structure or part of such a structure constructed for the purpose or vested in him or under his control.'.

(2)   Subsections (3) and (4) below apply where the Secretary of State enters into a contract with another person ('the contractor') for the provision by him of a prison.

(3)   Section 33(2) of the Prison Act 1952 shall have effect as if it also included references to—

(a)   any building or part of a building built by the contractor for the purpose or vested in him or under his control; and

(b)   any floating structure or part of such a structure constructed by the contractor for the purpose or vested in him or under his control.

(4)   Nothing in section 35(1) of that Act (prison property to be vested in the Secretary of State) shall require the prison or any real or personal property belonging to the prison to be vested in the Secretary of State.

Supplemental

101. Minor and consequential amendments

(1) In subsection (5) of section 85 of the 1991 Act (officers of contracted out prisons), for the words 'The contractor shall' there shall be substituted the words 'The contractor and any sub-contractor of his shall each'.

(2) In subsection (3)(b) of section 88 of that Act (intervention by the Secretary of State), for the words 'the contractor shall' there shall be substituted the words 'the contractor and any sub-contractor of his shall each'.

(3) In subsection (5) of that section, after the words 'the contractor,' there shall be inserted the words 'any sub-contractor of his,'.

(4) In subsection (3) of section 89 of that Act (certification of prisoner custody officers), for the words 'contracted out prison' there shall be substituted the words 'contracted out or directly managed prison'.

(5) In subsections (1) and (3) of section 90 of that Act (protection of prisoner custody officers), for the words from 'acting' to 'prison' there shall be substituted the words—

   '(a)   acting in pursuance of prisoner escort arrangements;
   (b)   performing custodial duties at a contracted out prison; or
   (c)   performing contracted out functions at a directly managed prison,'.

(6) In subsection (1) of section 91 of that Act (wrongful disclosure of information), for the words from 'is or has been' to 'prison' there shall be substituted the words—

   '(a)   is or has been employed (whether as a prisoner custody officer or otherwise) in pursuance of prisoner escort arrangements, or at a contracted out prison; or
   (b)   is or has been employed to perform contracted out functions at a directly managed prison,'.

(7) In subsection (1) of section 92 of that Act (interpretation of Part IV)—

   (a)   after the words 'In this Part' there shall be inserted the words 'unless the context otherwise requires';
   (b)   in the definitions of 'contracted out prison' and 'contractor', for the words 'section 84(2)' there shall be substituted the words 'section 84(4)';
   (c)   after those definitions there shall be inserted the following definitions—
   '"contracted out functions" and "directly managed prison" have the meanings given by section 88A(5) above;';
   (d)   after the definition of 'prison' there shall be inserted the following definitions—
   '"prison officer" means an officer of a directly managed prison;
   "prison rules" means rules made under section 47 of the 1952 Act;'; and
   (e)   after the definition of 'prisoner escort arrangements' there shall be inserted the following definition—
   '"sub-contractor" has the meaning given by section 84(4) above.'.

(8) After subsection (7) of section 102 of the 1991 Act (short title, commencement and extent) there shall be inserted the following subsection—

   '(7A)   Sections 80, 82 and 83 above, so far as relating to the delivery of prisoners to or from premises situated in a part of the British Islands outside England and Wales, extend to that part of those Islands.'.

(9) For sub-paragraph (1) of paragraph 3 of Schedule 10 to that Act (certification of prisoner custody officers) there shall be substituted the following sub-paragraph—

'(1) This paragraph applies where at any time—

(a) in the case of a prisoner custody officer acting in pursuance of prisoner escort arrangements, it appears to the prisoner escort monitor for the area concerned that the officer is not a fit and proper person to perform escort functions;

(b) in the case of a prisoner custody officer performing custodial duties at a contracted out prison, it appears to the controller of that prison that the officer is not a fit and proper person to perform custodial duties; or

(c) in the case of a prisoner custody officer performing contracted out functions at a directly managed prison, it appears to the governor of that prison that the officer is not a fit and proper person to perform custodial duties.'.

(10) In sub-paragraph (2) of that paragraph, for the words 'or controller' there shall be substituted the words 'controller or governor'.

CHAPTER II SCOTLAND

Prisoner escorts

102. Arrangements for the provision of prisoner excorts

(1) The Secretary of State may make arrangements for any of the functions specified in subsection (2) below ('escort functions') to be performed in such cases as may be determined by or under the arrangements by prisoner custody officers who are authorised to perform such functions.

(2) Those functions are—

(a) ' the transfer of prisoners from one set of relevant premises to another;

(b) the custody of prisoners held on court premises (whether or not they would otherwise be in the custody of the court) and their production before the court;

(c) the custody of prisoners temporarily held in a prison in the course of transfer from one prison to another; and

(d) the custody of prisoners while they are outside a prison for temporary purposes.

(3) In paragraph (a) of subsection (2) above, 'relevant premises' means—

(a) the premises of any court, prison, police station or hospital; or

(b) the premises of any other place from or to which a prisoner may be required to be taken under the Criminal Procedure (Scotland) Act 1975 or the Mental Health (Scotland) Act 1984;

and either (but not both) of the sets of premises mentioned in that paragraph may be situated in a part of the British Islands outside Scotland.

(4) Arrangements made by the Secretary of State under this section ('prisoner escort arrangements') may include entering into contracts with other persons for the provision by them of prisoner custody officers.

(5) Any person who, under a warrant or hospital order, is responsible for the performance of any such function as is mentioned in subsection (2) above shall be deemed to have complied with that warrant or order if he does all that he reasonably can to secure that the function is performed by a prisoner custody officer acting in pursuance of prisoner escort arrangements.

(6) In this section—

'hospital' has the same meaning as in the Mental Health (Scotland) Act 1984;
'hospital order' means an order for a person's detention in, or admission to and detention in, a hospital under section 174, 174A, 175, 375A or 376 of the Act of 1975 or section 70 of the Act of 1984; and
'warrant' means a warrant for committal, a warrant for arrest, a warrant under section 69, 73, 74 or 75 of the Act of 1984, a transfer direction under section 71 of that Act or any other warrant, order or direction under the Act of 1975 or the Act of 1984 requiring a person to be taken to a particular place.

103. Monitoring of prisoner escort arrangements

(1) Prisoner escort arrangements shall include the appointment of a prisoner escort monitor, that is to say, a Crown servant whose duty it shall be—

(a) to keep the arrangements under review and to report on them to the Secretary of State;

(b) to investigate and report to the Secretary of State on any allegations made against prisoner custody officers acting in pursuance of the arrangements; and

(c) to report to the Secretary of State on any alleged breaches of discipline on the part of prisoners for whose transfer or custody such officers so acting are responsible.

(2) In section 7(2) (functions of Her Majesty's Chief Inspector of Prisons for Scotland) of the 1989 Act—

(a) after 'Inspector' there shall be inserted '—(a)'; and

(b) at the end there shall be inserted—
'; and

(b) to inspect the conditions in which prisoners are transported or held in pursuance of prisoner escort arrangements (within the meaning of section 102 of the Criminal Justice and Public Order Act 1994) and to report to the Secretary of State on them.'.

104. Powers and duties of prisoner custody officers performing escort functions

(1) A prisoner custody officer acting in pursuance of prisoner escort arrangements shall have power to search—

(a) any prisoner for whose transfer or custody he is responsible in accordance with the arrangements; and

(b) any other person who is in or is seeking to enter any place where any such prisoner is or is to be held and any article in the possession of such a person.

(2) The power conferred by subsection (1)(b) above to search a person shall not be construed as authorising a prisoner custody officer to require a person to remove any of his clothing other than an outer coat, jacket, headgear and gloves.

(3) A prisoner custody officer shall, as respects prisoners for whose transfer or custody he is responsible in pursuance of prisoner escort arrangements, have the duty—

(a) to prevent their escape from legal custody;

(b) to prevent, or detect and report on, the commission or attempted commission by them of other unlawful acts;

(c) to ensure good order and discipline on their part;

(d) to attend to their wellbeing; and

(e) to give effect to any directions as to their treatment which are given by a court.

(4) Where a prisoner custody officer acting in pursuance of prisoner escort arrangements is on any premises in which a court of summary jurisdiction is sitting he shall have the duty to give effect to any order of the court under section 395(2) of the Criminal Procedure (Scotland) Act 1975 requiring an offender to be searched.

(5) The powers conferred by subsection (1) above and the powers arising by virtue of subsections (3) and (4) above shall include power to use reasonable force where necessary.

(6) Prison rules may make provision in relation to—

(a) the power conferred by subsection (1) above; and

(b) the duty imposed by subsection (3)(d) above.

105. Breaches of discipline by prisoners under escort

(1) Where a prisoner for whose transfer or custody a prisoner custody officer has been responsible in pursuance of prisoner escort arrangements is delivered to a prison, he shall be deemed, for the purposes of such prison rules as relate to breaches of discipline, to have been—

(a) in the custody of the governor of the prison; or

(b) in the case of a contracted out prison, in the custody of its director,

at all times during the period for which that officer was so responsible, and that officer may bring a charge of breach of such rules as so relate against the prisoner in respect of any such time.

(2) Nothing in subsection (1) above shall render a prisoner liable to be punished under prison rules for any act or omission of his for which he has already been punished by a court.

(3) In this section 'prison rules', in relation to a prison situated in a part of the British Islands outside Scotland, means rules made under any provision of the law of that part which corresponds to section 39 of the 1989 Act.

Contracted out prisons

106. Contracting out of prisons

(1) The Secretary of State may enter into a contract with another person for the provision or running (or the provision and running) by him, or (if the contract so provides) for the running by sub-contractors of his, of any prison or part of a prison in Scotland.

(2) While a contract under this section for the running of a prison or part of a prison is in force—

(a) the prison or part shall be run subject to and in accordance with—

(i) sections 107 and 108 below; and

(ii) the 1989 Act and prison rules and directions made under or by virtue of that Act (all as modified by section 110 below); and

(b) in the case of a part, that part and the remaining part shall each be treated for the purposes of sections 107 to 112 below as if they were separate prisons.

(3) Where the Secretary of State grants a lease for the purpose of any contract under this section, none of the following enactments shall apply to it—

(a) sections 4 to 7 of the Law Reform (Miscellaneous Provisions) (Scotland) Act 1985 (irritancy clauses); and

(b) the Agricultural Holdings (Scotland) Act 1991.

In this subsection 'lease' includes a sub-lease.

(4)   In this Chapter—
'contracted out prison' means a prison or part of a prison for the running of which a contract under this section is for the time being in force;
'the contractor', in relation to a contracted out prison, means the person who has contracted with the Secretary of State for the running of it; and
'sub-contractor', in relation to a contracted out prison, means a person who has contracted with the contractor for the running of it or any part of it.

107.   Officers of contracted out prisons
(1)   Instead of a governor, every contracted out prison shall have—
(a)   a director, who shall be a prisoner custody officer appointed by the contractor and specially approved for the purposes of this section by the Secretary of State; and
(b)   a controller, who shall be a Crown servant appointed by the Secretary of State,
and every officer of such a prison who performs custodial duties shall be a prisoner custody officer who is authorised to perform such duties or a prison officer who is temporarily attached to the prison.
(2)   Subject to subsection (3) below, the director shall have the same functions as are conferred on a governor by the 1989 Act and by prison rules.
(3)   The director shall not—
(a)   have any function which is conferred on a controller by virtue of subsection (4) below;
(b)   inquire into a disciplinary charge brought against a prisoner, conduct the hearing of such a charge or make, remit or mitigate an award in respect of such a charge; or
(c)   except in cases of urgency, order the removal of a prisoner from association with other prisoners, the temporary confinement of a prisoner in a special cell or the application to a prisoner of any other special control or restraint.
(4)   The controller shall have such functions as may be conferred on him by prison rules and shall be under a duty—
(a)   to keep under review, and report to the Secretary of State on, the running of the prison by or on behalf of the director; and
(b)   to investigate, and report to the Secretary of State on, any allegations made against prisoner custody officers performing custodial duties at the prison or prison officers who are temporarily attached to the prison.
(5)   The contractor and any sub-contractor of his shall each be under a duty to do all that he reasonably can (whether by giving directions to the officers of the prison or otherwise) to facilitate the exercise by the controller of all such functions as are mentioned in or conferred by subsection (4) above.
(6)   Every contracted out prison shall have a medical officer, who shall be a registered medical practitioner appointed by the contractor or, if the contract provides for the running of the prison by a sub-contractor, by the sub-contractor.

108.   Powers and duties of prisoner custody officers employed at contracted out prisons
(1)   A prisoner custody officer performing custodial duties at a contracted out prison shall have power to search—
(a)   any prisoner who is confined in the prison or for whose custody he is responsible; and

(b)   any other person who is in or is seeking to enter the prison and any article in the possession of such a person.

(2)   The power conferred by subsection (1)(b) above to search a person shall not be construed as authorising a prisoner custody officer to require a person to remove any of his clothing other than an outer coat, jacket, headgear and gloves.

(3)   A prisoner custody officer performing custodial duties at a contracted out prison shall, as respects the prisoners for whose custody he is responsible, have the duty—

(a)   to prevent their escape from legal custody;

(b)   to prevent, or detect and report on, the commission or attempted commission by them of other unlawful acts;

(c)   to ensure good order and discipline on their part; and

(d)   to attend to their wellbeing.

(4)   The powers conferred by subsection (1) above and the powers arising by virtue of subsection (3) above shall include power to use reasonable force where necessary.

109.   Breaches of discipline by prisoners temporarily out of contracted out prison

(1)   This section applies where a prisoner custody officer who performs custodial duties at a contracted out prison is responsible for the custody of a prisoner who is outside the prison for temporary purposes.

(2)   For the purposes of such prison rules as relate to breaches of discipline the prisoner shall be deemed to have been in the custody of the director of the prison at all times during the period for which the prisoner custody officer was so responsible, and that officer may bring a charge of breach of such rules as so relate against the prisoner in respect of any such time.

(3)   Nothing in subsection (1) above shall render a prisoner liable to be punished under prison rules for any act or omission of his for which he has already been punished by a court.

110.   Consequential modifications of 1989 Act, prison rules and directions

(1)   In relation to a contracted out prison, the provisions specified in subsections (2) to (7) below shall have effect subject to the modifications so specified.

(2)   In section 3 of the 1989 Act (general superintendence of prisons)—

(a)   in subsection (1), the words from 'who shall appoint' to the end shall be omitted; and

(b)   subsection (3) shall not apply.

(3)   In sections 9(5), 11(4), 15(1) and (3) (various functions of the governor of a prison), 33A (power of governor to delegate functions), 34 (duty of governor where prisoner dies), 39(8) and (12) (prison rules), 41(4) (detention of person suspected of bringing prohibited article into prison) and 41B(3) (testing prisoners for drugs) of that Act, in prison rules and in directions made by virtue of section 39(8) of that Act the reference to the governor shall be construed as a reference to the director.

(4)   In sections 11(4) (execution of certain warrants by prison officers etc.), 13(b) (legal custody of prisoners), 33A (power of governor to delegate functions), 40(1) (persons unlawfully at large), 41(3), (4), (6) and (8) (detention of person suspected of bringing prohibited article into prison) and 41B(1) (testing prisoners for drugs) of that Act, the reference to an officer of a prison (or, as the case may be, a prison

officer) shall be construed as a reference to a prisoner custody officer performing custodial duties at the prison or a prison officer temporarily attached to the prison.

(5)   Section 36 of that Act (vesting of prison property in Secretary of State) shall have effect subject to the provisions of the contract entered into under section 106 above.

(6)   Sections 37 (discontinuance of prison), 41(2A) and (2B) (power to search for prohibited articles) and 41A (powers of search by authorised employees) of that Act shall not apply.

(7)   In prison rules, in subsection (8) of section 39 of that Act (directions supplementing prison rules) and in any direction made by virtue of that subsection, the reference to an officer of a prison (or, as the case may be, a prison officer) shall be construed as including a reference to a prisoner custody officer performing custodial duties at the prison.

111.   Intervention by the Secretary of State

(1)   This section applies where, in the case of a contracted out prison, it appears to the Secretary of State—

(a)   that the director has lost or is likely to lose effective control of the prison or any part of it; and

(b)   that the making of an appointment under subsection (2) below is necessary in the interests of preserving the safety of any person or preventing serious damage to any property.

(2)   The Secretary of State may appoint a Crown servant to act as governor of the prison for the period—

(a)   beginning with the time specified in the appointment; and

(b)   ending with the time specified in the notice of termination under subsection (4) below.

(3)   During that period—

(a)   all the functions which would otherwise be exercisable by the director or the controller shall be exercisable by the governor;

(b)   the contractor and any sub-contractor of his shall each do all that he reasonably can to facilitate the exercise by the governor of those functions; and

(c)   the officers of the prison shall comply with any directions given by the governor in the exercise of those functions.

(4)   Where the Secretary of State is satisfied—

(a)   that the governor has secured effective control of the prison or, as the case may be, the relevant part of it; and

(b)   that the governor's appointment is no longer necessary as mentioned in subsection (1)(b) above,
he shall, by a notice to the governor, terminate the appointment at a time specified in the notice.

(5)   As soon as practicable after making or terminating an appointment under this section, the Secretary of State shall give a notice of the appointment, or a copy of the notice of termination, to the contractor, any sub-contractor of his, the director and the controller.

Contracted out functions

112.   Contracted out functions at directly managed prisons

(1)   The Secretary of State may enter into a contract with another person for any

functions at a directly managed prison to be performed by prisoner custody officers who are provided by that person and are authorised to perform custodial duties.

(2) Sections 108 and 109 above shall apply in relation to a prisoner custody officer performing contracted out functions at a directly managed prison as they apply in relation to such an officer performing custodial duties at a contracted out prison, but as if the reference in section 109(2) to the director of the contracted out prison were a reference to the governor of the directly managed prison.

(3) In relation to a directly managed prison, the references to an officer of a prison (or, as the case may be, a prison officer) in the provisions specified in subsection (4) below shall each be construed as including a reference to a prisoner custody officer performing custodial duties at the prison in pursuance of a contract under this section.

(4) Those provisions are—

(a) section 11(4) of the 1989 Act (execution of certain warrants by prison officers etc.);

(b) section 13(b) of that Act (legal custody of prisoners);

(c) section 33A of that Act (power of governor to delegate functions);

(d) subsection (8) of section 39 of that Act (directions supplementing prison rules) and directions made by virtue of that subsection;

(e) section 40(1) of that Act (persons unlawfully at large);

(f) section 41(3), (4), (6) and (8) of that Act (prohibited articles); and

(g) prison rules.

(5) Section 41(2A) and (2B) of the 1989 Act (search of person suspected of bringing prohibited article into prison) shall not apply in relation to a prisoner custody officer performing contracted out functions at a directly managed prison.

(6) Any reference in the foregoing provisions of this section to the performance of functions or custodial duties at a directly managed prison includes a reference to the performance of functions or such duties for the purposes of, or for purposes connected with, such a prison.

(7) In this Chapter—

'contracted out functions' means any functions which, by virtue of a contract under this section, fall to be performed by prisoner custody officers; and

'directly managed prison' means a prison which is not a contracted out prison.

Provision of new prisons

113. Provision of new prisons

(1) The Secretary of State may declare to be a prison—

(a) any building or part of a building built or adapted for the purpose; and

(b) any floating structure or part of such a structure constructed or adapted for the purpose,

whether vested in, or under the control of, the Secretary of State or any other person.

(2) Section 106(1) and subsection (1) above are without prejudice to the Secretary of State's powers under the 1989 Act with respect to the provision of prisons.

(3) A declaration under subsection (1) above—

(a) shall have effect for the purposes of the 1989 Act and any other enactment (including an enactment contained in subordinate legislation);

(b)   shall not be sufficient to vest the legal estate in any building or structure in the Secretary of State; and

(c)   may be revoked by the Secretary of State at any time other than a time when the prison to which it relates is a contracted out prison.

(4)   Nothing in section 36 of the 1989 Act (prison property to be vested in the Secretary of State) shall require the legal estate in—

(a)   any prison provided under a contract entered into under section 106(1) above;

(b)   any prison declared to be such under subsection (1) above and not vested in the Secretary of State; or

(c)   any heritable or moveable property belonging to any prison mentioned in paragraph (a) or (b) above,

to be vested in the Secretary of State.

Supplemental

114.   Prisoner custody officers: general provisions

(1)   In this Chapter 'prisoner custody officer' means a person in respect of whom a certificate is for the time being in force certifying—

(a)   that he has been approved by the Secretary of State for the purpose of performing escort functions or custodial duties or both; and

(b)   that he is accordingly authorised to perform them.

(2)   Schedule 6 to this Act shall have effect with respect to the certification of prisoner custody officers.

(3)   Prison rules may make provision regarding the powers and duties of prisoner custody officers performing custodial duties.

115.   Wrongful disclosure of information

(1)   A person who—

(a)   is or has been employed (whether as a prisoner custody officer or otherwise) in pursuance of prisoner escort arrangements, or at a contracted out prison; or

(b)   is or has been employed to perform contracted out functions at a directly managed prison,

shall be guilty of an offence if he discloses, otherwise than in the course of his duty or as authorised by the Secretary of State, any information which he acquired in the course of his employment and which relates to a particular prisoner.

(2)   A person guilty of an offence under subsection (1) above shall be liable—

(a)   on conviction on indictment, to imprisonment for a term not exceeding two years or a fine or both;

(b)   on summary conviction, to imprisonment for a term not exceeding six months or a fine not exceeding the statutory maximum or both.

116.   Minor and consequential amendments

(1)   In section 19(4)(b) of the 1989 Act (remand centres and young offenders institutions), for '33' there shall be substituted '33A'.

(2)   Section 33 of that Act (miscellaneous duties of prison governor) shall cease to have effect.

(3) After section 33 of that Act there shall be inserted the following section—

'33A.   Power of governor to delegate functions

Rules made under section 39 of this Act may permit the goveror of a prison to authorise an officer of the prison, or a class of such officers, to exercise on his behalf such of the governor's functions as the rules may specify.'.

(4)   In section 39 of that Act (prison rules)—

(a)   in subsection (1), after 'Act' there shall be inserted 'or any other enactment';

(b)   in subsection (8), for 'the purpose so specified' there shall be substituted 'any purpose specified in the rules'; and

(c)   after subsection (11), there shall be inserted the following subsection—

'(12)   Rules made under this section may (without prejudice to the generality of subsection (1) above) confer functions on a governor.'.

117.   Interpretation of Chapter II

(1)   In this Chapter, except where otherwise expressly provided—

'the 1989 Act' means the Prisons (Scotland) Act 1989;

'contracted out prison' and 'the contractor' have the meanings given by section 106(4) above;

'contracted out functions' and 'directly managed prison' have the meanings given by section 112(7) above;

'custodial duties' means custodial duties at a contracted out or a directly managed prison;

'escort functions' has the meaning given by section 102(1) above;

'prison' includes—

(a)   any prison other than a naval, military or air force prison; and

(b)   a remand centre or young offenders institution within the meaning of section 19 of the 1989 Act;

'prison officer' means an officer of a directly managed prison;

'prison rules' means rules made under section 39 of the 1989 Act;

'prisoner' means any person who is in legal custody or is deemed to be in legal custody under section 215 or 426 of the Criminal Procedure (Scotland) Act 1975;

'prisoner custody officer' has the meaning given by section 114(1) above;

'prisoner escort arrangements' has the meaning given by section 102(4) above; and

'sub-contractor' has the meaning given by section 106(4) above.

(2)   Any reference in this Chapter to custodial duties at a contracted out or directly managed prison includes a reference to custodial duties in relation to a prisoner who is outside such a prison for temporary purposes.

(3)   In sections 102(1) to (3), 104 and 105 above, 'prison'—

(a)   so far as relating to the transfer of prisoners to or from a prison situated in England and Wales, includes a young offender institution and a remand centre; and

(b)   so far as relating to the transfer of prisoners to or from a prison situated in Northern Ireland, includes a young offenders centre and a remand centre.

CHAPTER III   NORTHERN IRELAND

Prisoner escorts

118.   Arrangements for the provision of prisoner escorts

(1)   The Secretary of State may make arrangements for any of the following functions, namely—

    (a)   the delivery of prisoners from one set of relevant premises to another;

    (b)   the custody of prisoners held on the premises of any court (whether or not they would otherwise be in the custody of the court) and their production before the court;

    (c)   the custody of prisoners temporarily held in a prison in the course of delivery from one prison to another; and

    (d)   the custody of prisoners while they are outside a prison for temporary purposes;

to be performed in such cases as may be determined by or under the arrangements by prisoner custody officers who are authorised to perform such functions.

(2)   In paragraph (a) of subsection (1) above, 'relevant premises' means a court, prison, police station or hospital; and either (but not both) of the sets of premises mentioned in that paragraph may be situated in a part of the British Islands outside Northern Ireland.

(3)   Arrangements made by the Secretary of State under this section ('prisoner escort arrangements') may include entering into contracts with other persons for the provision by them of prisoner custody officers.

(4)   Any person who, under a warrant or a hospital order or remand, is responsible for the performance of any such function as is mentioned in subsection (1) above shall be deemed to have complied with that warrant, order or remand if he does all that he reasonably can to secure that the function is performed by a prisoner custody officer acting in pursuance of prisoner escort arrangements.

(5)   In this section—

    'hospital' has the same meaning as in the Mental Health (Northern Ireland) Order 1986;

    'hospital order' means an order for a person's admission to hospital under Article 44, 45, 49 or 50 of that Order, or section 11 or 13 of the Criminal Appeal (Northern Ireland) Act 1980;

    'hospital remand' means a remand of a person to hospital under Article 42 or 43 of the Mental Health (Northern Ireland) Order 1986;

    'warrant' means a warrant of commitment, a warrant of arrest or a warrant under Article 52, 53, 54, 56 or 79 of that Order.

119.   Monitoring etc. of prisoner escort arrangements

(1)   Prisoner escort arrangements shall include the appointment of a prisoner escort monitor, that is to say, a Crown servant whose duty it shall be to keep the arrangements under review and to report on them to the Secretary of State.

(2)   It shall also be the duty of a prisoner escort monitor to investigate and report to the Secretary of State on—

    (a)   any allegations made against prisoner custody officers acting in pursuance of the arrangements; and

    (b)   any alleged breaches of discipline on the part of prisoners for whose delivery or custody such officers so acting are responsible.

120.   Powers and duties of prisoner custody officers acting in pursuance of such arrangements

(1)   A prisoner custody officer acting in pursuance of prisoner escort arrangements shall have the following powers, namely—

(a) to search in accordance with rules made by the Secretary of State any prisoner for whose delivery or custody he is responsible in accordance with the arrangements; and

(b) to search any other person who is in or is seeking to enter any place where any such prisoner is or is to be held and any article in the possession of such a person.

(2) The powers conferred by subsection (1)(b) above to search a person shall not be construed as authorising a prisoner custody officer to require a person to remove any of his clothing other than an outer coat, hat, jacket or gloves.

(3) A prisoner custody officer shall have the following duties as respects prisoners for whose delivery or custody he is responsible in pursuance of prisoner escort arrangements, namely—

(a) to prevent their escape from lawful custody;

(b) to prevent, or detect and report on, the commission or attempted commission by them of other unlawful acts;

(c) to ensure good order and discipline on their part;

(d) to attend to their wellbeing; and

(e) to give effect to any directions as to their treatment which are given by a court,

and the Secretary of State may make rules with respect to the performance by prisoner custody officers of their duty under paragraph (d) above.

(4) Where a prisoner custody officer acting in pursuance of prisoner escort arrangements is on any premises in which a magistrates' court is sitting, it shall be his duty to give effect to any order of that court made under Article 110 of the Magistrates' Courts (Northern Ireland) Order 1981 (application of funds found upon defaulter).

(5) The powers conferred by subsection (1) above and the powers arising by virtue of subsections (3) and (4) above shall include power to use reasonable force where necessary.

(6) The power to make rules under this section shall be exercisable by statutory instrument which shall be subject to annulment in pursuance of a resolution of either House of Parliament.

121. Breaches of discipline by prisoners under escort

(1) This section applies where a prisoner for whose delivery or custody a prisoner custody officer has been responsible in pursuance of prisoner escort arrangements is delivered to a prison.

(2) For the purpose of such prison rules as relate to disciplinary offences, the prisoner shall be deemed to have been in the custody of the governor of the prison at all times during the period for which the prisoner custody officer was so responsible.

(3) In the case of any breach by the prisoner at any time during the period of such prison rules as so relate, a disciplinary charge may be laid against him by the prisoner custody officer.

(4) Nothing in this section shall enable a prisoner to be punished under prison rules for any act or omission of his for which he has already been punished by a court.

(5) In this section 'prison rules', in relation to a prison situated in a part of the British Islands outside Northern Ireland, means rules made under any provision of the law of that part which corresponds to section 13 of the Prison Act (Northern Ireland) 1953.

Supplemental

122. Certification of custody officers

(1) In this Chapter 'prisoner custody officer' means a person in respect of whom a certificate is for the time being in force certifying—

(a) that he has been approved by the Secretary of State for the purpose of performing escort functions; and

(b) that he is accordingly authorised to perform them.

(2) Schedule 7 to this Act shall have effect with respect to the certification of prisoner custody officers.

(3) In this section and Schedule 7 to this Act 'escort functions' means the functions specified in section 118(1) above.

123. Protection of prisoner custody officers

(1) Any person who assaults a prisoner custody officer acting in pursuance of prisoner escort arrangements shall be liable on summary conviction to a fine not exceeding level 5 on the standard scale or to imprisonment for a term not exceeding six months or to both.

(2) Article 18(2) of the Firearms (Northern Ireland) Order 1981 (additional penalty for possession of firearms when committing certain offences) shall apply to offences under subsection (1) above.

(3) Any person who resists or wilfully obstructs a prisoner custody officer acting in pursuance of prisoner escort arrangements shall be liable on summary conviction to a fine not exceeding level 3 on the standard scale.

(4) For the purposes of this section, a prisoner custody officer shall not be regarded as acting in pursuance of prisoner escort arrangements at any time when he is not readily identifiable as such an officer (whether by means of a uniform or badge which he is wearing or otherwise).

124. Wrongful disclosure of information

(1) A person who is or has been employed (whether as a prisoner custody officer or otherwise) in pursuance of prisoner escort arrangements shall be guilty of an offence if he discloses, otherwise than in the course of his duty or as authorised by the Secretary of State, any information which he acquired in the course of his employment and which relates to a particular prisoner.

(2) A person guilty of an offence under subsection (1) above shall be liable—

(a) on conviction on indictment, to imprisonment for a term not exceeding two years or a fine or both;

(b) on summary conviction, to imprisonment for a term not exceeding six months or a fine not exceeding the statutory maximum or both.

125. Interpretation of Chapter III

(1) In this Chapter—

'prison' includes a young offenders centre or remand centre;

'prisoner custody officer' has the meaning given by section 122(1) above;

'prison rules' means rules made under section 13 of the Prison Act (Northern Ireland) 1953;

'prisoner' means any person for the time being detained in lawful custody as the result of a requirement imposed by a court or otherwise that he be so detained;

'prisoner escort arrangements' has the meaning given by section 118(3) above.

(2) Sections 118, 119(1) and (2)(a), 120 and 122 to 124 above, subsection (1) above and Schedule 7 to this Act shall have effect as if—

(a) any reference in section 118(1), 119(1), 120 or 124 above to prisoners included a reference to persons remanded or committed to custody in certain premises under section 51, 74 or 75 of the Children and Young Persons Act (Northern Ireland) 1968 or ordered to be sent to a training school under section 74 or 78 of that Act; and

(b) any reference in section 118(1)(c) or (d) or (2) above to a prison included a reference to such premises or training school.

(3) In sections 118, 120 and 121 above, 'prison'—

(a) so far as relating to the delivery of prisoners to or from a prison situated in England and Wales, includes a remand centre or young offender institution; and

(b) so far as relating to the delivery of prisoners to or from a prison situated in Scotland, includes a remand centre or young offenders institution within the meaning of section 19 of the Prisons (Scotland) Act 1989.

CHAPTER IV   THE PRISON SERVICE

126.   Service in England and Wales and Northern Ireland

(1) The relevant employment legislation shall have effect as if an individual who as a member of the prison service acts in a capacity in which he has the powers or privileges of a constable were not, by virtue of his so having those powers or privileges, to be regarded as in police service for the purposes of any provision of that legislation.

(2) In this section 'the relevant employment legislation' means—

(a) the Employment Protection (Consolidation) Act 1978 and the Trade Union and Labour Relations (Consolidation) Act 1992; and

(b) the Industrial Relations (Northern Ireland) Order 1976, the Industrial Relations (No. 2) (Northern Ireland) Order 1976 and the Industrial Relations (Northern Ireland) Order 1992.

(3) For the purposes of this section a person is a member of the prison service if he is an individual holding a post to which he has been appointed for the purposes of section 7 of the Prison Act 1952 or under section 2(2) of the Prison Act (Northern Ireland) 1953 (appointment of prison staff).

(4) Except for the purpose of validating anything that would have been a contravention of section 127(1) below if it had been in force, subsection (1) above, so far as it relates to the question whether an organisation consisting wholly or mainly of members of the prison service is a trade union, shall be deemed always to have had effect and to have applied, in relation to times when provisions of the relevant employment legislation were not in force, to the corresponding legislation then in force.

(5) Subsection (6) below shall apply where—

(a) the certificate of independence of any organisation has been cancelled, at any time before the passing of this Act, in consequence of the removal of the name of that organisation from a list of trade unions kept under provisions of the relevant employment legislation; but

(b) it appears to the Certification Officer that the organisation would have remained on the list, and that the certificate would have remained in force, had that legislation had effect at and after that time in accordance with subsection (1) above.

(6)   Where this subsection applies—

(a)   the Certification Officer shall restore the name to the list and delete from his records any entry relating to the cancellation of the certificate;

(b)   the removal of the name from the list, the making of the deleted entry and the cancellation of the certificate shall be deemed never to have occurred; and

(c)   the organisation shall accordingly be deemed, for the purposes for which it is treated by virtue of subsection (4) above as having been a trade union, to have been independent throughout the period between the cancellation of the certificate and the deletion of the entry relating to that cancellation.

127.   Inducements to withhold services or to indiscipline

(1)   A person contravenes this subsection if he induces a prison officer—

(a)   to withhold his services as such an officer; or

(b)   to commit a breach of discipline.

(2)   The obligation not to contravene subsection (1) above shall be a duty owed to the Secretary of State.

(3)   Without prejudice to the right of the Secretary of State, by virtue of the preceding provisions of this section, to bring civil proceedings in respect of any apprehended contravention of subsection (1) above, any breach of the duty mentioned in subsection (2) above which causes the Secretary of State to sustain loss or damage shall be actionable, at his suit or instance, against the person in breach.

(4)   In this section 'prison officer' means any individual who—

(a)   holds any post, otherwise than as a chaplain or assistant chaplain or as a medical officer, to which he has been appointed for the purposes of section 7 of the Prison Act 1952 or under section 2(2) of the Prison Act (Northern Ireland) 1953 (appointment of prison staff),

(b)   holds any post, otherwise than as a medical officer, to which he has been appointed under section 3(1) of the Prisons (Scotland) Act 1989, or

(c)   is a custody officer within the meaning of Part I of this Act or a prisoner custody officer, within the meaning of Part IV of the Criminal Justice Act 1991 or Chapter II or III of this Part.

(5)   The reference in subsection (1) above to a breach of discipline by a prison officer is a reference to a failure by a prison officer to perform any duty imposed on him by the prison rules or any code of discipline having effect under those rules or any other contravention by a prison officer of those rules or any such code.

(6)   In subsection (5) above 'the prison rules' means any rules for the time being in force under section 47 of the Prison Act 1952, section 39 of the Prisons (Scotland) Act 1989 or section 13 of the Prison Act (Northern Ireland) 1953 (prison rules).

(7)   This section shall be disregarded in determining for the purposes of any of the relevant employment legislation whether any trade union is an independent trade union.

(8)   Nothing in the relevant employment legislation shall affect the rights of the Secretary of State by virtue of this section.

(9)   In this section 'the relevant employment legislation' has the same meaning as in section 126 above.

128.   Pay and related conditions

(1)   The Secretary of State may by regulations provide for the establishment, maintenance and operation of procedures for the determination from time to time of—

(a) the rates of pay and allowances to be applied to the prison service; and

(b) such other terms and conditions of employment in that service as may appear to him to fall to be determined in association with the determination of rates of pay and allowances.

(2) Before making any regulations under this section the Secretary of State shall consult with such organisations appearing to him to be representative of persons working in the prison service and with such other persons as he thinks fit.

(3) The power to make regulations under this section shall be exercisable by statutory instrument subject to annulment in pursuance of a resolution of either House of Parliament.

(4) Regulations under this section may—

(a) provide for determinations with respect to matters to which the regulations relate to be made wholly or partly by reference to such factors, and the opinion or recommendations of such persons, as may be specified or described in the regulations;

(b) authorise the matters considered and determined in pursuance of the regulations to include matters applicable to times and periods before they are considered or determined;

(c) make such incidental, supplemental, consequential and transitional provision as the Secretary of State thinks fit; and

(d) make different provision for different cases.

(5) For the purposes of this section the prison service comprises all the individuals who are prison officers within the meaning of section 127 above, apart from those who are custody officers within the meaning of Part I of this Act or prisoner custody officers within the meaning of Part IV of the Criminal Justice Act 1991 or Chapter II or III of this Part.

PART IX   MISCELLANEOUS AMENDMENTS: SCOTLAND

129. Transfer of persons detained by police and customs officers

(1) In subsection (1) of section 2 of the Criminal Justice (Scotland) Act 1980 (detention of suspect at police station or other premises)—

(a) after the word 'premises' there shall be inserted the words 'and may thereafter for that purpose take him to any other place'; and

(b) for the word 'there' there shall be substituted the words 'at the police station, or as the case may be the other premises or place'.

(2) In subsection (4) of that section—

(a) after paragraph (a) there shall be inserted the following paragraph—

'(aa) any other place to which the person is, during the detention, thereafter taken;'; and

(b) in paragraph (f), for the words 'departure from the police station or other premises' there shall be substituted the words 'release from detention'.

(3) In section 3(1)(b) of that Act (intimation to solicitor and other person of detention under section 2)—

(a) for the words 'in a police station or other premises' there shall be substituted the words 'and has been taken to a police station or other premises or place'; and

(b) for the words 'place where he is being detained' there shall be substituted the words 'police station or other premises or place'.

(4)   In subsection (1) of section 48 of the Criminal Justice (Scotland) Act 1987 (detention of suspect by customs officer)—

(a)   after the word 'premises' there shall be inserted the words 'and may thereafter for that purpose take him to any other place'; and

(b)   for the word 'there' there shall be substituted the words 'at the customs office, or as the case may be the other premises or place.'.

(5)   In subsection (5) of that section—

(a)   after paragraph (a) there shall be inserted the following paragraph—

'(aa)   any other place to which the person is, during the detention, thereafter taken;'; and

(b)   in paragraph (f), for the words 'departure from the customs office or other premises' there shall be substituted the words 'release from detention'.

(6)   In section 49(1) of that Act (intimation to solicitor and other person of detention under section 48)—

(a)   for the words 'at a customs office or other premises' there shall be substituted the words 'and has been taken to a customs office or other premises or place'; and

(b)   for the words 'place where he is being detained' there shall be substituted the words 'customs office or other premises or place'.

130.   Detention and release of children: Scotland

(1)   In section 7 of the Prisoners and Criminal Proceedings (Scotland) Act 1993 (children detained in solemn proceedings), after subsection (1) there shall be inserted—

'(1A)   The Secretary of State may by order provide—

(a)   that the reference to—

(i)   four years, in paragraph (a) of subsection (1) above; or

(ii)   four or more years, in paragraph (b) of that subsection,

shall be construed as a reference to such other period as may be specified in the order;

(b)   that the reference to—

(i)   half, in the said paragraph (a); or

(ii)   two thirds, in the said paragraph (b),

shall be construed as a reference to such other proportion of the period specified in the sentence as may be specified in the order.

(1B)   An order under subsection (1A) above may make such transitional provision as appears to the Secretary of State necessary or expedient in connection with any provision made by the order.'.

(2)   In section 45(3) of that Act (procedure in respect of certain orders), for the words '7(6)' there shall be substituted '7(1A) or (6)'.

(3)   In Schedule 6 to that Act (transitional provisions and savings)—

(a)   in paragraph 8, after the word 'revoked' there shall be inserted 'by virtue of paragraph 10 of this Schedule'; and

(b)   after paragraph 9 there shall be added—

'10.   Section 17 of this Act shall apply in respect of a release on licence under paragraph 4 of this Schedule as that section applies in respect of the release on licence, under Part I of this Act, of a long-term prisoner.'.

(4)   In section 39(7) of the Prisons (Scotland) Act 1989 (award of additional days), at the end there shall be added—

'; and the foregoing provisions of this subsection (except paragraph (b)) shall apply in respect of a person sentenced to be detained under section 206 of the 1975 Act, the detention not being without limit of time, as those provisions apply in respect of any such short-term or long-term prisoner.'.

131. Conditions in licence of released prisoner: requirement for Parole Board recommendations

In section 12(3)(a) of the Prisoners and Criminal Proceedings (Scotland) Act 1993 (requirement of Parole Board recommendations for inclusion of conditions in licences of certain released prisoners), after the word 'inclusion' there shall be inserted the words 'or subsequent insertion, variation or cancellation'.

132. Provision for standard requirements in supervised release orders in Scotland

In section 212A of the Criminal Procedure (Scotland) Act 1975 (which makes provision for the supervised release of short-term prisoners)—

(a)   in subsection (2)—

(i)   for the words from 'and', where it occurs immediately after paragraph (a), to the end of sub-paragraph (i) of paragraph (b), there shall be substituted—

'(b)   comply with—

(i)   such requirements as may be imposed by the court in the order;'; and

(ii)   at the end there shall be added—

'; and

(c)   comply with the standard requirements imposed by virtue of subsection (3)(a)(i) below'; and

(b)   in subsection (3), for paragraph (a) there shall be substituted—

'(a)   shall—

(i)   without prejudice to subsection (2)(b) above, contain such requirements (in this section referred to as the 'standard requirements'); and

(ii)   be as nearly as possible in such form, as may be prescribed by Act of Adjournal;'.

133. Extension of categories of prisoner to whom Part I of Prisoners and Criminal Proceedings (Scotland) Act 1993 applies

In section 10(4) of the Prisoners and Criminal Proceedings (Scotland) Act 1993 (interpretation of expression 'transferred life prisoner')—

(a)   in paragraph (a), after the word 'Scotland' there shall be inserted the words 'or a court-martial'; and

(b)   in paragraph (b)—

(i)   for the word '(whether' there shall be substituted—

', or in the case of a sentence imposed by a court martial in Scotland to a prison in Scotland (in either case whether';

(ii)   after sub-paragraph (ii) there shall be inserted—

'; or

(iii)   rules made under section 122(1)(a) of the Army Act 1955 (imprisonment and detention rules); or

(iv)   rules made under section 122(1)(a) of the Air Force Act 1955 (imprisonment and detention rules); or

(v)   a determination made under section 81(3) of the Naval Discipline
Act 1957 (place of imprisonment or detention),'; and
(iii)   at the end there shall be added—
'; and in this subsection 'prison' has the same meaning as in the 1989 Act.'.

**134.   Amendment of provisions continued in effect for certain prisoners by
Prisoners and Criminal Proceedings (Scotland) Act 1993**
(1)   In Schedule 6 to the Prisoners and Criminal Proceedings (Scotland) Act 1993
(transitional provisions and savings)—
(a)   in paragraph 1—
(i)   in the definition of 'existing provisions', at the end there shall be added
'except that an amendment or repeal effected by any enactment shall apply for the
purposes of the existing provisions if expressly stated to do so'; and
(ii)   in the definition of 'new provisions', after the word 'amended' there
shall be added 'by this Act'; and
(b)   in paragraph 2(1), for the words from 'and to' to 'Schedule' there shall be
substituted—
', to the following provisions of this Schedule and to the exception in the
definition of 'existing provisions' in paragraph 1 above,'.
(2)   Sections 18 (constitution and functions of Parole Board etc.), 22 (release on
licence of persons serving determinate sentences), 28 (revocation of licences and
conviction of prisoners on licence) and 42(3) (exercise of power to make rules etc.)
of the Prisons (Scotland) Act 1989, being provisions which, notwithstanding their
repeal by the Prisoners and Criminal Proceedings (Scotland) Act 1993, are 'existing
provisions' for the purposes of that Act of 1993, shall for those purposes be amended
in accordance with the following subsections.
(3)   In the said section 18, for subsections (3) and (4) there shall be substituted—
'(3A)   The Secretary of State may by rules make provision with respect to
the proceedings of the Board, including provision—
(a)   authorising cases to be dealt with in whole or in part by a prescribed
number of members of the Board in accordance with such procedure as may be
prescribed;
(b)   requiring cases to be dealt with at prescribed times; and
(c)   as to what matters may be taken into account by the Board (or by such
number) in dealing with a case.
(3B)   The Secretary of State may give the Board directions as to the matters
to be taken into account by it in discharging its functions under this Part of this
Act; and in giving any such directions the Secretary of State shall in particular
have regard to—
(a)   the need to protect the public from serious harm from offenders; and
(b)   the desirability of preventing the commission by offenders of further
offences and of securing their rehabilitation.'.
(4)   In each of the said sections 22 and 28, after subsection (1) there shall be
inserted—
'(1A)   The Secretary of State may by order provide that, in relation to such
class of case as may be specified in the order, subsection (1) above shall have
effect subject to the modification that for the word "may" there shall be
substituted the word "shall".'.

(5)   In the said section 22, at the beginning of subsection (7) there shall be inserted the words 'In a case where the Parole Board has recommended that a person be released on licence, and by virtue of subsection (1A) above such release is then mandatory, no licence conditions shall be included in the licence, or subsequently inserted, varied or cancelled in it, except in accordance with recommendations of the Board; and in any other case'.

(6)   In the said section 42—

(a)   in each of subsections (1) and (4), for the words '22(2)' there shall be substituted '22(1A) or (2), 28(1A),'; and

(b)   in subsection (3), for the word '(3)' there shall be substituted '(3A)'.

135.   Further amendment of Schedule 6 to the Prisoners and Criminal Proceedings (Scotland) Act 1993: application of 'new provisions'
In Schedule 6 to the Prisoners and Criminal Proceedings (Scotland) Act 1993 (transitional provisions and savings), after paragraph 6 there shall be inserted the following paragraphs—

'**6A.**

(1)   This paragraph applies where a prisoner sentenced before the relevant date to a sentence of imprisonment for life for an offence the sentence for which is not fixed by law has been (whether before, on or after that date) released on licence under the 1989 Act.

(2)   Without prejudice to section 22(6) of the 1989 Act, in a case to which this paragraph applies, the new provisions shall apply as if the prisoner were a discretionary life prisoner, within the meaning of section 2 of this Act, whose licence has been granted under subsection (4) of that section of this Act on his having served the relevant part of his sentence.

6B.

(1)   This paragraph applies where—

(a)   a prisoner was, at the relevant date, serving a sentence or sentences of imprisonment, on conviction of an offence, passed before that date and that sentence was for a term of, or as the case may be those sentences fall to be treated as for a single term of, two or more years; and

(b)   on or after that date he is, or has been, sentenced to a further term or terms of imprisonment, on conviction of an offence, to be served consecutively to, or concurrently with, the sentence or sentences mentioned in head (a) above.

(2)   In a case to which this paragraph applies—

(a)   the sentence or sentences mentioned in head (b) of sub-paragraph (1) above shall be treated as a single term with the sentences mentioned in head (a) of that sub-paragraph and that single term as imposed on or after the relevant date (so however that nothing in the foregoing provisions of this head shall affect the application of sections 39(7) (which makes provision as respects the award of additional days for breaches of discipline) and 24 (which makes provision as respects remission for good conduct) of the 1989 Act); and

(b)   the new provisions shall apply accordingly, except that—

(i)   where the prisoner is a long-term prisoner by virtue only of the aggregation provided for in head (a) of this sub-paragraph, he shall be released unconditionally on the same day as he would have been but for that aggregation;

(ii)   where, notwithstanding the aggregation so provided for, the prisoner remains a short-term prisoner, subsection (1) of section 1 of this Act shall in its application be construed as subject to the qualification that the prisoner shall be released no earlier than he would have been but for that aggregation;

      (iii)   that section shall in its application be construed as if for subsection (3) there were substituted—

'(3) Without prejudice to subsection (1) above and to sub-paragraph (2)(b)(i) of paragraph 6B of Schedule 6 to this Act, after a prisoner to whom that paragraph applies has either served one-third of the sentence, or as the case may be sentences, mentioned in sub-paragraph (1)(a) of that paragraph, or (if it results in a later date of release) has served twelve months of that sentence or those sentences, the Secretary of State may, if recommended to do so by the Parole Board under this section, release him on licence; and where such a prisoner has been released on licence under section 22 of the 1989 Act, that licence shall be deemed to have been granted by virtue of this subsection.';

      (iv)   section 11(1) shall in its application be construed as if the sentence referred to were the further term or terms mentioned in head (b) of sub-paragraph (1) above; and

      (v)   section 16 shall in its application be construed as if the original sentence (within the meaning of that section) were the further term or terms so mentioned.'.

PART X   CROSS-BORDER ENFORCEMENT

136. Execution of warrants

(1)   A warrant issued in England, Wales or Northern Ireland for the arrest of a person charged with an offence may (without any endorsement) be executed in Scotland by any constable of any police force of the country of issue or of the country of execution as well as by any other persons within the directions in the warrant.

(2)   A warrant issued in—

   (a)   Scotland; or

   (b)   Northern Ireland,

for the arrest of a person charged with an offence may (without any endorsement) be executed in England or Wales by any constable of any police force of the country of issue or of the country of execution as well as by any other persons within the directions in the warrant.

(3)   A warrant issued in—

   (a)   England or Wales; or

   (b)   Scotland,

for the arrest of a person charged with an offence may (without any endorsement) be executed in Northern Ireland by any constable of any police force of the country of issue or of the country of execution as well as by any other persons within the directions in the warrant.

(4)   A person arrested in pursuance of a warrant shall be taken, as soon as reasonably practicable, to any place to which he is committed by, or may be conveyed under, the warrant.

(5)   A constable executing a warrant—

   (a)   under subsection (1), (2)(b) or (3)(a) of this section may use reasonable force and shall have the powers of search conferred by section 139;

(b)   under subsection (2)(a) or (3)(b) of this section shall have the same powers and duties, and the person arrested the same rights, as they would have had if execution had been in Scotland by a constable of a police force in Scotland.

(6)   Any other person within the directions in a warrant executing that warrant under this section shall have the same powers and duties, and the person arrested the same rights, as they would have had if execution had been in the country of issue by the person within those directions.

(7)   This section applies as respects—

(a)   a warrant of commitment and a warrant to arrest a witness issued by a judicial authority in England, Wales or Northern Ireland as it applies to a warrant for arrest; and

(b)   a warrant for committal, a warrant to imprison (or to apprehend and imprison) and a warrant to arrest a witness issued by a judicial authority in Scotland as it applies to a warrant for arrest.

(8)   In this section 'judicial authority' means any justice of the peace or the judge of any court exercising jurisdiction in criminal proceedings; and any reference to a part of the United Kingdom in which a warrant may be executed includes a reference to the adjacent sea and other waters within the seaward limits of the territorial sea.

137.   Cross-border powers of arrest etc.

(1)   If the conditions applicable to this subsection are satisfied, any constable of a police force in England and Wales who has reasonable grounds for suspecting that an offence has been committed or attempted in England or Wales and that the suspected person is in Scotland or in Northern Ireland may arrest without a warrant the suspected person wherever he is in Scotland or in Northern Ireland.

(2)   If the condition applicable to this subsection is satisfied, any constable of a police force in Scotland who has reasonable grounds for suspecting that an offence has been committed or attempted in Scotland and that the suspected person is in England or Wales or in Northern Ireland may, as respects the suspected person, wherever he is in England or Wales or in Northern Ireland, exercise the same powers of arrest or detention as it would be competent for him to exercise were the person in Scotland.

(3)   If the conditions applicable to this subsection are satisfied, any constable of a police force in Northern Ireland who has reasonable grounds for suspecting that an offence has been committed or attempted in Northern Ireland and that the suspected person is in England or Wales or in Scotland may arrest without a warrant the suspected person wherever he is in England or Wales or in Scotland.

(4)   The conditions applicable to subsection (1) above are—

(a)   that the suspected offence is an arrestable offence; or

(b)   that, in the case of any other offence, it appears to the constable that service of a summons is impracticable or inappropriate for any of the reasons specified in subsection (3) of section 138.

(5)   The condition applicable to subsection (2) above is that it appears to the constable that it would have been lawful for him to have exercised the powers had the suspected person been in Scotland.

(6)   The conditions applicable to subsection (3) above are—

(a)   that the suspected offence is an arrestable offence; or

(b)   that, in the case of any other offence, it appears to the constable that service of a summons is impracticable or inappropriate for any of the reasons specified in subsection (3) of section 138.

(7)   It shall be the duty of a constable who has arrested or, as the case may be detained, a person under this section—

(a)   if he arrested him in Scotland, to take the person arrested either to the nearest convenient designated police station in England or in Northern Ireland or to a designated police station in a police area in England and Wales or in Northern Ireland in which the offence is being investigated;

(b)   if he arrested him in England or Wales, to take the person arrested to the nearest convenient police station in Scotland or to a police station within a sheriffdom in which the offence is being investigated or to the nearest convenient designated police station in Northern Ireland or to a designated police station in Northern Ireland in which the offence is being investigated;

(c)   if he detained him in England or Wales, to take the person detained to either such police station in Scotland as is mentioned in paragraph (b) above, or to the nearest convenient designated police station in England or Wales;

(d)   if he arrested him in Northern Ireland, to take the person arrested either to the nearest convenient designated police station in England or Wales or to a designated police station in a police area in England and Wales in which the offence is being investigated or to the nearest convenient police station in Scotland or to a police station within a sheriffdom in which the offence is being investigated;

(e)   if he detained him in Northern Ireland, to take the person detained to either such police station in Scotland as is mentioned in paragraph (b) above, or to the nearest convenient designated police station in Northern Ireland;
and to do so as soon as reasonably practicable.

(8)   A constable—

(a)   arresting a person under subsection (1) or (3) above, may use reasonable force and shall have the powers of search conferred by section 139;

(b)   arresting a person under subsection (2) above shall have the same powers and duties, and the person arrested the same rights, as they would have had if the arrest had been in Scotland; and

(c)   detaining a person under subsection (2) above shall act in accordance with the provisions applied by subsection (2) (as modified by subsection (6)) of section 138.

(9)   In this section—

'arrestable offence' and 'designated police station' have the same meaning as in the Police and Criminal Evidence Act 1984 and, in relation to Northern Ireland, have the same meaning as in the Police and Criminal Evidence (Northern Ireland) Order 1989; and

'constable of a police force', in relation to Northern Ireland, means a member of the Royal Ulster Constabulary or the Royal Ulster Constabulary Reserve.

(10)   This section shall not prejudice any power of arrest conferred apart from this section.

138.   Powers of arrest etc.: supplementary provisions

(1)   The following provisions have effect to supplement section 137 ('the principal section').

(2)   Where a person is detained under subsection (2) of the principal section, subsections (2) to (7) of section 2 (detention and questioning at police station) and subsections (1) and (3) to (5) of section 3 (right to have someone informed when

arrested or detained) of the Criminal Justice (Scotland) Act 1980 and section 28 (prints, samples etc. in criminal investigations) of the Prisoners and Criminal Proceedings (Scotland) Act 1993 shall apply to detention under that subsection of the principal section as they apply to detention under subsection (1) of the said section 2, but with the modifications mentioned in subsection (6) below.

(3)   The reasons referred to in subsections (4)(b) and (6)(b) of the principal section are that—

(a)   the name of the suspected person is unknown to, and cannot readily be ascertained by, the constable;

(b)   the constable has reasonable grounds for doubting whether a name furnished by the suspected person as his name is his real name;

(c)   either—

(i)   the suspected person has failed to furnish a satisfactory address for service; or

(ii)   the constable has reasonable grounds for doubting whether an address furnished by the suspected person is a satisfactory address for service;

(d)   the constable has reasonable grounds for believing that arrest is necessary to prevent the suspected person—

(i)   causing physical injury to himself or any other person;

(ii)   suffering physical injury;

(iii)   causing loss of or damage to property;

(iv)   committing an offence against public decency; or

(v)   causing an unlawful obstruction of a highway or road; or

(e)   the constable has reasonable grounds for believing that arrest is necessary to protect a child or other vulnerable person from the suspected person.

(4)   For the purposes of subsection (3) above an address is a satisfactory address for service if it appears to the constable—

(a)   that the suspected person will be at it for a sufficiently long period for it to be possible to serve him with process; or

(b)   that some other person specified by the suspected person will accept service of process for the suspected person at it.

(5)   Nothing in subsection (3)(d) above authorises the arrest of a person under sub-paragraph (iv) of that paragraph except where members of the public going about their normal business cannot reasonably be expected to avoid the person to be arrested.

(6)   The following are the modifications of sections 2 and 3 of the Criminal Justice (Scotland) Act 1980 which are referred to in subsection (2) above—

(a)   in section 2—

(i)   in subsection (2), the reference to detention being terminated not more than six hours after it begins shall be construed as a reference to its being terminated not more than four hours after the person's arrival at the police station to which he is taken under subsection (7)(c) of the principal section; and

(ii)   in subsections (4) and (7), references to 'other premises' shall be disregarded; and

(b)   in section 3(1), references to 'other premises' shall be disregarded.

139.   Search powers available on arrests under sections 136 and 137

(1)   The following powers are available to a constable in relation to a person arrested under section 136(1), (2)(b) or (3)(a) or 137(1) or (3).

(2)   A constable to whom this section applies may search the person if the constable has reasonable grounds for believing that the person may present a danger to himself or others.

(3)   Subject to subsections (4) to (6) below, a constable to whom this section applies may—

(a)   search the person for anything—

(i)   which he might use to assist him to escape from lawful custody; or

(ii)   which might be evidence relating to an offence; and

(b)   enter and search any premises in which the person was when, or was immediately before, he was arrested for evidence relating to the offence for which he was arrested.

(4)   The power to search conferred by subsection (3) above is only a power to search to the extent that is reasonably required for the purpose of discovering any such thing or any such evidence.

(5)   The powers conferred by this section to search a person are not to be construed as authorising a constable to require a person to remove any of his clothing in public other than an outer coat, jacket, headgear, gloves or footwear but they do authorise a search of a person's mouth.

(6)   A constable may not search a person in the exercise of the power conferred by subsection (3)(a) above unless he has reasonable grounds for believing that the person to be searched may have concealed on him anything for which a search is permitted under that paragraph.

(7)   A constable may not search premises in the exercise of the power conferred by subsection (3)(b) above unless he has reasonable grounds for believing that there is evidence for which a search is permitted under that paragraph.

(8)   In so far as the power of search conferred by subsection (3)(b) above relates to premises consisting of two or more separate dwellings, it is limited to a power to search—

(a)   any dwelling in which the arrest took place or in which the person arrested was immediately before his arrest; and

(b)   any parts of the premises which the occupier of any such dwelling uses in common with the occupiers of any other dwellings comprised in the premises.

(9)   A constable searching a person in the exercise of the power conferred by subsection (2) above may seize and retain anything he finds, if he has reasonable grounds for believing that the person searched might use it to cause physical injury to himself or to any other person.

(10)   A constable searching a person in the exercise of the power conferred by subsection (3)(a) above may seize and retain anything he finds, other than an item subject to legal privilege, if he has reasonable grounds for believing—

(a)   that he might use it to assist him to escape from lawful custody; or

(b)   that it is evidence of an offence, or has been obtained in consequence of the commission of an offence.

(11)   Nothing in this section shall be taken to affect the power conferred by section 15(3), (4) and (5) of the Prevention of Terrorism (Temporary Provisions) Act 1989.

(12)   In this section—

'item subject to legal privilege' has the meaning given to it—

(a)   as respects anything in the possession of a person searched in England and Wales, by section 10 of the Police and Criminal Evidence Act 1984;

(b)   as respects anything in the possession of a person searched in Scotland, by section 40 of the Criminal Justice (Scotland) Act 1987;

(c)   as respects anything in the possession of a person searched in Northern Ireland, by Article 12 of the Police and Criminal Evidence (Northern Ireland) Order 1989;

'premises'' includes any place and, in particular, includes—

(a)   any vehicle, vessel, aircraft or hovercraft;

(b)   any offshore installation; and

(c)   any tent or movable structure; and

'offshore installation' has the meaning given to it by section 1 of the Mineral Workings (Offshore Installations) Act 1971.

140.   Reciprocal powers of arrest

(1)   Where a constable of a police force in England and Wales would, in relation to an offence, have power to arrest a person in England or Wales under section 24(6) or (7) or 25 of the Police and Criminal Evidence Act 1984 (arrestable offences and non-arrestable offences in certain circumstances) a constable of a police force in Scotland or in Northern Ireland shall have the like power of arrest in England and Wales.

(2)   Where a constable of a police force in Scotland or in Northern Ireland arrests a person in England or Wales by virtue of subsection (1) above—

(a)   the constable shall be subject to requirements to inform the arrested person that he is under arrest and of the grounds for it corresponding to the requirements imposed by section 28 of that Act;

(b)   the constable shall be subject to a requirement to take the arrested person to a police station corresponding to the requirement imposed by section 30 of that Act and so also as respects the other related requirements of that section; and

(c)   the constable shall have powers to search the arrested person corresponding to the powers conferred by section 32 of that Act.

(3)   Where a constable of a police force in Scotland would, in relation to an offence, have power to arrest a person in Scotland, a constable of a police force in England and Wales or in Northern Ireland shall have the like power of arrest in Scotland.

(4)   Where a constable of a police force in England or Wales or in Northern Ireland arrests a person in Scotland by virtue of subsection (3) above, the arrested person shall have the same rights and the constable the same powers and duties as they would have were the constable a constable of a police force in Scotland.

(5)   Where a constable of a police force in Northern Ireland would, in relation to an offence, have power to arrest a person in Northern Ireland under Article 26(6) or (7) or 27 of the Police and Criminal Evidence (Northern Ireland) Order 1989 (arrestable offences and non-arrestable offences in certain circumstances) a constable of a police force in England and Wales or Scotland shall have the like power of arrest in Northern Ireland.

(6)   Where a constable of a police force in England and Wales or in Scotland arrests a person in Northern Ireland by virtue of subsection (5) above—

(a)   the constable shall be subject to requirements to inform the arrested person that he is under arrest and of the grounds for it corresponding to the requirements imposed by Article 30 of that Order;

(b)   the constable shall be subject to a requirement to take the arrested person to a police station corresponding to the requirement imposed by Article 32 of that Order and so as respects the other related requirements of that Article; and

(c)   the constable shall have powers to search the arrested person corresponding to the powers conferred by Article 34 of that Order.

(7)   In this section 'constable of a police force', in relation to Northern Ireland, means a member of the Royal Ulster Constabulary or the Royal Ulster Constabulary Reserve.

141.   Aid of one police force by another

(1)   The chief officer of police of a police force in England and Wales may, on the application of the chief officer of a police force in Scotland or the chief constable of the Royal Ulster Constabulary in Northern Ireland, provide constables or other assistance for the purpose of enabling the Scottish force or the Royal Ulster Constabulary to meet any special demand on its resources.

(2)   The chief officer of a police force in Scotland may, on the application of the chief officer of police of a police force in England and Wales or the chief constable of the Royal Ulster Constabulary in Northern Ireland, provide constables or other assistance for the purpose of enabling the English or Welsh force or the Royal Ulster Constabulary to meet any special demand on its resources.

(3)   The chief constable of the Royal Ulster Constabulary in Northern Ireland may, on the application of the chief officer of police of a police force in England and Wales or the chief officer of a police force in Scotland, provide constables or other assistance for the purpose of enabling the English or Welsh force or the Scottish force to meet any special demand on its resources.

(4)   If it appears to the Secretary of State to be expedient in the interests of public safety or order that any police force should be reinforced or should receive other assistance for the purpose of enabling it to meet any special demand on its resources, and that satisfactory arrangements under subsection (1), (2) or (3) above cannot be made, or cannot be made in time, he may direct the chief officer of police of any police force in England and Wales, the chief officer of any police force in Scotland or the chief constable of the Royal Ulster Constabulary, as the case may be, to provide such constables or other assistance for that purpose as may be specified in the direction.

(5)   While a constable is provided under this section for the assistance of another police force he shall, notwithstanding any enactment,—

(a)   be under the direction and control of the chief officer of police of that other force (or, where that other force is a police force in Scotland or the Royal Ulster Constabulary in Northern Ireland, of its chief officer or the chief constable of the Royal Ulster Constabulary respectively); and

(b)   have in any place the like powers and privileges as a member of that other force therein as a constable.

(6)   The police authority maintaining a police force for which assistance is provided under this section shall pay to the police authority maintaining the force from which that assistance is provided such contribution as may be agreed upon between those authorities or, in default of any such agreement, as may be provided by any agreement subsisting at the time between all police authorities generally, or, in default of such general agreement, as may be determined by the Secretary of State.

(7)   Any expression used in the Police Act 1964, the Police (Scotland) Act 1967 or the Police Act (Northern Ireland) 1970 and this section in its application to England and Wales, Scotland and Northern Ireland respectively has the same meaning in this section as in that Act.

(8)   In this section 'constable of a police force', in relation to Northern Ireland, means a member of the Royal Ulster Constabulary or the Royal Ulster Constabulary Reserve.

PART XI   SEXUAL OFFENCES

Rape

142.   Rape of women and men

For section 1 of the Sexual Offences Act 1956 (rape of a woman) there shall be substituted the following section—

'**1.   Rape of woman or man**

(1)   It is an offence for a man to rape a woman or another man.

(2)   A man commits rape if—

(a)   he has sexual intercourse with a person (whether vaginal or anal) who at the time of the intercourse does not consent to it; and

(b)   at the time he knows that the person does not consent to the intercourse or is reckless as to whether that person consents to it.

(3)   A man also commits rape if he induces a married woman to have sexual intercourse with him by impersonating her husband.

(4)   Subsection (2) applies for the purpose of any enactment.'.

Male rape and buggery

143.   Male rape and buggery

(1)   Section 12 of the Sexual Offences Act 1956 (offence of buggery) shall be amended as follows.

(2)   In subsection (1), after the words 'another person' there shall be inserted the words 'otherwise than in the circumstances described in subsection (1A) below'.

(3)   After subsection (1), there shall be inserted the following subsections—

'(1A)   The circumstances referred to in subsection (1) are that the act of buggery takes place in private and both parties have attained the age of eighteen.

(1B)   An act of buggery by one man with another shall not be treated as taking place in private if it takes place—

(a)   when more than two persons take part or are present; or

(b)   in a lavatory to which the public have or are permitted to have access, whether on payment or otherwise.

(1C)   In any proceedings against a person for buggery with another person it shall be for the prosecutor to prove that the act of buggery took place otherwise than in private or that one of the parties to it had not attained the age of eighteen.'.

Revised penalties for certain sexual offences

144.   Revised penalties for buggery and indecency between men

(1)   The following paragraphs of the Second Schedule to the Sexual Offences Act 1956 (which prescribe the punishments for offences of buggery and of indecency between men) shall be amended as follows.

(2) In paragraph 3—

(a) in sub-paragraph (a) (buggery), for the entry in the third column there shall be substituted 'If with a person under the age of sixteen or with an animal, life; if the accused is of or over the age of twenty-one and the other person is under the age of eighteen, five years, but otherwise two years.'; and

(b) in sub-paragraph (a) (attempted buggery), for the entry in the third column there shall be substituted 'If with a person under the age of sixteen or with an animal, life; if the accused is of or over the age of twenty-one and the other person is under the age of eighteen, five years, but otherwise two years.'.

(3) In paragraph 16—

(a) in sub-paragraph (a) (indecency between men), for the entry in the third column there shall be substituted 'If by a man of or over the age of twenty-one with a man under the age of eighteen, five years; otherwise two years.'; and

(b) in sub-paragraph (b) (attempted procurement of commission by a man of an act of gross indecency with another man), for the entry in the third column there shall be substituted 'If the attempt is by a man of or over the age of twenty-one to procure a man under the age of eighteen to commit an act of gross indecency with another man, five years; otherwise two years.'.

Homosexuality

145. Age at which homosexual acts are lawful

(1) In section 1 of the Sexual Offences Act 1967 (amendment of law relating to homosexual acts in private), for 'twenty-one' in both places where it occurs there is substituted 'eighteen'.

(2) In section 80 of the Criminal Justice (Scotland) Act 1980 (homosexual offences), for 'twenty-one' in each place where it occurs there is substituted 'eighteen'.

(3) In Article 3 of the Homosexual Offences (Northern Ireland) Order 1982 (homosexual acts in private), for '21' in both places where it occurs there is substituted '18'.

146. Extension of Sexual Offences Act 1967 to the armed forces and merchant navy

(1) Section 1(5) of the Sexual Offences Act 1967 (homosexual acts in the armed forces) is repealed.

(2) In section 80 of the Criminal Justice (Scotland) Act 1980—

(a) subsection (5) (homosexual acts in the armed forces) shall cease to have effect;

(b) in subsection (7)—

(i) after paragraph (b) there shall be inserted the word 'or'; and

(ii) paragraph (d) (homosexual acts on merchant ships) and the word '; or' immediately preceding that paragraph shall cease to have effect; and

(c) subsection (8) (interpretation) shall cease to have effect.

(3) Section 2 of the Sexual Offences Act 1967 (homosexual acts on merchant ships) is repealed.

(4) Nothing contained in this section shall prevent a homosexual act (with or without other acts or circumstances) from constituting a ground for discharging a

member of Her Majesty's armed forces from the service or dismissing a member of the crew of a United Kingdom merchant ship from his ship or, in the case of a member of Her Majesty's armed forces, where the act occurs in conjunction with other acts or circumstances, from constituting an offence under the Army Act 1955, the Air Force Act 1955 or the Naval Discipline Act 1957.

Expressions used in this subsection and any enactment repealed by this section have the same meaning in this subsection as in that enactment.

147.   Homosexuality on merchant ships and in the armed forces: Northern Ireland

(1)   In the Homosexual Offences (Northern Ireland) Order 1982, the following are revoked—

(a)   in article 3(1) (homosexual acts in private), the words 'and Article 5 (merchant seamen)'; and

(b)   article 5 (homosexual acts on merchant ships).

(2)   Article 3(4) of the Homosexual Offences (Northern Ireland) Order 1982 (homosexual acts in the armed forces) is revoked.

(3)   Nothing in this section shall prevent a homosexual act (with or without other acts or circumstances) from constituting a ground for discharging a member of Her Majesty's armed forces from the service or dismissing a member of the crew of a United Kingdom merchant ship from his ship or, in the case of a member of Her Majesty's armed forces, where the act occurs in conjunction with other acts or circumstances, from constituting an offence under the Army Act 1955, the Air Force Act 1955 or the Naval Discipline Act 1957.

Expressions used in this subsection and any enactment repealed by this section have the same meaning in this subsection as in that enactment.

148.   Amendment of law relating to homosexual acts in Scotland

In section 80(6) of the Criminal Justice (Scotland) Act 1980 (which defines 'homosexual act' for the purpose of section 80), after 'gross indecency' there is inserted 'or shameless indecency'.

PART XII   MISCELLANEOUS AND GENERAL

The Parole Board

149.   Incorporation of the Parole Board

In section 32 of the Criminal Justice Act 1991 (which provides the constitution and basic functions of the Parole Board), for subsection (1), there shall be substituted the following subsection—

'(1)   The Parole Board shall be, by that name, a body corporate and as such shall be constituted in accordance with, and have the functions conferred by, this Part.'.

150.   Powers to recall prisoners released on licence

In section 50 of the Criminal Justice Act 1991 (power by order to transfer certain functions to the Parole Board) subsection (4) shall cease to have effect and, in subsection (1), for the words '(2) to (4)' there shall be substituted the words '(2) or (3)'.

Prisons: powers in relation to prisoners, visitors and others

151. Power to test prisoners for drugs
(1)   After section 16 of the Prison Act 1952 there shall be inserted the following section—
  '16A. Testing prisoners for drugs
    (1)   If an authorisation is in force for the prison, any prison officer may, at the prison, in accordance with prison rules, require any prisoner who is confined in the prison to provide a sample of urine for the purpose of ascertaining whether he has any drug in his body.
    (2)   If the authorisation so provides, the power conferred by subsection (1) above shall include power to require a prisoner to provide a sample of any other description specified in the authorisation, not being an intimate sample, whether instead of or in addition to a sample of urine.
    (3)   In this section—
      'authorisation' means an authorisation by the governor;
      'drug' means any drug which is a controlled drug for the purposes of the Misuse of Drugs Act 1971;
      'intimate sample' has the same meaning as in Part V of the Police and Criminal Evidence Act 1984;
      'prison officer' includes a prisoner custody officer within the meaning of Part IV of the Criminal Justice Act 1991; and
      'prison rules' means rules under section 47 of this Act.'.
(2)   After section 41A of the Prisons (Scotland) Act 1989 there shall be inserted the following section—
  '41B. Testing prisoners for drugs
    (1)   If an authorisation is in force for the prison, any officer of the prison may, at the prison, in accordance with rules under section 39 of this Act, require any prisoner who is confined in the prison to provide a sample of urine for the purpose of ascertaining whether he has any drug in his body.
    (2)   If the authorisation so provides, the power conferred by subsection (1) above shall include power to require a prisoner to provide a sample of any other description specified in the authorisation, not being an intimate sample, whether instead of or in addition to a sample of urine.
    (3)   In this section—
      'authorisation' means an authorisation by the governor;
      'drug' means any drug which is a controlled drug for the purposes of the Misuse of Drugs Act 1971; and
      'intimate sample' means a sample of blood, semen or any other tissue fluid, saliva or pubic hair, or a swab taken from a person's body orifice.'.

152. Powers of search by authorised employees in prisons
(1)   In the Prison Act 1952, after section 8, there shall be inserted the following section—
  '8A. Powers of search by authorised employees
    (1)   An authorised employee at a prison shall have the power to search any prisoner for the purpose of ascertaining whether he has any unauthorised property on his person.
    (2)   An authorised employee searching a prisoner by virtue of this section—

(a)   shall not be entitled to require a prisoner to remove any of his clothing other than an outer coat, jacket, headgear, gloves and footwear;

(b)   may use reasonable force where necessary; and

(c)   may seize and detain any unauthorised property found on the prisoner in the course of the search.

(3)   In this section 'authorised employee' means an employee of a description for the time being authorised by the governor to exercise the powers conferred by this section.

(4)   The governor of a prison shall take such steps as he considers appropriate to notify to prisoners the descriptions of persons who are for the time being authorised to exercise the powers conferred by this section.

(5)   In this section 'unauthorised property', in relation to a prisoner, means property which the prisoner is not authorised by prison rules or by the governor to have in his possession or, as the case may be, in his possession in a particular part of the prison.'.

(2)   In the Prisons (Scotland) Act 1989, after section 41, there shall be inserted the following section—

'**41A.   Powers of search by authorised employees**

(1)   An authorised employee at a prison shall have the power to search any prisoner for the purpose of ascertaining whether he has any unauthorised property on his person.

(2)   An authorised employee searching a prisoner by virtue of this section—

(a)   shall not be entitled to require a prisoner to remove any of his clothing other than an outer coat, jacket, headgear, gloves and footwear;

(b)   may use reasonable force where necessary; and

(c)   may seize and detain any unauthorised property found on the prisoner in the course of the search.

(3)   In this section "authorised employee" means an employee of a description for the time being authorised by the governor to exercise the powers conferred by this section.

(4)   The governor of a prison shall take such steps as he considers appropriate to notify to prisoners the descriptions of employees who are for the time being authorised employees.

(5)   In this section—

"employee" means an employee (not being an officer of a prison) appointed under section 2(1) of this Act; and

"unauthorised property", in relation to a prisoner, means property which the prisoner is not authorised by rules under section 39 of this Act or by the governor to have in his possession or, as the case may be, in his possession in a particular part of the prison.'.

153.   Prohibited articles in Scottish prisons

(1)   Section 41 of the Prisons (Scotland) Act 1989 (unlawful introduction of tobacco, etc. into prison) shall be amended as follows.

(2)   In subsection (1), for the words from the beginning to 'shall be guilty' there shall be substituted—

'(1)   Any person who without reasonable excuse brings or introduces, or attempts by any means to bring or introduce, into a prison—

  (a)   any drug;
  (b)   any firearm or ammunition;
  (c)   any offensive weapon;
  (d)   any article to which section 1 of the Carrying of Knives etc.
(Scotland) Act 1993 applies; or
  (e)   without prejudice to paragraphs (a) to (d) above, any article which is
a prohibited article within the meaning of rules under section 39 of this Act,
shall be guilty'.
  (3)   After subsection (2) there shall be inserted the following subsections—
    '(2A)   Where an officer of a prison has reasonable grounds for suspecting
that a person who is in or is seeking to enter a prison has in his possession any
article mentioned in paragraphs (a) to (e) of subsection (1) above he shall,
without prejudice to any other power of search under this Act, have power to
search that person and any article in his possession and to seize and detain any
article mentioned in those paragraphs found in the course of the search.
    (2B) The power conferred by subsection (2A) above—
    (a)   shall be exercised in accordance with rules under section 39 of this Act;
    (b)   shall not be construed as authorising the physical examination of a
person's body orifices;
    (c)   so far as relating to any article mentioned in paragraph (c), (d) or (e)
of subsection (1) above (and not falling within paragraph (a) or (b) of that
subsection), shall not be construed as authorising an officer of a prison to require
a person to remove any of his clothing other than an outer coat, jacket, headgear,
gloves and footwear; and
    (d)   shall include power to use reasonable force where necessary.'.
  (4)   For subsection (3) there shall be substituted the following subsections—
    '(3)   Where an officer of a prison has reasonable grounds for suspecting that
any person has committed or is committing an offence under subsection (1)
above he may, for the purpose of facilitating investigation by a constable into
the offence, detain that person in any place in the prison in question and may,
where necessary, use reasonable force in doing so.
    (4)   Detention under subsection (3) above shall be terminated not more than
six hours after it begins or (if earlier)—
    (a)   when the person is detained in pursuance of any other enactment or
subordinate instrument;
    (b)   when the person is arrested by a constable; or
    (c)   where the governor of the prison or a constable investigating the
offence concludes that there are no such grounds as are mentioned in subsection
(3) above or the officer of the prison concludes that there are no longer such
grounds,
and the person detained shall be informed immediately upon the termination of
his detention that his detention has been terminated.
    (5)   Where a person has been released at the termination of a period of
detention under subsection (3) above he shall not thereafter be detained under
that subsection on the same grounds or on any grounds arising out of the same
circumstances.
    (6)   At the time when an officer of a prison detains a person under subsection
(3) above he shall inform the person of his suspicion, of the suspected offence

and of the reason for the detention; and there shall be recorded—

(a) the place where and the time when the detention begins;

(b) the suspected offence;

(c) the time when a constable or an officer of the police authority is informed of the suspected offence and the detention;

(d) the time when the person is informed of his rights in terms of subsection (7) below and the identity of the officer of the prison so informing him;

(e) where the person requests such intimation as is specified in subsection (7) below to be sent, the time when such request is—

(i) made; and

(ii) complied with; and

(f) the time when, in accordance with subsection (4) above, the person's detention terminates.

(7) A person who is being detained under subsection (3) above, other than a person in respect of whose detention subsection (8) below applies, shall be entitled to have intimation of his detention and of the place where he is being detained sent without delay to a solicitor and to one other person reasonably named by him and shall be informed of that entitlement when his detention begins.

(8) Where a person who is being detained under subsection (3) above appears to the officer of the prison to be under 16 years of age, the officer of the prison shall send without delay to the person's parent, if known, intimation of the person's detention and of the place where he is being detained; and the parent—

(a) in a case where there is reasonable cause to suspect that he has been involved in the alleged offence in respect of which the person has been detained, may; and

(b) in any other case, shall,

be permitted access to the person.

(9) The nature and extent of any access permitted under subsection (8) above shall be subject to any restriction essential for the furtherance of the investigation or the well-being of the person.

(10)

In this section—

"drug" means any drug which is a controlled drug for the purposes of the Misuse of Drugs Act 1971;

"firearm" and "ammunition" have the same meanings as in the Firearms Act 1968;

"offensive weapon" has the same meaning as in the Prevention of Crime Act 1953; and

"parent" includes a guardian and any person who has actual custody of a person under 16 years of age.'.

Harassment, alarm or distress

154. Offences of causing intentional harassment, alarm or distress

In Part I of the Public Order Act 1986 (offences relating to public order), after section 4, there shall be inserted the following section—

'4A. Intentional harassment, alarm or distress

(1) A person is guilty of an offence if, with intent to cause a person harassment, alarm or distress, he—

(a) uses threatening, abusive or insulting words or behaviour, or disorderly behaviour, or

(b) displays any writing, sign or other visible representation which is threatening, abusive or insulting,

thereby causing that or another person harassment, alarm or distress.

(2) An offence under this section may be committed in a public or a private place, except that no offence is committed where the words or behaviour are used, or the writing, sign or other visible representation is displayed, by a person inside a dwelling and the person who is harassed, alarmed or distressed is also inside that or another dwelling.

(3) It is a defence for the accused to prove—

(a) that he was inside a dwelling and had no reason to believe that the words or behaviour used, or the writing, sign or other visible representation displayed, would be heard or seen by a person outside that or any other dwelling, or

(b) that his conduct was reasonable.

(4) A constable may arrest without warrant anyone he reasonably suspects is committing an offence under this section.

(5) A person guilty of an offence under this section is liable on summary conviction to imprisonment for a term not exceeding 6 months or a fine not exceeding level 5 on the standard scale or both.'.

Offence of racially inflammatory publication etc. to be arrestable

155. Offence of racially inflammatory publication etc. to be arrestable

In section 24(2) of the Police and Criminal Evidence Act 1984 (arrestable offences), after the paragraph (h) inserted by section 166(4) of this Act, there shall be inserted the following paragraph—

'(i) an offence under section 19 of the Public Order Act 1986 (publishing, etc. material intended or likely to stir up racial hatred);'.

Prohibition on use of cells from embryos or foetuses

156. Prohibition on use of cells from embryos or foetuses

(1) The Human Fertilisation and Embryology Act 1990 shall be amended as follows.

(2) After section 3 there shall be inserted the following section—

'3A. Prohibition in connection with germ cells

(1) No person shall, for the purpose of providing fertility services for any woman, use female germ cells taken or derived from an embryo or a foetus or use embryos created by using such cells.

(2) In this section—

"female germ cells" means cells of the female germ line and includes such cells at any stage of maturity and accordingly includes eggs; and

"fertility services" means medical, surgical or obstetric services provided for the purpose of assisting women to carry children.'.

(3) In section 41(1)(a) (offences under the Act) after the words 'section 3(2)' there shall be inserted ', 3A'.

Increase in certain penalties

157. Increase in penalties for certain offences

(1) The enactments specified in column 2 of Part I of Schedule 8 to this Act which relate to the maximum fines for the offences mentioned (and broadly described) in column 1 of that Part of that Schedule shall have effect as if the maximum fine that may be imposed on summary conviction of any offence so mentioned were a fine not exceeding the amount specified in column 4 of that Part of that Schedule instead of a fine of an amount specified in column 3 of that Part of that Schedule.

(2) For the amount of the maximum fine specified in column 3 of Part II of Schedule 8 to this Act that may be imposed under the enactments specified in column 2 of that Part of that Schedule on summary conviction of the offences mentioned (and broadly described) in column 1 of that Part of that Schedule there shall be substituted the amount specified in column 4 of that Part of that Schedule.

(3) For the maximum term of imprisonment specified in column 3 of Part III of Schedule 8 to this Act that may be imposed under the enactments specified in column 2 of that Part of that Schedule on conviction on indictment, or on conviction on indictment or summary conviction, of the offences mentioned (and broadly described) in column 1 of that Part of that Schedule there shall be substituted the maximum term of imprisonment specified in column 4 of that Part of that Schedule.

(4) Any reference in column 2 of Part II of Schedule 8 to this Act to a numbered column of Schedule 4 to the Misuse of Drugs Act 1971 is a reference to the column of that number construed with section 2 5(2)(b) of that Act.

(5) Any reference in column 2 of Part III of Schedule 8 to this Act—

(a) to a numbered column of Schedule 6 to the Firearms Act 1968 is a reference to the column of that number construed with section 51(2)(b) of that Act; or

(b) to a numbered column of Schedule 2 to the Firearms (Northern Ireland) Order 1981 is a reference to the column of that number construed with Article 52(2)(b) of that Order.

(6) Section 143 of the Magistrates' Courts Act 1980 (power of Secretary of State by order to alter sums specified in certain provisions) shall have effect with the insertion, in subsection (2), after paragraph (p), of the following paragraph—

'(q)   column 5 or 6 of Schedule 4 to the Misuse of Drugs Act 1971 so far as the column in question relates to the offences under provisions of that Act specified in column 1 of that Schedule in respect of which the maximum fines were increased by Part II of Schedule 8 to the Criminal Justice and Public Order Act 1994.'.

(7) Section 289D of the Criminal Procedure (Scotland) Act 1975 (power of Secretary of State by order to alter sums specified in certain provisions of Scots law) shall have effect with the insertion, in subsection (1A), after paragraph (e), of the following paragraph—

'(ee)   column 5 or 6 of Schedule 4 to the Misuse of Drugs Act 1971 so far as the column in question relates to the offences under provisions of that Act specified in column 1 of that Schedule in respect of which the maximum fines were increased by Part II of Schedule 8 to the Criminal Justice and Public Order Act 1994.'.

(8) Article 17 of the Fines and Penalties (Northern Ireland) Order 1984 (power of Secretary of State by order to alter sums specified in certain provisions of the law

of Northern Ireland) shall have effect with the insertion, in paragraph (2), after sub-paragraph (j) of the following sub-paragraph—

    '(k)   column 5 or 6 of Schedule 4 to the Misuse of Drugs Act 1971 so far as the column in question relates to the offences under provisions of that Act specified in column 1 of that Schedule in respect of which the maximum fines were increased by Part II of Schedule 8 to the Criminal Justice and Public Order Act 1994.'.

  (9)   Subsections (1), (2) and (3) above do not apply to an offence committed before this section comes into force.

Extradition procedures

158. Extradition procedures

  (1)   The Extradition Act 1989 shall be amended as follows.

  (2)   In section 4 (extradition Orders), in subsection (5), for the words 'warrant his trial if' there shall be substituted the words 'make a case requiring an answer by that person if the proceedings were a summary trial of an information against him and'.

  (3)   In section 7 (extradition request and authority to proceed)—

    (a)   in subsection (2), in paragraph (b), after the word 'evidence' there shall be inserted the words 'or, in a case falling within subsection (2A) below, information'; and

    (b)   after subsection (2), there shall be inserted the following subsection—

    '(2A)   Where—

        (a)   the extradition request is made by a foreign state; and

        (b)   an Order in Council falling within section 4(5) above is in force in relation to that state,

it shall be a sufficient compliance with subsection (2)(b) above to furnish information sufficient to justify the issue of a warrant for his arrest under this Act.'.

  (4)   In section 8 (arrest for purposes of committal)—

    (a)   in subsection (3) after the word 'evidence' there shall be inserted the words 'or, in a case falling within subsection (3A) below, information'; and

    (b)   after subsection (3) there shall be inserted the following subsection—

    '(3A)   Where—

        (a)   the extradition request or, where a provisional warrant is applied for, the request for the person's arrest is made by a foreign state; and

        (b)   an Order in Council falling within section 4(5) above is in force in relation to that state,

it shall be sufficient for the purposes of subsection (3) above to supply such information as would, in the opinion of the person so empowered, justify the issue of a warrant of arrest.'.

  (5)   In section 9 (committal proceedings)—

    (a)   in subsection (2), for the words from 'jurisdiction' to the end there shall be substituted the words 'powers, as nearly as may be, including powers to adjourn the case and meanwhile to remand the person arrested under the warrant either in custody or on bail, as if the proceedings were the summary trial of an information against him; and section 16(1)(c) of the Prosecution of Offences Act 1985 (costs on dismissal) shall apply accordingly reading the reference to the dismissal of the information as a reference to the discharge of the person arrested.';

(b)   after subsection (2) there shall be inserted the following subsection—

'(2A)   If a court of committal in England and Wales exercises its power to adjourn the case it shall on so doing remand the person arrested in custody or on bail.';

(c)   in subsection (4), for the words from 'warrant the trial' to the end there shall be substituted the words 'make a case requiring an answer by the arrested person if the proceedings were the summary trial of an information against him.'; and

(d)   in subsection (8)(a), for the words from 'warrant his trial' to the end, there shall be substituted the words 'make a case requiring an answer by that person if the proceedings were the summary trial of an information against him.'.

(6)   In section 22 (International Convention cases), in subsection (5), for the words from 'warrant his trial' to the end, there shall be substituted the words 'make a case requiring an answer by that person if the proceedings were the summary trial of an information against him'.

(7)   In section 35 (interpretation), after subsection (2), there shall be inserted the following subsection—

'(3)   For the purposes of the application of this Act by virtue of any Order in Council in force under it or section 2 of the Extradition Act 1870, any reference in this Act to evidence making a case requiring an answer by an accused person shall be taken to indicate a determination of the same question as is indicated by a reference (however expressed) in any such Order (or arrangements embodied or recited in it) to evidence warranting or justifying the committal for trial of an accused person.'.

(8)   In Schedule 1 (provisions applying to foreign states in respect of which an Order in Council under section 2 of the Extradition Act 1870 is in force)—

(a)   in paragraph 6(1) (hearing of case), for the words from 'hear the case' to the end there shall be substituted the words 'have the same powers, as near as may be, including power to adjourn the case and meanwhile to remand the prisoner either in custody or on bail, as if the proceedings were the summary trial of an information against him for an offence committed in England and Wales; and section 16(1)(c) of the Prosecution of Offences Act 1985 (costs on dismissal) shall apply accordingly reading the reference to the dismissal of the information as a reference to the discharge of the prisoner.';

(b)   after paragraph 6(1) there shall be inserted the following sub-paragraph—

'(1A)   If the metropolitan magistrate exercises his power to adjourn the case he shall on so doing remand the prisoner either in custody or on bail.'; and

(c)   in paragraph 7(1) (committal or discharge of prisoner), for the words from 'justify the committal' to 'England or Wales' there shall be substituted the words 'make a case requiring an answer by the prisoner if the proceedings were for the trial in England and Wales of an information for the crime,'.

159.   Backing of warrants: Republic of Ireland

(1)   The Backing of Warrants (Republic of Ireland) Act 1965 shall be amended as follows.

(2)   In section 1 (conditions for endorsement of warrants issued in Republic of Ireland), in subsection (1)(b), after the word 'acts' there shall be inserted the words 'or on his way to the United Kingdom'.

(3)   In section 2 (proceedings for delivery of person arrested under endorsed

warrant), in subsection (2)(a) (excluded offences) the words from ', or an offence under an enactment' to 'control' shall be omitted.

(4) In section 4 (procedure for provisional warrants)—

(a) in subsection (1)(c), after the word 'acts' there shall be inserted the words 'or on his way to the United Kingdom';

(b) in subsection (2), for the words 'five days' there shall be substituted the words 'seven days'; and

(c) in subsection (3)(b), for the words 'three days' there shall be substituted the words 'seven days'.

(5) In the Schedule (proceedings before magistrates' court), in paragraph 3, for the words from 'and the proceedings' to the end, there shall be substituted the words 'as if the proceedings were the summary trial of an information against that person.'.

Constabulary powers in United Kingdom waters

160. Extension of powers, etc., of constables to United Kingdom waters

(1) Section 19 of the Police Act 1964 (area within which a constable's powers and privileges are exercisable) shall be amended as follows—

(a) in subsection (1), after the words 'England and Wales' there shall be inserted the words 'and the adjacent United Kingdom waters.';

(b) in subsection (2), after the words 'area for which he is appointed' there shall be inserted the words 'and, where the boundary of that area includes the coast, in the adjacent United Kingdom waters'; and

(c) after subsection (5), there shall be inserted the following subsection—

'(5A) In this section—

"powers" includes powers under any enactment, whenever passed or made;

"United Kingdom waters" means the sea and other waters within the seaward limits of the territorial sea;

and this section, so far as it relates to powers under any enactment, makes them exercisable throughout those waters whether or not the enactment applies to those waters apart from this provision.'.

(2) Section 17 of the Police (Scotland) Act 1967 (general functions and jurisdiction of constables) shall be amended as follows—

(a) in subsection (4), after the word 'Scotland' there shall be inserted the words 'and (without prejudice to section 1(2) of this Act) the adjacent United Kingdom waters'; and

(b) after subsection (7) there shall be inserted the following subsection—

'(7A) In this section—

"powers" includes powers under any enactment, whenever passed or made;

"United Kingdom waters" means the sea and other waters within the seaward limits of the territorial sea;

and this section, so far as it relates to powers under any enactment, makes them exercisable throughout those waters whether or not the enactment applies to those waters apart from this provision.'.

Obtaining computer-held information

161. Procuring disclosure of, and selling, computer-held personal information

(1) In section 5 of the Data Protection Act 1984 (prohibitions in relation to personal data, including disclosure), after subsection (5), there shall be inserted the

following subsections—

'(6) A person who procures the disclosure to him of personal data the disclosure of which to him is in contravention of subsection (2) or (3) above, knowing or having reason to believe that the disclosure constitutes such a contravention, shall be guilty of an offence.

(7) A person who sells personal data shall be guilty of an offence if (in contravention of subsection (6) above) he has procured the disclosure of the data to him.

(8) A person who offers to sell personal data shall be guilty of an offence if (in contravention of subsection (6) above) he has procured or subsequently procures the disclosure of the data to him.

(9) For the purposes of subsection (8) above, an advertisement indicating that personal data are or may be for sale is an offer to sell the data.

(10) For the purposes of subsections (7) and (8) above, ''selling'', or ''offering to sell'', in relation to personal data, includes selling, or offering to sell, information extracted from the data.

(11) In determining, for the purposes of subsection (6), (7) or (8) above, whether a disclosure is in contravention of subsection (2) or (3) above, section 34(6)(d) below shall be disregarded.'.

(2) In consequence of the amendment made by subsection (1) above—

(a) in subsection (5) of that section, after the word 'other' there shall be inserted the word 'foregoing'; and

(b) in section 28 (exemptions: crime and taxation), in subsection (3)—

(i) after the words 'section 26(3)(a) above' there shall be inserted the words 'or for an offence under section 5(6) above'; and

(ii) after the words 'to make' there shall be inserted the words 'or (in the case of section 5(6)) to procure'.

162. Access to computer material by constables and other enforcement officers

(1) In section 10 of the Computer Misuse Act 1990 (offence of unauthorised access not to apply to exercise of law enforcement powers), after paragraph (b), there shall be inserted the following words—

'and nothing designed to indicate a withholding of consent to access to any program or data from persons as enforcement officers shall have effect to make access unauthorised for the purposes of the said section 1(1).

In this section ''enforcement officer'' means a constable or other person charged with the duty of investigating offences; and withholding consent from a person ''as'' an enforcement officer of any description includes the operation, by the person entitled to control access, of rules whereby enforcement officers of that description are, as such, disqualified from membership of a class of persons who are authorised to have access.'.

(2) In section 17(5) of that Act (when access is unauthorised), after paragraph (b), there shall be inserted the following words—

'but this subsection is subject to section 10.'.

Closed-circuit television by local authorities

163. Local authority powers to provide closed-circuit television

(1) Without prejudice to any power which they may exercise for those purposes

under any other enactment, a local authority may take such of the following steps as they consider will, in relation to their area, promote the prevention of crime or the welfare of the victims of crime—

(a) providing apparatus for recording visual images of events occurring on any land in their area;

(b) providing within their area a telecommunications system which, under Part II of the Telecommunications Act 1984, may be run without a licence;

(c) arranging for the provision of any other description of telecommunications system within their area or between any land in their area and any building occupied by a public authority.

(2) Any power to provide, or to arrange for the provision of, any apparatus includes power to maintain, or operate, or, as the case may be, to arrange for the maintenance or operation of, that apparatus.

(3) Before taking such a step under this section, a local authority shall consult the chief officer of police for the police area in which the step is to be taken.

(4) In this section—

'chief officer of police', in relation to a police area in Scotland, means the chief constable of a police force maintained for that area;

'local authority'—

(a) in England, means a county council or district council;

(b) in Wales, means a county council or county borough council; and

(c) in Scotland, has the meaning given by section 235(1) of the Local Government (Scotland) Act 1973; and

'telecommunications system' has the meaning given in section 4 of the Telecommunications Act 1984 and 'licence' means a licence under section 7 of that Act.

(5) Until 1st April 1996, in this section 'local authority' means, in Wales, a county council or district council.

Serious fraud

164. Extension of powers of Serious Fraud Office and of powers to investigate serious fraud in Scotland

(1) Section 4 of the Criminal Justice (International Co-operation) Act 1990 (obtaining evidence in the United Kingdom for use overseas) shall be amended as follows—

(a) after subsection (2), there shall be inserted the following subsections—

'(2A) Except where the evidence is to be obtained as is mentioned in subsection (2B) below, if the Secretary of State is satisfied—

(a) that an offence under the law of the country or territory in question has been committed or that there are reasonable grounds for suspecting that such an offence has been committed; and

(b) that proceedings in respect of that offence have been instituted in that country or territory or that an investigation into that offence is being carried on there,

and it appears to him that the request relates to an offence involving serious or complex fraud, he may, if he thinks fit, refer the request or any part of the request to the Director of the Serious Fraud Office for him to obtain such of the evidence to which the request or part referred relates as may appear to the Director to be appropriate for giving effect to the request or part referred.

(2B)   Where the evidence is to be obtained in Scotland, if the Lord Advocate is satisfied as to the matters mentioned in paragraphs (a) and (b) of subsection (2A) above and it appears to him that the request relates to an offence involving serious or complex fraud, he may, if he thinks fit, give a direction under section 51 of the Criminal Justice (Scotland) Act 1987.';

(b)   in subsection (3), after the words 'subsection (2)' there shall be inserted the words '(2A) or (2B)'; and

(c)   in subsection (4), after the words 'subsection (2)(a) and (b)' there shall be inserted the words 'or (2A)(a) and (b)'.

(2)   Section 2 of the Criminal Justice Act 1987 (investigative powers of Director of Serious Fraud Office) shall be amended as follows—

(a)   in subsection (1), for the words from 'the Attorney-General' to 'the request' there shall be substituted 'an authority entitled to make such a request';

(b)   after subsection (1), there shall be inserted the following subsections—

'(1A)   The authorities entitled to request the Director to exercise his powers under this section are—

(a)   the Attorney-General of the Isle of Man, Jersey or Guernsey, acting under legislation corresponding to section 1 of this Act and having effect in the Island whose Attorney-General makes the request; and

(b)   the Secretary of State acting under section 4(2A) of the Criminal Justice (International Cooperation) Act 1990, in response to a request received by him from an overseas court, tribunal or authority (an ''overseas authority'').

(1B)   The Director shall not exercise his powers on a request from the Secretary of State acting in response to a request received from an overseas authority within subsection (1A)(b) above unless it appears to the Director on reasonable grounds that the offence in respect of which he has been requested to obtain evidence involves serious or complex fraud.';

(c)   after subsection (8), there shall be inserted the following subsections—

'(8A)   Any evidence obtained by the Director for use by an overseas authority shall be furnished by him to the Secretary of State for transmission to the overseas authority which requested it.

(8B)   If in order to comply with the request of the overseas authority it is necessary for any evidence obtained by the Director to be accompanied by any certificate, affidavit or other verifying document, the Director shall also furnish for transmission such document of that nature as may be specified by the Secretary of State when asking the Director to obtain the evidence.

(8C)   Where any evidence obtained by the Director for use by an overseas authority consists of a document the original or a copy shall be transmitted, and where it consists of any other article the article itself or a description, photograph or other representation of it shall be transmitted, as may be necessary in order to comply with the request of the overseas authority.'; and

(d)   in subsection (18), at the end, there shall be inserted the words '; and ''evidence'' (in relation to subsections (1A)(b), (8A), (8B) and (8C) above) includes documents and other articles.'.

(3)   In section 51(1) of the Criminal Justice (Scotland) Act 1987 (investigative powers of Lord Advocate as respects serious or complex fraud), at the end there shall

be added '; and he may also give such a direction by virtue of section 4(2B) of the Criminal Justice (International Cooperation) Act 1990 or on a request being made to him by the Attorney-General of the Isle of Man, Jersey or Guernsey acting under legislation corresponding to this section and sections 52 to 54 of this Act.'.

(4) In section 52 of the Criminal Justice (Scotland) Act 1987 (investigation by nominated officer)—

(a) after subsection (7) there shall be inserted—

'(7A) Any evidence obtained by the Lord Advocate by virtue of section 4(2B) of the Criminal Justice (International Cooperation) Act 1990 shall be furnished by him to the Secretary of State for transmission to the overseas authority in compliance with whose request (in the following subsections referred to as the "relevant request") it was so obtained.

(7B) If, in order to comply with the relevant request it is necessary for that evidence to be accompanied by any certificate, affidavit or other verifying document, the Lord Advocate shall also furnish for transmission such document of that nature as appears to him to be appropriate.

(7C) Where any evidence obtained by virtue of the said section 4(2B) consists of a document, the original or a copy shall be transmitted and where it consists of any other article the article itself or a description, photograph or other representation of it shall be transmitted, as may be necessary in order to comply with the relevant request.'; and

(b) in subsection (8), after the definition of 'documents' there shall be inserted—

'"evidence", in relation to a relevant request, includes documents and other articles;'.

Copyright and illicit recordings: enforcement of offences

165. Enforcement of certain offences relating to copyright and illicit recordings

(1) The Copyright, Designs and Patents Act 1988 shall be amended as follows.

(2) After section 107 (offences relating to copyright) there shall be inserted the following section—

'107A. Enforcement by local weights and measures authority

(1) It is the duty of every local weights and measures authority to enforce within their area the provisions of section 107.

(2) The following provisions of the Trade Descriptions Act 1968 apply in relation to the enforcement of that section by such an authority as in relation to the enforcement of that Act—

section 27 (power to make test purchases),

section 28 (power to enter premises and inspect and seize goods and documents),

section 29 (obstruction of authorised officers), and

section 33 (compensation for loss, &c. of goods seized).

(3) Subsection (1) above does not apply in relation to the enforcement of section 107 in Northern Ireland, but it is the duty of the Department of Economic Development to enforce that section in Northern Ireland.

For that purpose the provisions of the Trade Descriptions Act 1968 specified in subsection (2) apply as if for the references to a local weights and measures authority and any officer of such an authority there were substituted references to that Department and any of its officers.

(4)   Any enactment which authorises the disclosure of information for the purpose of facilitating the enforcement of the Trade Descriptions Act 1968 shall apply as if section 107 were contained in that Act and as if the functions of any person in relation to the enforcement of that section were functions under that Act.

(5)   Nothing in this section shall be construed as authorising a local weights and measures authority to bring proceedings in Scotland for an offence.'.

(3)   After section 198 (offences relating to illicit recordings) there shall be inserted the following section—

'**198A.   Enforcement by local weights and measures authority**

(1)   It is the duty of every local weights and measures authority to enforce within their area the provisions of section 198.

(2)   The following provisions of the Trade Descriptions Act 1968 apply in relation to the enforcement of that section by such an authority as in relation to the enforcement of that Act—

section 27 (power to make test purchases),

section 28 (power to enter premises and inspect and seize goods and documents),

section 29 (obstruction of authorised officers), and

section 33 (compensation for loss, &c. of goods seized).

(3)   Subsection (1) above does not apply in relation to the enforcement of section 198 in Northern Ireland, but it is the duty of the Department of Economic Development to enforce that section in Northern Ireland.

For that purpose the provisions of the Trade Descriptions Act 1968 specified in subsection (2) apply as if for the references to a local weights and measures authority and any officer of such an authority there were substituted references to that Department and any of its officers.

(4)   Any enactment which authorises the disclosure of information for the purpose of facilitating the enforcement of the Trade Descriptions Act 1968 shall apply as if section 198 were contained in that Act and as if the functions of any person in relation to the enforcement of that section were functions under that Act.

(5)   Nothing in this section shall be construed as authorising a local weights and measures authority to bring proceedings in Scotland for an offence.'.

Ticket touts

166.   Sale of tickets by unauthorised persons

(1)   It is an offence for an unauthorised person to sell, or offer or expose for sale, a ticket for a designated football match in any public place or place to which the public has access or, in the course of a trade or business, in any other place.

(2)   For this purpose—

(a)   a person is 'unauthorised' unless he is authorised in writing to sell tickets for the match by the home club or by the organisers of the match;

(b)   a 'ticket' means anything which purports to be a ticket; and

(c)   a 'designated football match' means a football match, or football match of a description, for the time being designated under section 1(1) of the Football (Offences) Act 1991.

(3)   A person guilty of an offence under this section is liable on summary conviction to a fine not exceeding level 5 on the standard scale.

(4)   In section 24(2) of the Police and Criminal Evidence Act 1984 (arrestable offences), after the paragraph (g) inserted by section 85(2) of this Act there shall be inserted the following paragraph—

'(h)   an offence under section 166 of the Criminal Justice and Public Order Act 1994 (sale of tickets by unauthorised persons);'.

(5)   Section 32 of the Police and Criminal Evidence Act 1984 (search of persons and premises (including vehicles) upon arrest) shall have effect, in its application in relation to an offence under this section, as if the power conferred on a constable to enter and search any vehicle extended to any vehicle which the constable has reasonable grounds for believing was being used for any purpose connected with the offence.

(6)   The Secretary of State may by order made by statutory instrument apply this section, with such modifications as he thinks fit, to such sporting event or category of sporting event for which 6,000 or more tickets are issued for sale as he thinks fit.

(7)   An order under subsection (6) above may provide that—

(a)   a certificate (a 'ticket sale certificate') signed by a duly authorised officer certifying that 6,000 or more tickets were issued for sale for a sporting event is conclusive evidence of that fact;

(b)   an officer is duly authorised if he is authorised in writing to sign a ticket sale certificate by the home club or the organisers of the sporting event; and

(c)   a document purporting to be a ticket sale certificate shall be received in evidence and deemed to be such a certificate unless the contrary is proved.

(8)   Where an order has been made under subsection (6) above, this section also applies, with any modifications made by the order, to any part of the sporting event specified or described in the order, provided that 6,000 or more tickets are issued for sale for the day on which that part of the event takes place.

Taxi touts

167.   Touting for hire car services

(1)   Subject to the following provisions, it is an offence, in a public place, to solicit persons to hire vehicles to carry them as passengers.

(2)   Subsection (1) above does not imply that the soliciting must refer to any particular vehicle nor is the mere display of a sign on a vehicle that the vehicle is for hire soliciting within that subsection.

(3)   No offence is committed under this section where soliciting persons to hire licensed taxis is permitted by a scheme under section 10 of the Transport Act 1985 (schemes for shared taxis) whether or not supplemented by provision made under section 13 of that Act (modifications of the taxi code).

(4)   It is a defence for the accused to show that he was soliciting for passengers for public service vehicles on behalf of the holder of a PSV operator's licence for those vehicles whose authority he had at the time of the alleged offence.

(5)   A person guilty of an offence under this section shall be liable on summary conviction to a fine not exceeding level 4 on the standard scale.

(6)   In this section—

'public place' includes any highway and any other premises or place to which at the material time the public have or are permitted to have access (whether on payment or otherwise); and 'public service vehicle' and 'PSV operator's licence' have the same meaning as in Part II of the Public Passenger Vehicles Act 1981.

(7)   In section 24(2) of the Police and Criminal Evidence Act 1984 (arrestable offences), after the paragraph (i) inserted by section 155 of this Act there shall be inserted the following paragraph—

'(j)   an offence under section 167 of the Criminal Justice and Public Order Act 1994 (touting for hire car services).'.

168.   Minor and consequential amendments and repeals

(1)   The enactments mentioned in Schedule 9 to this Act shall have effect with the amendments there specified (being minor amendments).

(2)   The enactments mentioned in Schedule 10 to this Act shall have effect with the amendments there specified (amendments consequential on the foregoing provisions of this Act).

(3)   The enactments mentioned in Schedule 11 to this Act (which include enactments which are spent) are repealed or revoked to the extent specified in the third column of that Schedule.

169.   Power of Secretary of State to make payments or grants in relation to crime prevention, etc.

(1)   The Secretary of State may, with the consent of the Treasury—

(a)   make such payments, or

(b)   pay such grants, to such persons,

as he considers appropriate in connection with measures intended to prevent crime or reduce the fear of crime.

(2)   Any grant under subsection (1)(b) above may be made subject to such conditions as the Secretary of State may, with the agreement of the Treasury, see fit to impose.

(3)   Payments under this section shall be made out of money provided by Parliament.

170.   Security costs at party conferences

(1)   The Secretary of State may, with the consent of the Treasury, pay grants towards expenditure incurred by a qualifying political party, or by a person acting for a qualifying political party, on measures to which this section applies.

(2)   This section applies to measures which are—

(a)   taken for the protection of persons or property in connection with a conference held in Great Britain for the purposes of the party, and

(b)   certified by a chief officer of police as having been appropriate.

(3)   A political party is a 'qualifying political party' for the purposes of this section if, at the last general election before the expenditure was incurred,—

(a)   at least two members of the party were elected to the House of Commons, or

(b)   one member of the party was elected to the House of Commons and not less than 150,000 votes were given to candidates who were members of the party.

(4)   Payments under this section shall be made out of money provided by Parliament.

171.   Expenses etc. under Act

There shall be paid out of money provided by Parliament—

(a)   any sums required by the Secretary of State for making payments
under contracts entered into under or by virtue of sections 2, 3, 7, 11, 96, 99, 100,
102(4), 106(1), 112(1) or 118(3) or paragraph 1 of Schedule 1;
    (b)   any administrative expenses incurred by the Secretary of State; and
    (c)   any increase attributable to this Act in the sums payable out of money so
provided under any other Act.

172.   Short title, commencement and extent

(1)   This Act may be cited as the Criminal Justice and Public Order Act 1994.

(2)   With the exception of section 82 and subject to subsection (4) below, this Act
shall come into force on such day as the Secretary of State or, in the case of sections
52 and 53, the Lord Chancellor may appoint by order made by statutory instrument,
and different days may be appointed for different provisions or different purposes.

(3)   Any order under subsection (2) above may make such transitional provisions
and savings as appear to the authority making the order necessary or expedient in
connection with any provision brought into force by the order.

(4)   The following provisions and their related amendments, repeals and
revocations shall come into force on the passing of this Act, namely sections 5 to 15
(and Schedules 1 and 2), 61, 63, 65, 68 to 71, 77 to 80, 81, 83, 90, Chapters I and IV
of Part VIII, sections 142 to 148, 150, 158(1), (3) and (4), 166, 167, 171, paragraph
46 of Schedule 9 and this section.

(5)   No order shall be made under subsection (6) of section 166 above unless a
draft of the order has been laid before, and approved by a resolution of, each House
of Parliament.

(6)   For the purposes of subsection (4) above—
    (a)   the following are the amendments related to the provisions specified in
that subsection, namely, in Schedule 10, paragraphs 26, 35, 36, 59, 60 and 63(1), (3),
(4) and (5);
    (b)   the repeals and revocations related to the provisions specified in that
subsection are those specified in the Note at the end of Schedule 11.

(7)   Except as regards any provisions applied under section 39 and subject to the
following provisions, this Act extends to England and Wales only.

(8)   Sections 47(3), 49, 61 to 67, 70, 71, 81, 82, 146(4), 157(1), 163, 169 and 170
also extend to Scotland.

(9)   Section 83(1) extends to England and Wales and Northern Ireland.

(10)   This section, sections 68, 69, 83(3) to (5), 88 to 92, 136 to 141, 156, 157(2),
(3), (4), (5) and (9), 158, 159, 161, 162, 164, 165, 168, 171 and Chapter IV of Part
VIII extend to the United Kingdom and sections 158 and 159 also extend to the
Channel Islands and the Isle of Man.

(11)   Sections 93, 95 and 101(8), so far as relating to the delivery of prisoners to
or from premises situated in a part of the British Islands outside England and Wales,
extend to that part of those Islands.

(12)   Sections 102(1) to (3), 104, 105 and 117, so far as relating to the transfer of
prisoners to or from premises situated in a part of the British Islands outside
Scotland, extend to that part of those Islands, but otherwise Chapter II of Part VIII
extends to Scotland only.

(13)   Sections 47(4), 83(2), 84(5) to (7), 87, Part IX, sections 145(2), 146(2), 148,
151(2), 152(2), 153, 157(7) and 160(2) extend to Scotland only.

(14)　Sections 118, 120, 121 and 125, so far as relating to the delivery of prisoners to or from premises situated in a part of the British Islands outside Northern Ireland, extend to that part of those islands, but otherwise Chapter III of Part VIII extends to Northern Ireland only.

(15)　Sections 53, 84(8) to (11), 85(4) to (6), 86(2), 145(3), 147 and 157(8) extend to Northern Ireland only.

(16)　Where any enactment is amended, repealed or revoked by Schedule 9, 10 or 11 to this Act the amendment, repeal or revocation has the same extent as that enactment; except that Schedules 9 and 11 do not extend to Scotland in so far as they relate to section 17(1) of the Video Recordings Act 1984.

SCHEDULES

Section 12　　SCHEDULE 1　ESCORT ARRANGEMENTS: ENGLAND AND WALES

Arrangements for the escort of offenders detained at secure training centres

1.—(1)　The Secretary of State may make arrangements for any of the following functions, namely—

(a)　the delivery of offenders from one set of relevant premises to another;

(b)　the custody of offenders held on the premises of any court (whether or not they would otherwise be in the custody of the court) and their production before the court;

(c)　the custody of offenders temporarily held in a secure training centre in the course of delivery from one secure training centre to another; and

(d)　the custody of offenders while they are outside a secure training centre for temporary purposes,

to be performed in such cases as may be determined by or under the arrangements by custody officers who are authorised to perform such functions.

(2)　In sub-paragraph (1)(a) above, 'relevant premises' means a court, secure training centre, police station or hospital.

(3)　Arrangements made by the Secretary of State under sub-paragraph (1) above ('escort arrangements') may include entering into contracts with other persons for the provision by them of custody officers.

(4)　Any person who, under a warrant or a hospital order or hospital remand is responsible for the performance of any such function as is mentioned in sub-paragraph (1) above shall be deemed to have complied with the warrant, order or remand if he does all that he reasonably can to secure that the function is performed by a custody officer acting in pursuance of escort arrangements.

(5)　In this paragraph—

'hospital' has the same meaning as in the Mental Health Act 1983;

'hospital order' means an order for a person's admission to hospital made under section 37, 38 or 44 of that Act, section 5 of the Criminal Procedure (Insanity) Act 1964 or section 6, 14 or 14A of the Criminal Appeal Act 1968;

'hospital remand' means a remand of a person to hospital under section 35 or 36 of the Mental Health Act 1983;

'warrant' means a warrant of commitment, a warrant of arrest or a warrant under section 46, 47, 48, 50 or 74 of that Act.

Monitoring etc. of escort arrangements

2.—(1)   Escort arrangements shall include the appointment of—

(a)   an escort monitor, that is to say, a Crown servant whose duty it shall be to keep the arrangements under review and to report on them to the Secretary of State; and

(b)   a panel of lay observers whose duty it shall be to inspect the conditions in which offenders are transported or held in pursuance of the arrangements and to make recommendations to the Secretary of State.

(2)   It shall also be the duty of an escort monitor to investigate and report to the Secretary of State on any allegations made against custody officers acting in pursuance of escort arrangements.

(3)   Any expenses incurred by members of lay panels may be defrayed by the Secretary of State to such extent as he may with the approval of the Treasury determine.

Powers and duties of custody officers acting in pursuance of escort arrangements

3.—(1)   A custody officer acting in pursuance of escort arrangements shall have the following powers, namely—

(a)   to search in accordance with rules made by the Secretary of State any offender for whose delivery or custody he is responsible in pursuance of the arrangements; and

(b)   to search any other person who is in or is seeking to enter any place where any such offender is or is to be held, and any article in the possession of such a person.

(2)   The powers conferred by sub-paragraph (1)(b) above to search a person shall not be construed as authorising a custody officer to require a person to remove any of his clothing other than an outer coat, headgear, jacket or gloves.

(3)   A custody officer shall have the following duties as respects offenders for whose delivery or custody he is responsible in pursuance of escort arrangements, namely—

(a)   to prevent their escape from lawful custody;

(b)   to prevent, or detect and report on, the commission or attempted commission by them of other unlawful acts;

(c)   to ensure good order and discipline on their part;

(d)   to attend to their wellbeing; and

(e)   to give effect to any directions as to their treatment which are given by a court,

and the Secretary of State may make rules with respect to the performance by custody officers of their duty under (d) above.

(4)   The powers conferred by sub-paragraph (1) above, and the powers arising by virtue of sub-paragraph (3) above, shall include power to use reasonable force where necessary.

(5)   The power to make rules under this paragraph shall be exercisable by statutory instrument which shall be subject to annulment in pursuance of a resolution of either House of Parliament.

Interpretation

4.   In this Schedule—

'escort arrangements' has the meaning given by paragraph 1 above; and 'offender' means an offender sentenced to secure training under section 1 of this Act.

'secure training centre' includes—

    (a)   a contracted out secure training centre;

    (b)   any other place to which an offender may have been committed or transferred under section 2 of this Act.

Section 12   SCHEDULE 2   CERTIFICATION OF CUSTODY OFFICERS: ENGLAND AND WALES

Preliminary

1.   In this Schedule—

    'certificate' means a certificate under section 12(3) of this Act;

    'the relevant functions', in relation to a certificate, means the escort functions or custodial duties authorised by the certificate.

Issue of certificates

2.—(1)   Any person may apply to the Secretary of State for the issue of a certificate in respect of him.

(2)   The Secretary of State shall not issue a certificate on any such application unless he is satisfied that the applicant—

    (a)   is a fit and proper person to perform the relevant functions; and

    (b)   has received training to such standard as he may consider appropriate for the performance of those functions.

(3)   Where the Secretary of State issues a certificate, then, subject to any suspension under paragraph 3 or revocation under paragraph 4 below, it shall continue in force until such date or the occurrence of such event as may be specified in the certificate.

(4)   A certificate authorising the performance of both escort functions and custodial duties may specify different dates or events as respects those functions and duties respectively.

Suspension of certificate

3.—(1)   This paragraph applies where at any time—

    (a)   in the case of a custody officer acting in pursuance of escort arrangements, it appears to the escort monitor that the officer is not a fit and proper person to perform escort functions;

    (b)   in the case of a custody officer performing custodial duties at a contracted out secure training centre, it appears to the person in charge of the secure training centre that the officer is not a fit and proper person to perform custodial duties; or

    (c)   in the case of a custody officer performing contracted out functions at a directly managed secure training centre, it appears to the person in charge of that secure training centre that the officer is not a fit and proper person to perform custodial duties.

(2)   The escort monitor or person in charge may—

    (a)   refer the matter to the Secretary of State for a decision under paragraph 4 below; and

(b)   in such circumstances as may be prescribed by regulations made by the Secretary of State, suspend the officer's certificate so far as it authorises the performance of escort functions or, as the case may be, custodial duties pending that decision.

(3)   The power to make regulations under this paragraph shall be exercisable by statutory instrument which shall be subject to annulment in pursuance of a resolution of either House of Parliament.

Revocation of certificate

4.   Where at any time it appears to the Secretary of State that a custody officer is not a fit and proper person to perform escort functions or custodial duties, he may revoke that officer's certificate so far as it authorises the performance of those functions or duties.

False statements

5.   If any person, for the purpose of obtaining a certificate for himself or for any other person—
(a)   makes a statement which he knows to be false in a material particular; or
(b)   recklessly makes a statement which is false in a material particular,
he shall be liable on summary conviction to a fine not exceeding level 4 on the standard scale.

Section 27   SCHEDULE 3   BAIL: SUPPLEMENTARY
                                    PROVISIONS

Bail Act 1976

1.   Section 5 of the Bail Act 1976 (supplementary provisions about decisions on bail) shall be amended as follows—
(a)   in subsection (1)(d), after the words 'a court' there shall be inserted the words 'or constable'; and
(b)   after subsection (10), there shall be inserted the following subsection—
'(11)   This section is subject, in its application to bail granted by a constable, to section 5A of this Act.'.
2.   After section 5 of the Bail Act 1976 there shall be inserted the following section—
'5A.   Supplementary provisions in cases of police bail
(1)   Section 5 of this Act applies, in relation to bail granted by a custody officer under Part IV of the Police and Criminal Evidence Act 1984 in cases where the normal powers to impose conditions of bail are available to him, subject to the following modifications.
(2)   For subsection (3) substitute the following—
"(3)   Where a custody officer, in relation to any person,—
(a)   imposes conditions in granting bail in criminal proceedings, or
(b)   varies any conditions of bail or imposes conditions in respect of bail in criminal proceedings,
the custody officer shall, with a view to enabling that person to consider requesting him or another custody officer, or making an application to a

magistrates' court, to vary the conditions, give reasons for imposing or varying the conditions.''.

(3) For subsection (4) substitute the following—

"(4) A custody officer who is by virtue of subsection (3) above required to give reasons for his decision shall include a note of those reasons in the custody record and shall give a copy of that note to the person in relation to whom the decision was taken.''.

(4) Subsections (5) and (6) shall be omitted.'.

Magistrates' Courts Act 1980

3. After section 43A of the Magistrates' Courts Act 1980 there shall be inserted the following section—

'43B. **Power to grant bail where police bail has been granted**

(1) Where a custody officer—

(a) grants bail to any person under Part IV of the Police and Criminal Evidence Act 1984 in criminal proceedings and imposes conditions, or

(b) varies, in relation to any person, conditions of bail in criminal proceedings under section 3(8) of the Bail Act 1976,

a magistrates' court may, on application by or on behalf of that person, grant bail or vary the conditions.

(2) On an application under subsection (1) the court, if it grants bail and imposes conditions or if it varies the conditions, may impose more onerous conditions.

(3) On determining an application under subsection (1) the court shall remand the applicant, in custody or on bail in accordance with the determination, and, where the court withholds bail or grants bail the grant of bail made by the custody officer shall lapse.

(4) In this section 'bail in criminal proceedings' and 'vary' have the same meanings as they have in the Bail Act 1976.'.

Section 44   SCHEDULE 4   TRANSFER FOR TRIAL
        PART I   PROVISIONS SUBSTITUTED FOR SECTIONS 4 OF
                MAGISTRATES' COURTS ACT 1980

Transfer for trial

4. Transfer for trial: preliminary

(1) Where—

(a) a person is charged before a magistrates' court with an offence which is triable only on indictment; or

(b) a person is charged before a magistrates' court with an offence triable either way and—

(i) the court has decided that the offence is more suitable for trial on indictment, or

(ii) the accused has not consented to be tried summarily,

the court and the prosecutor shall proceed with a view to transferring the proceedings for the offence to the Crown Court for trial.

(2) Where, under subsection (1) above or any other provision of this Part, a magistrates' court is to proceed with a view to transferring the proceedings for the

offence to the Crown Court for trial, sections 5 to 8C below, or such of them as are applicable, shall apply to the proceedings against the accused, unless—

(a)   the prosecutor decides to discontinue or withdraw the proceedings;

(b)   the Commissioners of Customs and Excise decide, under section 152(a) of the Customs and Excise Management Act 1979, to stay or compound the proceedings;

(c)   the court proceeds to try the information summarily under section 25(3) or (7) below; or

(d)   a notice of transfer under section 4 of the Criminal Justice Act 1987 or section 53 of the Criminal Justice Act 1991 is served on the court.

(3)   The functions of a magistrates' court under sections 5 to 8C below may be discharged by a single justice.

(4)   A magistrates' court may, at any stage in the proceedings against the accused, adjourn the proceedings, and if it does so shall remand the accused.

(5)   Any reference in this Part to a magistrates' court proceeding with a view to transfer for trial is a reference to the court and the prosecutor proceeding with a view to transferring the case to the Crown Court for trial and any reference to transferring for trial shall be construed accordingly.

5.   Prosecutor's notice of prosecution case

(1)   Where this section applies to proceedings against an accused for an offence, the prosecutor shall, within the prescribed period or within such further period as the court may on application by the prosecutor allow, serve on the magistrates' court a notice of his case which complies with subsection (2) below.

(2)   The notice of the prosecution case shall—

(a)   specify the charge or charges the proceedings on which are, subject to section 6 below, to be transferred for trial;

(b)   subject to subsection (5) below, include a set of the documents containing the evidence (including oral evidence) on which the charge or charges is or are based; and

(c)   contain such other information (if any) as may be prescribed;

and in this Part a 'notice of the prosecution case' means a notice which complies with this subsection.

(3)   The accused and any co-accused shall be given an opportunity to oppose in writing within the prescribed period the grant of an extension of time under subsection (1) above.

(4)   On serving the notice of the prosecution case on the magistrates' court, the prosecutor shall serve a copy of the notice on the accused, or each of the accused, unless the person to be served cannot be found.

(5)   There shall be no requirement on the prosecutor to include in the notice of the prosecution case copies of any documents referred to in the notice as having already been supplied to the court or the accused, as the case may be.

(6)   In this section 'co-accused', in relation to the accused, means any other person charged in the same proceedings with him.

6.   Application for dismissal

(1)   Where a notice of the prosecution case has been given in respect of proceedings before a magistrates' court, the accused, or any of them, may, within the prescribed period, or within such further period as the court may on application

allow, make an application in writing to the court ('an application for dismissal') for the charge or, as the case may be, any of the charges to be dismissed.

(2) If an accused makes an application for dismissal he shall, as soon as reasonably practicable after he makes it, send a copy of the application to—

(a) the prosecutor; and

(b) any co-accused.

(3) The prosecutor shall be given an opportunity to oppose the application for dismissal in writing within the prescribed period.

(4) The prosecutor and any co-accused shall be given an opportunity to oppose in writing within the prescribed period the grant of an extension of time under subsection (1) above.

(5) The court shall permit an accused who has no legal representative acting for him to make oral representations to the court when it considers his application for dismissal.

(6) An accused who has a legal representative acting for him and who makes an application for the dismissal of a charge may include in his application a request that, on the ground of the complexity or difficulty of the case, oral representations of his should be considered by the court in determining the application; and the court shall, if it is satisfied that representations ought, on that ground, to be considered, give leave for them to be made.

(7) The prosecutor shall be given an opportunity to oppose in writing within the prescribed period the giving of leave under subsection (6) above for representations to be made.

(8) If the accused makes the representations permitted under subsection (5) or (6) above, the court shall permit the prosecutor to make oral representations in response.

(9) Except for the purpose of making or hearing the representations allowed by subsection (5), (6) or (8) above, the prosecutor and the accused shall not be entitled to be present when the court considers the application for dismissal.

(10) The court, after considering the written evidence and any oral representations permitted under subsection (5), (6) or (8) above, shall, subject to subsection (11) below, dismiss a charge which is the subject of an application for dismissal if it appears to the court that there is not sufficient evidence against the accused to put him on trial by jury for the offence charged.

(11) Where the evidence discloses an offence other than that charged the court need not dismiss the charge but may amend it or substitute a different offence; and if the court does so the amended or substituted charge shall be treated as the charge the proceedings on which are to be transferred for trial.

(12) If the court permits the accused to make oral representations under subsection (6) above, but the accused does not do so, the court may disregard any document containing or indicating the evidence that he might have given.

(13) Dismissal of the charge, or any of the charges, against the accused shall have the effect of barring any further proceedings on that charge or those charges on the same evidence other than by preferring a voluntary bill of indictment.

(14) In this section 'co-accused' has the same meaning as in section 5 above.

7. Transfer for trial

(1) Where a notice of the prosecution case has been served on a magistrates' court with respect to any proceedings and—

    (a)   the prescribed period for an application for dismissal has expired without any such application, or any application for an extension of that time, having been made; or

    (b)   an application for dismissal has been made and dismissed, or has succeeded in relation to one or more but not all the charges,

the court shall, within the prescribed period, in the prescribed manner, transfer the proceedings for the trial of the accused on the charges or remaining charges to the Crown Court sitting at a place specified by the court.

    (2)   In selecting the place of trial, the court shall have regard to—

    (a)   the convenience of the defence, the prosecution and the witnesses;

    (b)   the expediting of the trial; and

    (c)   any direction given by or on behalf of the Lord Chief Justice with the concurrence of the Lord Chancellor under section 75(1) of the Supreme Court Act 1981.

    (3)   On transferring any proceedings to the Crown Court the magistrates' court making the transfer shall—

    (a)   give notice of the transfer and of the place of trial to the prosecutor and to the accused or each of the accused; and

    (b)   send to the Crown Court sitting at the place specified by the court a copy of the notice of the prosecution case and of any documents referred to in it as having already been supplied to the magistrates' court on which it was served and (where an application for dismissal has been made) a copy of any other evidence permitted under section 6 above.

8. Remand

    (1)   Where an accused has been remanded in custody, on transferring proceedings against him for trial a magistrates' court may—

    (a)   order that the accused shall be safely kept in custody until delivered in due course of law; or

    (b)   release the accused on bail in accordance with the Bail Act 1976, that is to say, by directing him to appear before the Crown Court for trial.

    (2)   Where—

    (a)   a person's release on bail under subsection (1)(b) above is conditional on his providing one or more sureties; and

    (b)   in accordance with subsection (3) of section 8 of the Bail Act 1976, the court fixes the amount in which the surety is to be bound with a view to the surety's entering into his recognisance subsequently in accordance with subsections (4) and (5) or (6) of that section,

the court shall in the meantime make an order such as is mentioned in subsection (1)(a) above.

    (3)   Where the court has ordered that a person be safely kept in custody in accordance with paragraph (a) of subsection (1) above, then, if that person is in custody for no other cause, the court may, at any time before his first appearance before the Crown Court, grant him bail in accordance with the Bail Act 1976 subject to a duty to appear before the Crown Court for trial.

    (4)   The court may exercise the powers conferred on it by subsection (1) above in relation to the accused without his being brought before it if it is satisfied—

    (a)   that he has given his written consent to the powers conferred by subsection (1) above being exercised in his absence;

(b)   that he had attained the age of 17 years when he gave that consent; and

(c)   that he has not withdrawn that consent.

(5)   Where proceedings against an accused are transferred for trial after he has been remanded on bail to appear before a magistrates' court on an appointed day, the requirement that he shall so appear shall cease on the transfer of the proceedings unless the magistrates' court transferring the proceedings states that it is to continue.

(6)   Where that requirement ceases by virtue of subsection (5) above, it shall be the duty of the accused to appear before the Crown Court at the place specified by the magistrates' court on transferring the proceedings against him for trial or at any place substituted for it by a direction under section 76 of the Supreme Court Act 1981.

(7)   If, in a case where the magistrates' court states that the requirement mentioned in subsection (5) above is to continue, the accused appears or is brought before the magistrates' court, the court shall have the powers conferred on a magistrates' court by subsection (1) above and, where the court exercises those powers, subsections (2) and (3) above shall apply as if the powers were exercised under subsection (1) above.

(8)   This section is subject to section 4 of the Bail Act 1976, section 41 below, regulations under section 22 of the Prosecution of Offences Act 1985 and section 25 of the Criminal Justice and Public Order Act 1994.

8A.   Reporting restrictions

(1)   Except as provided in this section, it shall not be lawful—

(a)   to publish in Great Britain a written report of an application for dismissal to a magistrates' court under section 6 above; or

(b)   to include in a relevant programme for reception in Great Britain a report of such an application,

if (in either case) the report contains any matter other than matter permitted by this section.

(2)   A magistrates' court may, on an application for the purpose made with reference to proceedings on an application for dismissal, order that subsection (1) above shall not apply to reports of those proceedings.

(3)   Where in the case of two or more accused one of them objects to the making of an order under subsection (2) above, the magistrates' court shall make the order if, and only if, the court is satisfied, after hearing the representations of the accused, that it is in the interests of justice to do so.

(4)   An order under subsection (2) above shall not apply to reports of proceedings under subsection (3) above, but any decision of the court to make or not to make such an order may be contained in reports published or included in a relevant programme before the time authorised by subsection (5) below.

(5)   It shall not be unlawful under this section to publish or include in a relevant programme a report of an application for dismissal containing any matter other than matter permitted by subsection (9) below where the application is successful.

(6)   Where—

(a)   two or more persons are charged in the same proceedings; and

(b)   applications for dismissal are made by more than one of them,

subsection (5) above shall have effect as if for the words 'the application is' there were substituted the words 'all the applications are'.

(7)   It shall not be unlawful under this section to publish or include in a relevant programme a report of an unsuccessful application for dismissal at the conclusion of the trial of the person charged, or of the last of the persons charged to be tried.

(8)   Where, at any time during its consideration of an application for dismissal, the court proceeds to try summarily the case of one or more of the accused under section 25(3) or (7) below, while dismissing the application for dismissal of the other accused or one or more of the other accused, it shall not be unlawful under this section to publish or include in a relevant programme as part of a report of the summary trial, after the court determines to proceed as aforesaid, a report of so much of the application for dismissal containing any matter other than matter permitted by subsection (9) below as takes place before the determination.

(9)   The following matters may be published or included in a relevant programme without an order under subsection (2) above before the time authorised by subsection (5) or (7) above, that is to say—

(a)   the identity of the magistrates' court and the names of the justices composing it;

(b)   the names, age, home address and occupation of the accused;

(c)   the offence, or offences, or a summary of them, with which the accused is or are charged;

(d)   the names of legal representatives engaged in the proceedings;

(e)   where the proceedings are adjourned, the date and place to which they are adjourned;

(f)   the arrangements as to bail;

(g)   whether legal aid was granted to the accused or any of the accused.

(10)   The addresses that may be published or included in a relevant programme under subsection (9) are addresses—

(a)   at any relevant time; and

(b)   at the time of their publication or inclusion in a relevant programme.

(11)   If a report is published or included in a relevant programme in contravention of this section, the following persons, that is to say—

(a)   in the case of a publication of a written report as part of a newspaper or periodical, any proprietor, editor or publisher of the newspaper or periodical;

(b)   in the case of a publication of a written report otherwise than as part of a newspaper or periodical, the person who publishes it;

(c)   in the case of the inclusion of a report in a relevant programme, any body corporate which is engaged in providing the service in which the programme is included and any person having functions in relation to the programme corresponding to those of the editor of a newspaper,

shall be liable on summary conviction to a fine not exceeding level 5 on the standard scale.

(12)   Proceedings for an offence under this section shall not, in England and Wales, be instituted otherwise than by or with the consent of the Attorney General.

(13)   Subsection (1) above shall be in addition to, and not in derogation from, the provisions of any other enactment with respect to the publication of reports of court proceedings.

(14)   In this section—

'publish', in relation to a report, means publish the report, either by itself or as part of a newspaper or periodical, for distribution to the public;

'relevant programme' means a programme included in a programme service (within the meaning of the Broadcasting Act 1990); and

'relevant time' means a time when events giving rise to the charges to which the proceedings relate occurred.

8B. Avoidance of delay

Where a notice of the prosecution case has been given in respect of proceedings before a magistrates' court, the court shall, in exercising any of its powers in relation to the proceedings, have regard to the desirability of avoiding prejudice to the welfare of any witness that may be occasioned by unnecessary delay in transferring the proceedings for trial.

8C. Public notice of transfer

Where a magistrates' court transfers proceedings for trial, the clerk of the court shall, within the prescribed period, cause to be displayed in a part of the court house to which the public have access a notice containing the prescribed information.

PART II
CONSEQUENTIAL AMENDMENTS

Preliminary

1. In this Part of this Schedule—
'the 1853 Act' means the Criminal Procedure Act 1853;
'the 1878 Act' means the Territorial Waters Jurisdiction Act 1878;
'the 1883 Act' means the Explosive Substances Act 1883;
'the 1933 Act' means the Administration of Justice (Miscellaneous Provisions) Act 1933;
'the 1948 Act' means the Criminal Justice Act 1948;
'the 1952 Act' means the Prison Act 1952;
'the 1955 Act' means the Army Act 1955;
'the 1957 Act' means the Naval Discipline Act 1957;
'the 1967 Act' means the Criminal Justice Act 1967;
'the 1968 Act' means the Firearms Act 1968;
'the 1969 Act' means the Children and Young Persons Act 1969;
'the 1973 Act' means the Powers of Criminal Courts Act 1973;
'the 1976 Act' means the Bail Act 1976;
'the 1978 Act' means the Interpretation Act 1978;
'the 1979 Act' means the Customs and Excise Management Act 1979;
'the 1980 Act' means the Magistrates' Courts Act 1980;
'the 1981 Act' means the Supreme Court Act 1981;
'the 1982 Act' means the Criminal Justice Act 1982;
'the 1983 Act' means the Mental Health Act 1983;
'the 1984 Act' means the County Courts Act 1984;
'the 1985 Act' means the Prosecution of Offences Act 1985;
'the 1986 Act' means the Agricultural Holdings Act 1986;
'the 1987 Act' means the Criminal Justice Act 1987;
'the 1988 Act' means the Legal Aid Act 1988;
'the 1991 Act' means the Criminal Justice Act 1991; and
'the 1992 Act' means the Sexual Offences (Amendment) Act 1992.

Criminal Procedure Act 1853 (c. 30.)

2. In section 9 of the 1853 Act (bringing up a prisoner to give evidence), for the words 'under commitment for trial' there shall be substituted the words 'pending his trial in the Crown Court'.

Territorial Waters Jurisdiction Act 1878 (c. 73.)

3. In section 4 of the 1878 Act (procedure under that Act), for the words 'committal of' there shall be substituted the words 'transfer of proceedings against'.

Explosive Substances Act 1883 (c. 3.)

4. In section 6(3) of the 1883 Act (inquiry by Attorney-General, and apprehension of absconding witnesses), for the words 'committing for trial of' there shall be substituted the words 'consideration of an application for dismissal under section 6 of the Magistrates' Courts Act 1980 made by such person for such crime or the transfer for trial of proceedings against'.

Children and Young Persons Act 1933 (c. 12.)

5. In section 42 of the Children and Young Persons Act 1933 (deposition of child or young person), for subsection (2)(a) there shall be substituted the following paragraph—

'(a)   if the deposition relates to an offence in respect of which proceedings have already been transferred to the Crown Court for trial, to the proper officer of the court to which the proceedings have been transferred; and'.

6. In section 56(1) of the Children and Young Persons Act 1933 (powers of courts to remit young offenders to youth court)—

(a)   for the words 'the offender was committed' there shall be substituted the words 'proceedings against the offender were transferred'; and

(b)   for the words 'he was not committed' there shall be substituted the words 'proceedings against him were not transferred'.

Administration of Justice (Miscellaneous Provisions) Act 1933 (c. 36.)

7.—(1)   Section 2 of the 1933 Act (procedure for indictment of offenders) shall be amended as follows.

(2)   In subsection (2)—

(a)   for paragraph (a) there shall be substituted the following paragraph—

'(a)   the proceedings for the offence have been transferred to the Crown Court for trial; or';

(b)   for proviso (i) there shall be substituted the following proviso—

'(i)   where the proceedings for the offence have been transferred to the Crown Court for trial, the bill of indictment against the person charged may include, either in substitution for or in addition to counts charging the offence in respect of which proceedings have been transferred, any counts founded on the evidence contained in the documents sent to the Crown Court by the magistrates' court on transferring the proceedings, being counts which may lawfully be joined in the same indictment;';

(c)   in proviso (iA)—

(i)   for the word 'material' there shall be substituted the words 'the evidence contained in the documents'; and

(ii)   after the words 'person charged' there shall be inserted the words 'or which is referred to in those documents as having already been sent to the person charged'; and

(d)   in proviso (ii), for the words 'the committal' there shall be substituted the words 'charge the proceedings on which were transferred for trial'.

(3)   In subsection (3), in proviso (b), for the words from 'a person' to 'for trial' there shall be substituted the words 'proceedings against a person have been transferred for trial and that person'.

Criminal Justice Act 1948 (c. 58.)

8.—(1)   The 1948 Act shall be amended as follows.

(2)   In section 27(1) (remand and committal of persons aged 17 to 20), for the words 'trial or sentence' there shall be substituted the words 'sentence or transfers proceedings against him for trial'.

(3)   In section 80(1) (interpretation of expressions used in the Act), in the definition of 'Court of summary jurisdiction', for the words from 'examining' to the end there shall be substituted the words 'a magistrates' court proceeding with a view to transfer for trial;'.

Prison Act 1952 (c. 52.)

9.—(1)   Section 43 of the 1952 Act (remand centres, etc.) shall be amended as follows.

(2)   In subsection (1)(a)—

(a)   the words 'trial or' shall be omitted; and

(b)   after the word 'sentence' there shall be inserted the words 'or are ordered to be safely kept in custody on the transfer of proceedings against them for trial'.

(3)   In subsection (2)—

(a)   in paragraph (b)—

(i)   the words 'trial or' shall be omitted; and

(ii)   after the word 'sentence' there shall be inserted the words 'or is ordered to be safely kept in custody on the transfer of proceedings against her for trial'; and

(b)   in paragraph (c)—

(i)   the words 'trial or' shall be omitted; and

(ii)   after the word 'sentence' there shall be inserted the words 'or ordered to be safely kept in custody on the transfer of proceedings against him for trial'.

10.   In section 47(5) of the 1952 Act (rules for the management of prisons, remand centres, etc.), for the words 'committed in custody' there shall be substituted the words 'ordered to be safely kept in custody on the transfer of proceedings against them'.

Army Act 1955 (c. 18.)

11.   In section 187(4) of the 1955 Act (proceedings against persons suspected of illegal absence

(a)   for the words from 'courts of' to 'justices' there shall be substituted the words 'magistrates' courts proceeding with a view to transfer for trial'; and

(b)   for the words 'so acting' there shall be substituted the words 'so proceeding'.

Air Force Act 1955 (c. 19.)

12. In section 187(4) of the Air Force Act 1955 (proceedings against persons suspected of illegal absence)—

(a) for the words from 'courts of' to 'justices' there shall be substituted the words 'magistrates' courts proceeding with a view to transfer for trial'; and

(b) for the words 'so acting' there shall be substituted the words 'so proceeding'.

Geneva Conventions Act 1957 (c. 52.)

13. In section 5 of the Geneva Conventions Act 1957 (reduction of sentence and custody of protected persons)—

(a) in subsection (1), for the word 'committal' there shall be substituted the words 'the transfer of the proceedings against him'; and

(b) in subsection (2)—

(i) for the word 'committal' the first time it occurs there shall be substituted the words 'the transfer of the proceedings against him'; and

(ii) for the words 'remand or committal order' there shall be substituted the words 'court on remanding him or transferring proceedings against him for trial'.

Naval Discipline Act 1957 (c. 53.)

14. In section 109(4) of the 1957 Act (proceedings against persons suspected of illegal absence)—

(a) for the words from ' 1952' to 'justices' there shall be substituted the words '1980, that is to say the provisions relating to the constitution and procedure of magistrates' courts proceeding with a view to transfer for trial'; and

(b) for the words 'so acting' there shall be substituted the words 'so proceeding'.

Criminal Justice Act 1967 (c. 80.)

15.—(1) The 1967 Act shall be amended as follows.

(2) In section 9 (general admissibility of written statements), in subsection (1), for the words 'committal proceedings' there shall be substituted the words 'proceedings under sections 4 to 6 of the Magistrates' Courts Act 1980'.

(3) In section 11 (notice of alibi), in subsection (8), in the definition of 'the prescribed period', for the words from 'the end' to 'or' there shall be substituted the words 'the transfer of the proceedings to the Crown Court for trial, or'.

Criminal Appeal Act 1968 (c. 19.)

16. In section 1(3) of the Criminal Appeal Act 1968 (limitation of right of appeal in case of scheduled offence), for the word 'committed' there shall be substituted the words 'transferred proceedings against'.

Firearms Act 1968 (c. 27.)

17. In paragraph 3(3) of Part II of Schedule 6 to the 1968 Act (trial of certain offences under that Act)—

(a) after the word 'If' there shall be inserted the words ', under section 6 of the said Act of 1980,';

(b)   for the words from 'determines' to 'for trial' there shall be substituted the words 'dismisses the charge against the accused';

(c)   in sub-subparagraph (a), for the words from 'inquire' to 'justices' there shall be substituted the words 'proceed with a view to transferring for trial proceedings for the listed offence';

(d)   in sub-subparagraph (b)—

   (i)   for the words 'inquire into' there shall be substituted the words 'proceed in respect of'; and

   (ii)   for the words from 'its inquiry' to 'justices' there shall be substituted the words 'a view to transferring for trial proceedings for that offence'.

Theft Act 1968 (c. 60.)

18.   In section 28(4) of the Theft Act 1968 (orders for restitution), for the words from ', the depositions' to the end there shall be substituted the words 'and, where the proceedings have been transferred to the Crown Court for trial, the documents sent to the Crown Court by the magistrates' court under section 7(3)(b) of the Magistrates' Courts Act 1980.'.

Children and Young Persons Act 1969 (c. 54.)

19.   In section 23(1) of the 1969 Act (remands and committals to local authority accommodation)—

(a)   in paragraph (a), for the words 'or commits him for trial or sentence' there shall be substituted the words ', transfers proceedings against him for trial or commits him for sentence'; and

(b)   for the words 'the remand or committal shall be' there shall be substituted the words 'he shall be remanded or committed'.

Powers of Criminal Courts Act 1973 (c. 62.)

20.   In section 21(2) of the 1973 Act (restriction on imposing sentences of imprisonment, etc., on persons not legally represented)—

(a)   for the words 'or trial' there shall be substituted the words 'or in respect of whom proceedings have been transferred to the Crown Court for trial'; and

(b)   after the words 'committed him' there shall be inserted the words 'or which transferred proceedings against him'.

21.   In section 32(1)(b) of the 1973 Act (enforcement, etc., of fines imposed and recognizances forfeited by Crown Court)—

(a)   the words 'tried or' shall be omitted; and

(b)   after the words 'dealt with' there shall be inserted the words 'or which transferred proceedings against him to the Crown Court for trial'.

Bail Act 1976 (c. 63.)

22.   In section 3 of the 1976 Act (incidents of bail in criminal proceedings)—

(a)   in subsection (8) (variation and imposition of bail conditions by court), for the words from 'committed' to 'trial or' there shall be substituted the words 'released a person on bail on transferring proceedings against him to the Crown Court for trial or has committed him on bail to the Crown Court'; and

(b)   in subsection (8A), for the words 'committed on bail' there shall be substituted the words 'released on bail on the transfer of proceedings against him'.

23.   In section 5 of the 1976 Act (supplementary provisions about decisions on bail)—

(a)   in subsection (6)(a)—

(i)   for the word 'committing' there shall be substituted the words 'transferring proceedings against'; and

(ii)   after the words 'Crown Court' where they occur first, there shall be inserted the words 'or has already done so'; and

(b)   in subsection (6A)(a), for sub-paragraph (i) there shall be substituted the following sub-paragraph—

'(i)   section 4(4) (adjournment when court is proceeding with a view to transfer for trial);'.

24.   In section 6(6)(b) of the 1976 Act (absconding by person released on bail), for the words from 'commits' to 'another offence' there shall be substituted the words 'transfers proceedings against that person for another offence to the Crown Court for trial'.

25.   In section 9(3)(b) of the 1976 Act (agreeing to indemnify sureties in criminal proceedings), for the words from 'commits' to 'another offence' there shall be substituted the words 'transfers proceedings against that person for another offence to the Crown Court for trial'.

Sexual Offences (Amendment) Act 1976 (c. 82.)

26.   In section 3 of the Sexual Offences (Amendment) Act 1976 (application of restrictions on evidence at trials for rape etc. to committal proceedings etc.), for subsection (1) there shall be substituted the following subsection—

'(1)   Where a magistrates' court considers an application for dismissal of a charge for a rape offence, then, except with the consent of the court, evidence shall not be adduced and a question shall not be asked at the consideration of the application which, if the proceedings were a trial at which a person is charged as mentioned in subsection (1) of the preceding section and each of the accused in respect of whom the application for dismissal is made were charged at the trial with the offences to which the application relates, could not be adduced or asked without leave in pursuance of that section.'.

27.   In section 4(6)(c) of the Sexual Offences (Amendment) Act 1976 (anonymity of complainants in rape etc. cases), for the words 'commits him for trial on' there shall be substituted the words 'transfers proceedings against him for trial for'.

Interpretation Act 1978 (c. 30.)

28.   In Schedule 1 to the 1978 Act—

(a)   in the definition of 'Committed for trial', paragraph (a) shall be omitted; and

(b)   after the definition of 'The Tax Acts' there shall be inserted the following definition—

'Transfer for trial' means the transfer of proceedings against an accused to the Crown Court for trial under section 7 of the Magistrates' Courts Act 1980.'.

Customs and Excise Management Act 1979 (c. 2.)

29.—(1) The 1979 Act shall be amended as follows.

(2)   In section 147 (proceedings for offences under customs and excise Acts), in subsection (2), for the words from the beginning to 'justices' there shall be

substituted the words 'Where, in England or Wales, on an application under section 6 of the Magistrates' Courts Act 1980 for dismissal of a charge under the customs and excise Acts, the court has begun to consider the evidence and any representations permitted under that section,'.

(3)   In section 155 (persons who may conduct proceedings under customs and excise Acts), in subsection (1), for the words 'examining justices' there shall be substituted the words 'magistrates' court proceeding with a view to transfer for trial'.

Reserve Forces Act 1980 (c. 9.)

30.   In paragraph 2(4) of Schedule 5 to the Reserve Forces Act 1980 (proceedings against persons suspected of illegal absence)—

(a)   for the words 'acting as examining justices' there shall be substituted the words 'proceeding with a view to transfer for trial'; and

(b)   for the words 'so acting' there shall be substituted the words 'so proceeding'.

Magistrates' Courts Act 1980 (c. 43.)

31.—(1)   Section 2 of the 1980 Act (Jurisdiction of magistrates' courts) shall be amended as follows.

(2)   In subsection (3), for the words from 'as examining' to 'any offence' there shall be substituted the words 'to proceed with a view to transfer for trial where the offence charged was'.

(3)   In subsection (4), for the words 'as examining justices' there shall be substituted the words 'to proceed with a view to transfer for trial'.

(4)   In subsection (5), for the words 'as examining justices' there shall be substituted the words 'to proceed with a view to transfer for trial'.

32.   In section 19 of the 1980 Act (court to consider mode of trial of either way offence), in subsection (4), for the words from 'to inquire' to the end of the subsection there shall be substituted the words 'with a view to transfer for trial.'.

33.   In section 20 of the 1980 Act (procedure where summary trial appears more suitable), in subsection (3)(b), for the words from 'to inquire' to the end there shall be substituted the words 'with a view to transfer for trial.'.

34.   In section 21 of the 1980 Act (procedure where trial on indictment appears more suitable), for the words from 'to inquire' to the end there shall he substituted the words 'with a view to transfer for trial.'.

35.—(1)   Section 23 of the 1980 Act (procedure where court proceeds to determine mode of trial in absence of accused) shall be amended as follows.

(2)   In subsection (4)(b)—

(a)   for the words from 'to inquire' to 'justices' there shall be substituted the words 'with a view to transfer for trial'; and

(b)   for the word 'hearing' there shall be substituted the word 'proceedings'.

(3)   In subsection (5)—

(a)   for the words from 'to inquire' to 'justices' there shall be substituted the words 'with a view to transfer for trial'; and

(b)   for the word 'hearing' there shall be substituted the word 'proceedings'.

36.—(1)   Section 24 of the 1980 Act (trial of child or young person for indictable offence) shall be amended as follows.

(2)   In subsection (1)—

(a) in paragraph (b), for the word 'commit' there shall be substituted the words 'proceed with a view to transferring the proceedings in relation to'; and

(b) for the words from 'commit the accused' to the end there shall be substituted the words 'proceed with a view to transferring the proceedings against the accused for trial.'.

(3) In subsection (2), for the words from 'commits' to 'him for trial' there shall be substituted the words 'proceeds with a view to transferring for trial the proceedings in relation to a person under the age of 18 years for an offence with which he is charged jointly with a person who has attained that age, the court may also proceed with a view to transferring for trial proceedings against him'.

37.—(1) Section 25 of the 1980 Act (court's power to change from summary trial to committal proceedings and vice versa) shall be amended as follows.

(2) In subsection (2)—

(a) for the words from 'to inquire' to 'justices' there shall be substituted the words 'with a view to transfer for trial'; and

(b) for the word 'hearing' there shall be substituted the word 'proceedings'.

(3) For subsection (3) there shall be substituted the following subsection—

'(3) Where on an application for dismissal of a charge under section 6 above the court has begun to consider the evidence and any representations permitted under that section, then, if at any time during its consideration it appears to the court, having regard to any of the evidence or representations, and to the nature of the case, that the offence is after all more suitable for summary trial, the court may—

(a) if the accused is present, after doing as provided in subsection (4) below, ask the accused whether he consents to be tried summarily and, if he so consents, may (subject to subsection (3A) below) proceed to try the information summarily; or

(b) in the absence of the accused—

(i) if the accused's consent to be tried summarily is signified by the person representing him, proceed to try the information summarily; or

(ii) if that consent is not so signified, adjourn the proceedings without remanding the accused, and if it does so, the court shall fix the time and place at which the proceedings are to be resumed and at which the accused is required to appear or be brought before the court in order for the court to proceed as provided in paragraph (a) above.'.

(4) In subsection (5), in paragraph (b), for the words from 'inquire' to 'fall' there shall be substituted the words 'consider the evidence and any representations permitted under section 6 above on an application for dismissal of a charge in a case in which, under paragraph (a) or (b) of section 24(1) above, the court is required to proceed with a view to transferring the proceedings to the Crown Court for trial,'.

(5) In subsection (6)—

(a) for the words from 'to inquire' to 'justices' there shall be substituted the words 'with a view to transfer for trial'; and

(b) for the word 'hearing' there shall be substituted the word 'proceedings'.

(6) In subsection (7), for the words 'the inquiry' there shall be substituted the words 'its consideration of the evidence and any representations permitted under section 6 above.'.

38. For section 26 of the 1980 Act (power to issue summons in certain circumstances) there shall be substituted the following section—

'**26.   Power to issue summons in certain circumstances**

Where, in the circumstances mentioned in section 23(1)(a) above, the court is not satisfied that there is good cause for proceeding in the absence of the accused, the justice or any of the justices of which the court is composed may issue a summons directed to the accused requiring his presence before the court; and if the accused is not present at the time and place appointed for the proceedings under section 19(1) or 22(1) above, as the case may be, the court may issue a warrant for his arrest.'.

39.   In section 28 of the 1980 Act (use in summary trial of evidence given in committal proceedings)—

(a)   for the words from 'inquire' to 'justices' there shall be substituted the words 'consider the evidence under section 6 above'; and

(b)   for the words from 'then' to 'any' there shall be substituted the words 'any oral'.

40.   In section 29 of the 1980 Act (remission of person under 18 to youth court for trial), in subsection (2)(b)(i), for the words from 'to inquire' to 'discharges him' there shall be substituted the words 'with a view to transfer for trial'.

41.   In section 42 of the 1980 Act (restriction on justices sitting after dealing with bail), in subsection (2), for the words 'committal proceedings' there shall be substituted the words 'proceedings before the court on an application for dismissal of a charge under section 6 above.'.

42.—(1)   Section 97 of the 1980 Act (summons to witness) shall be amended as follows.

(2)   In subsection (1)—

(a)   the words from 'at an inquiry' to 'be) or' shall be omitted; and

(b)   for the words 'such a court' there shall be substituted the words 'a magistrates' court for that county, that London commission area or the City (as the case may be)'.

(3)   After subsection (1) there shall be inserted the following subsection—

'(1A)   Where a magistrates' court is proceeding with a view to transferring proceedings against an accused for an offence to the Crown Court for trial, subsection (1) above shall apply in relation to evidence or a document or thing material to the offence subject to the following modifications—

(a)   no summons shall be issued by a justice of the peace after the expiry of the period within which a notice of the prosecution case under section 5 above must be served or the service of the notice of the prosecution case, if sooner; and

(b)   the summons shall require the person to whom it is directed to attend before the justice issuing it or another justice for that county, that London commission area or the City of London (as the case may be) to have his evidence taken as a deposition or to produce any document or thing.'.

(4)   In subsection (2)—

(a)   after the words 'subsection (1)' there shall be inserted the words 'or (1A)'; and

(b)   after the word 'court' there shall be inserted the words 'or justice, as the case may be,'.

(5)   In subsection (2A), after the words 'subsection (1)' there shall be inserted the words 'or (1A)'.

(6)   In subsections (3) and (4), after the words 'a magistrates' court' or 'the court' wherever they occur there shall be inserted the words 'or justice, as the case may be,'.

43.—(1)   Section 128 of the 1980 Act (remand in custody or on bail) shall be amended as follows.

(2)   In subsection (1)(b), for the words 'inquiring into or' there shall be substituted the words 'proceeding with a view to transferring the proceedings against that person for trial or is'.

(3)   In subsections (1A), (3A), (3C) and (3E), for the words 'section 5' there shall be substituted the words 'section 4(4)'.

(4)   In subsection (4)—

(a)   for the words from 'during an inquiry' to the words 'committed by him' there shall be substituted the words 'when it is proceeding with a view to transfer for trial'; and

(b)   in paragraph (c)—

(i)   for the word 'hearing' there shall be substituted the word 'proceedings'; and

(ii)   for the words from 'person' to 'committed' there shall be substituted the words 'proceedings against the person so bailed being transferred'.

44.   In section 129 of the 1980 Act (further remand), in subsection (4)—

(a)   for the words from 'commits' to 'bail' there shall be substituted the words 'transfers for trial proceedings against a person who has been remanded on bail'; and

(b)   for the words 'so committed' there shall be substituted the words 'in respect of whom proceedings have been transferred'.

45.   In section 130 of the 1980 Act (transfer of remand hearings), in subsection (1), for the words 'section 5' there shall be substituted the words 'section 4(4)'.

46.   In section 145(1)(f) of the 1980 Act (rules: supplementary provisions), for the word 'committed' there shall be substituted the words 'in respect of whom proceedings have been transferred'.

47.—(1)   Schedule 3 to the 1980 Act (corporations) shall be amended as follows.

(2)   In paragraph 1(1), for the words 'commit a corporation' there shall be substituted the words ', in the case of a corporation, transfer the proceedings'.

(3)   In paragraph 2(a), for the words from 'a statement' to 'to' there shall be substituted the words 'an application to dismiss'.

(4)   In paragraph 6, for the words 'inquiry into,' there shall be substituted the words 'transfer for trial'.

48.   In paragraph 5 of Schedule 5 to the 1980 Act (transfer of remand hearings), for the words 'sections 5' there shall be substituted the words 'sections 4(4)'.

Criminal Attempts Act 1981 (c. 47.)

49.   In section 2(2)(g) of the Criminal Attempts Act 1981 (application of procedural and other provisions to attempts), the words 'or committed for trial' shall be omitted.

Contempt of Court Act 1981 (c. 49.)

50.   In section 4(3)(b) of the Contempt of Court Act 1981 (contemporary reports of proceedings)—

(a)   for the words 'committal proceedings' there shall be substituted the words 'an application for dismissal under section 6 of the Magistrates' Courts Act 1980'; and

(b)   for the words from 'subsection (3)' to ' 1980' there shall be substituted the words 'subsection (5) or (7) of section 8A of that Act'.

Supreme Court Act 1981 (c. 54)

51.   In section 76 of the 1981 Act (alteration of place of Crown Court trial)—
    (a)   in subsection (1), for the words from 'varying the decision' to the end there shall be substituted the words 'substituting some other place for the place specified in a notice relating to the transfer of the proceedings to the Crown Court or by varying a previous decision of the Crown Court';
    (b)   in subsection (3), for the words from the beginning to the words 'varying the place of trial;' there shall be substituted the following words—
    'If he is dissatisfied with the place of trial—
        (a)   the defendant may apply to the Crown Court for a direction, or further direction, varying the place of trial specified in a notice relating to the transfer of the proceedings to the Crown Court or fixed by the Crown Court, or
        (b)   the prosecutor may apply to the Crown Court for a direction, or further direction, varying the place of trial specified in a notice given by the magistrates' court under section 7 of the Magistrates' Courts Act 1980 or fixed by the Crown Court;'; and
    (c)   after subsection (4) there shall be inserted the following subsection—
    '(5)   In this section any reference to a notice relating to the transfer of proceedings to the Crown Court is a reference to the notice given by the magistrates' court under section 7 of the Magistrates' Courts Act 1980 or by the prosecutor under section 4 of the Criminal Justice Act 1987 or section 53 of the Criminal Justice Act 1991.'.
52.—(1)   Section 77 of the 1981 Act (date of Crown Court trial) shall be amended as follows.
    (2)   In subsection (1), for the words from 'a person's committal' to 'beginning of the trial' there shall be substituted the words 'the transfer of proceedings for trial by the Crown Court and the beginning of the trial;'.
    (3)   In subsection (2)—
    (a)   for the words preceding paragraph (a) there shall be substituted the words 'The trial of a person on charges the proceedings on which have been transferred for trial to the Crown Court—'; and
    (b)   in paragraph (a), for the words 'his consent' there shall be substituted the words 'the consent of the person charged'.
    (4)   In subsection (3), for the word 'committal' there shall be substituted the word 'transfer'.
    (5)   After subsection (3) there shall be inserted the following subsections—
    '(4)   Where a notice of the prosecution case has been given in respect of any proceedings, the Crown Court before which the proceedings are to he tried shall, in exercising any of its powers in relation to the proceedings, have regard to the desirability of avoiding prejudice to the welfare of any witness that may be occasioned by unnecessary delay in bringing the proceedings to trial.
    (5)   In this section references to the transfer of proceedings for trial are references to a transfer by a magistrates' court under section 7 of the Magistrates' Courts Act 1980 or by the prosecutor under section 4 of the Criminal Justice Act 1987 or section 53 of the Criminal Justice Act 1991 and

the date of transfer for trial is the date on which the transfer is effected under the said section 7 or, where the transfer is by the prosecutor, the date specified in his notice of transfer.'.

53.   In section 80(2) of the 1981 Act (process to compel appearance before Crown Court), for the words from 'the person' to 'committed' there shall be substituted the words 'proceedings against the person charged have not been transferred'.

Criminal Justice Act 1982 (c. 48.)

54.   In section 1(2) of the 1982 Act (restrictions on custodial sentences for persons under 21)—

(a)   the words 'trial or' shall be omitted; and

(b)   after the word 'sentence' there shall be inserted the words 'or ordered to be safely kept in custody on the transfer of proceedings against him for trial'.

55.   In section 3(2) of the 1982 Act (restriction on imposing custodial sentences on persons under 21 not legally represented)—

(a)   for the words 'or trial' there shall be substituted the words 'or in respect of whom proceedings have been transferred to the Crown Court for trial'; and

(b)   after the words 'committed him' there shall be inserted the words 'or transferred proceedings against him'.

Mental Health Act 1983 (c. 20.)

56.—(1)   Section 52 of the 1983 Act (provisions relating to persons remanded by magistrates' courts) shall be amended as follows.

(2)   In subsection (2), for the words from 'accused' to 'or' there shall be substituted the words 'court, on transferring proceedings against the accused to the Crown Court for trial, orders him to be safely kept in custody, or commits the accused in custody to the Crown Court'.

(3)   In subsection (5), after the words 'expired or that' there shall be inserted the words 'proceedings against the accused are transferred to the Crown Court for trial or'.

(4)   In subsection (6), after the word 'If' there shall be inserted the words 'proceedings against the accused are transferred to the Crown Court for trial or'.

(5)   In subsection (7)—

(a)   for the words from 'inquire' to 'into' there shall be substituted the words 'proceed with a view to transferring for trial proceedings for'; and

(b)   for the words from 'commit' to '1980' there shall be substituted the words 'transfer proceedings against him for trial'.

County Courts Act 1984 (c. 28.)

57.   In section 57(1) of the 1984 Act (evidence of prisoners), for the words 'under committal' there shall be substituted the words 'following the transfer of proceedings against him'.

Police and Criminal Evidence Act 1984 (c. 60.)

58.   In section 62(10)(a) of the Police and Criminal Evidence Act 1984 (power of court to draw inferences from failure of accused to consent to provide intimate sample), for sub-paragraph (i) there shall be substituted the following sub-paragraph—

'(i)   whether to grant an application for dismissal made by that person under section 6 of the Magistrates' Courts Act 1980 (application for dismissal of charge in course of proceedings with a view to transfer for trial); or'.

Prosecution of Offences Act 1985 (c. 23.)

59.   In section 16 of the 1985 Act (defence costs)—

(a)   in subsection (1), for paragraph (b) there shall be substituted the following paragraph—

'(b)   a magistrates' court determines not to transfer for trial proceedings for an indictable offence;'; and

(b)   in subsection (2)(a), for the word 'committed' there shall be substituted the words 'in respect of which proceedings against him have been transferred'.

60.   In section 21(6) of the 1985 Act (interpretation, etc.), in paragraph (b), for the words from 'the accused' to 'but' there shall be substituted the words 'proceedings against the accused are transferred to the Crown Court for trial but the accused is'.

61.   In section 22 of the 1985 Act (time limits for preliminary stages of criminal proceedings), in subsection (11)—

(a)   in the definition of 'appropriate court', in paragraph (a) for the words from 'accused' to 'or' there shall be substituted the words 'proceedings against the accused have been transferred for trial or the accused has been'; and

(b)   in the definition of 'custody of the Crown Court', for paragraph (a) there shall be substituted the following paragraph—

'(a)   section 8(1) of the Magistrates' Court Act 1980 (remand of accused where court is proceeding with a view to transfer for trial); or'.

62.   In section 23 of the 1985 Act (discontinuance of proceedings in magistrates' courts), in subsection (2)(b)(i), for the words 'Accused has been committed' there shall be substituted the words 'proceedings against the accused have been transferred'.

Agricultural Holdings Act 1986 (c. 5.)

63.   In paragraph 12(1) of Schedule 11 to the 1986 Act (procedure on arbitrations under the Act), for the words 'under committal' there shall be substituted the words 'following the transfer of proceedings against him'.

Criminal Justice Act 1987 (c. 38.)

64.—(1)   The 1987 Act shall be amended as follows.

(2)   In section 4(1) (notices of transfer in serious fraud cases)—

(a)   in paragraph (b)(i), for the words from 'person' to 'trial' there shall be substituted the words 'proceedings against the person charged to be transferred for trial'; and

(b)   in paragraph (c), for the words from the beginning to 'justices' there shall be substituted the words 'not later than the time at which the authority would be required to serve a notice of the prosecution case under section 5 of the Magistrates' Courts Act 1980,'.

(3)   In section 5 (procedure for notices of transfer)—

(a)   in subsection (9)(a), for the words 'a statement of the evidence' there shall be substituted the words 'copies of the documents containing the evidence (including oral evidence)'; and

(b)   after subsection (9) there shall be inserted the following subsection—

'(9A)   Regulations under subsection (9)(a) above may provide that there shall be no requirement for copies of any documents referred to in the documents sent with the notice of transfer as having already been supplied to accompany the copy of the notice of the transfer.'.

(4)   In section 6(5) (applications for dismissal), for the words from 'a refusal' to the end there shall be substituted the words 'the dismissal of a charge or charges against an accused under section 6 of the Magistrates' Courts Act 1980.'.

Criminal Justice Act 1988 (c. 33.)

65.   In section 40 of the Criminal Justice Act 1988 (power to include counts for certain summary offences in indictment), in subsection (1), for the words from 'an examination' to the end, there shall be substituted the words 'the documents sent with the copy of a notice of the prosecution case to the Crown Court'.

66.—(1)   Section 41 of the Criminal Justice Act 1988 shall be amended as follows.

(2)   In subsection (1)—

(a)   for the words preceding paragraph (a) there shall be substituted the words 'Where a magistrates' court transfers to the Crown Court for trial proceedings against a person for an offence triable either way or a number of such offences, it may also transfer to the Crown Court for trial proceedings against a person for any summary offence with which he is charged and which—'; and

(b)   for the words from 'appears' to 'case' there shall be substituted the words 'was sent to the person charged with the notice of the transfer of the proceedings'.

(3)   In subsection (2)—

(a)   for the words from 'commits' to 'indictment' there shall be substituted the words 'transfers to the Crown Court for trial proceedings against a person'; and

(b)   for the words 'who is committed' there shall be substituted the words 'in respect of whom proceedings are transferred'.

(4)   In subsection (4), for the words 'committal of' there shall be substituted the words 'transfer for trial of proceedings against'.

Legal Aid Act 1988 (c. 34.)

67.   In section 20 of the 1988 Act (authorities competent to grant criminal legal aid), in subsection (4), after paragraph (a) there shall be inserted the following paragraph—

'(aa) which proceeds with a view to transferring proceedings to the Crown Court for trial,'.

68.   In section 21 of the 1988 Act (availability of criminal legal aid)—

(a)   in subsection (3)(a), for the words from 'a person' to 'his' there shall be substituted the words 'proceedings against a person who is charged with murder are transferred to the Crown Court for trial, for that person's'; and

(b)   in subsection (4), for the word 'commits' there shall be substituted the words 'transfers the proceedings against'.

69.—(1)   Schedule 3 to the 1988 Act (enforcement of contribution orders) shall be amended as follows.

(2)   In paragraph 1(b)—

(a)　for the words from 'who' to 'by a magistrates' court)' there shall be substituted the words 'against whom proceedings were transferred for trial or who was committed for sentence'; and

(b)　for the words 'committed him' there shall be substituted the words 'transferred the proceedings against him or committed him for sentence'.

(3)　In paragraph 9(b), for sub-subparagraph (i) there shall be substituted the following sub-subparagraph—

'(i)　in the proceedings against the legally assisted person being transferred to the Crown Court for trial or in the legally assisted person being committed to the Crown Court for sentence, or'.

(4)　In paragraph 10(2)(b), for sub-subparagraph (i) there shall be substituted the following sub-subparagraph—

'(i)　in the proceedings against the legally assisted person being transferred to the Crown Court for trial or in the legally assisted person being committed to the Crown Court for sentence, or'.

Coroners Act 1988 (c. 13.)

70.　In section 16 of the Coroners Act 1988 (adjournment of inquest)—

(a)　in subsection (1)(b), for the words 'examining justices' there shall be substituted the words 'a magistrates' court which is to proceed with a view to transferring proceedings against that person for trial,'; and

(b)　in subsection (8)—

(i)　for the words 'examining justices' there shall be substituted the words 'a magistrates' court considering an application for dismissal under section 6 of the Magistrates' Courts Act 1980'; and

(ii)　for the words from 'person' to 'committed' there shall be substituted the words 'proceedings against the person charged are transferred'.

71.　In section 17 of the Coroners Act 1988 (supplementary provisions applying on adjournment of inquest)—

(a)　in subsection (2)—

(i)　after the word 'Where' there shall be inserted the words 'proceedings against'; and

(ii)　for the words 'is committed' there shall be substituted the words 'are transferred'; and

(b)　in subsection (3)(b), for the words 'that person is committed' there shall be substituted the words 'proceedings against that person are transferred'.

War Crimes Act 1991 (c. 13.)

72.　In the War Crimes Act 1991—

(a)　in section 1(4) (introducing the Schedule providing a procedure for use instead of committal proceedings for certain war crimes), the words 'England, Wales or' shall be omitted; and

(b)　Part I of the Schedule (procedure for use in England and Wales instead of committal proceedings) shall be omitted.

Criminal Justice Act 1991 (c. 53.)

73.—(1)　The 1991 Act shall be amended as follows.

(2)   In section 53 (notices of transfer in certain cases involving children)—

(a)   in subsection (1)(a), for the words from 'person' to 'trial' there shall be substituted the words 'proceedings against the person charged to be transferred for trial'; and

(b)   in subsection (2), for the words from 'before' to the end, there shall be substituted the words 'not later than the time at which the Director would be required to serve a notice of the prosecution case under section 5 of the Magistrates' Courts Act 1980,'.

(3)   In paragraph 4 of Schedule 6 (procedure for notices of transfer)—

(a)   in sub-paragraph (1)(a) for the words 'a statement of the evidence' there shall be substituted the words 'copies of the documents containing the evidence (including oral evidence)'; and

(b)   after sub-paragraph (1) there shall be inserted the following sub-paragraph—

'(1A)   Regulations under sub-paragraph (1)(a) above may provide that there shall be no requirement for copies of any documents referred to in the documents sent with the notice of transfer as having already been supplied to accompany the copy of the notice of transfer.'.

(4)   In paragraph 5 of Schedule 6 (applications for dismissal), in sub-paragraph (7), for the words from 'a refusal' to the end there shall be substituted the words 'the dismissal of a charge or charges against an accused under section 6 of the Magistrates' Courts Act 1980.'.

(5)   In paragraph 6 of Schedule 6 (reporting restrictions), in sub-paragraph (8), for the words 'sub-paragraphs (5) and (6)' there shall be substituted the words 'sub-paragraphs (5) and (7)'.

Sexual Offences (Amendment) Act 1992 (c. 34.)

74.   In section 6(3)(c) of the 1992 Act, for the words 'commits him' there shall be substituted the words 'transfers proceedings against him'.

**Section 45   SCHEDULE 5   MAGISTRATES' COURTS:
DEALING WITH CASES WHERE ACCUSED PLEADS GUILTY**

Non-appearance of accused: plea of guilty

1.   For section 12 of the Magistrates' Courts Act 1980 ('the 1980 Act') there shall be substituted the following section—

'12.   Non-appearance of accused: plea of guilty

(1)   This section shall apply where—

(a)   a summons has been issued requiring a person to appear before a magistrates' court, other than a youth court, to answer to an information for a summary offence, not being—

(i)   an offence for which the accused is liable to be sentenced to be imprisoned for a term exceeding 3 months; or

(ii)   an offence specified in an order made by the Secretary of State by statutory instrument; and

(b)   the clerk of the court is notified by or on behalf of the prosecutor that the documents mentioned in subsection (3) below have been served upon the accused with the summons.

(2)   The reference in subsection (1)(a) above to the issue of a summons requiring a person to appear before a magistrates' court other than a youth court includes a reference to the issue of a summons requiring a person who has attained the age of 16 at the time when it is issued to appear before a youth court.

(3)   The documents referred to in subsection (1)(b) above are—

(a)   a notice containing such statement of the effect of this section as may be prescribed;

(b)   a concise statement in the prescribed form of such facts relating to the charge as will be placed before the court by or on behalf of the prosecutor if the accused pleads guilty without appearing before the court; and

(c)   if any information relating to the accused will or may, in those circumstances, be placed before the court by or on behalf of the prosecutor, a notice containing or describing that information.

(4)   Where the clerk of the court receives a notification in writing purporting to be given by the accused or by a legal representative acting on his behalf that the accused desires to plead guilty without appearing before the court—

(a)   the clerk of the court shall inform the prosecutor of the receipt of the notification; and

(b)   the following provisions of this section shall apply.

(5)   If at the time and place appointed for the trial or adjourned trial of the information—

(a)   the accused does not appear; and

(b)   it is proved to the satisfaction of the court, on oath or in such manner as may be prescribed, that the documents mentioned in subsection (3) above have been served upon the accused with the summons,

the court may, subject to section 11(3) and (4) above and subsections (6) to (8) below, proceed to hear and dispose of the case in the absence of the accused, whether or not the prosecutor is also absent, in like manner as if both parties had appeared and the accused had pleaded guilty.

(6)   If at any time before the hearing the clerk of the court receives an indication in writing purporting to be given by or on behalf of the accused that he wishes to withdraw the notification—

(a)   the clerk of the court shall inform the prosecutor of the withdrawal; and

(b)   the court shall deal with the information as if the notification had not been given.

(7)   Before accepting the plea of guilty and convicting the accused under subsection (5) above, the court shall cause the following to be read out before the court by the clerk of the court, namely—

(a)   the statement of facts served upon the accused with the summons;

(b)   any information contained in a notice so served, and any information described in such a notice and produced by or on behalf of the prosecutor;

(c)   the notification under subsection (4) above; and

(d)   any submission received with the notification which the accused wishes to be brought to the attention of the court with a view to mitigation of sentence.

(8)   If the court proceeds under subsection (5) above to hear and dispose of the case in the absence of the accused, the court shall not permit—

(a)   any other statement with respect to any facts relating to the offence charged; or

(b)   any other information relating to the accused,

to be made or placed before the court by or on behalf of the prosecutor except on a resumption of the trial after an adjournment under section 10(3) above.

(9)   If the court decides not to proceed under subsection (5) above to hear and dispose of the case in the absence of the accused, it shall adjourn or further adjourn the trial for the purpose of dealing with the information as if the notification under subsection (4) above had not been given.

(10)   In relation to an adjournment on the occasion of the accused's conviction in his absence under subsection (5) above or to an adjournment required by subsection (9) above, the notice required by section 10(2) above shall include notice of the reason for the adjournment.

(11)   No notice shall be required by section 10(2) above in relation to an adjournment—

(a)   which is for not more than 4 weeks; and

(b)   the purpose of which is to enable the court to proceed under subsection (5) above at a later time.

(12)   No order shall be made under subsection (1) above unless a draft of the order has been laid before and approved by resolution of each House of Parliament.

(13)   Any such document as is mentioned in subsection (3) above may be served in Scotland with a summons which is so served under the Summary Jurisdiction (Process) Act 1881'.'

Application of section 12 procedure where accused appears

2.   After section 12 of the 1980 Act there shall be inserted the following section—

'12A.   Application of section 12 where accused appears

(1)   Where the clerk of the court has received such a notification as is mentioned in subsection (4) of section 12 above but the accused nevertheless appears before the court at the time and place appointed for the trial or adjourned trial, the court may, if he consents, proceed under subsection (5) of that section as if he were absent.

(2)   Where the clerk of the court has not received such a notification and the accused appears before the court at that time and place and informs the court that he desires to plead guilty, the court may, if he consents, proceed under section 12(5) above as if he were absent and the clerk had received such a notification.

(3)   For the purposes of subsections (1) and (2) above, subsections (6) to (11) of section 12 above shall apply with the modifications mentioned in subsection (4) or, as the case may be, subsection (5) below.

(4)   The modifications for the purposes of subsection (1) above are that—

(a)   before accepting the plea of guilty and convicting the accused under subsection (5) of section 12 above, the court shall afford the accused an opportunity to make an oral submission with a view to mitigation of sentence; and

(b)   where he makes such a submission, subsection (7)(d) of that section shall not apply.

(5) The modifications for the purposes of subsection (2) above are that—

(a) subsection (6) of section 12 above shall apply as if any reference to the notification under subsection (4) of that section were a reference to the consent under subsection (2) above;

(b) subsection (7)(c) and (d) of that section shall not apply; and

(c) before accepting the plea of guilty and convicting the accused under subsection (5) of that section, the court shall afford the accused an opportunity to make an oral submission with a view to mitigation of sentence.'.

Consequential amendments

3.—(1) In consequence of the amendments made by paragraphs 1 and 2 above the Magistrates' Courts Act 1980 shall be further amended as follows.

(2) For section 13(4), there shall be substituted the following subsection—

'(4) This section shall not apply to an adjournment on the occasion of the accused's conviction in his absence under subsection (5) of section 12 above or to an adjournment required by subsection (9) of that section.'.

(3) In section 13(5), for '12(2)' there shall be substituted '12(5)'.

(4) In section 155(2), for '12(8)' there shall be substituted '12(13)'.

Section 114   SCHEDULE 6   CERTIFICATION OF PRISONER CUSTODY OFFICERS: SCOTLAND

Preliminary

1. In this Schedule—

'certificate' means a certificate under section 114 of this Act;

'the relevant functions', in relation to a certificate, means the escort functions or custodial duties authorised by the certificate.

Issue of certificates

2.—(1) The Secretary of State may, on the application of any person, issue a certificate in respect of that person.

(2) The Secretary of State shall not issue a certificate on any such application unless he is satisfied that the applicant—

(a) is a fit and proper person to perform the relevant functions; and

(b) has received training to such standard as he may consider appropriate for the performance of those functions.

(3) Where the Secretary of State issues a certificate, then, subject to any suspension under paragraph 3 or revocation under paragraph 4 below, it shall continue in force until such date or the occurrence of such event as may be specified in the certificate.

(4) A certificate authorising the performance of both escort functions and custodial duties may specify different dates or events as respects those functions and duties respectively.

Suspension of certificate

3.—(1) This paragraph applies where at any time—

(a) in the case of a prisoner custody officer acting in pursuance of prisoner escort arrangements, it appears to the prisoner escort monitor for the area concerned that the officer is not a fit and proper person to perform escort functions;

(b) in the case of a prisoner custody officer performing custodial duties at a contracted out prison, it appears to the controller of that prison that the officer is not a fit and proper person to perform custodial duties; or

(c) in the case of a prisoner custody officer performing contracted out functions at a directly managed prison, it appears to the governor of that prison that the officer is not a fit and proper person to perform custodial duties.

(2) The prisoner escort monitor, controller or governor may—

(a) refer the matter to the Secretary of State for a decision under paragraph 4 below; and

(b) in such circumstances as may be prescribed by prison rules, suspend the officer's certificate so far as it authorises the performance of escort functions or, as the case may be, custodial duties pending that decision.

Revocation of certificate

4. Where at any time (whether on a reference to him under paragraph 3(2)(a) above or otherwise) it appears to the Secretary of State that a prisoner custody officer is not a fit and proper person to perform escort functions or custodial duties, he may revoke that officer's certificate so far as it authorises the performance of those functions or duties.

False statements

5. If any person, for the purpose of obtaining a certificate for himself or for any other person—

(a) makes a statement which he knows to be false in a material particular; or

(b) recklessly makes a statement which is false in a material particular,

he shall be guilty of an offence and liable on summary conviction to a fine not exceeding level 4 on the standard scale.

Section 122(2)   SCHEDULE 7   CERTIFICATION OF
                PRISONER CUSTODY OFFICERS: NORTHERN IRELAND

Preliminary

1.   In this Schedule—

'certificate' means a certificate under section 122 of this Act;

'the relevant functions', in relation to a certificate, means the escort functions authorised by the certificate.

Issue of certificates

2.—(1) Any person may apply to the Secretary of State for the issue of a certificate in respect of him.

(2) The Secretary of State shall not issue a certificate on any such application unless he is satisfied that the applicant—

(a) is a fit and proper person to perform the relevant functions; and

(b) has received training to such standard as he may consider appropriate for the performance of those functions.

(3) Where the Secretary of State issues a certificate, then, subject to any suspension under paragraph 3 or revocation under paragraph 4 below, it shall continue in force until such date or the occurrence of such event as may be specified in the certificate.

Suspension of certificate

3.—(1)   This paragraph applies where at any time it appears to the prisoner escort monitor for the area concerned, that a prisoner custody officer is not a fit and proper person to perform the escort functions.

(2)   The prisoner escort monitor may—

(a)   refer the matter to the Secretary of State for a decision under paragraph 4 below; and

(b)   in such circumstances as may be prescribed by regulations made by the Secretary of State, suspend the officer's certificate so far as it authorises the performance of escort functions.

(3)   The power to make regulations under this paragraph shall be exercisable by statutory instrument which shall be subject to annulment in pursuance of a resolution of either House of Parliament.

Revocation of certificate

4.   Where at any time it appears to the Secretary of State that a prisoner custody officer is not a fit and proper person to perform escort functions, he may revoke that officer's certificate so far as it authorises the performance of those functions.

False statements

5.   If any person, for the purpose of obtaining a certificate for himself or for any other person—

(a)   makes a statement which he knows to be false in a material particular; or

(b)   recklessly makes a statement which is false in a material particular,

he shall be liable on summary conviction to a fine not exceeding level 4 on the standard scale.

Section 157   SCHEDULE 8   INCREASE IN PENALTIES

PART I   INCREASE OF FINES FOR CERTAIN SEA FISHERIES OFFENCES

(1) Enactment creating offence	(2) Penalty enactment	(3) Old maximum fine	(4) New maximum fine
SEA FISHERIES (SHELLFISH) ACT 1967 (c. 83).			
Offences under section 3(3) (dredging etc. for shellfish in contravention of restrictions etc. or without paying toll or royalty).	Section 3(3).	Level 2.	Level 5.
Offences under section 5(7) (obstruction of inspector or other person or refusal or failure to provide information to inspector etc.).	Section 5(7).	Level 3.	Level 5.
Offences under section 7(4) (fishing, dredging etc. in area where right of several fishery conferred or private oyster bed).	Section 7(4).	Level 3.	Level 5.
Offences under section 14(2) (contravention of order prohibiting the deposit or taking of shellfish, or importation of shellfish, or non-compliance with conditions of licences).	Section 14(2).	Level 4.	Level 5.
Offences under section 14(5) (obstruction of inspector).	Section 14(5).	Level 3.	Level 5.
Offences under section 16(1) (selling etc. of oysters between certain dates).	Section 16(1).	Level 1.	Level 4.
Offences under section 17(1) (taking and selling etc. of certain crabs).	Section 17(4).	Level 3.	Level 5.
Offences under section 17(3) (landing and selling etc. of certain lobsters).	Section 17(4).	Level 3.	Level 5.

PART II INCREASE OF FINES FOR CERTAIN MISUSE OF DRUGS OFFENCES

(1) Enactment creating offence	(2) Penalty enactment	(3) Old maximum fine	(4) New maximum fine
MISUSE OF DRUGS ACT 1971 (c. 38.)			
Offences under section 4(2) committed in relation to Class C drugs (production, or being concerned in the production of, a controlled drug).	Schedule 4, column 6.	£500	£2,500
Offences under section 4(3) committed in relation to Class C drugs (supplying or offering to supply a controlled drug or being concerned in the doing of either activity by another).	Schedule 4, column 6.	£500	£2,500
Offences under section 5(2) committed in relation to Class B drugs (having possession of a controlled drug).	Schedule 4, column 5.	£500	£2,500
Offences under section 5(2) committed in relation to Class C drugs (having possession of a controlled drug).	Schedule 4, column 6.	£200	£1,000
Offences under section 5(3) committed in relation to Class C drugs (having possession of a controlled drug with intent to supply it to another).	Schedule 4, column 6.	£500	£2,500
Offences under section 8 committed in relation to Class C drugs (being the occupier, or concerned in the management, of premises and permitting or suffering certain activities to take place there).	Schedule 4, column 6.	£500	£2,500
Offences under section 12(6) committed in relation to Class C drugs (contravention of direction prohibiting practitioner etc. from possessing, supplying etc. controlled drugs).	Schedule 4, column 6.	£500	£2,500
Offences under section 13(3) committed in relation to Class C drugs (contravention of direction prohibiting practitioner etc. from prescribing, supplying etc. controlled drugs).	Schedule 4, column 6.	£500	£2,500

PART III   INCREASE IN PENALTIES FOR CERTAIN FIREARMS OFFENCES

(1) *Enactment creating offence*	(2) *Penalty enactment*	(3) *Old maximum term of imprisonment*	(4) *New maximum term of imprisonment*
FIREARMS ACT 1968 (c.27).			
Offences under section 1(1) committed in an aggravated form within the meaning of section 4(4) (possessing etc. shortened shot gun or converted firearm without firearm certificate).	Schedule 6, column 4.	5 years.	7 years.
Offences under section 1(1) in any other case (possessing etc. firearms or ammunition without firearm certificate).	Schedule 6, column 4.	3 years.	5 years.
Offences under section 2(1) (possessing etc. shot gun without shot gun certificate).	Schedule 6, column 4.	3 years.	5 years.
Offences under section 3(1) (trading in firearms without being registered as a firearms dealer).	Schedule 6, column 4.	3 years.	5 years.
Offences under section 3(2) (selling firearms to person without a certificate).	Schedule 6, column 4.	3 years.	5 years.
Offences under section 3(3) (repairing, testing etc. firearm for person without a certificate).	Schedule 6, column 4.	3 years.	5 years.
Offences under section 3(5) (falsifying certificate, etc., with view to acquisition of firearm).	Schedule 6, column 4.	3 years.	5 years.
Offences under section 4(1) (shortening a shot gun).	Schedule 6, column 4.	5 years.	7 years.
Offences under section 4(3) (conversion of firearms).	Schedule 6, column 4.	5 years.	7 years.
Offences under section 5(1) (possessing or distributing prohibited weapons or ammunition).	Schedule 6, column 4	5 years.	10 years.

(1) Enactment creating offence	(2) Penalty enactment	(3) Old maximum term of imprisonment	(4) New maximum term of imprisonment
Offences under section 5(1A) (possessing or distributing other prohibited weapons).	Schedule 6, column 4.	(a) On summary conviction, 3 months. (b) On conviction on indictment, 2 years.	(a) On summary conviction, 6 months. (b) On conviction on indictment, 10 years.
Offences under section 19 (carrying loaded firearm other than air weapon in public place).	Schedule 6, column 4.	5 years.	7 years.
Offences under section 20(1) (trespassing with firearm other than air weapon in a building).	Schedule 6, column 4.	5 years.	7 years.
Offences under section 21(4) (contravention of provisions denying firearms to ex-prisoners and the like).	Schedule 6, column 4	3 years.	5 years.
Offences under section 21(5) (supplying firearms to person denied them under section 21).	Schedule 6, column 4.	3 years.	5 years.
Offences under section 42 (failure to comply with instructions in firearm certificate when transferring firearm to person other than registered dealer; failure to report transaction to police).	Schedule 6, column 4.	3 years.	5 years.
FIREARMS (NORTHERN IRELAND) ORDER 1981 (SI 1981/155 (NI 2))			
Offences under Article 3(1) (possessing etc. firearms or ammunition without firearm certificate).	Schedule 2, column 4	3 years.	5 years.
Offences under Article 4(1) (trading in firearms without being registered as a firearms dealer).	Schedule 2, column 4.	3 years.	5 years.
Offences under Article 4(2) (selling firearms to person without a certificate).	Schedule 2, column 4.	3 years.	5 years.

(1) Enactment creating offence	(2) Penalty enactment	(3) Old maximum term of imprisonment	(4) New maximum term of imprisonment
Offences under Article 4(3) (repairing, testing etc. firearm for person without a certificate).	Schedule 2, column 4.	3 years.	5 years.
Offences under Article 4(4) (falsifying certificate, etc., with view to acquisition of firearm).	Schedule 2, column 4.	3 years.	5 years.
Offences under Article 5(1) (shortening a shot gun).	Schedule 2, column 4.	5 years.	7 years.
Offences under Article 5(3) (conversion of firearms).	Schedule 2, column 4.	5 years.	7 years.
Offences under Article 6(1) (possessing or distributing prohibited weapons or ammunition).	Schedule 2, column 4.	5 years.	10 years.
Offences under Article 6(1A) (possessing or distributing other prohibited weapons).	Schedule 2, column 4.	(a) On summary conviction, 3 months. (b) On conviction on indictment, 2 years.	(a) On summary conviction, 6 months. (b) On conviction on indictment, 10 years.
Offences under Article 22(5) (contravention of provisions denying firearms to ex-prisoners and the like).	Schedule 2, column 4.	3 years.	5 years.
Offences under Article 22(7) (supplying firearms to person denied them under Article 22).	Schedule 2, column 4.	3 years.	5 years.
Offences under Article 43 (failure to comply with instructions in firearm certificate when transferring firearm to person other than registered dealer; failure to report transaction to police).	Schedule 2, column 4	3 years.	5 years.

Section 168(1)   SCHEDULE 9   MINOR AMENDMENTS

Poaching: increase in penalties

1.—(1) The Game Act 1831 shall be amended as follows.

(2) In section 30 (trespassing in search or pursuit of game)—
    (a) for the words 'level 1' there shall be substituted the words 'level 3'; and
    (b) for the words 'level 3' there shall be substituted the words 'level 4'.

(3) In section 32 (searching for or pursuing game with a gun and using violence, etc.), for the words 'level 4' there shall be substituted the words 'level 5'.

(4) The Game (Scotland) Act 1832 shall be amended as follows.

(5) In section 1 (trespassing in search or pursuit of game)—
    (a) for the words 'level 1' there shall be substituted the words 'level 3'; and
    (b) for the words 'level 3' there shall be substituted the words 'level 4'.

(6) In section 6 (penalty for assaults on persons acting under the Act), for the words 'level 1' there shall be substituted the words 'level 3'.

(7) The amendments made by this paragraph shall not apply to offences committed before this paragraph comes into force.

Sexual offences: procurement of women

2. In sections 2(1) and 3(1) of the Sexual Offences Act 1956 (procurement of women to have unlawful sexual intercourse by threats or false pretences), the word 'unlawful' shall be omitted.

Electronic transmission of obscene material

3. In section 1(3) of the Obscene Publications Act 1959 (definition of publication for purposes of that Act), in paragraph (b), after the words 'projects it' there shall be inserted the words ', or, where the matter is data stored electronically, transmits that data.'.

Poaching: forfeiture of vehicles

4. After section 4 of the Game Laws (Amendment) Act 1960 there shall be inserted the following section—

    '4A.   Forfeiture of vehicles

    (1) Where a person is convicted of an offence under section thirty of the Game Act 1831 as one of five or more persons liable under that section and the court is satisfied that any vehicle belonging to him or in his possession or under his control at the relevant time has been used for the purpose of committing or facilitating the commission of the offence, the court may make an order for forfeiture under this subsection in respect of that vehicle.

    (2) The court may make an order under subsection (1) above whether or not it also deals with the offender in respect of the offence in any other way and without regard to any restriction on forfeiture in any enactment.

    (3) Facilitating the commission of the offence shall be taken for the purposes of subsection (1) above to include the taking of any steps after it has been committed for the purpose of—
      (a) avoiding apprehension or detection; or
      (b) removing from the land any person or property connected with the offence.

(4)   An order under subsection (1) above shall operate to deprive the offender of his rights, if any, in the vehicle to which it relates, and the vehicle shall (if not already in their possession) be taken into the possession of the police.

(5)   Where any vehicle has been forfeited under subsection (1) above, a magistrates' court may, on application by a claimant of the vehicle, other than the offender from whom it was forfeited under subsection (1) above, make an order for delivery of the vehicle to.the applicant if it appears to the court that he is the owner of the vehicle.

(6)   No application shall be made under subsection (5) above by any claimant of the vehicle after the expiration of six months from the date on which an order in respect of the vehicle was made under subsection (1) above.

(7)   No such application shall succeed unless the claimant satisfies the court either that he had not consented to the offender having possession of the vehicle or that he did not know, and had no reason to suspect, that the vehicle was likely to be used for a purpose mentioned in subsection (1) above.

(8)   An order under subsection (5) above shall not affect the right of any person to take, within the period of six months from the date of an order under subsection (5) above, proceedings for the recovery of the vehicle from the person in possession of it in pursuance of the order, but on the expiration of that period the right shall cease.

(9)   The Secretary of State may make regulations for the disposal of vehicles, and for the application of the proceeds of sale of vehicles, forfeited under subsection (1) above where no application by a claimant of the property under subsection (5) above has been made within the period specified in subsection (6) above or no such application has succeeded.

(10)   The regulations may also provide for the investment of money and the audit of accounts.

(11)   The power to make regulations under subsection (9) above shall be exercisable by statutory instrument which shall be subject to annulment in pursuance of a resolution of either House of Parliament.

(12)   In this section, 'relevant time', in relation to a person convicted of an offence such as is mentioned in subsection (1) above, means the time when the vehicle was used for the purpose of committing or facilitating the commission of the offence, or the time of the issue of a summons in respect of the offence.'.

Magistrates' courts'jurisdiction in cases involving children and young persons

5.   In section 18 of the Children and Young Persons Act 1963 (jurisdiction of magistrates' courts in certain cases involving children and young persons)—

(a)   in paragraph (a), for the words 'the age of seventeen' there shall be substituted the words 'the age of eighteen'; and

(b)   in paragraph (b), for the words 'the age of seventeen' there shall be substituted the words 'the age of eighteen'.

Service of documents by first class post

6.—(1)   In section 9(8) of the Criminal Justice Act 1967 (which relates to the service of a written statement to be admitted as evidence in criminal proceedings)—

(a)   in paragraph (c), after the word 'service' there shall be inserted the words 'or by first class post'; and

(b)   in paragraph (d), after the word 'service' there shall be inserted the words 'or by first class post'.

(2)   In section 11(7) of the Criminal Justice Act 1967 (which provides for the means by which a notice of alibi may be given), after the word 'service' there shall be inserted the words 'or by first class post'.

(3)   In section 1 of the Road Traffic Offenders Act 1988 (which requires warning of prosecution for certain offences to be given), after subsection (1), there shall be inserted the following subsection—

'(1A)   A notice required by this section to be served on any person may be served on that person—

(a)   by delivering it to him;

(b)   by addressing it to him and leaving it at his last known address; or

(c)   by sending it by registered post, recorded delivery service or first class post addressed to him at his last known address.'.

Transfers of proceedings

7.   In section 11 of the Criminal Justice Act 1967 (notice of alibi), in subsection (8)—

(a)   in the definition of 'the prescribed period' (as amended by paragraph 2 of Schedule 2 to the Criminal Justice Act 1987), for the words 'section 4 of the Criminal Justice Act 1987' there shall be substituted the words 'a relevant transfer provision'; and

(b)   after that definition there shall be inserted the following definition—

'"relevant transfer provision" means—

(a)   section 4 of the Criminal Justice Act 1987; or

(b)   section 53 of the Criminal Justice Act 1991.'.

Offences aggravated by possession of firearms

8.   In Schedule 1 to the Firearms Act 1968 (which lists the offences to which section 17(2) (possession of firearms when committing or being arrested for specified offences) relates)—

(a)   in paragraph 4, after the word 'Theft' there shall be inserted the word 'robbery'; and

(b)   after paragraph 5, there shall be inserted the following paragraphs—

'5A.   An offence under section 90(1) of the Criminal Justice Act 1991 (assaulting prisoner custody officer).

5B.   An offence under section 13(1) of the Criminal Justice and Public Order Act 1994 (assaulting secure training centre custody officer).'.

Notice of proceedings

9.   In section 34(2) of the Children and Young Persons Act 1969 (which requires notice of certain proceedings to be given to a probation officer), for the words 'the age of seventeen' there shall be substituted the words 'the age of eighteen'.

Treatment of mental condition of offenders placed on probation

10.—(1)   Paragraph 5 of Schedule 1A to the Powers of Criminal Courts Act 1973 (requirement in probation order for treatment of offender's mental condition) shall be amended as follows.

(2)   In sub-paragraph (2)—

(a)   after the words 'such part' there shall be inserted the words 'or parts'; and

(b)   after the words 'medical practitioner' there shall be inserted the words 'or a chartered psychologist (or both, for different parts)'.

(3)   In sub-paragraph (3)(c), after the words 'medical practitioner' there shall be inserted the words 'or chartered psychologist (or both)'.

(4)   In sub-paragraphs (6) and (8), after the words 'medical practitioner' (wherever they occur) there shall be inserted the words 'or chartered psychologist'.

(5)   In sub-paragraph (10), after the words 'In this paragraph' there shall be inserted the words '—

'chartered psychologist' means a person for the time being listed in the British Psychological Society's Register of Chartered Psychologists; and'.

Rehabilitation of offenders placed on probation

11.—(1)   In section 5 of the Rehabilitation of Offenders Act 1974 (rehabilitation periods for particular sentences)—

(a)   in Table A in subsection (2), in the entry relating to fines or other sentences subject to rehabilitation under that Act, after the words ,'subsections (3)' there shall be inserted the words ', (4A)'.

(b)   in subsection (4), the words 'or placed on probation,' and 'or probation order' shall be omitted; and

(c)   after subsection (4), there shall be inserted the following subsection—

'(4A)   Where in respect of a conviction a person was placed on probation, the rehabilitation period applicable to the sentence shall be—

(a)   in the case of a person aged eighteen years or over at the date of his conviction, five years from the date of conviction;

(b)   in the case of a person aged under the age of eighteen years at the date of his conviction, two and a half years from the date of conviction or a period beginning with the date of conviction and ending when the probation order ceases or ceased to have effect, whichever is the longer.'.

(2)   The amendments made by this paragraph shall apply only in relation to persons placed on probation after the date on which this paragraph comes into force.

Transfers of proceedings

12.   In section 3 of the Bail Act 1976 (general provisions)—

(a)   in subsection (8A) (inserted by paragraph 9 of Schedule 2 to the Criminal Justice Act 1987), for the words 'section 4 of the Criminal Justice Act 1987' there shall be substituted the words 'a relevant transfer provision'; and

(b)   after subsection (9) there shall be inserted the following subsection—

'(10)   In subsection (8A) above 'relevant transfer provision' means—

(a)   section 4 of the Criminal Justice Act 1987, or

(b)   section 53 of the Criminal Justice Act 1991.'.

Anonymity of victims of certain offences

13.   In section 4 of the Sexual Offences (Amendment) Act 1976 (anonymity of victims in rape etc. cases), after subsection (6) there shall be inserted the following subsection—

'(6A) For the purposes of this section, where it is alleged or there is an accusation that an offence of incitement to rape or conspiracy to rape has been committed, the person who is alleged to have been the intended victim of the rape shall be regarded as the alleged victim of the incitement or conspiracy or, in the case of an accusation, as the complainant.'.

Execution of warrants for non-payment

14.—(1) In section 38A(6) of the Criminal Law Act 1977 (execution of warrants for imprisonment for non-payment of fine), for the words 'the age of 17 years' there shall be substituted the words 'the age of 18 years'.

(2) In section 38B(6) of the Criminal Law Act 1977 (execution of warrants for commitment for non-payment of due sum), for the words 'the age of 17 years' there shall be substituted the words 'the age of 18 years'.

Committals for sentence

15. In section 38 of the Magistrates' Courts Act 1980 (power of magistrates' court to commit offender to Crown Court for sentence), in subsection (2)(b)—

(a) the words from 'committed' to '21 years old' shall be omitted; and

(b) for the words 'sentence of imprisonment' there shall be substituted the words 'custodial sentence'.

Conditional or absolute discharge: appeal to Crown Court

16. In section 108(1A) of the Magistrates' Courts Act 1980 (right of appeal to Crown Court in case of conditional or absolute discharge), for the words 'Section 13' there shall be substituted the words 'Section 1C'.

Transfers of proceedings

17. In section 76 of the Supreme Court Act 1981 (alteration by Crown Court of place of trial) (as amended by paragraph 10 of Schedule 2 to the Criminal Justice Act 1987)—

(a) in subsection (1), for the words 'section 4 of the Criminal Justice Act 1987' there shall be substituted the words 'a relevant transfer provision';

(b) in subsection (3), for the words 'section 4 of the Criminal Justice Act 1987' there shall be substituted the words 'a relevant transfer provision'; and

(c) after subsection (4) there shall be inserted the following subsection—

'(5) In this section 'relevant transfer provision' means—

(a) section 4 of the Criminal Justice Act 1987, or

(b) section 53 of the Criminal Justice Act 1991.'.

The amendments made by this paragraph shall cease to have effect on the coming into force of the amendments made by paragraph 51 of Schedule 4 to this Act.

Transfers of proceedings

18. In section 77 of the Supreme Court Act 1981 (date of trial) (as amended by paragraph 11 of Schedule 2 to the Criminal Justice Act 1987)—

(a) in subsection (1), for the words 'section 4 of the Criminal Justice Act 1987' there shall be substituted the words 'a relevant transfer provision';

(b) in subsection (2), after the words 'committed by a magistrates' court' there shall be inserted the words 'or in respect of whom a notice of transfer under a relevant transfer provision has been given';

(c)   in subsection (3), after the words 'committal for trial' there shall be inserted the words 'or of a notice of transfer'; and
    (d)   after subsection (3), there shall be inserted the following subsection—
        '(4)   In this section 'relevant transfer provision' means—
          (a)   section 4 of the Criminal Justice Act 1987, or
          (b)   section 53 of the Criminal Justice Act 1991.'.
The amendments made by this paragraph shall cease to have effect on the coming into force of the amendments made by paragraph 52 of Schedule 4 to this Act.

Transfers of proceedings

19.   In section 81 of the Supreme Court Act 1981 (bail by Crown Court)—
    (a)   in subsection (1)(a) (as amended by paragraph 12 of Schedule 2 to the Criminal Justice Act 1987), for the words 'section 4 of the Criminal Justice Act 1987' there shall be substituted the words 'a relevant transfer provision'; and
    (b)   after subsection (6), there shall be inserted the following subsection—
        '(7)   In subsection (1) above 'relevant transfer provision' means—
          (a)   section 4 of the Criminal Justice Act 1987, or
          (b)   section 53 of the Criminal Justice Act 1991.'.

Electronic transmission of obscene material (Scotland)

20.   In section 51(8) of the Civic Government (Scotland) Act 1982, after the words 'otherwise reproducing' there shall be inserted the words ', or, where the material is data stored electronically, transmitting that data'.

Fines for breach of attendance centre orders or rules

21.   In section 19 of the Criminal Justice Act 1982 (breach of attendance centre orders or rules), for the subsection (3A) inserted by section 67(5) of the Criminal Justice Act 1991 there shall be substituted the following subsection—
        '(3A)   A fine imposed under subsection (3) above shall be deemed, for the purposes of any enactment, to be a sum adjudged to be paid by a conviction.'.

Video recordings

22.   In section 1 of the Video Recordings Act 1984 (which provides for the interpretation of, among other terms, 'video work' and 'video recordings')—
    (a)   in subsection (2), in paragraph (a), the word 'or' before the words 'magnetic tape' shall be omitted and after those words there shall be inserted the words 'or any other device capable of storing data electronically'; and
    (b)   in subsection (3), the word 'or' before the words 'magnetic tape' shall be omitted and after those words there shall be inserted the words 'or any other device capable of storing data electronically'.

Standard period of validity of search warrants

23.   In the following enactments there shall be omitted the words from 'within' to 'warrant' (which prescribe the period of validity of warrants under those enactments for which section 16(3) of the Police and Criminal Evidence Act 1984 prescribes a standard period of one month), namely—
    (a)   section 4(2) of the Protection of Children Act 1978; and
    (b)   section 17(1) of the Video Recordings Act 1984.

Transfers of proceedings

24. In section 62(10) of the Police and Criminal Evidence Act 1984 (power of court to draw inferences from failure of accused to consent to provide intimate sample), after paragraph (a) there shall be inserted the following paragraph—

'(aa) a judge, in deciding whether to grant an application made by the accused under—

(i) section 6 of the Criminal Justice Act 1987 (application for dismissal of charge of serious fraud in respect of which notice of transfer has been given under section 4 of that Act); or

(ii) paragraph 5 of Schedule 6 to the Criminal Justice Act 1991 (application for dismissal of charge of violent or sexual offence involving child in respect of which notice of transfer has been given under section 53 of that Act); and'.

Transfers of proceedings

25. In section 16 of the Prosecution of Offences Act 1985 (defence costs)—

(a) in subsection (2)(aa) (inserted by paragraph 14 of Schedule 2 to the Criminal Justice Act 1987), for the words 'section 4 of the Criminal Justice Act 1987' there shall be substituted the words 'a relevant transfer provision'; and

(b) after subsection (I 1) there shall be inserted the following subsection—

'(12) In subsection (2)(aa) 'relevant transfer provision' means—

(a) section 4 of the Criminal Justice Act 1987, or

(b) section 53 of the Criminal Justice Act 1991.'.

Award of costs against accused

26. In section 18(5) of the Prosecution of Offences Act 1985 (award of costs against accused), for the words 'the age of seventeen' there shall be substituted the words 'the age of eighteen'.

Transfers of proceedings

27. In section 22 of the Prosecution of Offences Act 1985 (time limits for preliminary stages of criminal proceedings), in subsection (11), in the definition of 'custody of the Crown Court', after paragraph (c) (inserted by paragraph 104 of Schedule 15 to the Criminal Justice Act 1988), there shall be inserted the following paragraph, preceded by the word ', or', namely—

'(d) paragraph 2(1)(a) of Schedule 6 to the Criminal Justice Act 1991 (custody after transfer order in certain cases involving children).'.

Confiscation orders in drug trafficking cases: variation of sentences

28. In section 1A of the Drug Trafficking Offences Act 1986 (inserted by section 8 of the Criminal Justice Act 1993) (power of court to postpone determinations required before a confiscation order can be made), after subsection (9) there shall be inserted the following subsection—

'(9A) Where the court has sentenced the defendant under subsection (7) above during the specified period it may, after the end of that period, vary the sentence by imposing a fine or making any such order as is mentioned in section 1(5)(b)(ii) or (iii) of this Act so long as it does so within a period corresponding to that allowed by section 47(2) or (3) of the Supreme Court Act 1981 (time allowed for varying a sentence) but beginning with the end of the specified period.'.

Transfer of fraud cases

29.   In section 4 of the Criminal Justice Act 1987 (transfer of certain fraud cases to Crown Court), in subsection (1)(b)(ii), for the words 'seriousness and complexity' there shall be substituted the words 'seriousness or complexity'.

Fraud cases: preparatory hearings

30.   In section 7 of the Criminal Justice Act 1987 (preparatory hearings for certain fraud cases), in subsection (1), for the words 'seriousness and complexity' there shall be substituted the words 'seriousness or complexity'.

Transfers of proceedings

31.   In section 25(1) of the Criminal Justice Act 1988 (principle to be followed by court in certain proceedings), in paragraph (a), after head (iii) there shall be inserted the following—

'(iv)   on the hearing of an application under paragraph 5 of Schedule 6 to the Criminal Justice Act 1991 (applications for dismissal of charges in certain cases involving children transferred from magistrates' court to Crown Court); or'.

Evidence through television links

32.   In section 32 of the Criminal Justice Act 1988 (evidence through television links), in subsection (3B) (inserted by section 55(4) of the Criminal Justice Act 1991), for the words 'subsection (3) above' there shall be substituted the words 'subsection (3A) above'.

Competence of children

33.   In section 33A of the Criminal Justice Act 1988 (inserted by section 52(1) of the Criminal Justice Act 1991), after subsection (2) there shall be inserted the following subsection—

'(2A)   A child's evidence shall be received unless it appears to the court that the child is incapable of giving intelligible testimony.'.

Reviews of sentencing

34.   In section 35 of the Criminal Justice Act 1988 (kinds of case referable for review of sentence)—

(a)   in subsection (3), for the words following 'case' there shall be substituted the following words—

'—
(a)   of a description specified in an order under this section; or
(b)   in which sentence is passed on a person—
(i)   for an offence triable only on indictment; or
(ii)   for an offence of a description specified in an order under this section'; and

(b)   in subsection (4), after the word 'case', there shall be inserted the words 'of a description specified in the order or to any case'.

Assaulting prisoner custody officer triable with indictable offence

35.   In section 40(3) of the Criminal Justice Act 1988 (summary offences triable with indictable offences), after paragraph (a), there shall be inserted the following paragraphs—

'(aa)   an offence under section 90(1) of the Criminal Justice Act 1991 (assaulting a prisoner custody officer);

(ab)   an offence under section 13(1) of the Criminal Justice and Public Order Act 1994 (assaulting a secure training centre custody officer)'.

Confiscation orders: variation of sentence

36.   In section 72A of the Criminal Justice Act 1988 (inserted by section 28 of the Criminal Justice Act 1993) (power of court to postpone determinations required before a confiscation order can be made), after subsection (9) there shall be inserted the following subsection—

'(9A)   Where the court has sentenced the defendant under subsection (7) above during the specified period it may, after the end of that period, vary the sentence by imposing a fine or making any such order as is mentioned in section 72(5)(b) or (c) above so long as it does so within a period corresponding to that allowed by section 47(2) or (3) of the Supreme Court Act 1981 (time allowed for varying a sentence) but beginning with the end of the specified period.'.

Extradition from the United Kingdom

37.—(1)   The Extradition Act 1989 shall be amended as follows.

(2)   In section 2(4) (law of, and conduct in, parts or dependencies of foreign States)—

(a)   for the words 'subsections (1) to (3) above' there shall be substituted the words 'this Act, except Schedule 1'; and

(b)   at the end there shall be inserted the following paragraph preceded by the word '; but'—

'(d)   reference shall be made to the law of the colony or dependency of a foreign state or of a designated Commonwealth country, and not (where different) to the law of the foreign state or Commonwealth country, to determine the level of punishment applicable to conduct in that colony or dependency.'.

(3)   In section 7 (procedure for making and implementing extradition requests)—

(a)   in subsection (1)—

(i)   after the word 'made' there shall be inserted the words 'to the Secretary of State';

(ii)   for paragraph (a) there shall be substituted the following paragraph—

'(a)   by—

(i)   an authority in a foreign state which appears to the Secretary of State to have the function of making extradition requests in that foreign state, or

(ii)   some person recognised by the Secretary of State as a diplomatic or consular representative of a foreign state; or' and

(iii)   after paragraph (b), there shall be inserted the words—

'and an extradition request may be made by facsimile transmission and an authority to proceed issued without waiting to receive the original';

(b)   in subsection (2)—
(i)   in paragraph (c), after the word 'warrant' there shall be inserted the words 'or a duly authenticated copy of a warrant'; and
(ii)   in paragraph (d), after the word 'certificate' there shall be inserted the words 'or a duly authenticated copy of a certificate'; and
(c)   after subsection (6), there shall be inserted the following subsection—
'(7)   Where an extradition request is made by facsimile transmission this Act (including subsection (2) above) shall have effect as if the foreign documents so sent were the originals used to make the transmission and receivable in evidence accordingly.'.

Remands and committals of young persons to secure accommodation

38.   In section 21 of the Children Act 1989 (provision of accommodation for children on remand, etc.), in subsection (2)(c)(i), after the words 'on remand' there shall be inserted the words '(within the meaning of the section)'.

Non-intimate samples: samples of hair

39.   In Article 63 of the Police and Criminal Evidence (Northern Ireland) Order 1989 (regulation of taking of non-intimate samples), at the end, there shall be inserted the following paragraph—
'(10)   Where a sample of hair other than pubic hair is to be taken the sample may be taken either by cutting hairs or by plucking hairs with their roots so long as no more are plucked than the person taking the sample reasonably considers to be necessary (in point of quantity or quality) for the purpose of enabling information to be produced by means of analysis used or to be used in relation to the sample.'.

Pre-sentence reports

40.—(1)   The Criminal Justice Act 1991 shall be amended as follows.
(2)   In section 3 (requirement to obtain pre-sentence reports before passing custodial sentences)—
(a)   in subsection (2), the words from the beginning to 'indictment,' shall be omitted;
(b)   after subsection (2), there shall be inserted the following subsection—
'(2A)   In the case of an offender under the age of eighteen years, save where the offence or any other offence associated with it is triable only on indictment, the court shall not form such an opinion as is mentioned in subsection (2) above or subsection (4A) below unless there exists a previous pre-sentence report obtained in respect of the offender and the court has had regard to the information contained in that report, or, if there is more than one such report, the most recent report.';
(c)   in subsection (4)—
(i)   the words from 'which is' to 'applies' shall be omitted;
(ii)   for the words 'comply with that subsection' there shall be substituted the words 'obtain and consider a pre-sentence report before forming an opinion referred to in subsection (1) above'; and
(iii)   in paragraph (a), after the word 'shall' there shall be inserted the words ', subject to subsection (4A) below,'; and

(d)   after subsection (4) there shall be inserted the following subsection—

'(4A)   Subsection (4)(a) above does not apply if the court is of the opinion—

(a)   that the court below was justified in forming an opinion that it was unnecessary to obtain a pre-sentence report, or

(b)   that, although the court below was not justified in forming that opinion, in the circumstances of the case at the time it is before the court, it is unnecessary to obtain a pre-sentence report.'.

(3)   In section 7 (requirement to obtain pre-sentence reports before passing certain community sentences)—

(a)   in subsection (3), at the beginning, there shall be inserted the words 'Subject to subsection (3A) below,';

(b)   after subsection (3), there shall be inserted the following subsections—

'(3A)   Subsection (3) above does not apply if, in the circumstances of the case, the court is of the opinion that it is unnecessary to obtain a pre-sentence report.

(3B)   In the case of an offender under the age of eighteen years, save where the offence or any other offence associated with it is triable only on indictment, the court shall not form such an opinion as is mentioned in subsection (3A) above or subsection (5) below unless there exists a previous pre-sentence report obtained in respect of the offender and the court has had regard to the information contained in that report, or, if there is more than one such report, the most recent report.';

(c)   in subsection (4)—

(i)   for the words 'comply with' there shall be substituted the words 'obtain and consider a pre-sentence report before forming an opinion referred to in'; and

(ii)   in paragraph (a), after the word 'shall' there shall be inserted the words ', subject to subsection (5) below,';

(d)   after subsection (4) there shall be inserted the following subsection—

'(5)   Subsection (4)(a) above does not apply if the court is of the opinion—

(a)   that the court below was justified in forming an opinion that it was unnecessary to obtain a pre-sentence report, or

(b)   that, although the court below was not justified in forming that opinion, in the circumstances of the case at the time it is before the court, it is unnecessary to obtain a pre-sentence report.'.

Curfew orders

41.   In section 12 of the Criminal Justice Act 1991 (curfew orders) after subsection (4) there shall be inserted the following subsection—

'(4A)   A court shall not make a curfew order unless the court has been notified by the Secretary of State that arrangements for monitoring the offender's whereabouts are available in the area in which the place proposed to be specified in the order is situated and the notice has not been withdrawn.'.

Fines

42.—(1)   Sections 18 and 20 of the Criminal Justice Act 1991 (which relate respectively to the fixing of fines and financial circumstances orders) shall be amended as provided in sub-paragraphs (2) and (3) below.

(2)   In section 18—

(a)   for subsection (1), there shall be substituted the following subsection—
  '(1)   Before fixing the amount of any fine to be imposed on an offender who is an individual, a court shall inquire into his financial circumstances.'; and

(b)   in subsection (3), after the word 'fine' there shall be inserted the words 'to be imposed on an offender (whether an individual or other person)'.

(3)   In section 20, in subsections (1), (1A), (1B), (1C), (2) and (3) for the words 'a person' and 'any person' there shall be substituted the words 'an individual' and 'any individual'.

(4)   In section 57(4) of that Act (application to local authorities of power to order fines to be paid by a parent or guardian), paragraph (b) shall be omitted.

(5)   The amendments made by this paragraph apply in relation to offenders convicted (but not sentenced) before the date on which this paragraph comes into force as they apply in relation to offenders convicted after that date.

False statements as to financial circumstances

43.   After section 20 of the Criminal Justice Act 1991 there shall be inserted the following section—

'20A.   False statements as to financial circumstances

(1)   A person who is charged with an offence who, in furnishing a statement of his financial circumstances in response to an official request—

(a)   makes a statement which he knows to be false in a material particular;

(b)   recklessly furnishes a statement which is false in a material particular; or

(c)   knowingly fails to disclose any material fact,

shall be liable on summary conviction to imprisonment for a term not exceeding three months or a fine not exceeding level 4 on the standard scale or both.

(2)   For the purposes of this section an official request is a request which—

(a)   is made by the clerk of the magistrates' court or the appropriate officer of the Crown Court, as the case may be; and

(b)   is expressed to be made for informing the court, in the event of his being convicted, of his financial circumstances for the purpose of determining the amount of any fine the court may impose.

(3)   Proceedings in respect of an offence under this section may, notwithstanding anything in section 127(1) of the 1980 Act (limitation of time), be commenced at any time within two years from the date of the commission of the offence or within six months from its first discovery by the prosecutor, whichever period expires the earlier.'.

Effect of previous probation orders and discharges

44.—(1)   Section 29 of the Criminal Justice Act 1991 (as substituted by section 66(6) of the Criminal Justice Act 1993) (effect of previous convictions and offending while on bail and treatment of certain orders as sentences and convictions) shall be amended as follows.

(2)   In subsection (4), for the words 'conditional discharge order' there shall be substituted the words 'an order discharging the offender absolutely or conditionally'.

(3)   After subsection (4) there shall be inserted the following subsections—
  '(5)   A conditional discharge order made after 30th September 1992 (which, by virtue of section 1A of the Powers of Criminal Courts Act 1973, would

otherwise not be a sentence for the purposes of this section) is to be treated as a sentence for those purposes.

(6) A conviction in respect of which an order discharging the offender absolutely or conditionally was made after 30th September 1992 (which, by virtue of section 1C of the Powers of Criminal Courts Act 1973, would otherwise not be a conviction for those purposes) is to be treated as a conviction for those purposes.'.

(4) The amendments made by this paragraph shall apply in relation to offenders convicted (but not sentenced) before the date on which this paragraph comes into force as they apply in relation to offenders convicted after that date.

Sexual offences

45.—(1) In section 31(1) of the Criminal Justice Act 1991 (which defines, amongst other expressions, 'sexual offence'), for that definition, there shall be substituted the following definition—

'"sexual offence" means any of the following—

(a) an offence under the Sexual Offences Act 1956, other than an offence under section 30, 31 or 33 to 36 of that Act;

(b) an offence under section 128 of the Mental Health Act 1959;

(c) an offence under the Indecency with Children Act 1960;

(d) an offence under section 9 of the Theft Act 1968 of burglary with intent to commit rape;

(e) an offence under section 54 of the Criminal Law Act 1977;

(f) an offence under the Protection of Children Act 1978;

(g) an offence under section 1 of the Criminal Law Act 1977 of conspiracy to commit any of the offences in paragraphs (a) to (f) above;

(h) an offence under section 1 of the Criminal Attempts Act 1981 of attempting to commit any of those offences;

(i) an offence of inciting another to commit any of those offences;'.

(2) The amendment made by this paragraph shall apply in relation to offenders convicted (but not sentenced) before the date on which this paragraph comes into force as it applies in relation to offenders convicted after that date.

Discretionary life prisoners

46.—(1) In section 34 of the Criminal Justice Act 1991 (duty to release discretionary life prisoners after they have served the relevant part of their sentence and the Parole Board has directed their release)—

(a) in subsection (6), for the words after 'sentence' there shall be substituted the following words—

(a) account shall be taken of any corresponding relevant period; but

(b) no account shall be taken of any time during which the prisoner was unlawfully at large within the meaning of section 49 of the Prison Act 1952 ('the 1952 Act').'; and

(b) after that subsection, there shall be inserted the following subsection—

'(6A) In subsection (6)(a) above, 'corresponding relevant period' means the period corresponding to the period by which a determinate sentence of imprisonment imposed on the offender would fall to be reduced under section 67 of the Criminal Justice Act 1967 (reduction of sentences to take account of police detention or remands in custody).'.

(2)   In paragraph 9(2) of Schedule 12 to that Act (application of early release provisions of the Act to existing life prisoners), after paragraph (b) there shall be inserted the following paragraph, preceded by the word 'and'—

'(c)   in section 34 of this Act, paragraph (a) of subsection (6) and subsection (6A) were omitted.'.

Committals for sentence

47.   In section 40(3) of the Criminal Justice Act 1991 (power of magistrates' court to commit offender convicted of new offence during currency of previous sentence to Crown Court for sentence), in paragraph (b), for the words from 'in accordance with' to the end there shall be substituted the words '; and the Crown Court to which he has been so committed may make such an order with regard to him as is mentioned in subsection (2) above.'.

Extradited persons: sentence of imprisonment to reflect custody

48.—(1)   In section 47 of the Criminal Justice Act 1991 (computation of sentences of imprisonment of persons extradited to United Kingdom), in subsection (4), in the definition of 'extradited to the United Kingdom', after paragraph (iv), there shall be inserted the following paragraph, preceded by the word 'or'—

'(v)   in pursuance of arrangements with a foreign state in respect of which an Order in Council under section 2 of the Extradition Act 1870 is in force;'.

(2)   In each of sections 218(3) and 431(3) of the Criminal Procedure (Scotland) Act 1975 (corresponding provisions for Scotland), after paragraph (c) there shall be inserted the following paragraph—

'(cc)   in pursuance of arrangements with a foreign state in respect of which an Order in Council under section 2 of the Extradition Act 1870 is in force;'.

Transfers of proceedings

49.   In section 53 of the Criminal Justice Act 1991 (notices of transfer in certain cases involving children)—

(a)   in subsection (1), for the words 'served' and 'on' there shall be substituted the words 'given' and 'to';

(b)   in subsection (2), for the word 'served' there shall be substituted the word 'given';

(c)   in subsection (3), for the word 'service' there shall be substituted the word 'giving'; and

(d)   in subsection (4), for the word 'serve' there shall be substituted the word 'give'.

Community sentences: binding over of parent or guardian

50.   In section 58(2) of the Criminal Justice Act 1991 (power of court to bind over parent or guardian of young offender), at the end, there shall be inserted the following paragraph—

'Where the court has passed on the relevant minor a community sentence (within the meaning of section 6 above) it may include in the recognisance a provision that the minor's parent or guardian ensure that the minor complies with the requirements of that sentence.'.

Confiscation orders in terrorist-related activities cases: variation of sentences

51.—(1)   In section 48 of the Northern Ireland (Emergency Provisions) Act 1991 (postponed confiscation orders etc.), after subsection (3B) there shall be inserted the following subsection—
    '(3C) Where the court has sentenced the defendant under subsection (2) or (3) above during the specified period it may, after the end of that period, vary the sentence by imposing a fine or making any such order as is mentioned in subsection (5)(b) or (c) below so long as it does so within a period corresponding to that allowed by section 49(2) or (3) of the Judicature (Northern Ireland) Act 1978 (time allowed for varying a sentence) but beginning with the end of the specified period.'.
(2)   For the purposes of section 69 of the Northern Ireland (Emergency Provisions) Act 1991 (temporary provisions) the amendment made in that Act by this paragraph shall be treated, as from the time when this paragraph comes into force, as having been continued in force by the order made under subsection (3) of that section which has effect at that time.

Anonymity of victims of certain offences

52.—(1)   The Sexual Offences (Amendment) Act 1992 shall be amended as follows.
(2)   In section 2(1) (offences to which the Act applies), after paragraph (e) there shall be inserted the following paragraphs—
    '(f)   any conspiracy to commit any of those offences;
    (g)   any incitement of another to commit any of those offences.'.
(3)   In section 6 (interpretation)—
    (a)   after subsection (2) there shall be inserted the following subsection—
    '(2A)   For the purposes of this Act, where it is alleged or there is an accusation that an offence of conspiracy or incitement of another to commit an offence mentioned in section 2(1)(a) to (d) has been committed, the person against whom the substantive offence is alleged to have been intended to be committed shall be regarded as the person against whom the conspiracy or incitement is alleged to have been committed.
    In this subsection, "the substantive offence" means the offence to which the alleged conspiracy or incitement related.'; and
    (b)   in subsection (3), after the words 'references in' there shall be inserted the words 'subsection (2A) and in'.

Application of 1993 Act powers to precommencement offences

53.   Section 78(6) of the Criminal Justice Act 1993 (application of Act to pre-commencement offences) shall have effect, and be deemed always to have had effect, with the substitution, for the words from 'or the powers' to the end, of the words 'and, where it confers a power on the court, shall not apply in proceedings instituted before the coming into force of that provision.'.

Section 168(2)   SCHEDULE 10
                        CONSEQUENTIAL AMENDMENTS

Bail: exclusion in homicide and rape cases

1.   In section 2 of the Habeas Corpus Act 1679 (bail for persons released from custody under habeas corpus while awaiting trial), after the words 'brought as aforesaid shall' there shall be inserted the words ', subject to section 25 of the Criminal Justice and Public Order Act 1994,'.

Evidence of accused in criminal proceedings

2.   In section 1 of the Criminal Evidence Act 1898 (competency of accused to give evidence in criminal proceedings), proviso (b) shall be omitted.

Evidence of accused in criminal proceedings

3.   In section 1 of the Criminal Evidence Act (Northern Ireland) 1923 (competency of accused to give evidence in criminal proceedings)—
     (a)   after the words 'Provided as follows:—' there shall be inserted the following proviso—
     '(a)   A person so charged shall not be called as a witness in pursuance of this Act except upon his own application;';
     (b)   proviso (b) shall be omitted.

Responsibility for fine for breach of requirements of secure training order

4.   In section 55(1A) of the Children and Young Persons Act 1933 (power of court to order parent or guardian to pay fine imposed on child or young person), after paragraph (b) there shall be inserted the following paragraph—
     '(c)   a court would impose a fine on a child or young person under section 4(3) of the Criminal Justice and Public Order Act 1994 (breach of requirements of supervision under secure training order),'.

Bail: exclusion in homicide and rape cases

5.   In section 56(3) of the Children and Young Persons Act 1933 (powers of courts remitting young offenders to youth court), after the word 'may' there shall be inserted the words ', subject to section 25 of the Criminal Justice and Public Order Act 1994,'.

Bail: exclusion in homicide or rape cases

6.   In section 37(1) of the Criminal Justice Act 1948 (power of High Court to grant bail on case stated or application for certiorari)—
     (a)   in paragraph (b), after the word 'may' there shall be inserted the words ', subject to section 25 of the Criminal Justice and Public Order Act 1994,'; and
     (b)   in paragraph (d), after the word 'may' there shall be inserted the words ', subject to section 25 of the Criminal Justice and Public Order Act 1994,'.

Modernisation of 'servant' in Prison Act

7.   In section 3(1) of the Prison Act 1952 (officers and servants at prisons), for the word 'servants' there shall be substituted the words 'employ such other persons'.

Use of young offender institutions as secure training centres

8.   In section 37(4) of the Prison Act 1952 (prisons not deemed closed where used as remand centres etc.), at the end, there shall be inserted the words 'or secure training centre'.

Young offenders absconding from secure training centres

9.—(1)   Section 49 of the Prison Act 1952 (persons unlawfully at large) shall be amended as follows.

(2)   In subsection (1), after the words 'young offenders institution' there shall be inserted the words 'or a secure training centre'.

(3)   In subsection (2), for the words between 'detained in a' and 'is unlawfully' there shall be substituted the words 'young offenders institution or in a secure training centre'.

(4)   In subsection (2), in proviso (a), for the words after 'prison' there shall be substituted the words 'remand centre, young offenders institution or secure training centre'.

Bail: exclusion in homicide and rape cases

10.   In section 4(2) of the Administration of Justice Act 1960 (power of High Court to grant bail to persons appealing to the House of Lords), after the words 'Divisional Court shall' there shall be inserted the words ', subject to section 25 of the Criminal Justice and Public Order Act 1994,'.

Young offenders: application of prison rules

11.   In section 23(4) of the Criminal Justice Act 1961 (which applies provisions relating to prison rules to other institutions), before the words 'and remand centres' there shall be inserted the words 'secure training centres'.

Young offenders: transfer, supervision and recall within British Islands

12.—(1)   Part III of the Criminal Justice Act 1961 (transfer, supervision and recall within British Islands) shall have effect with the following amendments.

(2)   In section 29—

(a)   in subsection (1), for the words from 'youth custody centre' to 'young offenders institution' there shall be substituted the words 'or institution for young offenders to which this subsection applies';

(b)   after subsection (2), there shall be inserted the following subsection—

'(2A)   The institutions for young offenders to which subsection (1) above applies are the following: a remand centre, young offenders institution or secure training centre and, in Northern Ireland, a young offenders centre.'.

(3)   In section 30—

(a)   in subsection (3), for the words between 'prison' and 'in any part' there shall be substituted the words 'or institution for young offenders to which this subsection applies';

(b)   after subsection (3), there shall be inserted the following subsection—

'(3A)   The institutions for young offenders to which subsection (3) above applies are the following: a young offenders institution or secure training centre and, in Northern Ireland, a young offenders centre.'.

(4)   In section 32, in subsection (2), after paragraph (k), there shall be inserted the following paragraph—
   '(1)   sections 1 and 3 of the Criminal Justice and Public Order Act 1994.'.
(5)   In section 38(3), for paragraph (a), there shall be substituted the following paragraph—
   '(a)   the expression 'imprisonment or detention' means imprisonment, custody for life, detention in a young offenders institution or in a secure training centre or detention under an equivalent sentence passed by a court in the Channel Islands or the Isle of Man;'.

Payment of damages by police authority

13.   In section 48(4) of the Police Act 1964 (payment by police authority of damages awarded against constables), after the words 'section 14 of this Act' there shall be inserted the words 'or section 141 of the Criminal Justice and Public Order Act 1994'.

Cross-border enforcement: extension of protection

14.   In section 51 of the Police Act 1964 (assaults on, and obstruction of, constables), after subsection (3), there shall be inserted the following subsection—
   '(4)   This section also applies to a constable who is a member of a police force maintained in Scotland or Northern Ireland when he is executing a warrant or otherwise acting in England or Wales by virtue of any enactment conferring powers on him in England and Wales.'.

Bail: exclusion in homicide and rape cases

15.   In section 22(1) of the Criminal Justice Act 1967 (power of High Court to grant bail), after the word 'may', there shall be inserted the words ', subject to section 25 of the Criminal Justice and Public Order Act 1994,'.

Young offenders: detention under secure training order

16.   Section 67 of the Criminal Justice Act 1967 (computation of sentences of imprisonment or detention passed in England and Wales) shall be amended by the insertion in subsection (5), after paragraph (b), of the following paragraph—
   '(c)   to secure training orders under section 1 of the Criminal Justice and Public Order Act 1994;'.

Payment of damages by Scottish police authority

17.   In section 39(4) of the Police (Scotland) Act 1967 (payment by police authority of damages awarded against constables), after the words 'section 11 of this Act' there shall be inserted the words 'or section 141 of the Criminal Justice and Public Order Act 1994'.

Assaults on constables etc.

18.   In section 41 of the Police (Scotland) Act 1967 (assaults on constables etc.), after subsection (2), there shall be inserted the following subsection—
   '(3)   This section also applies to a constable who is a member of a police force maintained in England and Wales or in Northern Ireland when he is executing a warrant or otherwise acting in Scotland by virtue of any enactment conferring powers on him in Scotland.'.

Bail: exclusion in homicide and rape cases

19.   In section 8(2)(a) of the Criminal Appeal Act 1968 (powers of Court of Appeal on retrial), after the words 'custody or' there shall be inserted the words ', subject to section 25 of the Criminal Justice and Public Order Act 1994,'.

Bail: exclusion in homicide and rape cases

20.   In section 11(5) of the Criminal Appeal Act 1968 (powers of Court of Appeal on quashing interim hospital order), after the word 'may' there shall be inserted the words ', subject to section 25 of the Criminal Justice and Public Order Act 1994,'.

Bail: exclusion in homicide and rape cases

21.   In section 16(3)(b) of the Criminal Appeal Act 1968 (powers of Court of Appeal on allowing an appeal against a finding that a person is under a disability), after the word 'may' there shall be inserted the words ', subject to section 25 of the Criminal Justice and Public Order Act 1994,'.

Bail: exclusion in homicide and rape cases

22.   In section 19(1) of the Criminal Appeal Act 1968 (power of Court of Appeal to grant bail), after the word 'may', there shall be inserted the words ', subject to section 25 of the Criminal Justice and Public Order Act 1994.'.

Bail: exclusion in homicide and rape cases

23.   In section 36 of the Criminal Appeal Act 1968 (power of Court of Appeal to grant bail on appeal by defendant), after the word 'may' there shall be inserted the words ', subject to section 25 of the Criminal Justice and Public Order Act 1994'.

Young offenders: possession of firearms

24.—(1)   The Firearms Act 1968 shall be amended as follows.

(2)   In section 21 (possession of firearms by persons previously convicted of crime)—

(a)   in subsection (2), after the word 'Scotland' there shall be inserted the words 'or who has been subject to a secure training order'; and

(b)   for subsection (2A) there shall be substituted—

'(2A)   For the purposes of subsection (2) above, 'the date of his release' means—

(a)   in the case of a person sentenced to imprisonment with an order under section 47(1) of the Criminal Law Act 1977 (prison sentence partly served and partly suspended), the date on which he completes service of so much of the sentence as was by that order required to be served in prison;

(b)   in the case of a person who has been subject to a secure training order—

(i)   the date on which he is released from detention under the order;

(ii)   the date on which he is released from detention ordered under section 4 of the Criminal Justice and Public Order Act 1994; or

(iii)   the date halfway through the total period specified by the court in making the order,

whichever is the later.'.

(3)   In section 52(1) (forfeiture and disposal of firearms), in paragraph (a), after the word 'Scotland' there shall be inserted the words 'or is subject to a secure training order'.

Cross-border enforcement: extension of protection

25.   In section 7 of the Criminal Justice (Miscellaneous Provisions) Act (Northern Ireland) 1968 (assaults on, and obstruction of, constables), after subsection (3), there shall be inserted the following subsection—

'(4)   This section also applies to a constable who is a member of a police force maintained in England and Wales or Scotland when he is executing a warrant or otherwise acting in Northern Ireland by virtue of any statutory provision conferring powers on him in Northern Ireland.'.

Sexual offences: male rape

26.   In section 9(2) of the Theft Act 1968 (offences which if intended by a trespasser constitute burglary), for the words 'raping any woman' there shall be substituted the words 'raping any person'.

Payment of damages by Police Authority for Northern Ireland

27.   In section 14(5) of the Police Act (Northern Ireland) 1970 (payment by Police Authority of damages awarded against persons serving with the Royal Ulster Constabulary), for the words 'section 19' there shall be substituted the words 'section 141 of the Criminal Justice and Public Order Act 1994'.

Jury service: penalty for serving when not qualified

28.   In section 20(5) of the Juries Act 1974 (offences in connection with jury service), at the end of paragraph (d) there shall be inserted '; or

(e)   knowing that he is not qualified for jury service by reason of section 40 of the Criminal Justice and Public Order Act 1994, serves on a jury,'.

Custody officers: ineligibility for jury service

29.   In Part I of Schedule 1 to the Juries Act 1974, in Group B (ineligibility for jury service of certain persons concerned with the administration of justice), after the entry for prisoner custody officers within the meaning of Part IV of the Criminal Justice Act 1991, there shall be inserted the following entry—

'Custody officers within the meaning of Part I of the Criminal Justice and Public Order Act 1994'.

Rehabilitation of offenders subject to secure training orders

30.   In section 5(6) of the Rehabilitation of Offenders Act 1974 (rehabilitation periods for particular sentences), after paragraph (c), there shall be inserted the following paragraph, preceded by the word 'or'—

'(d)   a secure training order under section 1 of the Criminal Justice and Public Order Act 1994;'.

Prisoner custody officers: ineligibility for jury service

31.   In Schedule 2 to the Juries (Northern Ireland) Order 1974 (exemptions from jury service) in the group headed 'Persons connected with the administration of justice', at the end there shall be inserted—

'Prisoner custody officers within the meaning of section 122(1) of the Criminal Justice and Public Order Act 1994.'.

Bail: exclusion in homicide and rape cases

32. In section 4 of the Bail Act 1976 (entitlement to bail), after subsection (7), there shall be inserted the following subsection—
'(8) This section is subject to section 25 of the Criminal Justice and Public Order Act 1994 (exclusion of bail in cases of homicide and rape).'.

Police bail: variation by magistrates

33. In section 4(2) of the Bail Act 1976 (occasions for implementation of right to bail), in paragraph (b), after the words 'for bail' there shall be inserted the words 'or for a variation of the conditions of bail'.

Bail: no right for persons offending while on bail

34. In Part III of Schedule 1 to the Bail Act 1976, in paragraph 2, at the end, there shall be inserted the words '; and so as respects the reference to an offence committed by a person on bail in relation to any period before the coming into force of paragraph 2A of Part I of this Schedule.'.

Sexual offences: male rape

35.—(1) The Sexual Offences (Amendment) Act 1976 shall be amended as follows,
(2) In section 1(2) (reasonable grounds for belief in consent to intercourse), after the word 'woman' there shall be inserted the words 'or man'.
(3) In section 2(3) (restrictions on evidence at trials for rape etc.), after the word 'woman' there shall be inserted the words 'or man'.
(4) In section 7(2) (interpretation of terms used in the Act)—
(a) the words from 'references' to 'only);' shall be omitted; and
(b) for the words 'and section 46 of that Act' there shall be substituted the words 'section 46 of the Sexual Offences Act 1956'.

Sexual offences: male rape

36.—(1) Section 4 of the Sexual Offences (Amendment) Act 1976 (anonymity of complainants in rape etc. cases) shall be amended as follows.
(2) In subsection (1)—
(a) in paragraph (a)—
(i) after the word 'woman' in both places where it occurs there shall be inserted the words 'or man';
(ii) for the words 'woman's name nor her address' there shall be substituted the words 'name nor the address of the woman or man';
(iii) after the words 'of her' there shall be inserted the words 'or him';
(iv) for the words 'her lifetime' there shall be substituted the words 'that person's lifetime'; and
(v) for the words 'identify her' there shall be substituted the words 'identify that person'; and
(b) in paragraph (b)—
(i) after the word 'woman' there shall be inserted the words 'or man'; and

(ii)   for the words 'her lifetime' there shall be substituted the words 'that person's lifetime'.

(3)   In subsection (5A), after the word 'woman' there shall be inserted the words 'or man'.

(4)   In subsection (5B), for the words 'woman's peace or comfort' there shall be substituted the words 'peace or comfort of the woman or man'.

(5)   In subsection (6), in the definition of 'complainant', after the word 'woman' there shall be inserted the words 'or man'.

Indecent photographs etc.

37.—(1)   The Protection of Children Act 1978 shall be amended as follows.

(2)   In section 2(3), after the words 'proceedings under this Act' there shall be inserted the words 'relating to indecent photographs of children'.

(3)   In section 4—

(a)   in subsection (1), after the word 'photograph' there shall be inserted the words 'or pseudo-photograph'; and

(b)   in subsection (2), after the word 'photographs' there shall be inserted the words 'or pseudo-photographs'.

(4)   In section 5(2), (5) and (6), after the word 'photographs' there shall be inserted the words 'or pseudo-photographs'.

Indecent photographs etc. (Northern Ireland)

38.—(1)   The Protection of Children (Northern Ireland) Order 1978 shall be amended as follows.

(2)   In Article 4(1)—

(a)   after the word 'photograph' there shall be inserted the words 'or pseudo-photograph'; and

(b)   after the word 'photographs' there shall be inserted the words 'or pseudo-photographs'.

(3)   In Article 5(3) and (5), after the word 'photographs' there shall be inserted the words 'or pseudo-photographs'.

(4)   In Article 6(1), after the word 'photographs' there shall be inserted the words 'or pseudo-photographs'.

(5)   In Article 7(1), after the word 'Order' there shall be inserted the words 'relating to indecent photographs of children'.

Secure training orders: absence of accused

39.   In section 11(3) of the Magistrates' Courts Act 1980 (certain sentences and orders not to be made in absence of accused), after the word 'make' there shall be inserted the words 'a secure training order or'.

Procedure for young offenders in cases of grave crimes

40.   In section 24(1)(a) of the Magistrates' Courts Act 1980 (exception to summary trial of children or young persons) the words 'he has attained the age of 14 and' shall be omitted.

Bail: exclusion in homicide and rape cases

41. In section 29(4)(b) of the Magistrates' Courts Act 1980 (person under 18 remitted to youth court for trial), after the word 'may' there shall be inserted the words ', subject to section 25 of the Criminal Justice and Public Order Act 1994,'.

Bail: exclusion in homicide and rape cases

42. In section 37(1) of the Magistrates' Courts Act 1980 (committal to Crown Court for sentence), after the word 'may' there shall be inserted the words ', subject to section 25 of the Criminal Justice and Public Order Act 1994,'.

Police bail

43. In section 43(1) of the Magistrates' Courts Act 1980 (bail under the Police and Criminal Evidence Act 1984), after the words 'bail under' there shall be inserted the words 'Part IV of'.

Bail: exclusion in homicide or rape cases

44. In section 113(1) of the Magistrates' Courts Act 1980 (power of magistrates' court to grant bail on appeal to Crown Court or by way of case stated), after the word 'may' there shall be inserted the words ', subject to section 25 of the Criminal Justice and Public Order Act 1994,'.

Prisoner custody officers: ineligibility for jury service

45. In Part I of Schedule 1 to the Law Reform (Miscellaneous Provisions) (Scotland) Act 1980 (which makes ineligible for jury service persons connected with the administration of justice), in Group B, after paragraph (o) there shall be inserted the following paragraph—

'(oo)   prisoner custody officers within the meaning of section 114(1) of the Criminal Justice and Public Order Act 1994;'.

Young offenders: detention in the custody of a constable and others

46. In section 6 of the Imprisonment (Temporary Provisions) Act 1980 (detention in the custody of a constable)—

(a)   in subsection (1), after the words 'remand centre' there shall be inserted the words 'secure training centre';

(b)   in subsection (2), after the words 'remand centre' there shall be inserted the words 'secure training centre'; and

(c)   after the subsection (3) inserted by section 94 of this Act, there shall be inserted the following subsection—

'(4)   Any reference in this section to a constable includes a reference to a custody officer (within the meaning of section 12 of the Criminal Justice and Public Order Act 1994) acting in pursuance of escort arrangements (within the meaning of Schedule 1 to that Act).'.

Detention by constables and officers of a prison etc.: maximum period

47. In section 2 of the Criminal Justice (Scotland) Act 1980 (detention and questioning at police station etc.)—

(a)   at the beginning of subsection (3A) there shall be inserted 'Subject to subsection (3B) below,'; and

(b)   after subsection (3A) there shall be inserted the following subsection—

'(3B)   Subsection (3A) above shall not apply in relation to detention under section 41(3) of the Prisons (Scotland) Act 1989 (detention in relation to introduction etc. into prison of prohibited article), but where a person was detained under section 41(3) immediately prior to his detention under subsection (1) above the period of six hours mentioned in subsection (2) above shall be reduced by the length of that earlier detention.'.

Bail: exclusion in homicide and rape cases

48.   In section 81(1) of the Supreme Court Act 1981 (power of Crown Court to grant bail), after the word 'may', there shall be inserted the words ', subject to section 25 of the Criminal Justice and Public Order Act 1994,'.

Young offenders: legal representation

49.   In section 3(1) of the Criminal Justice Act 1982 (restriction on certain sentences where offender not legally represented), after paragraph (d) there shall be inserted the following paragraph, preceded by the word 'or'—

'(e)   make a secure training order,'.

Young offenders: early release

50.   In section 32 of the Criminal Justice Act 1982 (early release by order of classes of prisoners and other persons), after subsection (7), there shall be inserted the following subsection—

'(7A)   Subsections (1) and (4) above shall apply in relation to secure training centres and persons detained in such centres as they apply, by virtue of section 43(5) of the Prison Act 1952, to young offenders institutions and to persons detained in such institutions.'.

Bail: exclusion in homicide and rape cases

51.   In section 51(4) of the Mental Health Act 1983 (power of court to remit or release on bail detained person), after the words 'above or' there shall be inserted the words ', subject to section 25 of the Criminal Justice and Public Order Act 1994,'.

Video recordings

52.—(1)   The Video Recordings Act 1984 shall be amended as follows.

(2)   In section 13, after subsection (2), there shall be inserted the following subsection—

'(3) A person guilty of an offence under this section shall be liable, on summary conviction, to a fine not exceeding level 5 on the standard scale.'.

(3)   For section 15 there shall be substituted the following section—

'15.   Time limit for prosecutions

(1)   No prosecution for an offence under this Act shall be brought after the expiry of the period of three years beginning with the date of the commission of the offence or one year beginning with the date of its discovery by the prosecutor, whichever is earlier.

(2) In Scotland, the reference in subsection (1) above to the date of discovery by the prosecutor shall be construed as a reference to the date on which evidence sufficient in the opinion of the Lord Advocate to warrant proceedings came to his knowledge.

(3) For the purposes of subsection (2) above—

(a) a certificate signed by the Lord Advocate or on his behalf and stating the date on which evidence came to his knowledge shall be conclusive evidence of that fact;

(b) a certificate purporting to be signed as mentioned in paragraph (a) above shall be presumed to be so signed unless the contrary is proved; and

(c) a prosecution shall be deemed to be brought on the date on which a warrant to apprehend or to cite the accused is granted provided that the warrant is executed without undue delay.'.

Interim possession order: power of entry

53. In section 17 of the Police and Criminal Evidence Act 1984 (police powers of entry to effect arrest etc.)—

(a) in subsection (1)(c), after sub-paragraph (iii), there shall be inserted the following sub-paragraph—

'(iv) section 76 of the Criminal Justice and Public Order Act 1994 (failure to comply with interim possession order);';

(b) in subsection (3), after the words 'subsection (1)(c)(ii)' there shall be inserted the words 'or (iv)'.

Bail: exclusion in homicide and rape cases

54. In section 38(1) of the Police and Criminal Evidence Act 1984 (duty of custody officer to release on bail or without bail after charge), after the word 'shall' there shall be inserted the words ', subject to section 25 of the Criminal Justice and Public Order Act 1994,'.

Searches of persons detained at police stations

55. In section 54(1)(b) of the Police and Criminal Evidence Act 1984 (searches of persons detained at police stations), for the words 'under section 47(5) above' there shall be substituted the words ', as a person falling within section 34(7), under section 37 above'.

Fingerprinting: speculative searches

56. In section 61 of the Police and Criminal Evidence Act 1984 (which regulates the taking of fingerprints)—

(a) after subsection (7) there shall be inserted the following subsection—

'(7A) If a person's fingerprints are taken at a police station, whether with or without the appropriate consent—

(a) before the fingerprints are taken, an officer shall inform him that they may be the subject of a speculative search; and

(b) the fact that the person has been informed of this possibility shall be recorded as soon as is practicable after the fingerprints have been taken.'; and

(b) in subsection (8), after the word 'them' there shall be inserted the words 'and, in the case failing within subsection (7A) above, the fact referred to in paragraph (b) of that subsection'.

Intimate samples: speculative searches

57.   In section 62 of the Police and Criminal Evidence Act 1984 (which regulates the taking of intimate body samples)—
(a)   after subsection (7) there shall be inserted the following subsection—
'(7A)   If an intimate sample is taken from a person at a police station—
(a)   before the sample is taken, an officer shall inform him that it may be the subject of a speculative search; and
(b)   the fact that the person has been informed of this possibility shall be recorded as soon as practicable after the sample has been taken.'; and
(b)   in subsection (8), after the words 'subsection (7)' there shall be inserted the words 'or (7A)'.

Non-intimate samples: speculative searches

58.   In section 63 of the Police and Criminal Evidence Act 1984 (which regulates the taking of non-intimate body samples)—
(a)   after the subsection (8A) inserted by section 55 of this Act, there shall be inserted the following subsection—
'(8B)   If a non-intimate sample is taken from a person at a police station, whether with or without the appropriate consent—
(a)   before the sample is taken, an officer shall inform him that it may be the subject of a speculative search; and
(b)   the fact that the person has been informed of this possibility shall be recorded as soon as practicable after the sample has been taken.'; and
(b)   in subsection (9), after the words '(8A)' there shall be inserted the words 'or (8B)'.

Sexual offences: male rape and buggery

59.   In Part I of Schedule 5 to the Police and Criminal Evidence Act 1984 (serious arrestable offences mentioned in section 116(2)(a) of that Act), for item 7 (buggery) there shall be substituted—
'7.   Buggery with a person under the age of 16.'.

Trespassory assemblies

60.   In section 15(1) of the Public Order Act 1986 (delegation of functions), for '14' there shall be substituted '14A'.

Inferences from accused's silence

61.—(1)   The Criminal Evidence (Northern Ireland) Order 1988 shall be amended as follows.
(2)   In Article 3(1)(a), after the word 'questioned' there shall be inserted the words 'under caution'.
(3)   In Article 4—
(a)   in paragraph (1)—
(i)   for the words 'to (7)' there shall be substituted the words 'and (4)';
(ii)   in sub-paragraph (b), the words 'be called upon to' shall be omitted;
(iii)   for the words from 'if' onwards there shall be substituted the words ', at the conclusion of the evidence for the prosecution, his legal representative

informs the court that the accused will give evidence or, where he is unrepresented, the court ascertains from him that he will give evidence';

(b) for paragraphs (2) and (3) there shall be substituted the following paragraph—

'(2) Where this paragraph applies, the court shall, at the conclusion of the evidence for the prosecution, satisfy itself (in the case of proceedings on indictment conducted with a jury, in the presence of the jury) that the accused is aware that the stage has been reached at which evidence can be given for the defence and that he can, if he wishes, give evidence and that, if he chooses not to give evidence, or having been sworn, without good cause refuses to answer any question, it will be permissible for the court or jury to draw such inferences as appear proper from his failure to give evidence or his refusal, without good cause, to answer any question.';

(c) in paragraph (4)—

(i) at the beginning there shall be inserted the words 'Where this paragraph applies,';

(ii) in sub-paragraph (a), for the words 'from the refusal as appear proper' there shall be substituted the words 'as appear proper from the failure of the accused to give evidence or his refusal, without good cause, to answer any question';

(d) in paragraph (5), for the words 'refusal to be sworn' there shall be substituted the words 'failure to do so'; and

(e) paragraphs (9) and (10) shall be omitted.

(4) In Article 5(1)(b), for the words 'the constable' there shall be substituted the words 'that or another constable investigating the case'.

(5) In Article 5(2), after sub-paragraph (a), for the word 'and' there shall be substituted the following sub-paragraph—

'(aa) a judge, in deciding whether to grant an application made by the accused under Article 5 of the Criminal Justice (Serious Fraud) (Northern Ireland) Order 1988 (application for dismissal of charge where a case of fraud has been transferred from a magistrates' court to the Crown Court under Article 3 of that Order); and'.

(6) In Article 5, after paragraph 3, there shall be inserted the following paragraph—

'(3A) This Article applies in relation to officers of customs and excise as it applies in relation to constables.'.

(7) In Article 6(1)(b), for the words 'the constable' there shall be substituted the words 'that or another constable investigating the case'.

(8) In Article 6(2), after sub-paragraph (a), for the word 'and' there shall be substituted the following sub-paragraph—

'(aa) a judge, in deciding whether to grant an application made by the accused under Article 5 of the Criminal Justice (Serious Fraud) (Northern Ireland) Order 1988 (application for dismissal of charge where a case of fraud has been transferred from a magistrates' court to the Crown Court under Article 3 of that Order); and'.

(9) In Article 6, after paragraph 2, there shall be inserted the following paragraph—

'(2A) This Article applies in relation to officers of customs and excise as it applies in relation to constables.'.

(10)   In Article 6(3), for the words 'do so' there shall be substituted the words 'comply with the request'.

Samples: application to terrorist suspects

62.—(1)   The Prevention of Terrorism (Temporary Provisions) Act 1989 shall be amended as provided in sub-paragraphs (2) and (3) below.

(2)   In section 15 (provisions supplementary to powers to arrest and detain suspected persons), after subsection (10), there shall be inserted the following subsections—

'(11)   Section 62(1) to (11) of the Police and Criminal Evidence Act 1984 (regulation of taking of intimate samples) shall apply to the taking of an intimate sample from a person under subsection (9) above as if—

(a)   for subsection (2) there were substituted—

"(2)   An officer may only give an authorisation under subsection (1) or (1A) above for the taking of an intimate sample if he is satisfied that it is necessary to do so in order to assist in determining—

(a)   whether that person is or has been concerned in the commission, preparation or instigation of acts of terrorism to which section 14 of the Prevention of Terrorism (Temporary Provisions) Act 1989 applies; or

(b)   whether he is subject to an exclusion order under that Act;

or if the officer has reasonable grounds for suspecting that person's involvement in an offence under any of the provisions mentioned in subsection (1)(a) of that section and for believing that an intimate sample will tend to confirm or disprove his involvement''; and

(b)   in subsection (6), after the word 'includes', there were inserted the words ''where relevant''.

(12)   In this section, ''intimate sample'' has the same meaning as in section 65 of the Police and Criminal Evidence Act 1984.

(13)   Section 63(1) to (9) of the Police and Criminal Evidence Act 1984 (regulation of taking of non-intimate samples) shall apply to the taking of a non-intimate sample from a person by a constable under subsection (9) above as if—

(a)   for subsection (4) there were substituted—

"(4)   An officer may only give an authorisation under subsection (3) above for the taking of a non-intimate sample if he is satisfied that it is necessary to do so in order to assist in determining—

(a)   whether that person is or has been concerned in the commission, preparation or instigation of acts of terrorism to which section 14 of the Prevention of Terrorism (Temporary Provisions) Act 1989 applies; or

(b)   whether he is subject to an exclusion order under that Act;

or if the officer has reasonable grounds for suspecting that person's involvement in an offence under any of the provisions mentioned in subsection (1)(a) of that section and for believing that a non-intimate sample will tend to confirm or disprove his involvement''; and

(b)   in subsection (7), after the word ''includes'' there were inserted the words ''where relevant''.

(14)   In this section, ''non-intimate sample'' has the same meaning as in section 65 of the Police and Criminal Evidence Act 1984.'.

(3)   In Schedule 5, in paragraph 7 (provisions supplementary to powers to detain persons pending examination etc.), after sub-paragraph (6), there shall be inserted the following sub-paragraphs—

'(6A)   Section 62(1) to (11) of the Police and Criminal Evidence Act 1984 (regulation of taking of intimate samples) shall apply to the taking of an intimate sample from a person under sub-paragraph (5) above as if—

(a)   for subsection (2) there were substituted—

"(2)   An officer may only give an authorisation under subsection (1) or (1A) above for the taking of an intimate sample if he is satisfied that it is necessary to do so in order to assist in determining—

(a)   whether that person is or has been concerned in the commission, preparation or instigation of acts of terrorism to which paragraph 2 of Schedule 5 to the Prevention of Terrorism (Temporary Provisions) Act 1989 applies; or

(b)   whether he is subject to an exclusion order under that Act; or

(c)   whether there are grounds for suspecting that he has committed an offence under section 8 of that Act"; and

(b)   in subsection (6), after the word "includes", there were inserted the words "where relevant".

(6B)   In this paragraph, "intimate sample" has the same meaning as in section 65 of the Police and Criminal Evidence Act 1984.

(6C)   Section 63(1) to (9) of the Police and Criminal Evidence Act 1984 (regulation of taking of non-intimate samples) shall apply to the taking of a non-intimate sample from a person by a constable under sub-paragraph (5) above as if—

(a)   for subsection (4) there were substituted—

"(4)   An officer may only give an authorisation under subsection (3) above for the taking of a non-intimate sample if he is satisfied that it is necessary to do so in order to assist in determining—

(a)   whether that person is or has been concerned in the commission, preparation or instigation of acts of terrorism to which paragraph 2 of Schedule 5 to the Prevention of Terrorism (Temporary Provisions) Act 1989 applies;

(b)   whether he is subject to an exclusion order under that Act; or

(c)   whether there are grounds for suspecting that he has committed an offence under section 8 of that Act"; and

(b)   in subsection (7), after the word "includes", there were inserted the words "where relevant".

(6D)   In this paragraph, "non-intimate sample" has the same meaning as in section 65 of the Police and Criminal Evidence Act 1984.'.

(4)   In consequence of the foregoing amendments—

(a)   in section 62 of the Police and Criminal Evidence Act 1984 (which regulates the taking of intimate body samples), at the end there shall be inserted the following subsection—

'(12)   Nothing in this section, except as provided in section 15(11) and (12) of, and paragraph 7(6A) and (6B) of Schedule 5 to, the Prevention of Terrorism (Temporary Provisions) Act 1989, applies to a person arrested or detained under the terrorism provisions.';

(b)   in section 63 of the Police and Criminal Evidence Act 1984 (which regulates the taking of non-intimate body samples), at the end there shall be inserted the following subsection—

'(10)   Nothing in this section, except as provided in section 15(13) and (14) of, and paragraph 7(6C) and (6D) of Schedule 5 to, the Prevention of Terrorism (Temporary Provisions) Act 1989, applies to a person arrested or detained under the terrorism provisions.'; and

(c)   in section 28(2) of the Prevention of Terrorism (Temporary Provisions) Act 1989 (extent), in paragraph (b) (provisions extending only to England and Wales), after the words 'section 15(10)' there shall be inserted the words 'to (14)' and after the words 'paragraph 7(6)' there shall be inserted the words 'to (6D)'.

(5)   For the purposes of section 27 of the Prevention of Terrorism (Temporary Provisions) Act 1989 (temporary provisions), the amendments made by this paragraph shall be treated, as from the time when those amendments come into force, as having been continued in force by the order under subsection (6) of that section which has effect at that time.

Prevention of terrorism: consents for prosecutions etc.

63.—(1)   The Prevention of Terrorism (Temporary Provisions) Act 1989 shall be amended as follows.

(2)   In section 17(1)(b) (purposes of investigations), for the words 'section 21(4) of that Act' there shall be substituted the words 'section 28(3) of that Act'.

(3)   In section 19(1) (consents required for prosecutions), after paragraph (a), there shall be inserted the following paragraph—

'(aa)   in England and Wales for an offence under section 13A, 16A or 16B except by or with the consent of the Director of Public Prosecutions;'.

(4)   In section 28(2) (extent), in paragraph (a) (provisions not extending to Northern Ireland), for the words 'and section 15(1)', there shall be substituted the words ', sections 13A and 15(1) and Part IVA'.

(5)   For the purposes of section 27 (temporary provisions), the amendments made by this paragraph shall be treated, as from the time when those amendments come into force, as having been continued in force by the order under subsection (6) of that section which has effect at that time.

Young offenders: powers to search and to test for drugs

64.   In section 19(4) of the Prisons (Scotland) Act 1989 (remand centres and young offenders institutions), for the words 'and 41 ' there shall be substituted the words '41, 41A and 41B'.

Non-appearance of accused:plea of guilty

65.   In section 20(1A) of the Criminal Justice Act 1991 (power of court to make financial circumstances order in absence of accused where guilty plea notified), for the words 'section 12(2)' there shall be substituted the words 'section 12(4)'.

Young offenders: secure training order a custodial sentence

66.   In section 31(1) of the Criminal Justice Act 1991 (which defines, amongst other expressions, 'custodial sentence'), in paragraph (b) of that definition, after the

words '1982 Act', there shall be inserted the words, 'or a secure training order under section 1 of the Criminal Justice and Public Order Act 1994'.

Bail: exclusion in homicide and rape cases

67. In section 40(3)(b) of the Criminal Justice Act 1991 (committal for sentence of offender convicted of offence during currency of original sentence), at the beginning, there shall be inserted the words 'subject to section 25 of the Criminal Justice and Public Order Act 1994,'.

Contracted out prisons: exclusion of search powers

68. In section 87(3) of the Criminal Justice Act 1991 (provisions of Prison Act 1952 not applying to contracted out prisons), after the word 'officers)' there shall be inserted the words 'and section 8A (powers of search by authorised employees)'.

Testing prisoners for drugs: director's function

69. In section 87(4) of the Criminal Justice Act 1991 (certain functions as governor to be functions of director of contracted out prisons), after '13(1)' insert '16A'.

The Parole Board

70. For Schedule 5 to the Criminal Justice Act 1991 (supplementary provisions about the Parole Board) there shall be substituted the following Schedule—

'SCHEDULE 5 THE PAROLE BOARD: SUPPLEMENTARY PROVISIONS

Status and capacity

1.—(1) The Board shall not be regarded as the servant or agent of the Crown or as enjoying any status, immunity or privilege of the Crown; and the Board's property shall not be regarded as property of, or held on behalf of, the Crown.

(2) It shall be within the capacity of the Board as a statutory corporation to do such things and enter into such transactions as are incidental to or conducive to the discharge of its functions under Part II of this Act.

Membership

2.—(1) The Board shall consist of a chairman and not less than four other members appointed by the Secretary of State.

(2) The Board shall include among its members—

   (a) a person who holds or has held judicial office;

   (b) a registered medical practitioner who is a psychiatrist;

   (c) a person appearing to the Secretary of State to have knowledge and experience of the supervision or after-care of discharged prisoners; and

   (d) a person appearing to the Secretary of State to have made a study of the causes of delinquency or the treatment of offenders.

(3) A member of the Board—

   (a) shall hold and vacate office in accordance with the terms of his appointment;

(b)   may resign his office by notice in writing addressed to the Secretary of State;

and a person who ceases to hold office as a member of the Board shall be eligible for re-appointment.

Payments to members

3.—(1)   The Board may pay to each member such remuneration and allowances as the Secretary of State may determine.

(2)   The Board may pay or make provision for paying to or in respect of any member such sums by way of pension, allowances or gratuities as the Secretary of State may determine.

(3)   If a person ceases to be a member otherwise than on the expiry of his term of office and it appears to the Secretary of State that there are special circumstances that make it right that he should receive compensation, the Secretary of State may direct the Board to make to that person a payment of such amount as the Secretary of State may determine.

(4)   A determination or direction of the Secretary of State under this paragraph requires the approval of the Treasury.

Proceedings

4.—(1)   Subject to the provisions of section 32(5) of this Act, the arrangements relating to meetings of the Board shall be such as the Board may determine.

(2)   The arrangements may provide for the discharge, under the general direction of the Board, of any of the Board's functions by a committee or by one or more of the members or employees of the Board.

(3)   The validity of the proceedings of the Board shall not be affected by any vacancy among the members or by any defect in the appointment of a member.

Staff

5.—(1)   The Board may appoint such number of employees as it may determine.

(2)   The remuneration and other conditions of service of the persons appointed under this paragraph shall be determined by the Board.

(3)   Any determination under sub-paragraph (1) or (2) shall require the approval of the Secretary of State given with the consent of the Treasury.

(4)   The Employers' Liability (Compulsory Insurance) Act 1969 shall not require insurance to be effected by the Board.

6.—(1)   Employment with the Board shall be included among the kinds of employment to which a scheme under section 1 of the Superannuation Act 1972 can apply, and accordingly in Schedule 1 to that Act (in which those kinds of employment are listed) at the end of the list of Other Bodies there shall be inserted—

"Parole Board.".

(2)   The Board shall pay to the Treasury, at such times as the Treasury may direct, such sums as the Treasury may determine in respect of the increase attributable to this paragraph in the sums payable under the Superannuation Act 1972 out of money provided by Parliament.

Financial provisions

7.—(1)   The Secretary of State shall pay to the Board—

(a)   any expenses incurred or to be incurred by the Board by virtue of paragraph 3 or 5; and

(b)   with the consent of the Treasury, such sums as he thinks fit for enabling the Board to meet other expenses.

(2)   Any sums required by the Secretary of State for making payments under sub-paragraph (1) shall be paid out of money provided by Parliament.

Authentication of Board's seal

8.   The application of the seal of the Board shall be authenticated by the signature of the Chairman or some other person authorised for the purpose.

Presumption of authenticity of documents issued by Board

9.   Any document purporting to be an instrument issued by the Board and to be duly executed under the seal of the Board or to be signed on behalf of the Board shall be received in evidence and shall be deemed to be such an instrument unless the contrary is shown.

Accounts and audit

10.—(1)   It shall be the duty of the Board—

(a)   to keep proper accounts and proper records in relation to the accounts;

(b)   to prepare in respect of each financial year a statement of accounts in such form as the Secretary of State may direct with the approval of the Treasury; and

(c)   to send copies of each such statement to the Secretary of State and the Comptroller and Auditor General not later than 31st August next following the end of the financial year to which the statement relates.

(2)   The Comptroller and Auditor General shall examine, certify and report on each statement of accounts sent to him by the Board and shall lay a copy of every such statement and of his report before each House of Parliament.

(3)   In this paragraph, 'financial year' means the period beginning with the date on which the Board is incorporated and ending with the next following 31st March, and each successive period of twelve months.

Reports

11.   The Board shall as soon as practicable after the end of each financial year make to the Secretary of State a report on the performance of its functions during the year; and the Secretary of State shall lay a copy of the report before Parliament.'.

Bail: exclusion in homicide and rape cases

71.   In Schedule 6 to the Criminal Justice Act 1991 (procedure on notice of transfer in certain cases involving children), in paragraph 2(1), after the word '1976' where it occurs first there shall be inserted the words ', section 25 of the Criminal Justice and Public Order Act 1994'.

Probation officers for offenders subject to secure training orders

72. In section 4 of the Probation Service Act 1993 (functions of probation committee)—

(a)   in subsection (1), after paragraph (d), there shall be inserted the following paragraph—

'(dd)   to make arrangements for the selection, from the probation officers appointed for or assigned to a petty sessions area within their probation area, of an officer to supervise any person subject to supervision by a probation officer under a secure training order (within the meaning of section 1 of the Criminal Justice and Public Order Act 1994) naming as that petty sessions area the petty sessions area within which the person to be supervised resides for the time being;'; and

(b)   in subsection (4), for the words 'paragraph (c) or (d)' there shall be substituted the words 'paragraph (c), (d) or (dd)'.

Secure training orders: cost of supervision by probation officer

73. In section 17 of the Probation Service Act 1993 (probation committee expenditure)—

(a)   in subsection (1), for the words 'and (5)' there shall be substituted the words '(5) and (5A)'; and

(b)   after subsection (5) there shall be inserted the following subsection—

'(5A)   Nothing in sections 18 or 19 requires there to be paid out of the metropolitan police fund or defrayed by a local authority any expenses of a probation committee which are defrayed by the Secretary of State under section 3(6) of the Criminal Justice and Public Order Act 1994.'.

Section 168(3)   SCHEDULE II   REPEALS

Chapter	Short title	Extent of repeal
1848 c. 42.	Indictable Offences Act 1848.	Sections 12, 14 and 15.
1898 c. 36.	Criminal Evidence Act 1898.	In section 1, proviso (b).
1923 c. 9 (N.I.).	Criminal Evidence Act (Northern Ireland) 1923.	In section 1, proviso (b).
1925 c. 86.	Criminal Justice Act 1925.	Section 13(3). Section 49(2).
1952 c. 52.	Prison Act 1952.	In section 43(1)(a), the words 'trial or'. In section 43(1), the word 'and' at the end of paragraph (b). In section 43(2)(b) and (c), the words 'trial or'.
1956 c. 69.	Sexual Offences Act 1956.	In section 2(1), the word 'unlawful'. Section 2(2). In section 3(1), the word 'unlawful'. Section 3(2). Section 4(2). Section 22(2). Section 23(2).
1963 c. 37.	Children and Young Persons Act 1963.	In section 57(2), the words 'Section 49 of the principal Act and' and 'an appeal by case stated or'.
1965 c. 45.	Backing of Warrants (Republic of Ireland) Act 1965.	In section 2(2)(a), the words from ', or an offence under an enactment' to 'control'.
1965 c. 69.	Criminal Procedure (Attendance of Witnesses) Act 1965.	Section 1.
1967 c. 60.	Sexual Offences Act 1967.	In section 1(1), the words 'but subject to the provisions of the next following section'. Section 1(5). Section 2. Section 3.
1967 c. 77.	Police (Scotland) Act 1967.	Section 18.

Chapter	Short title	Extent of repeal
1967 c. 80.	Criminal Justice Act 1967.	Section 7. In section 36(1), the definition of 'committal proceedings'. In section 67(5), the word 'and' at the end of paragraph (a).
1968 c. 19.	Criminal Appeal Act 1968.	In Schedule 2, paragraph 1, the words from 'section 13(3)' to 'but'.
1968 c. 52.	Caravan Sites Act 1968.	Sections 6 to 12. In section 16, the definition of 'gipsies'.
1969 c. 54.	Children and Young Persons Act 1969.	Section 10(1) and (2). In section 57(4), the words '49 and the said sections'.
1969 c. 63.	Police Act 1969.	Sections 1, 3, 6 and 7.
1970 c. 9 (N.I.).	Police Act (Northern Ireland) 1970.	Sections 19 and 20.
1972 c. 71.	Criminal Justice Act 1972.	In section 46(1), the following words— 'Section 102 of the Magistrates' Courts Act 1980 and'; 'which respectively allow'; 'committal proceedings and in other'; 'and section 106 of the said Act of 1980'; 'which punish the making of'; '102 or'; ', as the case may be'. Section 46(2).
1973 c. 62.	Powers of Criminal Courts Act 1973.	In section 32(1)(b), the words 'tried or'.
1974 c. 23.	Juries Act 1974.	In section 10, the words 'physical disability or'.
1974 c. 53.	Rehabilitation of Offenders Act 1974.	In section 5(4), the words 'or placed on probation,' and 'or probation order'.
1976 c. 63.	Bail Act 1976.	Section 1(4). In section 3(6), the words '(but only by a court)'.

Chapter	Short title	Extent of repeal
1976 c. 82.	Sexual Offences (Amendment) Act 1976.	Section 1(1). In section 7(2), the words from 'references' to 'only);'.
1977 c. 45.	Criminal Law Act 1977.	Section 6(3). Section 38.
1978 c. 30.	Interpretation Act 1978.	In Schedule 1, paragraph (a) of the definition of 'Committed for trial'.
1978 c. 37.	Protection of Children Act 1978.	In section 1(1)(a), the words following 'child'. In section 4(2), the words from 'within' to 'warrant'.
1980 c. 43.	Magistrates' Courts Act 1980.	In section 22(1), the words 'subject to subsection (7) below'. In section 24(1)(a) the words 'he has attained the age of 14 and'. In section 38(2)(b), the words from 'committed' to '21 years old'. In section 97(1), the words from 'at an inquiry' to 'be) or'. Section 102. Section 103. Section 105. Section 106. Section 145(1)(e). In section 150(1), the definition of 'committal proceedings'. In Schedule 5, paragraph 2.
1980 c. 62.	Criminal Justice (Scotland) Act 1980.	In section 80, subsection (5); in subsection (7), paragraph (d) and the word '; or' immediately preceding that paragraph; and subsection (8).
1981 c. 47.	Criminal Attempts Act 1981.	In section 2(2)(g), the words 'or committed for trial'.

Chapter	Short title	Extent of repeal
1982 c. 48.	Criminal Justice Act 1982.	In section 1(2), the words 'trial or'. Section 12(6), (7) and, in subsection (11), paragraph (b) and the word 'and'. Section 67(5). In Schedule 14, paragraph 8.
S.I. 1982/1536 (N.I. 19).	Homosexual Offences (Northern Ireland) Order 1982.	In Article 3, in paragraph (1), the words 'and Article 5 (merchant seamen)' and paragraph (4). Article 5.
1984 c. 39.	Video Recordings Act 1984.	In section 1, in subsection (2)(a), the word 'or' and in subsection (3), the word 'or' where it occurs first. In section 17(1), the words from 'within' to 'warrant'.
1984 c. 60.	Police and Criminal Evidence Act 1984.	Section 37(1)(b), together with the word 'or' preceding it. Section 47(5). In section 62(10), the word following 'proper'. In section 118(1), the definition of 'intimate search'.
1985 c. 23.	Prosecution of Offences Act 1985.	In Schedule 1, paragraph 1.
1986 c. 64.	Public Order Act 1986.	Section 39. In section 42(2), '39'.
1987 c. 38.	Criminal Justice Act 1987.	In Schedule 2, paragraphs 10 and 11.
1988 c. 33.	Criminal Justice Act 1988.	In section 25(1)(a)(ii), the word 'or'. Section 32A(10). In section 34(2), the words from 'in relation to' to the end. Section 126. In section 160, in subsection (1), the words from '(meaning' to '16)' and subsection (5).

Chapter	Short title	Extent of repeal
1988 c. 34.	Legal Aid Act 1988.	In section 20(4)(a), the words 'trial or'. Section 20(4)(bb). Section 20(5).
S.I. 1988/1987 (N.1.20).	Criminal Evidence (Northern Ireland) Order 1988.	In Article 4, in paragraph (1)(b) the words 'be called called upon to' and paragraphs (9) and (10).
1989 c. 45.	Prisons (Scotland) Act 1989.	Section 33.
1989 c. 54.	Children Act 1989.	In Schedule 5, paragraph 7(2)(f). In Schedule 6, paragraph 10(2)(j).
1990 c. 42.	Broadcasting Act 1990.	In Schedule 20, in paragraph 3(2), the words 'and 49'.
1991 c. 13.	War Crimes Act 1991.	In section 1(4), the words 'England, Wales or'. Part I of the Schedule.
1991 c. 24.	Northern Ireland (Emergency Provisions) Act 1991.	In Schedule 7, paragraph 5(3)(c).
1991 c. 53.	Criminal Justice Act 1991.	In section 3(2), the words from the beginning to 'indictment,'. In section 3(4), the words from 'which is' to 'applies'. Section 50(4). Section 52(2). Section 57(4)(b), together with the word 'and' preceding it. Section 64.
S.I. 1992/1829.	Parole Board (Transfer of Functions) Order 1992.	In Article 3, the words from 'and 39' to 'licence)' and the words 'and (4)'.
1993 c. 24.	Video Recordings Act 1993.	Section 3.
1993 c. 36.	Criminal Justice Act 1993.	Section 67(2).

Note: The repeals that are to come into force on the passing of this Act are the following, namely, the repeals in the Sexual Offences Act 1967, the Caravan Sites Act 1968, the Sexual Offences (Amendment) Act 1976, the Public Order Act 1986, the Criminal Justice (Scotland) Act 1980 and the Homosexual Offences (Northern Ireland) Order 1982.

Index